# THE RISE OF NECRO/NARCO CITIZENSHIP

# THE RISE OF NECRO/NARCO CITIZENSHIP

Belonging and Dying in the Southwest North American Region

Carlos G. Vélez-Ibáñez

THE UNIVERSITY OF ARIZONA PRESS
TUCSON

The University of Arizona Press
www.uapress.arizona.edu

We respectfully acknowledge the University of Arizona is on the land and territories of Indigenous peoples. Today, Arizona is home to twenty-two federally recognized tribes, with Tucson being home to the O'odham and the Yaqui. Committed to diversity and inclusion, the University strives to build sustainable relationships with sovereign Native Nations and Indigenous communities through education offerings, partnerships, and community service.

© 2025 by The Arizona Board of Regents
All rights reserved. Published 2025

ISBN-13: 978-0-8165-5469-0 (hardcover)
ISBN-13: 978-0-8165-5468-3 (paperback)
ISBN-13: 978-0-8165-5470-6 (ebook)

Cover design by Leigh McDonald
Cover photograph of Roberto Primero Luis and his wife, Katy Sunún, courtesy of Lucas Primero Luis
Typeset by Sara Thaxton in 10.5/14 Warnock Pro with Worker, Forma DJR Display, and Adobe Caslon Pro

Publication of this book is made possible in part by the proceeds of a permanent endowment created with the assistance of a Challenge Grant from the National Endowment for the Humanities, a federal agency.

Library of Congress Cataloging-in-Publication Data
Names: Vélez-Ibañez, Carlos G., 1936– author.
Title: The rise of necro/narco citizenship : belonging and dying in the southwest North American region / Carlos G. Vélez-Ibáñez.
Description: Tucson : University of Arizona Press, 2025. | Includes bibliographical references and index.
Identifiers: LCCN 2024032650 (print) | LCCN 2024032651 (ebook) | ISBN 9780816554690 (hardcover) | ISBN 9780816554683 (paperback) | ISBN 9780816554706 (ebook)
Subjects: LCSH: Militarization—Mexican-American Border Region. | Mexican-American Border Region—Social conditions—21st century. | Mexican-American Border Region— Economic conditions—21st century.
Classification: LCC F787 .V454 2025 (print) | LCC F787 (ebook) | DDC 972.08/4—dc23/eng/20241118
LC record available at https://lccn.loc.gov/2024032650
LC ebook record available at https://lccn.loc.gov/2024032651

Printed in the United States of America
♾ This paper meets the requirements of ANSI/NISO Z39.48-1992 (Permanence of Paper).

*To Maria Luz Cruz Torres, one of the bravest women I know, who undertook fieldwork in the most trying of circumstances and excelled as a scholar, humanist, and friend to all those she met and won over with her singular and unlimited capacity to tell the truth without embellishment or ego-saving concern. For her, there are no shortcuts in creating the necessary avenues for this craft we call anthropology and in the narratives that we create from the daily realities we experience and explore in the worlds we seek to understand. To Nayely Vélez-Cruz, an extraordinary scholar and literate who taught herself physics and all matter of mathematics, leading to two doctorate degrees in different sciences but highly fed by the nutrients of Russian, Latin American, Japanese, and American literatures for balance and cosmic convergences, my deepest respect. Finally, to all my children and grandchildren, and the last, the santito lindo, Santi Toriello Vélez, who is the future of us all, mi cariño y afecto.*

# CONTENTS

| | |
|---|---|
| *List of Illustrations* | *ix* |
| *Acknowledgments* | *xi* |

| | | |
|---|---|---|
| | Introduction | 3 |
| 1. | The Necro/Narco Trans-state Network Emergence and Their Wars of Commission and Omission | 17 |
| 2. | The Rise of Necrocitizenship and Narcocitizenship Cultural and Social Compensations | 25 |
| 3. | Belonging and Dying: Genesis and Ethnographies of Necrocitizenship in Wars of Commission and Omission | 57 |
| 4. | Dislocations, Corruption, Impunity, Murder, and the Normalization of Violence: Genesis and Ethnographies of Narcocitizenship | 85 |
| 5. | The Transborder Dynamics on Familial and Quotidian Realities of Everyday Life: Here and There and Here Again, the Cosalá Case<br>NAYELI BURGUEÑO A. | 111 |
| 6. | Casualties of Wars of Commission and Omission: Youth at the Crossroads | 129 |

| | | |
|---|---|---|
| 7. | Journaling in Sinaloa: Between Uncertainty and Fear | 151 |
| | ARTURO SANTAMARÍA GÓMEZ | |
| 8. | Landing on Souls of Young Folks: The Deterritorialization of the Narcocorrido | 199 |
| | Commentary and Conclusions | 217 |
| | *Notes* | *223* |
| | *Bibliography* | *257* |
| | *Index* | *289* |

# ILLUSTRATIONS

## Figures

| | | |
|---|---|---|
| 1. | Map of the ecological regions of the U.S.-Mexico borderlands | 5 |
| 2. | Robotic surveillance dog on the U.S.-Mexico border | 23 |
| 3. | U.S. Army constructing concertina wire, Nogales, Arizona, February 2019 | 32 |
| 4. | U.S. Army concertina wire completed, Nogales, Arizona, February 2019 | 33 |
| 5. | A video game titled *Border Security Wall Construction AP* by TwoTwenty Games | 33 |
| 6. | Permanent U.S.-Mexico border checkpoints in August 2009 | 34 |
| 7. | Arizona checkpoints, Tucson sector | 35 |
| 8. | U.S. Border Patrol sign between Las Cruces and Hatch, New Mexico | 36 |
| 9. | *Toe Tag Wall Prototype* at Phillips Museum of Art, Franklin & Marshall College, Undocumented Migration Project pop-up exhibit | 37 |
| 10. | Bird Nest Hill in the Sonoran Desert near Sells, Arizona | 38 |
| 11. | Roberto Primero Luis and his wife, Katy Sunún, in Guatemala a few months before his death journey | 38 |
| 12. | Altar to slain Texcoco mayor Gisela Mota | 45 |
| 13. | Puro Cartél del Golfo | 46 |
| 14. | Mexico military expenditure in millions of dollars, 2023 | 48 |

| | | |
|---|---|---|
| 15. | El Chapo commodities | 51 |
| 16. | A family network gathers to eat carne asada next to the border wall | 54 |
| 17. | Heber López Vásquez | 106 |
| 18. | Roberto Toledo | 106 |
| 19. | Margarito Martínez Esquivel | 106 |
| 20. | Lourdes Maldonado López | 107 |
| 21. | Marco Ernesto Islas Flores | 107 |
| 22. | José Luis Gamboa Arenas | 107 |
| 23. | Jorge Camero Zazueta | 108 |
| 24. | Juan Carlos Muñiz | 108 |
| 25. | Amando Linares López | 108 |
| 26. | Baby-faced Sinaloa Cartel recruits awaiting orders during the second Culiacán takeover, January 5, 2023 | 131 |

## Tables

| | | |
|---|---|---|
| 1. | Selected LIC equipment present in immigration and drug enforcement in the U.S.-Mexico border region, 1978–1992 | 29 |
| 2. | Selected LIC operational characteristics present in immigration and drug enforcement in the U.S.-Mexico border region, 1978–1992 | 30 |

# ACKNOWLEDGMENTS

I wish to thank Nora Martinez, who provided invaluable editorial and substantive assistance to the completion of this work. And thanks to Sheila McMahon, an extraordinary wordsmith and editor with a very sharp pen, for her directions and her extraordinary editing and guidance. To my dear friend Roberto Alvarez, *mil gracias* for his pithy and often deadeye reckonings of concepts and the necessity for shortening windiness. I'm grateful to my colleague James B. Greenberg for his theoretical commentary and clarity; my colleague Margaret Dorsey for her insightful remarks and suggestions on very early drafts; and Josiah Heyman for his remarkable attention to the theoretical basis of this work. Thank you to the reviewers, who were exacting in their reviews and extremely helpful in their suggestions and added materials and citations. Also, this book could not have been possible without the sabbatical provided by Arizona State University in 2021 or without the director of the School of Transborder Studies, Irasema Coronado. To my many informed informants who must remain nameless, bless you and your families. You are often in harm's way, and yet you persist in—sometimes impossibly—dealing with the dangers of context to support and educate your children on both sides of the bifurcation of this huge geography of the border region.

# THE RISE OF NECRO/NARCO CITIZENSHIP

# Introduction

This book is about the manner in which warring of various types has led to the creation of violence-dependent material, human, and symbolic cultural networks that cross and recross an imposed border dividing what I have termed the "Southwest North American Region" (SWNAR). It details the genesis and history of the violent dynamics penetrating multiple aspects of daily life on both sides of the border, such as the dislocation of thousands of people, which often forces the best and the brightest to flee for their lives.

As an introductory example, such is the case for Clarissa Gómez (pseudonym). Clarissa was a real estate developer in a coastal town noted for its thousands of years of Maya presence, whose ritual altars still dot the coastline. Long used as beacons for Maya seafarers, these altars are now shadowed by hotels crowding the formerly pristine beaches. Clarissa used her law degree to negotiate the often arcane and cloudy laws pertaining to foreign ownership of houses and property, and successfully managed her lucrative office for ten years. After a divorce, while raising two very bright daughters and being surrounded by extensive family networks, Clarissa became involved with an American entrepreneur and builder. Five years later, after a number of vacations and long-distance romantic commuting, they married and started a development and real estate company. With Clarissa clearing the legal and extralegal barriers and using her familial networks for contacts in banking and financial circles, she and her husband soon became known as an international power couple in a very lucrative beach market. They did extremely well, sharing homes in Mexico and the United States.

However, she started receiving repeated telephone calls demanding payment for keeping her business open. It seems that for many years she had been protected by a cousin deeply associated with one of the cartels—but that organization had been usurped by another. Thus, this example—which is elaborated in chapter 4—is only a single case of the far-reaching consequences of the militarization and the violent processes overtaking the region.

The SWNAR, encompassing northern Mexico and the southwestern United States, is an ecological architecture consisting of huge mountain ranges buttressed by the huge Chihuahuan and Sonoran Deserts, interspersed by adjoining diverse archipelagos and plains and coastal systems all crosscut by crucial riverine systems (figure 1).[1] Excluding Mesoamerica and including the northern Mexican states and North American border states as political entities, its ecological expanse and space are larger than most of Western Europe, including the United Kingdom. It is a huge region held together by the massive Chihuahuan and Sonoran Deserts, the Sierra Madre and Rocky Mountains, the diverse Madrean Archipelago, and bounded smaller ecosystems. Crosscut by valleys, riverine systems, mountain ranges, and nourished by the Colorado and Rio Grande Rivers emerging from the north in the Rocky Mountains, its outlets flow into the Sea of Cortez and the Gulf of Mexico. The region in its entirety is a complex of peoples and continuing methods of extraction and exploitation.

For thousands of years, human populations have adopted diverse and complex methods of exploitation in the SWNAR—from monumental centers like those of Chaco Canyon of New Mexico to Casas Grandes of Chihuahua, interspersed with small-scale rancherias, farms, and temporary mobile settlements. It has been colonized by more than 400 years of Spanish hegemony, is part of the birthplace to the Mexican nation, and was a site of conquest by the United States in the nineteenth century. And for the past 175 years, these historical and sociocultural factors developed a region of great economic contradiction and dependence, with

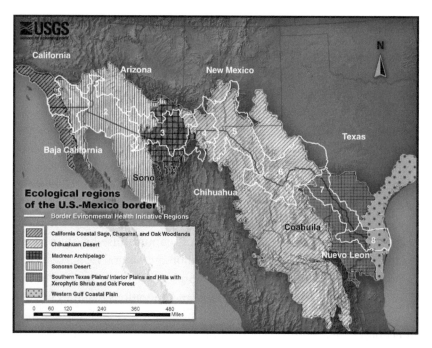

FIGURE 1 Map of the ecological regions of the U.S.-Mexico borderlands. U.S.-Mexico Border Environmental Health Initiative (2015), redrawn by Enrique Borges. Reprinted from Carlos G. Vélez-Ibáñez, *Hegemonies of Language and Their Discontents: The Southwest North American Region Since 1540* (Tucson: University of Arizona Press, 2017), 26.

enormous reliance on Mexican labor on both sides of the geographic bifurcation.

From the nineteenth century to the present, economic policies, investments, and extractions of value in diverse formats developed and emerged in the region.[2] Over the past fifty years, most of my anthropological narratives of Mexican-origin populations on both sides of the bifurcation we call the "border" have presented relatively promising messages for the populations involved, from political struggles in central urban Mexico to the economic and social practices of highly mobile transnational populations. Marked by deliberate political actions of diverse sorts—from physical confrontations to negotiated "settlements" between communities and overwhelmingly strong economic and political institutions and authorities—these populations gained a bit of an edge in the aftermath of their actions. Equally important in this long rendering was the first transnational narrative of rotating savings and credit associations of participating populations from Tapachula, Chiapas, to Washington State. These were crucial to these highly mobile populations to create substantial funds for investment, housing, schooling, and ritual activities, all reflecting the density and "thickness" of social relations within networks of relatives, friends, and coworkers and the central core value of *confianza*, or mutual trust. Like the political actors described, these "economic" actors survived, excelled, and made it possible for following generations to edge away from the effects of poverty, underemployment, and the extraction of value from their labor.

But in the present late stage of global capitalism, these phenomena seem linked strongly to a debilitated and compromised system of extraction, filled with the exploitation of labor and natural resources. Over the past fifty years, political entities representing their "nations" introduced military know-how, assumptions, and operations that they funded, transmitted, and adopted in congruent cooperation, resulting in a pattern of economic and political transnational networks of questionable coda and moral centers. In a blog post for the North American Congress on Latin America (NACLA), Paul Ashby describes this process in terms of "policing." Ashby writes:

> During this summer's [2014] child migrant crisis and the accompanying frenzy around "security" along the U.S.-Mexico boundary, a spotlight was shone on Mexico's role in protecting the U.S. "homeland." It helped illuminate what Washington considers the United States' territorial boundaries: those of the countries associated with the North American Free Trade Agreement (NAFTA). In other words, the territories of Canada and Mexico are part of the U.S. policing regime, under a regional security framework we might call "NAFTA-land Security."[3]

I prefer the term *militarization* for what Ashby calls *NAFTA-land security*. I would call late-stage capitalism's extensive neoliberal economic policies of structural readjustment as central to what will be developed as the "War of Omission." More simply, late-stage capitalism is the incorporation of all world economies into a global pattern of accumulation

INTRODUCTION

that knows no national or cultural boundaries and leaves out millions as casualties of the War of Omission.

In 1991, Michael Kearney published "Borders and Boundaries of State and Self at the End of Empire," which discusses with theoretical complexity nationalisms, the nation-state, transnationalisms, ethnicity, and anthropology in the context of contemporary capitalism.[4] In it, Kearney expounds the "decline of the unitedstatesian empire which is experiencing a . . . dissolution in the spatial, and symbolic distinction between itself and its dependencies."[5] Just as importantly, he points to the spatial separation of the site of the purchase and expenditure of labor and thus a national separation of the sites of production and reproduction. It is my contention that in the thirty years since Kearney's insightful article appeared, the increasing important reliance on military processes— both legal and extralegal—by the United States and Mexico have led to the emergence of an intense and continuous militarized transnational superstate-like network. This emerging superstate network functions as a primary mechanism of control, surveillance, suppression, exploitation, and violence against inhabitants from southern Mexico (Tapachula) to the southwestern United States (Tucson), and beyond in both directions. The result, I argue, has produced profound social dislocations of populations, constrictions of civil freedoms, and the development of "warrior" cultural formations on both sides of the bifurcation.

The present work concentrates on how low-intensity military doctrine is basically "total war at the grassroots level," as opposed to global warfare leading to annihilation.[6] It varies in intensity according to circumstances but essentially it is marked by the use of local forces against insurgents, technical and material assistance by a superior military source, sales of arms and communication networks, and the establishment of a strategy attracting local support in its efforts. In various degrees, it has permeated the daily lives of millions of populations, especially in the Southwest North American Region, but beyond it as well. The American drug market is a major immediate and present core element of broader militarized functions. However, there are much larger processes responsible for the establishment of this particular market, its attending impacts, and the continued debility of state political structures and their basic adjusted militarized transnational networks. From the nations of the United States and Mexico to local towns and households on both sides of the bifurcation of the "border," the processes of militarization emerge in the SWNAR from boundaryless sources and have diverse impacts from Tucson to Tapachula and beyond. The picture is not a pretty one. Indeed, the effects of ever-present violent death and psychological distresses are wide-ranging, deeply effective, and detrimental to the development of following generations. Civic and civil social, political, and cultural structures dissolve, dislocate, and deaden, and are replaced with fear, intimidation, avoidance, and cultural rationalizations of legitimacy and expression. All these consequences emanate, to different degrees, from the asymmetry of economic relations and structures of a flailing global economy.

## The Dynamics of Economy and Inequality

From the nineteenth century to the present, the interdependent but asymmetrical economies of the United States and Mexico created and demanded Mexican labor to establish industrial agriculture, mining, ranching, and urbanization. Periodic economic depressions have been used to justify deportations, expulsions, criminalizations of persons as "illegals," and dislocations of Mexican families, followed by periods of restabilization and growth in which their replacements return or are brought back. These cycles of attraction and expulsion were exacerbated in the twentieth century by the expansion of neoliberal ideologies and implementations.

In Mexico, "three decades of neoliberalism . . . has destroyed the country's industrial and agricultural productive structure as well as its public institutions," according to Asa Cristina Laurell.[7] The 1983 debt crisis put into place an International Monetary Fund–dictated neoliberal policy resulting in a "redistribution of income between capital (48 percent to 64 percent) and labor (42 percent to 29 percent), a 30 percent to 40 percent decrease in wages and salaries and a significant rise of unemployment and precarious jobs by 12 percent."[8] Furthermore, says Laurell, "total public expenditure also dropped and about 60 percent was channeled to pay debt, while social public expenditure was reduced by about 35 percent between 1982 and 1988."[9] Constitutional amendments transformed cooperative farms into private property and eliminated rural subsidies. Simultaneously, "public companies were privatized; land reform was reversed; higher public education could legally be charged to students; and Mexico's transnational processes sealed by deregulating and liberalization of capital flows, but not of labor."[10] Neoliberal policy peaked with the implementation of NAFTA in 1994 under Carlos Salinas del Gortari's presidency and was a strategic imposition guaranteeing these processes.[11]

The implementation of neoliberal and structural adjustment policies in the United States and Mexico in the 1970s and 1980s, respectively, and the rise of a colossal drug market in the United States created a perfect economic storm in the region. As a result of accelerated neoliberal policies and the denationalization of the financial system, foreign financial groups came to control almost 100 percent of Mexican banking assets. Meanwhile, the wholesale extraction of natural resources through mining enormously increased. Even further, these changes were accompanied by large-scale migration of landless or out-subsidized farmers, rural peoples, and both underemployed and unemployed urban populations to the United States.[12] With the loss of necessary social programs and agricultural subsidies, millions of people were pushed out from rural areas, and the result was large-scale migrations to the United States and to cities and towns in Mexico in the 1970s–1990s. Josiah Heyman notes, "This impulse to liberalize Mexico's economic institutions without addressing underdeveloped oversight measures and governmental units without the ability to withstand corrupting influences which only led to the further concentration of ill-gotten and capitalist wealth accumulation."[13]

Simultaneously, enormous profitmaking by drug cartels and organizations created an illegal arms trade, using narco dollars as payment for a highly militarized and organized cultural architecture. As numerous commentators have indicated, it is at this point that the criminal economy began to spread its influence without political control; this was the case under the Institutional Revolutionary Party (Partido Revolucionario Institucional, PRI) in Mexico. Without it, the criminal economy extended enormous influence politically, socially, economically, and culturally into the present.[14]

The sale of opiates and cocaine and the creation of transnational criminal gangs permitted low-intensity warfare doctrine to penetrate many aspects of life in the United States and Mexico. The Mexican version of this militarization involves the Mexican military's receipt of millions of dollars of U.S. aid and the increasing roles of the military in public works such as airport, railway, and highway developments, as well as seaport and airport custom and fiscal controls. These activities all circumvent general fund allocations.

Just as the American drug market greatly gave energy to these phenomena, so too have the highly militarized low-intensity warfare doctrines and funding support promulgated by every U.S. presidential administration since Richard Nixon. His administration created the "five schedules" of drugs, later amplified by other administrations. These schedules were used as the focus points for the "War on Drugs" that followed. The powerful subdoctrine of a "War on Drugs" resulted eventually in the further migration of documented and undocumented Mexicans to the United States over the past thirty years. Coupled with hysterical public policy and media representation concerning immigration, the United States has created the basic architecture for diverse "low-intensity" warfare doctrines, with sharply focused militarization arising in the aftermath of the events of 9/11.[15] What evolved among white Americans was the integration of 9/11 fears of fatal terrorist attacks with fantastic fears of a border easily penetrated by alleged masses of racialized Mexicans, falsely characterized as bringing with them a drug market capable of infiltrating all corners of the United States.

These compounding developments over the past thirty years have led to the creation of an American necro/state structure and its accompanying Mexican narco/state structure, inexorably linked by multiple articulations. Thus, on both sides of the bifurcated region, a well-funded twin-state necro/narco network structure is developing. In this book, I discuss how this necro/narco network is felt in diverse ways on both sides of the border bifurcation but especially onerously in the Southwest North American Region and beyond. This militarized system is characterized by multiple spatial and behavioral domains and affects the daily lives of millions of persons in diverse classes on both sides of the bifurcation—civilly, politically, socially, economically, and culturally. Young generations are often caught in the structure's web of multiple legalities and aspirations, leading to often tensely negotiated and temporary relations with significant others, such as in youth gangs—as will be discussed in chapter 6. A diversity of persons often caught between and betwixt social and political structures must become expert conductors of interstitial relations and contexts. This includes economically "living at a slant," which is basically a survival strategy by populations in disadvantaged social and economic positions that avoid confrontations, create functional reciprocal networks, and induce positive decisions with powerholders.[16] The approach for this entire narrative centers on great attention to structural impediments, processes, and impacts; the quotidian realities negotiated by those populations affected by the necro/narco structure; and the adaptive and maladaptive consequences they experience in their lives. These are further discussed in chapters 1 and 2.

## Overview of This Book

To support the central foci of the book, I combine archival, ethnographic, statistical, autoethnobiographical, and historical sources. Archival material was gleaned from multiple governmental sources from both sides of the region, while statistical information was extracted from major reports, academic sources, and public information sources, including newspapers, periodicals, journals, editorial commentary, and specialized online sources. Ethnographic sources include published works, from which vignettes are reproduced with intervening commentaries, as well as original participant observation conducted on both sides of the region by the lead author and Nayeli Burgueño A.

This book draws upon original transborder field observations from many junctures throughout my career. More specifically, this book relies on fieldwork conducted during summers, winter vacations, and research leaves between 2019 and 2023 on both sides of the border bifurcation in the region, mostly in northern Mexican states and Arizona. I further rely on original field notes of the Marine Corps League of Tucson, Arizona, initially conducted in the late 1980s; oral history interviews with some of its members in the 1990s; two reconstructed conversations between my uncle and my father in the late 1940s, followed by a discussion between my uncle and myself; and, fifty years later, reconstructed information from a relative in the late 1990s and supported by further interviews of the same in 2022. Most names and places are masked where a consideration of either security issues or sensitivities to the individuals were warranted and especially interviews and observations made in situ in northern Mexican states and in southwestern American states. Other places and persons in the public record made such masking impossible. All English translations are mine from all sources.

The narrative is structured as eight chapters followed by a conclusion. Importantly, two of these eight chapters are contributions. The first contribution is chapter 5, by Nayeli Burgueño A., who provides a vivid ethnography of the struggle of returning migrants to Cosalá, Sinaloa, in the aftermath of U.S. immigration policies. The second, chapter 7, is an ethnobiography by Arturo Santamaría Gómez of his decades-long struggles against state and local corruption and as a scholar and journalist revealing the influences and powerful forces imbedded in political and educational institutions.

In chapter 1, I establish where and how global capitalism fits within the political ecology of the SWNAR and its constant reliance on Mexican labor for its basic functions since the nineteenth century and its unequal interdependent relation of extraction and commoditization. Undergirding this work is Nina Glick-Schiller's concept of the "global historical conjuncture," which forms "an approach to history that places transformations in political and social formations within an analysis of dominant forms of the accumulation and concentration of wealth and power."[17] As I demonstrate in this chapter, the development of the necro/narco transstate network is a consequence of global capitalism's "global historical conjuncture." I further argue that this emergent network, formed by the building blocks of low-intensity warfare and their cultural and behavioral dynamics, is the mechanism of force and legitimacy that provides the foundational structures of this global historical conjuncture and its accompanying phenomena.

I refer to these phenomena as the consequences of the Wars of Omission—that is, the expected results of poor wages, low incomes, poor infrastructure, low educational outcomes, and continued economic exploitation (like those of the maquiladoras) created by this late stage of capital. The millions of individuals in these circumstance are the real casualties of these wars. Further, the violent attempts to maintain or protect the status quo are aspects of the Wars of Commission and are usually promulgated by state actors or those in opposition.

In chapter 2, I explore how the aforementioned phenomena of Wars of Commission and Omission give rise to the development of two cultural complexes: necrocitizenship and narcocitizenship. The former is marked in the United States by a penchant for symbolically and politically identifying with militarized symbols, rituals, and behaviors as well as political positions of global and local dimensions, while the latter appears in the Mexican region/state characterized by low-intensity warfare, violence, and nonstate political and authority-controlled spaces that parallel and counter existing civil and political regimes—with profound cultural impacts. Cultural manifestations of narcocitizenship include the development of generations of youth that mix masculinities with adherence to a drug culture of impunity, violence, and glorification of wealth and an early demise. For those not involved in narcotrafficking activity, narcocitizenship entails daily negotiations of avoidance, denial, and suppressed fear. Empirical and historical data and examples of practices provide the underlying support for these constructs.

In chapter 3, I seek to understand both the genesis and the developmental aspects of necrocitizenship, a cultural complex of the necro/narco trans-state network. Necrocitizenship includes patinas of patriotism, rationales of justifications, and a host of ritual and behavioral indicators of a willingness to use violence in all its forms, local and global. Ethnographic narratives and examples are provided as empirical supports for this analysis focusing on the works of Texas and Arizona patriotic associations. I consider in this chapter not only Mexican-origin U.S. populations but also Puerto Ricans, as they share colonial and conquest characteristics that are unlike those of any other Latina/o/x population. For these populations, their historical conquest, continued misuse and use of their labors, and unequal economic relations continuously contribute to their omission from the rewards of the global economy, and their participation in long Wars of Commission places them in unviable social and cultural contradictions whose major escape is to be willing to die to belong in global and local conflicts. Thus, those engaged in Wars of Omission at the local level may creep into Wars of Commission as responses to their psychological, economic, or cultural dissatisfaction.

In chapter 4, I examine narcocitizenship, the companion cultural complex of necrocitizenship, as an ever-evolving and emergent symbolic, material, and "distributive" process combining illegal sale and transmission of drugs by well-organized cartels. It is accompanied by extreme violence, both defensive and offensive; symbolic and expressive folklore, rituals, and language; public cultural expressions of music, dress, and attire; and deeply engineered military tactics, strategies, and political influences and control. However, to different degrees, the violence, threats, firefights, and the impunity of cartel-associated actors have created among the general population feelings of discord, uncertainty, and fear. These feelings are casually coupled to dislocations and unwanted migrations from points of origin to other parts of Mexico and the United States, and with them deep human resource losses to their original contexts. Simultaneously, Wars of Omission are visited among the population by labor exploitation and social inequality. I use statistical, historical, and ethnographic materials from both original and published works that reveal the quotidian realities of populations caught in the glare of inequality, institutional and political decay of wide swaths of the juridical and legislative system enforcement, control, and civil life.

Chapter 5 is a translation of a chapter written by Dr. Nayeli Burgueño A. of the Universidad Autónoma de Sinaloa for this book and partially reported in her own recent work, *Retorno a la comunidad: Migración y los fondos de identidad trasnacional*.[18] Using original field research conducted in the town of Cosolá, Sinaloa, in 2000, Burgueño analyzes the behaviors needed to sustain a semblance of familial and personal security, compensation and adaptation to fear and insecurity, and the manner in which social relations of returned transnational families are negotiated and sustained or disrupted. The lack of institutional support for returned families, the stresses of adaptation of U.S.-born children in schools, and the extreme reduction of needed resources for familial stability are all part of the many issues these families have had to undergo. These are compounded by the insecurities they suffer because of the uncertainties of community life due to the penetration of drug-influenced economic and legal issues and the forced outmigration and familial disruptions of U.S.-born children who had accompanied their parents.

Chapter 6 focuses on how sectors of the Mexican-origin population on the northern side of the border region, especially in rural areas, are extremely affected by addiction in the daily lives of youth. Sectors of Mexican youth in rural areas on the southern side have become part of the universe of users instead of being observers of drugs passing by. Thus, inhaling, ingesting, consuming, and dying from products of eventual destruction, many youths on both sides of the border are daily ensconced in narcoculture, created by a dearth of opportunities and by structural dimensions and pressures that have relatively little surcease. Such conditions are made possible by global drug markets of self-destruction and generational self-consumption. These circumstances form part of a regional version of a globalizing process beyond necro and narcocitizenship that will influence generations of wasted youth. I use strong ethnographic material from published sources, statistical and quantitative data, and historical documentation to triangulate how Wars of Commission and Omission impact the daily lives of many youths on both sides of the Southwest North American Region and are the wellsprings of the tragic consequences established in the narrative.

Chapter 7 is an autoethnobiography written specifically for this book in 2023 by Dr. Arturo Santamaría Gómez, also from the Universidad Autónoma de Sinaloa. Based on Santamaría's ethnobiographical reconstruction and his own published work, and translated and introduced by myself, this chapter provides a historical and autoethnobiographical narrative detailing how over forty years, the democratization of Mexico has led to the muting of any real participatory political process and enabled the creation of parallel and sometimes integrated bodies of political power completely outside of possible institutional control and with more of a narcocitizenship bent than previous versions of government traditionally controlled by a one-party state. Santamaría details the hijacking of democratic processes in the guise of political participation, aided and abetted by unsavory elements with the eventual impressive oppression of the free expression of ideas and issues of representation. The chapter is presented first in English and then in its original Spanish. The Spanish version is imperative because of its importance in revealing for Spanish-speaking readers the interlocking aspects of political corruption and academic silencing adhered to deeply emotional stresses and quiet desperation.

Chapter 8 is an examination of transnational public culture as expressed in music that broaches and articulates the warring dynamics of the process of necro/narco citizenship. The narcocorrido is a public, deterritorialized cultural production revealing its intentional creation and targeting of a youthful audience on both sides of the border bifurcation. The songs have become the unofficial anthems of the Wars of Commission and Omission. Their implications are mixed as to impact or influence, but their meta-messages seem to be based on an underlying architecture of the self-consumption of this late stage of accumulation and its acceptance by many youths as the primary consumers. For some youth, different versions of the messaging of narcocorridos are congruent with the realities of their quotidian experience, and for others there are injected mythical solutions via violence, objectified women, and extravagant consumption—what I have termed the "American Mexican Triangle."

In the commentary and conclusions, what must be emphasized is that there is an unexpected but certain consequence of assembling and constructing this complex of relations, political structures, cultural practices and beliefs, economic asymmetries, and disconnected productions, including drug markets. These relations emerged and were derived from their situated ethnographic contexts and human actions. Thus, there is no doubt that without such contexts the quotidian struggles in which people are engaged in the Southwest North American Region and globally cannot be fully understood—and worse, too, are often ahistorically represented only by enumerated references. Providing the quotidian realities of those engaged, from the most corrupt of relationships to those refusing to become victims of such corruption, reinforces Eric Wolf's admonition that ethnography has never been more important for ferreting out the myriad historical complexities of connections of economy, politics, social relations, cultural systems, behaviors, and their attending patterns of political ecology in this late stage of human self-absorption.[19]

Thus, this work seeks to uncover the hidden dimensions of this situated global process in which low-intensity Wars of Commission and Omission play the central roles in the struggle over the value of labor, the value of work, and the imposed value of materiality. Attending this struggle are the cultural and social dimensions created by intended and unintended practices and behaviors. These behaviors are expressed in myriad ways ritually and by what I have termed the American Mexican Triangle of narcocorridos providing youthful anthems to necro/narco citizenship.

# CHAPTER 1

## The Necro/Narco Trans-state Network Emergence and Their Wars of Commission and Omission

The necro/narco trans-state network of the United States and Mexico is, I argue, the latest phase of the process in which globalization has structurally replaced local, community, regional, and national economies, creating a global export economy largely in the hands of international corporations with allegiance to none but profit. The Southwest North American Region (SWNAR) is part of a War of Omission: an extractive late-stage capitalism circumstance that began in the nineteenth century and left in its wake profound social disturbances and millions of low-income casualties. The necro/narco trans-state network that consequently emerged was formed by low-intensity warfare and its cultural and behavioral practices. It is the weaponized medium ostensibly created to counter those Wars of Omission disturbances—especially those created by the transnational American drug market.

In this chapter, I examine American necrocitizenship and its nonidentical twin Mexican narcocitizenship as characteristic of culturally diverse complexes arising in tandem as consequences of the long history of Wars of Commission and Omission. I take up for discussion global capitalism, its weaknesses and contradictions, and at this late stage of development, *where* and *how* it fits within the political ecology of the SWNAR. Undergirding this work is Nina Glick-Schiller's concept of the "global historical conjuncture," which forms "an approach to history that places transformations in political and social formations within an analysis of dominant forms of the accumulation and concentration of wealth and power."[1] These are the structural foundations of the Wars of Omission. The resulting necro/narco trans-state network of the United States and Mexico as such is a current example of Glick-Schiller's "accumulation and concentration of wealth and power." Their Wars of Commission and Omission constitute their systemic artifacts.

In the SWNAR, global capitalism persists through a constant reliance on Mexican labor—a dependence that has lasted since the nineteenth century—and the unequal relation of extraction and commoditization. This is especially the case for Mexico after the implementation of NAFTA in 1994 and following versions of the same policy, which has been integrated into other advanced countries.[2] It is marked by the replacement of imports of major industries like automobile and steel production, mining, agriculture, and other major sectors with export-oriented strategies managed by foreign investors, or foreign direct investments (FDIs). These substitutions contribute to real underlying structural issues, as summarized by Özlem Onaran: "In the case of FDI, there is no evidence of a positive effect on the manufacturing wage share. In Mexico the high inflow of capital, particularly after NAFTA[,] might even have a negative, albeit low effect on the wage share. The lack of positive FDI effects is related to the dominance of the efficiency[-]seeking FDI with low domestic backward linkages."[3] This "efficiency" sought by FDIs is especially marked by its threats of moving capital and further alienation from local markets.

Or, to sum up: FDI corporations in Mexico are far removed from the national economy, depend on low wages, and tend to leave when profit margins are more attractive in other countries, leaving behind husks of what they established. They offer little real share for workers and threaten workers and country into low-wage spirals. FDIs are in fact the expected consequences of the Wars of Omission and are symptomatic of late-stage capital accumulation seeking to scrape value from every corner of production. This extractivism combines with disastrous ecological impacts from floods, drought, earthquakes, and pandemics in Central America and the Caribbean to create a perfect economic and ecological storm that displaces hundreds of thousands of people. Migrating north or south is one of the few remaining choices for individuals and families to respond to the local, regional, and national vacuums created by the structural debilitation of postindustrial capitalism and natural disasters.

It also results in the creation of sectors of drug seekers and drug suppliers. Drug-seeking sectors are concentrated in Europe and North America, while Mexico, South America, and Asia make up the drug-supplier sectors. These drug sectors eventually culminate in regional policies. The "War on Drugs," though promulgated by the United States, was emulated and networked by Mexico through numerous treaties, agreements, economic assistance, and the technical and personnel presence of Department of Homeland Security (DHS) and Drug Enforcement Administration (DEA) agents. These constitute "Wars of Commission" and are of the "low-intensity" type, which mostly use indirect means of intervention but also rely on home countries' "boots on the ground" action. "Boots on the ground" includes attention to "pacification" programs of various sorts as well as tactics mirroring those of the opponents. Regardless of terminology, from the outset with the Nixonian War on Drugs, followed by the Clintonian "Colombia Plan" of the 1990s and subsequent "Mérida Initiative / Plan Mexico," and into the present, these campaigns place great emphasis on the hallmarks of "low-intensity warfare." They rely on the same tactical approaches of interdiction, technical assistance, military equipment and training, and military, DEA, and, later, Homeland Security personnel on the ground.[4] Low-intensity warfare has been practiced especially since the "banana wars" of the early twentieth century in Central America, interventions in Haiti, and honed to a fine point in Vietnam.

Crucially, what emerges here is the development of a trans-state network promulgating self-serving policies and transborder control. These "policing" policies must be understood within the political ecology of the region and the underlying architecture of inequalities, hegemonies, and conquests of populations and their accompanying cultural, social, economic, and often racialized impositions of the region and beyond. As Heyman asserts:

> They all represent the U.S. state desire to control illicit flows through prohibition and the policing regimes are a projection of US military power under the rubric of foreign policy and diplomacy. These take on the form of unilateral exertions of policing control. And the desire for control of

political actors in the U.S. government's legislative and executive branches should be viewed cynically. Policing regimes are also effective political theater as Peter Andreas pointed out in *Border Games: The Politics of Policing the U.S.-Mexico Divide.*[5]

## Historical Junctures of Imperial and Colonial Settler Hegemonies and the Criminalization of Mexicans

There is a long history of imperial and colonial settler hegemonies that provide the historical context for the present phase of militarization of the SWNAR and beyond. These established the underlying structural relations of ecology, economy, politics, social stratifications, and racialisms and provided the cultural rationalizations for the present circumstances. For the most part, the current circumstances of hegemonies and global historical conjuncture in the SWNAR began in the fifteenth century, with the penetration of the Spanish Empire. This was then replaced with a nascent Mexican political state in 1821, and then the region was conquered by the United States in 1848.

All these versions of colonial hegemony—Spanish colonialism followed by a Mexican Republican rationalization, and then the American manifest destiny—were based on an imperial design akin to what Juanita Sundberg refers to as *"a way of life"* that permeates all.[6] Thus, the Spanish rationalized their mercantile and imperial hegemony as a mechanism for saving Indigenous populations from perdition. Indigenous systems were replaced with a celestial version of Catholicism further rationalized by civil legalisms pertaining to vassalage, rights of discovery, their accompanying declarations, and institutions of requerimiento, repartimiento, and encomienda.[7] These acts were made possible by ritual, language, and especially by violence and military force.[8] Thus, the cross, the pen, and the sword established a fragile but three-hundred-year oppressive hegemony—but not without its discontents.[9]

For the next twenty-five years after Mexican independence in 1821, the new Mexican Republic tried to establish a national version of sovereignty over its domains. The Republic sought to establish mestizo hegemony over Indigenous populations in the name of national identity and democratic principles of representation, but to no avail. Internal dissensions, conflict, and class and caste strife impeded their efforts. And, of course, these efforts were mostly without the consent of most Indigenous populations.

In 1835, Mexico lost Texas by revolution, sparked by resistance to the abolition of slavery by the Mexican government on the part of immigrant Anglo Texans, and opposition to the Mexican centralized government by Native Tejanos.[10] By 1846, the country was invaded by the United States. Two years after the U.S. occupation of Mexico City by American troops and Mexico's subsequent loss, Mexico signed the Treaty of Guadalupe Hidalgo. Five years later, the Treaty of the Mesilla established what came to be the border for the most part. Between 1845 and 1852, the United States annexed the following Mexican territories: the slave state of Texas; the conquered lands of Nevada, Utah, most of New Mexico, Arizona, and Colorado; parts of Oklahoma, Kansas, and Wyoming; and much of California. It also purchased southern Arizona and New Mexico in 1852, in a sale that was likely forced by the United States' threats during negotiations to declare war again if Mexico did not agree to the terms.[11] All in all, more than half of Mexico became a possession of the United States, mostly by military conquest or its threat.

Beginning in 1880 with the introduction of the railroad, European settler colonists immigrated to the newly conquered regions on the American side and politically and demographically displaced the remaining Mexican populations. Over the next fifty years, Mexican colonial settlers were replaced by American versions of mostly European settlers now considered "Americans." Indigenous populations were cornered into reservations and Mexicans became foreigners in the region marked by the newly imposed border line.

As mining, agriculture, ranching, railroads, and urbanization by foreign companies in Mexico and in their adjoining American states created large-scale industrial modes of production, Mexican labor became a much used and abused commodity in all industrial enterprises on both sides of the bifurcation, regardless of "legality." Employing a strategy that continues to this day, nineteenth-century Anglo enterprises used Mexican laborers when economic circumstances necessitated it and expulsed them when their work was no longer needed. Through the twentieth and early twenty-first centuries, an economic rationale referred to as "labor elasticity" arose. Labor elasticity rationalizes the recruitment of Mexican labor—both authorized and unauthorized—regardless of where needed from California to the Carolinas. So when industries and enterprises need low-paid labor, Mexicans become desired labor pools.[12] This spiked especially after the illegalization of Mexican laborers and their reduction to criminal subjects, particularly by state policy such as the infamous and unconstitutional SB 1070 of the state of Arizona.[13] With such circumstances glued to the emergence of the transnational and now global drug economy, migrations of thousands to the north are painted with the brush of illegality—and, importantly, criminally subject to arrest, incarceration, and deportation.

## Militarization and the Creation of the Necro/Narco Trans-state Network

In the present, unauthorized and authorized migrations seem to be conflated by American publics—a conflation that is especially promulgated by politicians like Donald Trump who paint all migrants with the brush of "illegals," and in so doing attach a criminal trope as an adhesive definition, as Leo R. Chavez has pointed out in his numerous works.[14] Conflated under the category of "illegal," migration is then further criminalized by association with cross-border narcotrafficking. Both nations rely fundamentally on military doctrine and operations to enforce bans on the transportation of drugs, and in this way, Mexicans who cross the border for all reasons are objectified as military subjects and subject to doctrine and operational tactics. This is evidenced by the adoption of high-tech weapons of war and numerous other militarized deployments among U.S. boundary enforcers and their supporting edifices—weapons of war that include night-vision equipment, drones, all-terrain vehicles, and mobile border surveillance posts.

The most recent addition to the enforcers' arsenal is the military-grade robo-dogs made by Ghost Robotics, initially designed to be deployed in the Arizona–Sonora boundary area (figure 2).[15] The quadruped autonomous robots are strong and fast, can upright themselves, and can be armed. Operationally and culturally, they neutralize human emotion and empathy, both necessary for military-level doing and thinking. Enforcers

FIGURE 2 Robotic surveillance dog on the U.S.-Mexico border. Reprinted from Katy Murdza, "New Border Surveillance Technology Raises Privacy Concerns and Could Increase Deaths," Immigration Impact, March 4, 2022, https://immigrationimpact.com/2022/03/04/border-surveillance-technology-privacy-deaths/.

view the robo-dogs as potential force multipliers in border control along the U.S.-Mexico boundary area.[16]

Over the past decade, the U.S. state has made enormous expenditures in support of the Department of Homeland Security. Between 2017 and 2021, the DHS had a five-year average of 211,000 federal employees, 1,431 contracting employees, and 1,438 active opportunities. In this same period, their five-year average for annual contract obligations was $18.2 billion, and their total allocated budget was $91 billion.[17] These funding allocations have created thousands of quasi-military control agents and specialized multiple units of the U.S. Border Patrol (USBP), averaging 20,000 officers over ten years—slightly smaller than the 1st Marine Division.[18] By 2022, this increased to 25,756 officers, half of whom are Mexican origin and/or other Latina/o/x origins. Out of the entire force, approximately a third are military veterans; there is a strong push specially to hire Iraq and Afghanistan veterans.[19] DHS's administrative and operational locus for permanent and roving militarized checkpoints on U.S. soil use "low-intensity warfare" policies extending to Central America. The boundary space is buttressed by its system of internal and boundary-enforcement apparatus controlled by the DHS, and militarized communication networks linking local, state, national, and international policing agencies. This enforcement apparatus is further augmented and made possible by the transformation of the desert regions into "death funnels" to prevent border crossings. The region has been weaponized with the most advanced "low-intensity warfare" technologies and arms and by the assignment of military units as well as special border units as operational control and intervention enforcers.

The border wall is the militarized line of departure, and the COVID-19 pandemic has empowered these enforcement agents even further, particularly through the power to exclude potential "health threats" under Section 265 in U.S. Code Title 42. The combined militarized policies and practices from all agents, south and north, have affected the daily lives of millions of people on both sides of the border region. On the Mexican side, the effects range from human dislocations and the unraveling of civil authority in towns and cities to violence and heinous deaths. And the American side has seen intensive militarized activities from the border to one hundred miles north, with legal and juridical rights of residents set aside for the sake of enforcement.

From such circumstances at this point of history, cultural, social, economic, and political phenomena emerge with unintended, unplanned, unpredictable, and destructive consequences. Yet there is no doubt that militarization promulgated by the United States is the formal dynamic that makes violence the normative energy underlying it all. It is expressed culturally, behaviorally, certainly economically, and politcally using low-intensity warfare as the medium of expression.

# CHAPTER 2

# The Rise of Necrocitizenship and Narcocitizenship Cultural and Social Compensations

The state, funded by citizen taxes and contributions, constitutes a powerful apparatus to implement and perpetuate necrocitizenship. This is often exemplified through symbols such as the Pledge of Allegiance, the Marine Corps Hymn, the national anthem, and tattered but standing regimental and national flags and banners.[1] It also includes rationalization through appealing constructs such as "protecting our borders," "safeguarding jobs," or eliminating foreign workers and their unfair competition.[2] Such discourse is sometimes communicated in the guise of medical rationales of maintaining cleanliness, free from the infections of the "Others," as Chavez has so well shown.[3] And of course, tropes like "invasions," "out of control," "amassing," and "erasing of the border" are repeated to create a sense of fear and to justify violent actions as only offering "protection" to legal citizens and safe spaces for children to grow and prosper. Analyzing the employment of these tropes, Chavez provides valuable exposition of the layers of emotional energy that sustain necrocitizenry.[4] He provides dozens of examples, drawing from processes of engagement, public restatements, media complicity, and, importantly, television talking heads like Sean Hannity, Lou Dobbs, Tucker Carlson, and Laura Ingraham, among others.

Thus, necrocitizenship is double-faced and hydra-headed; not binary, but complex and made up of cultural layers discoverable but too often so normalized that the Pledge of Allegiance is seen as just another elementary school practice and not as an initiation of necrocitizenship. This begins the economic and social dynamics necessary for its long-term integration.

These necro/narco citizenships are theoretically drawn from Achille Mbembe's idea of "necropower and occupation in late modernity."[5] They are directly related to "the writing of new spatial relations."[6] Space as well as the topographies of place inhabited by subjugated peoples become central to the imposition of state power fueled by capturing taxes on capital. Space, in this sense, is a critical lever of sovereignty, not co-extensive with it but critical to its exercise.[7] The Southwest North American Region is such a spatial entity with constant attempts to discipline its inhabitants and reborder its boundaries, especially through militarized policing and low-intensity warfare.

## The Border Patrol Strategy: Rebordering the State

From the point of view of the state, a crucial element to constructing necrocitizenship is rebordering state sovereignty through building borders and walls, as Miguel Díaz-Barriga and Margaret E. Dorsey have insightfully noted.[8] This is accomplished by extending the legal use of surveillance, violence, force, and repression prior to and beyond its concertina wire and twenty-foot border walls with slicing capacities. We can think of the walls as part of the expression of the development and creation of necrostate processes, expressed and manifested through public cultural mediums. Thus, the U.S. Border Patrol strategy emphasizes low-intensity warfare tactics of interdiction and further accentuates the rebordering process with interior checkpoints and in-country raids specifically targeting migrants.

In a document published in 2004, the national border patrol strategy of the U.S. Customs and Border Protection (CPB) was described as consisting of "six core elements: (1) securing the right combination of personnel, technology and infrastructure; (2) improving mobility and rapid deployment to quickly counter and interdict based on shifts in smuggling routes and tactical intelligence; (3) deploying defense-in-depth that makes full use of interior checkpoints and enforcement operations calculated to deny successful migration; (4) coordinating and partnering with other law enforcement agencies to achieve our goals; (5) improving border awareness and intelligence; and (6) strengthening the Headquarters command structure."[9] None of these address the proliferation of arms in Mexico and the drug-dependent populations in the United States, nor the economic basis for drug smuggling as well as for human migration.

As they have done since the creation of the Border Patrol in 1924, agents deploy a broad set of activities related to "border enforcement" and "border security," drawing on low-intensity warfare tactics that emphasize command, control, interdiction, penetrating operational actions, and coordination of actions and operations. Further tactics include networking between local and national agencies, all geared up through a centralized control mechanism. On any given day, thousands of U.S. citizens and noncitizens confront the multiple forms of surveillance, stops, personal inspections (routine and special inspections), questioning, and inspections of vehicles, laptops, and cell phones. Within the one-hundred-mile border zone and international airports, federal Border Patrol, Customs, and Immigration and Customs Enforcement (ICE) agents can carry out routine inspections without probable cause. Thus, in a compressed "typical day," CPB will have carried out the following activities:

Processed: 650,178 passengers and pedestrians
169,842 incoming international air passengers and crew
35,795 passengers and crew on arriving ship/boat
444,541 incoming land travelers
187,049 incoming privately owned vehicles
77,895 truck, rail, and sea containers
$6.64 million worth of imported goods
Conducted 1,107 apprehensions between US ports of entry
Arrested 39 wanted criminals at US ports of entry
Encountered 634 inadmissible persons at US ports of entry
Intercepted 269 fraudulent documents
Discovered 250 pests at US ports of entry and 3,091 materials for
    quarantine—plant, meat, animal byproduct, and soil
Seized: 3,677 pounds of narcotics

$386,195.5 undeclared or illicit currency

$3.6 million worth of products with Intellectual Property Rights violations

Collected approximately $216 million in duties, taxes, and other fees, including more than $204 million in duties

Employed 63,685 men and women including law enforcement and trade personnel:

25,756 CBP officers

2,638 CBP agriculture specialists

19,740 Border Patrol agents

621 air interdiction agents (pilots)

328 marine interdiction agents

338 aviation enforcement agents

1,033 trade personnel

Deployed 1,434 canine teams and 127 horse patrols

Flew 207 enforcement hours at and beyond the border, and within the nation's interior

Underway 74 float hours of enforcement missions in the U.S.

Conducted operations in: 106 countries with more than 697 CBP employees working internationally

328 ports of entry within 20 field offices

131 Border Patrol stations within 20 sectors including 36 immigration checkpoints

74 Air and Marine Operations locations, including branches and units, National Air Security Operations Centers, and the Air and Marine Operations Center[10]

Lest one thinks these are but recent artifacts of low-intensity warfare, such militarization harkens back to much earlier projects. One dimension of the militarization on the part of the U.S. state is the war-inspired arsenal granted to border enforcement agencies between 1978 and 1992, as shown in tables 1 and 2. Nevertheless, the costs of such articulation of policy, equipment, and operations—excluding state and local expenditures—between 1990 and 2020 was $4.09 billion, quadrupling during both Democratic and Republican presidential administrations.[11]

After 9/11, from 2003 to 2022, the central coordinating agency of Homeland Security (which encompasses Customs, Border Patrol, and ICE) has increased fifteenfold in personnel and armaments. They have

# THE RISE OF NECROCITIZENSHIP

TABLE 1  Selected LIC equipment present in immigration and drug enforcement in the U.S.-Mexico border region, 1978–1992

| LIC Equipment | INS* Equipment in the Border Region |
|---|---|
| Helicopters | Increased from 2 in 1980 to 58 in 1992 (most from military) |
| Night-vision equipment | • 335 night-vision scopes by the mid-1980s, & numerous subsequent expansions<br>• Extensive loans of various types of night-vision equipment from the military<br>• Low-light-level television surveillance systems (in portions of 6 out of 9 southwest Border Patrol sectors) |
| Electronic intrusion-detection ground sensors | 1,221 replaced & upgraded by 1984, & numerous subsequent expansions (in all 9 southwest Border Patrol sectors) |

*INS was renamed and placed within DHS
Source: Timothy J. Dunn, *The Militarization of the U.S.-Mexico Border, 1998–1972: Low-Intensity Conflict Doctrine Comes Home* (Austin: CMAS Books, 1996), 150–51.

switched from pistols to M-16s—which are automatic weapons and were first used in Vietnam in 1965—and created SWAT and special operations teams. Some of the latter were introduced by the Trump administration to quell protests in American cities arising from the Black Lives Matter movement. The agency is equipped with detection dogs, vehicle barriers, and surveillance equipment such as censors, floodlights, trip-wire cameras, mobile observation towers, radar blimps, P-3 Orion Surveillance aircraft, helicopters, and drones. Further, Homeland Security has integrated with state and local law enforcement alerts, databases, and communication links.[12]

A salient element strongly associated with this necroprocess is the use of terror to disguise, prevent, or remove any and all incriminating or oppositional communications of arrest, detention, and violations of law and procedure. A recent example of this is the attempted suppression by ICE of a three-year film project that shows how ICE became an instrument of repression and terror, according to a review of the Netflix series *Immigrant Nation* by Caitlin Dickerson for the *New York Times*.[13] The first episode of the series shows people who were arrested by ICE—including someone who was not the target.

TABLE 2  Selected LIC operational characteristics present in immigration and drug enforcement in the U.S.-Mexico border region, 1978–1992

| LIC Operational Characteristics | Border-Region Enforcement Examples |
| --- | --- |
| Coordination & integration of distinct forces (especially police with military) | • Alien Border Control Committee: a multiagency federal task force that designed contingency plans in the mid-1980s for the mass roundup of targeted aliens & for sealing the border<br>• Loosening of legal restrictions on the use of the U.S. military in domestic law enforcement, thereby allowing joint military-police efforts (mainly antidrug)<br>• Operation Alliance: a joint antidrug effort (established in 1986) of federal & state law enforcement agencies (LEAs), with military support<br>• Joint Task Force 6 (JTF-6): a military antidrug unit established in late 1989 to support LEAs in the U.S.-Mexico border region (JTF-6 conducted 775 missions of various types from 1990 to 1992) |
| Military training of local forces | Reconnaissance, intelligence gathering, & small-unit tactics training provided by the military to border-region LEAs |
| Military training exercises outside military bases | Various types of training exercises conducted by military units in border region to support LEAs, primarily in drug enforcement (e.g., JTF-6 conducted 384 operational missions, 1990–1992, though not all were outside bases) |
| Emphasis on intelligence efforts | • Deployment of INS field agents in Mexico & Central America to gather intelligence information on undocumented immigration flows<br>• Sharing of immigration intelligence information among the INS, CIA, & State Department<br>• Formation of the Southwest Border Intelligence Task Force (focused on drug enforcement) |

*Source*: Timothy J. Dunn, *The Militarization of the U.S.-Mexico Border, 1998–1972: Low-Intensity Conflict Doctrine Comes Home* (Austin: CMAS Books, 1996), 150–51.

## Deadly Walls, Canals, and Dying à la Trump: Wars of Commission Artifacts

From link fences and concertina wire to steel and concrete, the border wall constructions are designed to hurt, designed for the use of violence and force "à la Trump." Cemented-in boulders lie in wait, protruding, so that if a person attempting to climb the wall slips and falls, they are not just knocked unconscious but grievously hurt, with limbs, necks, spines, and heads broken. The clear presence of extreme violence related to the wall is evident in the numerous cross-border shootings by Border Patrol officers, exemplified by a Border Patrol officer who shot an unarmed teenager through the slats of the steel barrier in Nogales.[14] To varying degrees, the examples that follow are Wars of Commission artifacts.

The expectation of death at the border wall did not begin with Trump's "Beautiful Wall." The All-American Canal, whose construction started in the 1930s and was completed in 1942, channels water from the Colorado River to the Yuma Valley and the Imperial Valley over eighty-two miles and is considered the most dangerous body of water in the United States. More than six hundred migrants are known to have died in the canal.[15] However, the assumption of warfare at the border is accentuated by the concertina razor wire. Installed during the Trump administration and continued under Joe Biden, the injurious wire further martializes the region as a barrier to invasion—or, as in Vietnam, as a measure to keep attacking forces at bay or slowed down to be further intercepted by force of arms. The installation of the razor wire in Nogales, Arizona, is depicted in figures 3 and 4. Not pictured here is the San Diego–Tijuana border, where the wire was also installed—evidently, local wags there have removed stretches of the wire and installed them as home protection.[16]

Moreover, lest we think that the border is only symbolic and its cultural impact has not been effective, the digital "game" within the *Border Security Wall Construction AP* by TwoTwenty Games (figure 5) is an indication of the cultural embeddedness of the edifice. Players are able "to play the role of building and defending," that is, to "enjoy the army duty games for the country defence and for your home defence."[17] However, it is a placard for the underlying ideology for a War of Commission.

FIGURE 3  U.S. Army constructing concertina wire, Nogales, Arizona, February 2019. Photo by Jonathan Clark. Reprinted from Alexa Lardieri, "Arizona City Officials Demand Government Remove Razor Wire from Border Wall," *U.S. News*, February 7, 2019, https://www.usnews.com/news/politics/articles/2019-02-07/arizona-city-officials-demand-government-remove-razor-wire-from-border-wall.

Thus, the integration of the border fence and the border of the home are accomplished as part of a cognitive infrastructure to be repeated and manipulated, so that at every successive turn, not only does the player receive satisfaction of accomplishing a goal, but the goal of interdiction of eliminating the danger from the player's family becomes interlocked without reflection and accentuates the normalcy of the act itself. The player "learns to learn" multiple layers of meaning reinforced by seeming play and pleasure, creating the foundation for uncritical acceptance of violent, militarized borders—or of an already accepted violent picture that is expanded effortlessly by creating the best and most effective border wall impediment.

Building the wall also involves other forms of violence. Its construction requires setting aside conservation, riparian, and environmental protection laws as well as the generally sacrosanct notion of "private property." Laws have been ignored to enable the installation of these and other similar projects as well as the development of internal surveillance

FIGURE 4  U.S. Army concertina wire completed, Nogales, Arizona, February 8, 2019. Photo by Jonathan Clark. Reprinted from Associated Press, "Arizona City Officials Want Troop-Installed Razor Wire Removed from Border Wall," *Military Times*, February 6, 2019, https://www.militarytimes.com/news/your-army/2019/02/07/arizona-city-officials-want-troop-installed-razor-wire-removed-from-border-wall.

FIGURE 5  A video game titled *Border Security Wall Construction AP* by Two-Twenty Games. Reprinted from "Border Security Wall Construction for Android," mob.org, accessed January 3, 2023, https://mob.org/en/android/games/g-border_security_wall_construction.

apparatuses, checkpoints, and roving checkpoints as far as one hundred miles north of the border itself. Needless to say, not only is wholesale violation of Indigenous tribal lands of the Arizona Sonora border commonplace but both federal and state impediments are and continue to be forcibly introduced regardless of opposition by tribal authorities.[18]

The last element of the necrostate and its violent War of Commission is the most death-dealing instrument: the weaponization of the political ecology of the region to funnel migrants into the deadly Arizona/Sonora and Chihuahuan Deserts, buttressed by internal checkpoints. Figures 6 and 7 show the major checkpoints along the border (figure 6) and the rolling checkpoints set up randomly (figure 7). Figure 8 shows a sign installed by the U.S. Border Patrol between Las Cruces and Hatch, New Mexico, enumerating "alien removals" and pounds of narcotics seized, equating drug interdiction with immigration capture.

## Necrostate Violence: "Prevention Through Deterrence"

The primary tool for the policy of "prevention through deterrence" is the use of the Chihuahua and Sonora Deserts as well as the All-American

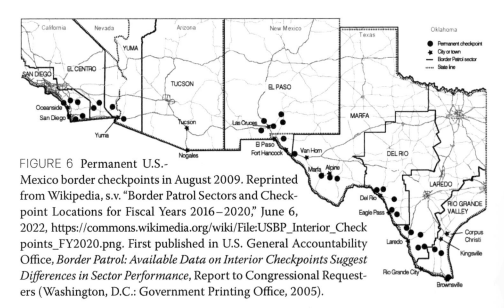

FIGURE 6  Permanent U.S.-Mexico border checkpoints in August 2009. Reprinted from Wikipedia, s.v. "Border Patrol Sectors and Checkpoint Locations for Fiscal Years 2016–2020," June 6, 2022, https://commons.wikimedia.org/wiki/File:USBP_Interior_Checkpoints_FY2020.png. First published in U.S. General Accountability Office, *Border Patrol: Available Data on Interior Checkpoints Suggest Differences in Sector Performance*, Report to Congressional Requesters (Washington, D.C.: Government Printing Office, 2005).

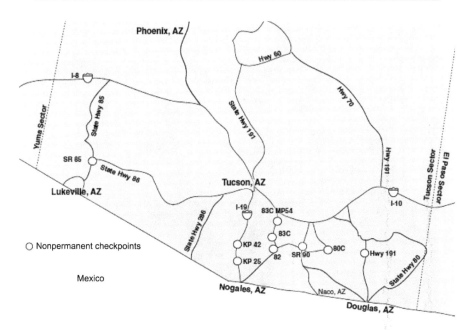

FIGURE 7  Arizona checkpoints, Tucson sector. Reprinted from Wikipedia, s.v. "US Internal Border Checkpoints in the Tucson Sector," July 1, 2005, https://commons.wikimedia.org/wiki/File:GAO-05-435_Figure_14.gif. First published in U.S. General Accountability Office, *Border Patrol: Available Data on Interior Checkpoints Suggest Differences in Sector Performance*, Report to Congressional Requesters (Washington, D.C.: Government Printing Office, 2005).

Canal as weapons for the funneling of northbound migrants. The policy itself was first drafted in 1993 by Sandia National Laboratories, a subsidiary of Lockheed Martin, at the request of the Bill Clinton administration.[19] Within this policy of deterrence were various measurements for its efficacy. One predicted indicator of "the effectiveness of the strategy to deter illegal entry along the southwest border," according to the U.S. General Accounting Office, was "deaths of aliens attempting entry." If the strategy were successful, deaths might increase.[20] The policy is estimated to be responsible for 7,236 deaths between fiscal years 1998 and 2017, and it is highly likely that the number of deaths was twice that. In 2020, an art installation consisting of "a 16–20 foot long map of the Arizona/Mexico border with ~3,200 hand written toe tags" represented "the recovered bodies of people who have died between 2000 and 2020 crossing the US/Mexico border through the Sonoran Desert" and was

FIGURE 8  U.S. Border Patrol sign between Las Cruces and Hatch, New Mexico. Photo taken by the author between Las Cruces and Hatch, New Mexico, May 1999.

exhibited at the Phillips Museum of Art, Franklin & Marshall College (figure 9). The tags were placed on the map in the exact locations where the bodies of the individuals were found.[21]

Figure 10 shows part of the killing grounds of the Sonoran Desert: Bird Nest Hill, where twenty-three-year-old Roberto Primero Luis was found face down, nearly mummified.[22] The *New York Times*' original too-graphic description, however, contrasts tragically and vividly with figure 11, which shows the humanity of displayed affection by Roberto and his wife, Katy Sunún.[23] Their dreams for expanding their successful barbershop through Roberto seeking work in the United States were destroyed by the nightmare of his death, created by a policy designed to kill in the 100,000 square miles (258,998.81 sq. km.) of desert, an area larger than Britain, in 120-degree (48.8 Celsius) heat and no water at all, functioning like a giant incendiary howitzer.

And many of these tragedies will continue and become worsened by competition for the rival use of this space, since the U.S. and Mexican

# THE RISE OF NECROCITIZENSHIP

FIGURE 9  *Toe Tag Wall Prototype* at Phillips Museum of Art, Franklin & Marshall College, Undocumented Migration Project pop-up exhibit. Reprinted from "Pop-Up Installation Synopsis," Undocumented Migration Project, accessed November 10, 2022, https://www.undocumentedmigrationproject.org/installation.

governments have declared the region a zone of two militarized conflicts: "the war on terror"—that is, the aftermath of 9/11—and the "War on Drugs," justifying legal exceptions and the lethal use of weapons on migrants and refugees. Both conflicts constitute Wars of Commission.[24]

## The Rise of the Narco Trans-state Networks and the Emergence of Narcocitizenry

Connected to these developments is the emergence of drug cartels and many of their attending behavioral and symbolic influences. They emerge as conduct of a non-state version of a War of Commission. These developments occurred significantly in the U.S. market and have given shape to, and strongly influence, the quotidian lives of Mexicans by way of cartel violence. The cultural effects of the cartels include impunity of action

FIGURE 10  Bird Nest Hill in the Sonoran Desert near Sells, Arizona. Photo by Kevin Cooley. Reprinted from James Verini, "How U.S. Policy Turned the Sonoran Desert into a Graveyard for Migrants," *New York Times Magazine*, August 18, 2020.

FIGURE 11  Roberto Primero Luis and his wife, Katy Sunún, in Guatemala a few months before his death journey. Photo provided by the family and reprinted by permission.

and influence of many parts of the political and security structure of the Mexican state, aspirational influences among poor youth, and artistic and musical expressions. Mexico is increasingly coming to resemble a narcostate as well, in which many branches of government are heavily penetrated by drug money and influence.[25] Simultaneously, Mexican versions of the drug war are carried out, with the concomitant loss of soldiers and citizens and with its repressions and disappearances carried out by military units. This creates an indistinguishable non-state political and civic process, accompanied by extreme militarization. Local communities on both sides of the region are subject to displacements, forced migration, deep physical and psychic distress, and the abrogation of civil rights.

Narcocitizenship is manifested in multiple and contradictory ways. First, there is a sort of citizen "normalization" of violent death that happens to others, so that little feeling or concern is expressed toward young men in cartels or gangs being murdered, as Howard Campbell has so eloquently noted.[26] At the same time, hundreds of mothers search for their missing sons in possible mass burial grounds throughout Mexican states. Innocent victims are handed over by police for wholesale murder by cartels—as was the case for forty-three male students from the Ayotzinapa Rural Teachers' College who were forcibly abducted and then disappeared in Iguala, Guerrero, Mexico. Arrests were not made until eight years later.[27] Even with a great national and international uproar, the main investigator of the crime has himself disappeared and is probably in Israel.[28] Second, narcocitizenry is manifested by dislocations of regions throughout the "Golden Triangle" area of Durango, Zacatecas, and Sinaloa, and certainly to different degrees throughout Mexico and marked especially in states like Michoacán, Guerrero, and the northern states of Baja California, Sonora, Tamaulipas, Chihuahua, and Nuevo León. Thousands of people in the middle class have moved themselves and their businesses from cities like Tijuana, Juárez, Nogales, and Monterrey to their adjoining U.S. counterparts of San Diego, El Paso, Nogales, Laredo, and Brownsville. But Mexicans also adapt to normalize the fear and impunity of the cartels by negotiating daily adjustments of avoidance and care.[29]

The low-intensity warfare doctrine in Mexico and the creation of an American market-driven web of Mexican criminal nodes have undermined whatever existing weak civil authority existed in Mexico and replaced it with networks of cartels that influence and manage political authority. Both use violence or its threats to establish this dynamic mirroring and militarization of the region, often expressed in the deaths of thousands. Here, then, lie the enormous contradictions that have emerged over the past forty-plus years, and especially since 1978: the rise of the American necrostate apparatus that now extends directly and indirectly to El Salvador; and the rise of the narcostate that extends into Mexico and on to the border arenas, where it exerts control over commerce, trade for guns, and the infusion of millions of dollars of drugs for a hungry American market. Extralegal authority of the cartels has developed to such an extent that even in some areas of northern Mexico, pathways to crossing the border by drug traffickers are controlled by a sort of cartel custom house, with a barrier stopping human traffic before it can enter the environs of U.S. desert territory. Yet elements creating this forty-year process have much earlier roots, during early stages of capitalist industrial production in the late nineteenth century with the introduction of Chinese labor into northern Mexico and eventually maturing especially through World War II and to the present of cartel-driven Wars of Commission.

## Historical Tidbits on Opium

One of the linchpins that eventually created conditions for the rise of the necro/narco trans-state networks was opium. The Spanish colony originally introduced the poppy to the region as an ornamental plant, the psychotropic properties of which were not yet known.[30] But according to Héctor R. Olea, Chinese workers in the late nineteenth century introduced the narcotic species after having noted that the ornamental version grew readily in the western Sierra Madre region. When they did so, they introduced knowledge about its medicinal and psychotropic uses as well.[31] A local cottage industry serving recreational opium users as well as those seeking medicinal treatments was established, especially through local *boticas* (drug stores); the use of opium at that time was not considered a social problem.[32] However, the export north was and has been a major impetus for drug production and its connection between Mexican political institutions and the drug trade, according to Benjamin T. Smith.[33] Smith asserts that from the postrevolutionary period, politicians sought to harness the revenues from the illegal drug trade north by offering convenient protection against authorities who enforced legal prohibitions against drug producers and traffickers in exchange for a percent of the profits. In this way, various state agents served as facilitators and protectors, and states controlled the flow of drugs north and operated by state police, who ensured that the entire range of political levels and structures benefited from this arrangement.[34]

During the Manuel Ávila Camacho presidency, between 1940 and the end of World War II, poppies were massively and extensively cultivated as part of a compact between the American Mafia and leading politicians and members of Camacho's presidential office. Mexican poppy cultivation was part of the production chain for morphine used to treat Americans who were wounded during the war.[35] According to Antonio Hass, opium then morphed from a cottage industry to an extensive industrial model.[36] But there also seems to have been great impetus during the post–World War II period, during the presidency of Miguel Alemán. According to Arturo Santamaría Gómez, Luis Antonio Martínez Peña, and Pedro Brito Osuna, a woman named Virginia Hill, who was known by the Federal Bureau of Investigation (FBI) as the "Queen of the Mafia" and an American mob love of Benjamin Siegel, an underling of Lucky Luciano, seduced a number of high-ranking military officers and officials in Alemán's government and further facilitated the export of Mexican opium that had been initiated during World War II.[37] Thus, it was the American Mafia and their Mexican facilitators who massively upscaled drug exports from Sinaloa, Durango, and Chihuahua to the United States.

In time, a nexus of profit-earning enterprises arose, attached to civil authorities and politicians, peasants, and agricultural workers. From the Sierras, this nexus penetrated the Sinaloa political system and its multiplying organizational of versions now referred to as cartels, myriad sectors of Mexico from Baja California to the Gulf Coast, and all its major states and urban cities. Eventually this production apparatus contributed to local populations not migrating to cities or to the north, except as greater violence and militarization became rooted in those same areas over the next forty years.[38] These populations became the casualties of war, but doubly so by victimization by the War of Commission driven to a state of War of Omission.

Yet it was postwar American policy that initiated early versions of the War on Drugs, including opium. Transborder militarization began, from its array of blockades to the building of walls on the necro side and its extension to the narco side by the Mexican military. This process started very early in 1970. Under the Nixon administration, in 1969 "Operation Intercept" prompted the initial military-style blockage through a three-minute automobile individual inspection in thirty Mexican border crossings. Further, radar domes were established in strategic nonobserved areas, the U.S. Navy was deployed in the Gulf of Mexico, and in 1973, twenty-seven international airports in the United States with flights from Mexico were made "border equivalents" by the U.S. Supreme Court.[39]

In January 1970, the Mexican counterpart became part of a Mexican War of Commission and initiated military operations with U.S. equipment, logistics, and cooperation after meeting in Culiacán. A virtual war began in the highlands of the Sinaloa sierras, in which the army killed twelve civilians. By 1977, Operation Condor possessed a force of ten thousand soldiers commanded by General José Hernández, who had participated in the military use of violence against students at the Universidad Nacional Autónoma de México, La Nicolaita, and the state of Sonora. Through Operation Condor, the military invaded the sierras of Sinaloa, Durango, and Chihuahua. There, using the Vietnam-era herbicide "paraquat" to destroy diverse drug plants, thousands of acres—including interconnecting towns and hamlets—were sprayed. People in the area suffered the resultant health maladies. Similar to what occurred during the bigger Operation Condor in South and Central America, the military tortured many townspeople for information, assassinated alleged drug producers, practiced violence against women, sacked homes and towns, and made illegal arrests of innocents.[40] This violence created further casualties and drove many into migration, greater poverty, and great uncertainty.

A brilliant essay from 2012 by Nery Córdova Solís covers the historical and sociocultural characteristics of the Sinaloa drug enterprise. Córdova Solís summarizes Condor's impact: "It paradoxically resulted in the national fortification of the drug industry [and] in the towns dedicated to its production and cultivation of prohibited drugs, the daily life of its inhabitants has been, and is, subject to a kind of primary complicity, which translates into an elementary rule of survival."[41]

After countless major military operations, intercessions, raids, and arrests, and 150,000 persons killed, between 30 and 35 percent of the territory of Mexico was in the hands of organized crime as of 2021. Further, a number of cartel-controlled areas developed, including the "Golden Triangle" of the Sierras shared by Sinaloa, Durango, and Zacatecas, and the coastal states of Guerrero, Veracruz, and Baja California. Concentrations of cartel activity to one degree or another exist, of course, in all other Mexican states. This prevalence of organized crime in the region is one of the major reasons for the increase in the number of migrants across the U.S. border.[42] Thus the War of Commission became a transnational phenomenon resulting in many populations seeking escape north.

## Narcostate/Military Cartel Apparatus and Networks

The cartels are mostly responsible for an American market drug trade. People who use drugs in the United States spent on the order of $150 billion on cocaine, heroin, marijuana, and methamphetamine in 2016. The marijuana market is roughly the size of the cocaine and methamphetamine markets combined, and the size of the retail heroin market is now closer to the size of the marijuana market than it is to the other drugs.[43] Thus, the cartels account for a sizeable amount of foreign currency earnings from these sources alone. They often splinter and regroup because of military action or internal wars for plazas, areas of control. Larger cartels will support splinter groups within an opposition cartel to undermine the authority of the competition and weaken its hold over the territory, in order to eventually move in.

The impact of cartel violence in Mexico is egregious. New cartel morphs are emerging as they break up because of interdiction or internal violence used to gain greater territorialization.[44] According to a report published by the Congressional Research Service in 2020, "Overall, since 2006, many sources maintain that Mexico experienced roughly 150,000 murders related to organized crime, which is about 30 percent to 50 percent of total intentional homicides. In addition, the government assesses more than 40,000 Mexicans disappeared."[45] The international War on Drugs, from its origin to the present presidency of Mexico, has resulted in fragmentations of the cartels. Simultaneously, cartel violence is rising;

in 2019, 17,000 homicides in a six-month period were committed. For the entire year of 2019, almost 35,000 murders were committed and do not account for the many abducted whose bodies are never found and often buried in mass graves or dissolved in acid.[46]

In 2019, the Sinaloa Cartel took over Culiacán, the capital city of the state of Sinaloa, when Ovidio Guzmán López, son of kingpin Joaquín "El Chapo" Guzmán Loera, was arrested by President Andrés Manuel López Obrador's new national police force and the Mexican Army. The state military forces were outgunned and tactically outmaneuvered by the cartel, and the president himself ordered Guzmán López's release; Ovidio was captured again in January 2023 (with his brother Joaquín and Israel "El Mayo" Zambada García arrested in July 2024, as described at the end of chapter 7). Further north of Culiacán, sixty miles south of Nogales, Arizona, is the town of Magdalena, Sonora. Founded in 1688 by Father Eusebio Kino, Magdalena is a town where I spent my childhood walking from my aunt and uncle's home to drink ice-cold lemonade in the plaza. In the warm evenings, young men and women would walk in opposite directions, flirting. At times, bands would play to accompany the beat from the cicadas. But things have changed drastically since then. Magdalena has been taken over by cartel gunmen and the music there now is created by assassins shooting AK-47s and M-16s.[47] Caborca, Sonora, was taken over by twenty armed cartel trucks and one tank on February 18, 2022. The cartel killed two people, kidnapped two young athletes, and terrorized the town with police and federal troops only minutes away. In what seems to have been the only defense for lack of response on the part of authorities, Sonoran police officials stated that the kidnapping was more than likely an error.[48]

Cartels possess unlimited funds to use for bribing top officials in police and judicial enforcement. One example of how far-reaching cartel influence has been and continues to be among these officials is Genaro García Luna of the Felipe Calderón administration (2006–12), arrested in 2019 by the United States for the enormous bribes he received from the Sinaloa Cartel. If bribes are not accepted or journalists not cowed, violence is the most assured method of stirring public fear. Cartels killed twelve journalists in 2019 and thirty-seven mayors in 2018. In one case, a mayor was killed two hours after taking office. Figure 12 shows Gisela Mota, mayor of Texcoco (my original field site), who was killed on her

FIGURE 12  Altar to slain Texcoco mayor Gisela Mota, who was killed by gunmen in the town of Temixco, Mexico, on her second day in office in 2016. Reprinted from Noelia de Marcos Collado, "Asesinada Gisela Mota Ocampo horas después de asumir su cargo," *Periodismo Internacional*, January 4, 2016, https://periodismointernacional.org/asesinada-gisela-mota-ocampo-horas-despues-de-asumir-su-cargo/.

second day in office in 2016.[49] These are all clear indications of civil suppression by the cartels.

Such killings are made possible by an intensive market for weapons illegally imported by the cartels. According to data from the Bureau of Alcohol, Tobacco, Firearms and Explosives (ATF), of the 106,001 guns recovered by law enforcement as part of criminal investigations in Mexico from 2011 to 2016 and submitted for tracing, 70 percent were originally purchased from a licensed gun dealer in the United States. These U.S.-linked guns likely represent only a fraction of the total number of guns that cross the southern border. Other estimates suggest that close to 213,000 firearms are smuggled across the U.S.-Mexico border each year. According to the U.S. Government Accountability Office (GAO), nearly half of the U.S.-sourced guns recovered in Mexico are long guns, which include high-caliber semiautomatic rifles, such as AK and AR variants.[50] This is a concern for Mexican law enforcement officials, who have reported that assault rifles have become the weapons of choice for

Mexican drug-trafficking organizations, in part because they can easily be converted into fully automatic rifles. The GAO also reports that, from 2009 to 2014, the majority of the crime guns recovered in Mexico that were originally purchased in the United States came from three southern border states: 41 percent from Texas, 19 percent from California, and 15 percent from Arizona.

Even more alarming is the increased militarization of the cartels through the incorporation of former Mexican and Guatemalan special forces and special operations soldiers. Originally recruited by the Los Zetas cartel, these former military personnel then took over the organization. What followed were recruitments of these specialists by other cartels to even things up, resulting in the creation of trained insurgent companies of highly militarized cartel gangs, compared to standard cartel gangs (figure 13). All are well weaponized.

In response, both the Mexican Army and Navy have been engaged in cartel suppression, but the former is often tainted by corruption among some of the top divisional generals. General Salvador Cienfuegos, former secretary of defense under Enrique Peña Nieto, was arrested on October 15, 2020, in Los Angeles for trafficking and money laundering under a U.S. Drug Enforcement Administration warrant. He was later released by the direct intervention of President López Obrador and the Trump administration. The Navy, despite having a small Marine infantry complement and special operations group, has been very successful until recently. However, these forces have been pulled from active operations, leading some to believe that they were too successful and incorruptible.

FIGURE 13  Puro Cártel del Golfo. Reprinted from "Cártel del Golfo y CJNG: La infame alianza que amenaza con una guerra en Tamaulipas," Infobae, July 1, 2021, https://www.infobae.com/america/mexico/2021/07/01/cartel-del-golfo-y-cjng-la-infame-alianza-que-amenaza-con-una-guerra-en-tamaulipas/.

Both the Army and Marines, on the other hand, have been involved in extrajudicial killings—the latter less so, but in 2021 thirty Marines were arrested for their involvement in the disappearance of numerous civilians, including an American citizen, in the Mexican state of Tamaulipas since their deployment there.[51] This proved so embarrassing to an otherwise admired branch of service that the Navy gave a public apology, which no Mexican armed force had ever done before.[52]

So-called tactical training is an important subtopic under the "low-intensity warfare" approach to suppression and removal, according to the Mexico Violence Resource Project of the Center for U.S.–Mexico Studies at UC San Diego. After 2011, tactical training "expanded dramatically." Mexican Marines received the bulk of this training between 2007 and 2012, representing 60 percent of all students.[53]

But as disconcerting for the long term is the continued and now budgetarily supported militarization of the Mexican state itself. To combat corruption, seaports and custom crossing points as well as customs at airports were all moved under the control and supervision of the military. According to a report from 2020:

> Nowhere has the role of the army grown more than in construction. In addition to the new Mexico City airport, the army is building 150 barracks for the National Guard and 2,700 new branches of government-run banks across the country to distribute the president's social benefits. Once the airport is finished, the army will be tasked with building two large sections of a planned, nearly 950-mile tourist train line in the Yucatán Peninsula that is expected to cost some $6.3 billion.[54]

Additionally, the National Defense budget of the public sector budget has increased dramatically (figure 14).

Another budgetary issue is revenue accrued from seaports, airports, construction projects, and other military-run enterprises that circumvent the general budget and in some cases directly profit the military itself. In this manner, the private sector is ruled out and the military steps in to initiate, develop, manage, and become fiscally responsible for all these arenas. Simultaneously, it acquires important almost autonomous budgetary agreements from the president of Mexico:

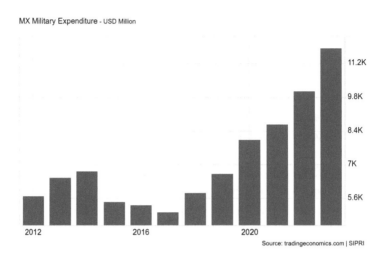

FIGURE 14  Mexico military expenditure in millions of dollars, 2023. Reprinted from "Mexico Military Expenditure," *Trading Economics*, 2023, https://tradingeconomics.com/mexico/military-expenditure.

Under this arrangement, the military will keep some of the profits, giving it power vis-à-vis current and future presidential administrations. On the surface, the National Guard that López Obrador created in 2019 to assume the military's public-safety role would seem to clip its wings. But in practice, the armed forces exert budgetary and operational control over the National Guard, and a new proposal would put it under the full control of the Secretariat of National Defense.[55]

Thus, there is a devolution of mirroring processes in which a necro/narco state apparatus has most recently been at the forefront of what I would consider serious "structural adjustments." This means that the United States has, to greater degrees, integrated a regional "low-intensity warfare" strategy as part of a transborder War of Commission for the region, including the many elements discussed and expanded under the Trump administration. Its counterpart, the drug-infused polity of Mexico, participates, promulgating a similar "low-intensity" war against drugs and its own version of a War of Commission. This has a most serious consequence: the recruitment of and integration of the same strategy among cartels. And, just as importantly, we see the creation of the narcostate network as a parallel structure.

## The Ethnography of Corruption Within Government Institutions and Civil Dislocations

The criminal involvement of state governors with the cartels and other criminals reflects the extent of corruption in the layers of government and across parties in Mexico. In 2018, twenty former state governors, many from the long-dominant Institutional Revolutionary Party (PRI), were under investigation or in jail. Over the six years of PRI president Peña Nieto's term (2012–18), Mexico fell thirty-two places in Transparency International's "Corruption Perceptions Index."[56] But there is not a sector that is left untouched in one manner or another, so it is probable that it is only a one- to two-step process to link with a criminal connection. Money laundering is extensive as well, as the legitimate and forced acquisition of legitimate businesses—especially in the hotel, tourist, and service sectors—rounds out the criminals' business portfolios.

Consider the following scene that took place among friends sipping wine at a bourgeois party in a major seaport city:

> **Friend 1**: *¿Por qué los gringos tienen tanto miedo de lo que cruza la frontera?* (Why are Americans so afraid of what crosses the border?)
> **Friend 2**: *Porque tienen miedo de que los terroristas islámicos crucen también.* (They are afraid that the Islamic terrorists also cross.)
> **Friend 3** (*Slowly approaching from a few feet away and obviously having heard the interchange*): *No pasan.* (They won't get across.)
> **Friend 2**: *Y ¿por qué no?* (And why not?)
> **Friend 3**: *Porque no.* (Because no.)
> **Friend 3** (*Smiles briefly and walks away.*)
> **Friend 2**: *¿Está situado?* (Is he situated [meaning, cartel]?)
> **Friend 1** (*In a low voice*): *Parece.* (Seems like it.)
> **Friend 2** (*Turns away and nods almost imperceptibly, and sips on his Cabernet Sauvignon.*)

Even in a celebration such as this, and seemingly out of the blue, some cultural aspect and element of possible unwanted or desired associations of narcocitizenship becomes articulated and expressed, contaminating even the most innocent conversation. There is no way to predict whether and how a social setting might eventually become touched by aspects of narcocitizenship, either directly or indirectly. And as in this case, aspects are kept foggy and unclear so that unease with a conclusion may be more normative than not. There is an almost constant inkling that an association with narcoculture is just around the corner. Seemingly innocent references or remarks create daily fears and anxiety, and things can become touchy easily, leading many people to do their best to avoid any topic that may lead to a suspected possibility. It is best not to discuss in any serious manner aspects of narcocitizenship that may become problematic, and the topic is assiduously avoided with frank statements like "No hablo de eso" (I don't speak about that). Thus, many in the Mexican working, middle, and elite sectors just keep their heads down and remain silent about the ongoing murders of judges, police chiefs, federal enforcement officers, police officers, soldiers, and judicial authorities, and the associated corruption and political impunity.[57] Even then, however, there are no guarantees of security given the myriad ways in which insecurity and indeterminacy are present and exhibited.

## Dislocation of Populations: From Peasants to Entrepreneurs and Murder

Especially detrimental for the long-term cultural and social capital of all of Mexico is the dislocation of large numbers of people, including professional, entrepreneurial, and largely well-educated populations as well as important rural populations in an assortment of class, gender, and ethnic sectors. The movement of rural populations to cities, to border regions, and to other areas of Mexico has been exponential since Americanized low-intensity warfare emerged as a central focus and major policy from among the first sweeps during the 1970s through Felipe Calderón's very bloody presidency (2004–12). Calderón now admits that this policy was a halfway measure without American interest in the necessary and sufficient condition of the American economic support of that which the necro/narco network of states seeks to eradicate. On September 10, 2010, two years before his term expired, Calderón stated, "We live next to the world's largest drug consumer, and all the world wants to sell them drugs through our door and our window. And we live next to the world's largest arms seller, which is supplying the criminals."[58] From such contradictions develop attending Wars of Commission, while an accentuation of a War of Omission spreads further and a plethora of casualties are created.

Drug money has become one of the top five sources of foreign exchange for Mexico and not too far from remittances, which now supersede oil revenue. But to provide a final sense of the pervasiveness of drug culture, we can turn to the array of public culture paraphernalia and media devoted to its continued acceptance (figure 15).

FIGURE 15  El Chapo commodities. Reprinted from Loan Grillo, "Opinion: How Mexico's Drug Cartels Are Profiting from the Pandemic," *New York Times*, July 7, 2020. Credit: Fernando Carranza/Reuters/Redux.

Among the strongest indicators of narcocitizenship in public culture—which will be discussed in depth in chapter 7—are the transborder narcorridos like those of Chalino Sánchez that gained a great deal of recognition among Mexican youth on both sides of the border. Another example is narcodramas such as the telenovela *La Reina del Sur*, based on the novel by Arturo Pérez-Reverte, wherein the film's female protagonist, played by Kate del Castillo, eventually in real life accepted an opportunity to visit El Chapo Guzmán along with actor Sean Penn. Even anthropologists watch the Mexican *El Señor de los Cielos* and the Colombian *Sin senos no hay paraíso*.

## Semifinal Comments and Large Flies in the Ointment: Trumpian License—Civil Rights Amended—Necrocitizenship—ALMO, ALMO, Where Art Thou—Slanting and Jiving and Getting By

Trump built his wall, blocked asylum seekers from entering the United States, and effectively moved the U.S. border line to the southern Mexican border. Biden closely followed suit. Meanwhile, López Obrador is sending his new national police force to prevent people like Roberto Primero Luis from crossing the border and is doubling down on the use of the desert as killing grounds in exchange for not being tariffed to death.

Trump used national defense funds to build sections of the wall not funded by Congress, which of course goes against Trump's political platform of having Mexico fund this impediment. Equally as important to the wall itself—which has been breached more than three thousand times since its construction—is the zone of tenuous civil rights that surrounds it, ostensibly within one hundred miles of the border, but in fact agents raid and intercept much beyond those limits. Walter A. Ewing describes this aspect of necrocitizenry, which is a direct result of congressional and presidential efforts:

> In 2008, the American Civil Liberties Union (ACLU) described the U.S. border as a "Constitution-Free Zone," referring to a 100-mile wide strip of territory around the "external boundary" of the nation within which Fourth Amendment protections against random and arbitrary stops and searches by law-enforcement officials do not apply. According to the ACLU, the 197.4 million people residing in this zone—roughly two-thirds of the US population—are subject to "administrative" stops by the Border Patrol or other federal authorities for the purpose of guarding the nation's borders from security threats.... The inland checkpoints where the Border Patrol conducts "administrative" stops and searches are mostly clustered near the southwest borderlands of California, Arizona, and Texas, but are also found along the northern border in Washington state and could, in principle, appear anywhere else along U.S. land or coastal borders.[59]

These searches do continually take place in the most northeastern states, especially in Vermont around its maple-producing groves and dairy milk farms. Mexican and Guatemalan workers and families work seven days a week at these farms, are largely cloistered, and avoid even casual trips to the store, having food purchased for them by others or delivered by delivery trucks, so as to steer clear of checkpoints.[60]

So where does this leave us? Although Biden was part of the Barack Obama administration that deported more Mexicans and Guatemalans than the previous three presidents, as well as Trump, we can hope that at least the low-intensity warfare in the region will shift back to a nonmilitarized law enforcement position. There is also hope that Mexico will manage to gain some sort of political authority that renders the market-driven drug trade less attractive to generations of Mexicans now laid low by the impact of the COVID-19 pandemic. But there is, in addition to the narco/military development of the Mexican state—which seems to be headed toward even more low-intensity warfare—the control of major sectors of the Mexican economy by the military and the directly budgetary access of the military itself. These do not bode well for long-term civilian institutional development.

On the other hand, at the quotidian level on both sides of the border, populations of Mexican-origin peoples deal with the aftermath and impacts of these processes on a day-to-day basis. They do so mostly by slanting past impediments, jiving and dancing around powerful forces, and trying to get by. They depend mostly on extended family members, friends in low places, and educating their children the best they can while surviving when they should not and excelling when they should not. In Mazatlán, families that stroll along the Malecón on Sundays will pass the condominium where El Chapo Guzmán was captured, while in Brownsville, family networks gather for carne asada next to a section of the border wall (figure 16).[61] Underlying both scenes are the behavioral, material, and symbolic architectures of necro- and narcocitizenship as the frames and substances of a transborder cultural complex treated in the following chapters.

Finally, there is the perspective proposed by Jeremy Slack and Daniel E. Martínez:

> We argue that incidental exposure to violence and crime began as an implicit aspect of immigration enforcement and has grown into one of the central tenets of current policy.... These practices are directly connected to the current wave of policies aimed at stopping asylum seekers, including "metering," where people are made to wait at the border to apply for asylum at the port of entry, and the Remain in Mexico program (otherwise known as the Migrant Protection Protocols). We argue that enforcement is more complex than "prevention through deterrence" narratives and exposure to nonstate violence in Mexico has slowly become a more integral part of enforcement plans.[62]

FIGURE 16  A family network gathers to eat carne asada next to the border wall. Reprinted from Aaron Nelsen, "Former UT Brownsville President to Teach Course on Border Wall at UT RGV," *San Antonio Express-News*, December 23, 2017.

From the point of view I adopt in this work, these are the effects of low-intensity warfare policies and the creation of necro/narco trans-state networks. From these networks emerge cultural complexes in conjunction with a northern (U.S.) enterprise, which is dominant and hegemonic over the southern (Mexican) version. We can rationally conclude that militarized enforcement of entire regions—initiated by cartel violence and American drug appetites and coupled to the "elastic" use and misuse of Mexican labor—has become the major weaponized measure extended by both twins of the necro/narco nexus of militarization. As discussed, the enforcement strategies constitute Wars of Commission and Omission. These measures are used to discipline unruly persons seeking to find a better life for themselves and their families as well as those capitalizing on or dependent on drugs.

Finally, the trans-state network is flexible, unequal, and asymmetrical, but with profound cultural impacts. Militarization is the formal dynamic that makes violence the normative energy underlying it all. In the broad theoretical architecture, this is a product of late-stage postindustrial global capitalism weakly held up by nineteenth-century political structures and seeming solutions. As we will see, these processes have produced and reproduced diverse versions of necro- and narcocitizenship as cultural complexes affecting following generations in real and imagined ways.

# CHAPTER 3

## Belonging and Dying

*Genesis and Ethnographies of Necrocitizenship
in Wars of Commission and Omission*

Necrocitizenship is a construct of fealty that overcomes the concept of civil actions as citizens use violent action, including death, to support its underlying use and ritualized character. As an important characteristic of the Wars of Commission, it includes various depths and intensities, patinas and layers of patriotism, and rationales for its justifications. Miguel Díaz-Barriga and Margaret Dorsey most insightfully apply this concept to the U.S.-Mexico border zone by showing the "normalization of militarism and military engagement within Mexican-American Culture."[1] In a dialogic manner, they differentiate between "patriotic citizenship" and "necrocitizenship" in order to explore its signification for an "othered" population. Necrocitizenship is a long-standing phenomenon integral to nation-states in which citizens are convinced of the efficacy of death as a final arbiter of association of belonging to a citizenship category. It consists of a host of ritual and behavioral indicators that mask and express the development, creation, displays, and their behavioral manifestations, often filled with contradictions. It includes a willingness to use violence in all its formats in the name of acceptance to a national body. Necrocitizenship is in fact a highly weaponized expression of "patriotism," which in many cases provides an uncritical syndrome of acceptance.

It becomes the final arbiter of civilly associated citizenship, often unquestioned and very much part of ideological arguments designed to nudge the public into uncritically accepting its premises. These premises range from "defending the homeland," as has been suggested against an externally perceived or actual foe, to reenacting such convictions in ritualized formats, such as pledges of allegiance, saluting a flag, and attending ceremonies honoring those killed in action. Most national entities have anniversaries marking their founding, ritualized representations of wars conducted in their stead, and collective remembrances of those who participated in one or more wars. Most participants in necrocitizenship actions and rituals are impressed with war service narratives from an early age so that they will carry out the difficult and horrendous tasks associated with the violence of wars and combat. To internalize the emotion and emotionally laden values associated with necrocitizenship, it is necessary that these youths learn, repeat, and be acted upon by premises and hopes supporting that participation uncritically. And so, educational, religious, commercial, and secular institutions for private and public domains express through myriad mediums the messages, intentions, and rationalizations to impress generations of youths to become full "necrocitizens" willing to die and kill for their nation. Thus, many have died to belong.

But the outstanding characteristic of necrocitizenship is not just its reliance on death as a requirement of acceptance. Underlying its development and multiple expressions is a structure of legitimacy both coded and uncoded by varying levels of articulation by the states and nation. For example, "Be all you can be," an Army recruitment slogan repeated in many mediums of communication from television to social media, has overt and covert messages. The most obvious is that it resonates with the American ideals of equality, opportunity, achievement, and success. It subsumes an assumption of "hard work" as its underlying architecture. Military participation is presented as an action and direction toward this goal, offering structures and steps of rank and standing toward total achievement and acceptance. It is differentiated from other cultural messages by symbols and medal displays, uniforms, and rites of passage such as boot camp training. Repeated ideologies, mythic narratives, and glorification of standing by and adhering to the underlying architectures of the institution are messages that transcend generations, institutions, and contexts. They are embedded symbolically, in curricula, in classrooms, in legal architectures, and in juridical and legislative systems from local to national levels of articulation displayed prominently and subtly—most obviously on flagpoles. In a sense, necrocitizenship is a total institutionalized cultural complex learned early, ritualized, internalized, and uncritically accepted as normal by many people of the nation-state.

Facsimiles of the hardships, sufferings, and common scripts of admiration and imitation of those gone before repeat across mediums, creating diverse generational social bonds and reconstituted identities. These are received by necrocitizens on a spectrum of participation that ranges from passive acceptance and nonreflection to actively engaging in rituals and behaviors driving one toward death—one's own or others'. For some, these are eventually tested in the cruelty of combat. Despite the persistence of representations in film, television, and literature, the specifics experienced in combat are almost impossible to convey to nonparticipants. This experience consists of many molecular levels of traumatic and sometimes joyful impressions, glued by diverse emotions and trailed by unexpected and expected reactions and involvements. Later in life, a twitch, a glint, a pungent smell, a tiny image, a felt wetness, or a click may recall the reaction never lost. Nevertheless, these facsimile representations still have the effect of transmitting, to those who admire the standing of those serving but who themselves do not participate directly, the metamessages of citizenship as a death-supporting medium and dying as part of the cost of whatever values are articulated. In this way, watching the action or ceremony on television, or ritually participating by attending, donating, or supporting associations focused on necrocitizenship, binds participants in common identities of belonging, which ultimately is considered a righteous standing.

It involves the acceptance and practice of highly ritualized expressions, from primary school through reserve officer training corps programs at colleges and universities, from reciting the pledge of allegiance in first grade to military swearing-in ceremonies as a young adult to joining postwar associations. All these rituals and expressions reinforce the necessity and totality of necrocitizenship. Even American sporting events are surrounded by banners, flags, emblems, and performances, thriving and exploding with militarized sounds and sights for attendees and the millions watching on television. Performers march to militarized musical compositions and ersatz skyrockets burst in the air, and as both intended and unintended consequences "make citizens like children, infantilized, passive, and overdependent on the 'immense tutelary power' of the state."[2]

Often, the youths who are most targeted by the nation-state's messages of necrocitizenship are those who are marginalized to the dominant class, caste, or racialized categories prominently influencing their destinies and who try to reach a standing of "un-other." For Mexican-origin populations in the United States, the price for reaching this standing has been high since the Civil War, only a few years after their own territorial and population conquest, and through every war in which the United States has been engaged for the past 160 years. In every major conflict in which this population has served, they have endured an over-representation among those killed and wounded. The norm is that the dead and dying are finally "un-othered."[3]

Necrocitizenship is culturally constructed, through historically derived representations, ritualized repetitive practices, socially approved behaviors, mythic outlines of connections, integrations of values and beliefs that support an array of symbolic representations, and institutional and public cultural demonstrations. All are configured to rationalize and support the possibility of dying to support the goals of Wars of Commission. For decades, Mexican and Latina/o/x populations in the United States have participated in these aspects of necrocitizenship as a means of ensuring their cultural acceptance and to counter white Americans' perceptions of them as foreigners, especially in the Southwest North American Region (SWNAR), which itself was conquered by a second set of colonial settlers. These populations display and manifest their participation primarily by their service in every American war from the Civil War to the present, and by suffering egregiously by their overrepresentation as casualties. After each war, this population has organized to express and maintain their sacrifices through political action and veterans' associations.

## The Genesis and Distribution of Necrocitizenship and Militarization

If we are to fully understand the genesis and historical unfolding of the military association and necrocitizenship for Mexican-origin populations of the SWNAR, we must begin by looking to its own conquest in the nineteenth century, the racialized identity thoughtlessly induced as part of this conquest, and the populations' almost desperate striving to belong in opposition to that imposition. Thus militarization in the region begins very early in the history of the United States, and especially in the use of conquest and occupation as the major means of establishing hegemony over former Mexican territory. But the imposition of regimes of immigration from 1790 to the present rationalizes the later and more spiritual renditions of justification, carrying necrologies of rationales into the present. Under the Naturalization Act of 1790, the U.S. law that "set the first uniform rules for the granting of United States citizenship by naturalization," any noncitizen, "'being a free white person,' could apply for citizenship, so long as he or she lived in the United States for at least two years, and in the state where the application was filed for at least a year. The new law also provided that 'children of citizens of the United States that may be born . . . out of the limits of the United States shall be considered as natural born citizens.'"[4] The law "excluded indentured servants, free blacks and slaves, who were regarded as 'property' and not 'persons.'"[5] But Mexicans were not excluded from being rendered as "white." The Treaty of Guadalupe Hidalgo of 1848, which ended the war between the United States and Mexico, made remaining Mexicans in captured Mexican territories—including present-day Texas, California, Nevada, Utah, New Mexico, and parts of Arizona, Colorado, Oklahoma, Kansas, and Wyoming—not transported to Mexico eligible to be American citizens, thus shoehorning them in as "white." Thus "whiteness" seems to have been lent to Mexicans since only white men could be citizens; they were slipped into that racial category politically, but hardly socially or culturally. Later amendments to the law eliminated the "white" insistence.

However, this penchant for "whiteness" and being "pure of blood" has its own marked presence inherited through the racialized caste system of three hundred years of Spanish colonial rule but given further credence by the Immigration Law itself. Thus Mexicans simultaneously were excluded from Jim Crow laws legally but often typecast as racial mongrels through the twentieth century as I have shown elsewhere.[6]

Regardless of birthplace and regardless of which side of the border line they lived on, and even with an acquired social hue, Mexicans became the enemy of the state after the conquest of the Mexican population.[7] Long-standing prejudices concerning "mongrelization" persisted, especially among white southerners, leading to legal and social prohibitions on interracial relationships even as slave masters fathered children with enslaved people and white ranchers with Mexican women.[8] For the next 150 years, Mexicans and formerly enslaved persons faced segregated schools, poll taxes ensuring unequal representation, job discrimination, land encroachments, educational disparities, and severe economic inequality of wages. All the while, they served in every U.S. war during that period.

Certainly, military occupation of occupied territories in the nineteenth century was the norm given the conqueror's rationalization to counter any uprisings by Mexicans or Native peoples by establishing numerous military bases throughout the region. This occurred in New Mexico, resulting in the assassination of the American governor and various uprisings in Texas and from Californio postwar resistance in the nineteenth century.[9] The nineteenth century was also marked by American incursions into Mexico to control newly conquered Mexican territory and Indigenous populations in the form of "filibuster expeditions" and forays of American troops into Mexican territory, with the aim of forcibly removing Native peoples from their traditional lands or to conduct revenge raids.

From the middle of the nineteenth century on, there also arose the development and operational employment and deployment of "low-intensity warfare" by militarized police and civilian groups as well as military forces. In *Militarizing the Border: When Mexicans Became the Enemy*, Miguel Antonio Levario describes the characteristics of low-intensity warfare doctrine of the northern side of the region, but I would suggest certainly extending south without boundaries. Levario explains: "The doctrine orders for integrated and coordinated efforts of police, paramilitary, and military forces to establish and maintain social control over a targeted civilian population. However, . . . that militarization went far beyond policing and into aggressive acts of war. Militarization at the turn of the twentieth century contributed to a historical construction of ethnic Mexicans as an 'enemy other' rather than simply as a racialized other."[10] This was coupled with the commodification of Mexican labor to posit the "enemy other" as a danger to wages and unions.

For the most part, Mexicans continue to be regarded by swaths of the American public only through the denigrating lens of "cheap labor," that is, human beings in aggregate, of little value regardless of knowledge, regardless of experience, and reduced to a nonhuman artifact but also perennially tied to a medical model of apparent danger to the health and welfare of Americans. The most recent expression of this is the Trumpian enforcement of Title 42, which "authorizes the Director of the Centers for Disease Control and Prevention (CDC) to suspend entry of individuals into the United States to protect public health."[11] This continues to be enforced by the Biden administration, especially upon asylum seekers, so that Mexicans and others from the Northern Triangle of Central America are the primary targets of exclusion on this basis. By extending the Trump "national emergency," Biden continued its enforcement for COVID-19 in February 2022 in response to increased immigration by Venezuelans, Haitians, and Cubans, while the Supreme Court allowed it to remain in place after it was scheduled to end in March 2022.[12]

Thus the "Mexican enemy other" is a layered construct that generations of Mexicans on both sides of the border bifurcation have had to negotiate, combat, adjust, and protest. One way they have found to do so is to assume the trappings and identifications of a "necrocitizen" willing to die for nation and flag as well as to attend to their accompanying rituals and symbolic meanings. There have been individual oppositions to this process in some instances, but other than the period of the Vietnam War, most Mexicans on both sides of the bifurcation participated in U.S. wars from the Civil War to the present as supporters, workers, participants, passive observers, and active dead.

## Mexicans and Puerto Ricans in American Wars

The association between the military and Mexican-origin and Puerto Rican communities has been a long one, beginning with the expansion of U.S. military power into Mexico and the Caribbean in the middle and late nineteenth century. This relationship has had to be characterized by both accommodation and participation, rejection and resistance, depending on the political and social circumstances of the time. For Mexican-origin populations and Puerto Ricans, their initial relationship with the U.S.

military emerged as the aftermath of the expansion of the United States through military conquest.[13] Thus, the relationship between the U.S. military, the national society, and these populations differs from that of other populations except for Native Americans, who themselves were conquered by the U.S. military, the Spanish, and Mexican ancestors. Yet Latinas/os have not only fulfilled their military duty but use this experience as the basis to further their civil rights and to fight the daily conflicts for employment, education, and social justice in often intolerable conditions. Equally important are the many roles and changes that women filled and initiated, from espionage to suffering in combat. These roles created the social templates and dynamics for fighting sexual discrimination and harassment and the filling of crucial jobs in wartime and in the caring professions. Thus, this combination of factors plays crucial roles in the acquisition of "necrocitizenship," since the willingness to join the military and work in defense plants are also steppingstones to the acquisition of a layer of the social identity of necrocitizenship.

The initial specific interaction that led to necrocitizenship for Mexicans depended on the ongoing historical relations between nations. In this way, the American-Mexican War of 1846–48 produced frequently contradictory relations between populations of what then was Mexico and the United States.[14] That war itself was part of territorial expansionism following the dictums of manifest destiny and those seeking the further increase of slaveholding states.[15] Slaveholding populations (Texans) had earlier successfully overthrown the neophyte Mexican nation's political control in Texas in 1835, and some Mexican Texans (Tejanos) had in fact fought against Mexico to protest political centralization and later against the United States in the American-Mexican War.[16]

The importance of the American-Mexican War to understand the importance of necrocitizenship for Mexican-origin populations cannot be overstated, for it set the stage for the American Civil War in which Mexican-origin populations would fight for the Union *and* the Confederacy. More than thirteen thousand people of Mexican origin and Cubans served in the Confederate Army, especially from Texas, Louisiana, and Florida.[17] On the other hand, numerous companies of Mexican-origin populations organized for the Union, such as Romero's Independent Company, Co. A, Militia Infantry, New Mexico; Perea's Independent Company, New Mexico Volunteers USA; Gonzales Company, New

Mexico Militia USA; Montoya's Company, Perea's Battalion, New Mexico Militia Infantry; El Valle's Co., Perea's Battalion, New Mexico USA Militia Infantry; Aragon's Company, Company I, 2nd New Mexico USA Infantry; Duran's Company, New Mexico Military Militia USA; Baca's Company, Perea's Battalion, New Mexico Militia Infantry.[18] Latinas are represented in the war as well. Loreta Janeta Velazquez, a Cuban woman, was said to have fought disguised as a Confederate soldier. *The Woman in Battle* is her account of her adventures as Lieutenant Harry Buford. She enlisted in the Confederate Army disguised as a man and fought at First Manassas, Ball's Bluff, and Shiloh. Discharged when her gender was discovered, she rejoined and fought at Fort Pillow as a man. Discovered again, she became a successful Confederate spy as a woman.[19]

Latinos continued to serve in the U.S. military throughout the nineteenth century and even fought against Spaniards in the Spanish-American War, with the assistance of Cuban irregulars who had previously defeated the Spaniards. Mexican-origin populations from New Mexico, Texas, and California fought with Theodore Roosevelt's Rough Riders as well as other units at San Juan Hill and other engagements.[20] Thus, Captain Maximiliano Luna of Santa Fe, New Mexico, led the F Troop, a platoon-sized unit of about a hundred men, all of whom were Spanish-speaking citizens from the state of New Mexico. But this war also created the basis of the relationship between Puerto Ricans and the United States. At the cusp of becoming independent from Spain, Puerto Rico became and remained a territorial colony of the United States, whose populations would extensively serve in the U.S. military from colonization to the present. It is largely mythic that U.S. citizenship for Puerto Ricans was shoehorned into the Jones Act of 1917 one month before the declaration of war by the United States as a means of ensuring manpower for that conflict.[21]

World War I engaged two hundred thousand Latinos, and especially Mexican Americans. Some who had been born in the United States chose to move to Mexico rather than serve in the bloody trenches of France. However, there were numerous young men who served in the U.S. military, and some were awarded the Medal of Honor. Puerto Ricans served in all–Puerto Rican units, which, in the aftermath of the Spanish-American War, were formed in six segregated infantry regiments, guarding key installations in Puerto Rico and the Panama Canal Zone.[22]

In spite of mistreatment, David Barkley Cantu, a Mexican American from Laredo, Texas, chose to serve in the 89th Infantry Division's 356th Infantry Regiment. Cantu was awarded the Medal of Honor posthumously for his actions near Pouilly, France, on November 9, 1918.[23] Many others served with distinction, such as Private First Class Jose C. Salazar, U.S. Army 128th Infantry Regiment, 32nd Infantry Division, who died on November 10, 1918—the last day of the war. Salazar is buried at Plot B, Row 04, Grave 38, Meuse-Argonne American Cemetery, Romagne, France.[24] Others wrote of their experience, like J. Luz Saenz of southern Texas, who published his diary *Los mexico-americanos en la Gran Guerra: Y su contingente en pro de la democracia, la humanidad y la justicia.* Saenz's diary illustrates the wish to serve faithfully in the military of the United States while simultaneously having to cope with the reality of Texan racism and ethnocentrism in that period.[25]

Military service also moved returning veterans to fight for their rights and against discrimination. While not a veterans' organization, the League of United Latin American Citizens (LULAC) was founded in 1929 and was influenced by returning veterans like Saenz, who served on its board of directors early on.[26] Mexican-origin women played an important role in developing LULAC, as its auxiliary organization was crucial in the total organization's development. More than likely, Latinas served as part of the thirty-three thousand women who were enlisted in the armed services during that period, while other Latinas filled in crucial labor roles in factories, businesses, and agriculture.[27]

This pattern of returning veterans influencing and organizing associations in the struggle against racial and ethnic discrimination had its apogee after the intense service in all branches of the military by Mexican Americans, Puerto Ricans, and some Cubans. Yet there were also internal struggles in the services themselves, with Latinos at times being less eligible for promotion and unrecognized for their actions on the battlefield.[28] On the other hand, many Latinos were honored and received great kudos for valor and leadership. Among the five hundred thousand Latinos who served in World War II, the 158th Infantry Regiment, the "Bushmasters"—a quarter of which were Mexican Americans—was lauded by General Douglas MacArthur as "one of the greatest fighting combat teams ever deployed for battle."[29]

Large segments of the Mexican American population, as well as Mexicans who were not yet citizens, joined elite units of the army like the paratroopers or the marines and were drafted in large numbers into combat units. Some—like Antonio Alcaraz and his sisters, whose parents had migrated to Tucson, Arizona, from Sinaloa, Mexico, shortly after the Mexican Revolution—were all sent back to Mexico during the infamous "repatriation" period in the 1930s while he was enrolled at Tucson High School. Shortly afterward, he "illegally" returned to the United States to enlist and served with the 551st Parachute Regiment. Later, only a few weeks after becoming a U.S. citizen, he was wounded in the Battle for Salerno.[30] Others became aces, such as Francis Perdomos or Richard Candelaria, both born in El Paso, Texas, but raised in Los Angeles, California. The former became the last USAAF pilot to become an "Ace in a Day," when he shot down five Japanese planes in a single day while serving with the 464th Fighter Squadron. Candelaria, on April 7, 1945, singlehandedly engaged seventeen German combat aircraft, including two jets, and shot down four German fighters to add to the two he had downed previously.[31] Marine Edward Romero of Tucson survived two wounds through the battles of Saipan, Tinian, and was in the first wave of the invasion of Iwo Jima, in which 90 percent suffered casualties, and later included fierce hand-to-hand combat.[32] Many combat units were made up almost exclusively of Mexican-origin soldiers. These included Company E of the 141st Infantry Regiment of the 36th Division; the 7th, 30th, and 142nd Infantry Regiments of the 3rd Division; the 22nd Infantry Regiment of the 4th Division; the 23rd Infantry Regiment of the 2nd Division; and the 79th Infantry Regiment of the 7th Division. In total, eleven Mexican-origin soldiers were awarded the Medal of Honor, among them Marcario García of Villa de Castaño, Mexico, of the 4th Infantry Division.[33]

While thousands of Mexico-origin and Puerto Rican Marine, Army, Navy, and Air Corps volunteers served for the United States in World War II, three hundred thousand Mexicans under the Mexico-United States Borrowed Workmanship Program—also known as the Bracero Program—replaced their brethren and non-Latino workers who had gone off to war. Mexican braceros worked in California, Montana, Washington, Colorado, Michigan, Arizona, Wisconsin, and Minnesota between 1942 and 1946. Some considered themselves "soldiers of agriculture, construction and of the railroads."[34] Thus, while Mexican labor much antedated this period, they also became, after the war, an inexhaustible source of agricultural labor too often exploited, underpaid, and unprotected, in part leading to the Farmworkers movement of the 1960s.

Sixty-five thousand Puerto Ricans also served in the U.S. armed forces. Four Puerto Ricans received the Congressional Medal of Honor, while hundreds of Boricuas died in the Pacific and Europe, establishing part of the basis for their legitimate claims to necrocitizenship.[35] Many Puerto Rican servicemembers served in segregated units, like the Regular Army's 65th Infantry Regiment or the Puerto Rican National Guard's 295th and 296th Infantry Regiments in Puerto Rico, Panama, the Caribbean, Hawai'i, North Africa, Italy, and the Maritime Alps of France and Germany.[36] Those who served in nonsegregated units were subjected to visual appraisals of their skin color—one method reported anecdotally but not confirmed in official documentation is that appraising officers and noncommissioned officers had Puerto Ricans remove their shirts to examine their backs. If they were gauged as "dark," the soldiers were placed in segregated units. Those deemed "white" were placed in unsegregated units; some in this latter category achieved important standings and recognition.[37] A case in point of "white" Puerto Rican inclusion was Annapolis graduate Lieutenant General Pedro del Valle, of the United States Marine Corps of Puerto Rico. As a lieutenant colonel, del Valle was the architect of all artillery on Guadalcanal; without his tactical and strategic use of arms, that very tenuous battle would certainly have been lost. He commanded the 11th Marines (artillery regiment of the 1st Marine Division), the Artillery of the 3rd Amphibious Corps on Guadalcanal and Guam, and the 1st Marine Division during the Okinawa Campaign.[38] His awards and decorations include the Distinguished Service Medal and the Legion of Merit with Gold Star, the Navy and Marine Corps Medal, Ethiopia, 1935–1936, among others.[39]

Like many of their World War I predecessors, the World War II generation of Mexican Americans struggled for civil rights. Veterans returning to their homes were denied their earned education, housing, and medical benefits. Some funeral homes refused to inter the bodies of battle-slain Mexican American veterans in other than segregated cemeteries.[40] Mexican American veterans of World War II declared "no más" (no more) to discrimination, founding the American GI Forum. The forum was responsible for many of the gains made against segregated schools, poor housing and restricted covenants, voting rights, and employment opportunities, and were among the many that took advantage of the GI Bill to earn university degrees. Equally important were American Legion Associations like Post 41 of Phoenix, Arizona, made up of wholly Mexican members because the non-Latino American Legion did not accept Mexican veterans after World War II. Post 41 was instrumental in removing housing covenants against Mexican veterans as well as removing barriers to their prevention of obtaining housing loans from local banks.[41]

Puerto Ricans also faced appalling social and economic conditions upon their return to the island. Thousands migrated from Puerto Rico to New York, where they faced similar issues to those confronting Mexicans in the Southwest: poor employment opportunities, limited educational opportunities, racial and linguistic discrimination, housing covenants, and economic disparities in salaries and wages, as well as exclusion from union representation. They, too, developed veteran-led independent organizations as well as others under the GI Forum banner.

World War II was also a watershed for American women, and for Latinas especially so. Given the much higher birth rates of Latino families in comparison to the general population, Latina mothers suffered especially heavy losses to their families during the war. The Varas, Garcia, and Ortega families, for example, each had six sons engaged in combat from New Guinea to Iwo Jima, from the skies over Germany to the invasion of the beaches of Normandy.[42] Many Latinas also served in the Navy, Marine Corps, Army, and Army Air Force as officers and enlisted women as nurses and in quartermaster, communications, instructional, and transportation roles, like Tucsonans Lieutenant Carmen Romero, U.S. Army, and Ensign Beatrice Amado, U.S. Navy, who both served crucial roles as nurses in healing hundreds of wounded veterans.[43]

On the home front, Latinas took over jobs from which they had been kept out and created new ones when millions of men left for the services, and they fought ethnic and gender discrimination on the job and in the military. Mexican-origin women, for example, replaced male railroad workers in firing up locomotive engines for the Southern Pacific Railroad and took the first important steps in breaking down the occupational "color" barriers suffered by Mexican-origin men. In 1943, they successfully had men fired for sexual harassment, which may make them among the first women in the United States to do so in the workplace. Other women of Mexican origin represented by the Amalgamated Clothing Workers of America worked in the copper mines of Arizona; these women organized wildcat strikes protesting poor working conditions and sexual harassment.[44] Many would go on to form auxiliary women's organizations with their returning husbands and brothers, who would once again face employment discrimination for the very jobs their spouses and sisters filled.

But there is one overriding characteristic of Latino participation: their overrepresentation among the KIAs and WIAs in World War II and in almost every conflict. I performed a capsule analysis made of Mexican-origin casualties of Maricopa County, Arizona, in World War II by looking at an alphabetical snapshot of surnames between A and H. Of these, 20 percent of the killed in action (KIA) were of Mexican origin at a time that they made up 3.25 percent of the eligible age population. In fact, of the three counties in Arizona in which most Mexican-origin populations lived during this period, the following are the KIA casualty rates in comparison to the eligible population: Maricopa County, 21 percent; Pima County, 32 percent; Santa Cruz, 56 percent, with a total average of 36 percent. Even though each county accounted for the greatest percentage of eligible Mexican-origin youth, no county consisted of eligible male youths in more than single-digit numbers. The original document does not include youths killed in the Marine Corps, Coast Guard, or Navy.[45]

Unlike U.S. participation in World War II, the role of the United States in the Korean War was at the time a contentious development. Among the general U.S. population, there was little understanding as to the whys and wherefores of the "police action" that cost many lives. This war was also a mixed proposition for many Latinos/as, since those who went into combat in Korea were in the midst of battling the civil rights issues at home—the first civil rights bills had not yet passed. President Harry S. Truman's 1948 executive order mandating the integration of the armed forces did have many implications, especially for Puerto Rican soldiers, many of whom served in nonsegregated units since "race" no longer was the central arbiter in separating them one from the other and in segregated units. Despite the desegregation order, Puerto Ricans in Korea were placed in segregated units, including the well-regarded 65th Army Regiment that had seen service in World War I and World

War II. In Korea, a hundred of the regiment's men refused to fight in one ill-organized and futile battle. They had already suffered heavy casualties due to leadership incompetence of officers and non-Spanish-speaking noncommissioned officers. Eventually, the men of the 65th were exonerated and all courts-martial were rescinded. The 65th also served with distinction in helping guard the flanks of the 1st Marine Division, many of whom were of Mexican descent, as it extricated itself from the infamous Chosin Reservoir.[46]

Additionally, a large percentage of the Marine Reserve Easy Company were Mexicans and Mexican Americans from Tucson, Arizona. Some who were sixteen and still in high school were called up in June 1950, and with very limited training, they fought valiantly through the Inchon invasion, the battle for the City of Seoul, and to the Yalu River bordering China. Some returned to graduate from Tucson High School, many wounded and all suffering from battle trauma. Some Marine officers in Korea derided units with many Mexican Americans as only "Mexican Marines" and racially denigrated them, but these units were defended hotly with fists and hearts by other Marine officers, such as Captain Herbert Oxnam.[47] Latina women again would suffer because of the larger size of their families, and many of their sons would enter combat units like those of Easy Company and not return. Cathy Ramirez lived in hope and dread when her older brother, Joe M. Valenzuela, was reported missing in December 1950, a month after his wife, Elsa, had given birth to their daughter, Elaine. He unfortunately was confirmed to have been killed.[48]

As in World War II, the Medals of Honor that were awarded to Latino veterans of the Korean conflict were mostly posthumous: six of Mexican decent, a Puerto Rican, and a Cuban.[49] This generation would also return to the United States to fight for civil rights and gain college degrees, and they created many opportunities for following generations—such as Sergeant Eugene Suarez, the only Mexican American Marine combat photographer to have served in either World War II or Korea.[50] The Korean War—like World War II—served as an important step toward greater civil and educational equity for Latinas and Latinos, with many men and women returning from war also joining the GI Forum, developing civil associations like the Mexican American Political Association and the Mexican American League. Just as importantly, they took advantage of the GI Bill that offered similar support to that of the World

War II version. Suarez returned to complete his university degree and successfully achieved a long career in law enforcement.

Among the costliest of wars in which Latinos were disproportionately represented in dead and wounded was that of Vietnam.[51] Between 1961 and 1973, Latinos suffered many casualties, terrible psychic wounds were incurred, and families were torn apart by loss. An analysis of the distribution of Latino soldiers, marines, and sailors in combat units, their total casualty rates suffered of dead and wounded, and the aftereffects on families has not yet been accomplished in the study of this terrible tragedy. However, we do know that between January 1961 and February 1967, slightly less than 20 percent of those killed in Vietnam from the Southwest United States were of Mexican origin, and between December 1967 and March 1969, 19 percent were of Mexican origin—United States and Mexico born.[52] Between 1961 and 1969, 19 percent were killed from a southwestern state, when only 13.8 percent were of military age. For the entire period of the war, 1961–73, 1 in 2 Latinos served in combat units, 1 in 3 were wounded, and 1 in 5 were killed. Latinos became the second-largest American minority in Vietnam, representing more than 19 percent of those killed or wounded at a period in which the total Latino population in that age cohort was less than 14 percent.[53]

Thus, during this period, especially between 1968 and 1973, these casualty rates were felt by many communities whose sons perished in a very unpopular war. These casualties also became known and questioned among many sectors of the Latino community. In response, Latino university and high school students, professionals, farmworkers, blue-collar workers, and numerous community organizations and individuals carried out and organized widespread protests not unlike those expressed by millions of other Americans. The Chicano Moratorium of Los Angeles against the war, attended by thousands on August 29, 1970, was among the largest but was ended ignominiously by a combination of Los Angeles riot police and Los Angeles County sheriff's deputies.

Unlike their fathers and grandfathers who served in the previous two wars, Latino veterans returning from Vietnam did not generally join veterans' associations. Like many other veterans of the unpopular war, they hid from the open hostility heaped on them and escaped into neighborhoods to attend school and jobs. In many cases they suffered alone for many years from the shock of battle. According to the National Vietnam

Veterans Readjustment Study, 29 percent of Latinos who went to war in Vietnam at some point in their adult lives met the full diagnostic criteria for post-traumatic stress disorder, in comparison to a lifetime prevalence rate of 20 percent and 14 percent for African Americans and white European Americans, respectively.[54] This Latino percentage is superseded only by Native American veterans, at 30 percent.[55]

Yet like their fathers and grandfathers before them, this generation earned Medals of Honor, and while whole units were no longer segregated or composed mostly of Latinos, the sheer percentage of Latinos serving in combat units supports the conclusion that Vietnam was fought by too many youths whose basic recommendation for combat was the lack of a college deferment. As in World War II and Korea, noncitizens like Marines Jose Francisco Jimenez from Mexico City and Alfred V. Rascon from Chihuahua, Mexico, gave their lives for others and were posthumously awarded the Medal of Honor. Puerto Ricans were awarded four Medals of Honor, as many in Vietnam as in World War II.

Twenty thousand Latinos served in the Gulf War (1990–91), and by 1997 a third of the combat troops in Bosnia were Latinos. But the U.S. intervention in Iraq in the early 2000s once again raised the issue of Latinos engaged mostly in combat units, and often in harm's way and regardless of citizenship. The first two marines killed in that war were not citizens of the United States but of Guatemala and Mexico; the third was the son of an immigrant from Mexico.[56] Joe V. Aldaz Jr., of the D'Aniello Institute for Veterans and Military Families, writes, "According to the Congressional Research Service in 2017, of those killed in Iraq, 450 were Latino and 52 killed in Afghanistan were Latino. That is[,] 10.6% of the casualties in Iraq were Latino and 7.9% in Afghanistan were Latino."[57] If the historical pattern holds, most were of Mexican and Puerto Rican origin and overrepresented in relation to the eligible percentage of mostly males between the ages of eighteen and twenty-five. In satellite remarks to the League of United Latin American Citizens Convention in 2004, President George W. Bush stated, "Some 85,000 Latinos have served in Operation Enduring Freedom and Operation Iraqi Freedom. More than 100 have given their lives. Over 400 have been injured in combat."[58]

Indeed, among the armed service branches, the Marine Corps presently has the highest percentage of Latinos and Latinas (15 percent), in part due to the allure of an elite combat force, and—in many cases—the quest for legitimacy through the military.[59] Given the population density of Mexican- and Puerto Rican–identifying Latinos, it is highly likely that the largest percentages of the Marine Corps are of Mexican and Puerto Rican origin.[60]

Mexican-origin, Puerto Rican, and other Latino populations have served valiantly and with distinction in the American Civil War, the Spanish-American War, World War I, and World War II, as well as the conflicts in Korea, Vietnam, Iraq, and Afghanistan, and in 2022 more than one hundred military assistance programs globally, most through the Department of Defense. Each war has provided the means by which returning veterans were able to resist the political and social conditions of the time, and the dead were constant reminders to Latinos that they did not have to accept the status quo. But at the same time that they resisted conditions still present in parts of the United States, they also often strongly internalized an uncritical necrocitizenship. Ironically, such civil rights gains reinforce the underlying mythic architecture of "being all you can be" through accepting necrocitizenship and being willing or unwilling to pay—symbolically or in actuality—the eventual double duties of dying for others and having others die in one's stead. Thus, this willingness accentuates the mythic and ideological substances of Wars of Commission.

## Los Chavalones of E Company: A Bit of Ethnography of the Continuing Process

Necrocitizenship often emerges unexpectedly to bring together bands of brothers from the same neighborhoods, cultural contexts, educational experiences, work and labor, and group identities, localized and internationalized at the same time.[61] With this bit of ethnography, I provide a small narrative in order to explore the parameters and intensity of the category that became a crucially important identity marker for a generation of young men who were members of a Marine Corps infantry reserve unit in Tucson, Arizona, that was called into combat service in Korea after World War II. But it is also a narrative of how this service was developed into a highly regarded and ritualized postwar association of young men and their spouses and families.

I refer to them as "Los Chavalones of E Company" because, for the most part, the original cast who joined the reserve units were not veterans but sixteen- to nineteen-year-old neophytes hardly trained and barely recognizable as marines. There were cadres of World War II veterans who had served in the Pacific War who were highly seasoned, some wounded in combat and others highly decorated for bravery. These were, for the most part, the noncommissioned officers, as well as a representation of officers who were also veterans of the Pacific conflict. Yet of the 225 young men in E Company of the 13th Infantry Reserve, most were untrained and had at most a few two-week summertime tastes of military discipline and narratives. Many had not yet become expert with their weapons and were less than physically capable of the strains of combat. Many were still in high school or working in nonmilitary jobs, some were professionals among the officers, and some had older brothers and sisters who were veterans who were attending the University of Arizona under the GI Bill, but in general most worked and came from working-class, Mexican-origin households and were living in Mexican barrios or neighborhoods.

These youngsters were not simply the children of Mexican immigrants. Many had ancestors who experienced the Spanish Colony of Tucson and, more recently, the Mexican Revolution on both sides of the recently imposed border. The young soldiers of the company in 1950 had been born during the Depression in the very late twenties and through the thirties while older siblings had been drafted or joined the armed services during World War II. Some had parents who had been "repatriated" during the Depression as part of the infamous expulsions of thousands of Mexican-origin persons, both citizens and noncitizens. There probably was not a family in Tucson of that generation who had not known the pain of loss of a brother, a cousin, or an uncle killed in Europe or the Pacific as well as the joy of returned veterans who had survived. Many of these youngsters had buried a relative or welcomed one back from the world conflict. For a short period of five years, these growing young men had known peace—until 1950, when the Korean War broke out and those in the Marine Corps Reserve unit were unceremoniously called in and shipped off on a train from Tucson.

It has been said that heroism is the act of ordinary people engaged in extraordinary actions in extraordinary events. War, by definition, is an extraordinary event; its levels of physical and psychological stress and trauma are unimaginable to anyone who has not experienced it, and to defend or rescue one's comrades requires the kind of self-sacrifice that few of us in any circumstances could or would conceive. How, then, did mostly untrained, young, and inexperienced Tucsonans who were shipped out on July 31, 1950, not only engage in extraordinary actions in Korea but in large part—except for the twelve brave men who were overcome in battle—return home? How, in fact, did most of the 225 or so mostly teenage boots who had, at best, slightly more than three weeks of training make the amphibious landings at Inchon, participate in bitter street-to-street fighting in Seoul, and engage and defeat a determined, skilled, and experienced enemy who outnumbered them in some cases ten to one in the frozen hills and mountains of North Korea?

It defies all logic for them to have done so. Few should have been able to sustain the difficulty of combat in each of these extraordinary actions without intense and lengthy training. Amphibious assaults are tricky, dangerous, and take months of repetitive training and practice so that relatively large bodies of men can move smoothly together to achieve the necessary coordination. On the other hand, to fight in cities takes an entirely different approach in which only the smallest units participate, and door-to-door fighting requires each member to cover the other in small, almost mini-actions. While practice makes perfect in city combat, it is among the most harrowing and difficult forms of combat to learn— and to survive.

Steep-hill-terrain combat, which became common in Korea, most marines will admit, is the most uncompromising of all extraordinary ac- tions. Trudging up and down steep hills not only exhausts you but offers little in cover, concealment, or protection from a determined enemy that does not want to let you up. Preparing for this type of combat, then, requires not only intense conditioning, forced marches, and endurance but a special kind of courage to endure almost open-terrain warfare. Yet, for the most part, none of these ordinary young men—mostly from the barrios of Tucson, from families who lived in Menlo Park, Hollywood, El Hoyo, South Tucson, El Barrio Libre, the Indigenous reservation, and in a few cases from the ritzier Drachman neighborhood—had this train- ing and in some cases had not even been to boot camp. They learned to fire the M1 rifles, machine guns, and bazookas between Treasure Island, California, and Japan.

How, too, were they able to face a winter in North Korea—as one author puts it, "a cold howling beast"? By day the temperature hovered somewhere between zero and twenty degrees Fahrenheit, and by night it stood at twenty degrees below zero and in some cases fell to thirty below. Weapons froze, rations froze, human flesh froze, and the carbine became a useless stick to be used only for clubbing—but not much, because it became too brittle and broke with the first stroke. How were these Chicanos, Chinos, Native Americans, Jews, and Anglos from hot Tucson able to withstand a cold that froze rivers and choked the gorges with snow?

In this awful cold, which almost guaranteed frostbite, these mostly sixteen- to nineteen-year-old Chavalones were yet able to fight off 100,000 men who were led by General Song Shilun, who led the 9th Chinese Army Group. Robert Lecke writes:

> Song was a master of warfare. He had been handling men in combat since his graduation from Whampoa Military Academy at the age of seventeen, had commanded a regiment on the famous Chinese Long March, and fought the Japanese for years. General Song had been specifically selected to lead his hundred thousand troops against the Chavalones and the first Marine division in order to carry out one single function: to wipe them out.[62]

How did these ordinary kids from largely working-class homes—who had gone to Safford, Roskruge, and Tucson High, played pelota in the sandlot in front of Herbert Street, ate tamales on Christmas, danced at the Blue Moon, saw Mickey Mouse and Donald Duck at the Lyric and Pedro Armendariz and Maria Felix at the Plaza, and spent Friday night's paychecks on Saturday night—confront these extraordinary events? The clue does not lie in combat training. We know that for the most part these ordinary young men were unprepared and ill-trained for the extraordinary events in which they participated. Rather, I argue that it lies in all the other intangibles that these young men had as a community: a sense of family, of responsibility, of commonality, of willingness to help others when they are down, and, most of all, a genuine love for each other as people in spite of their differences. The Chavalones who left that day were already extraordinary because they came from ordinary homes that had fought in the extraordinary event of survival—surviving revolutions in Mexico, ethnocentrism and discrimination in the United States, underemployment, poor education, and lack of opportunity.

The Chavalones came from homes in which families did not surrender to conditions but rather made the best of the worst; they created opportunities and helped others when necessary. These young men already had developed this mental and spiritual preparation prior to Korea. Many of their parents had survived the Mexican Revolution, which had killed a million Mexicans. Another million had crossed the recent border. For the most part, then, the Prices, the Jaymes, the Cocios, the Nacho Cruzes, the Gaspar Aldriches, the Zimmermans, the Fishers, the Suarezes, and all the others who went to Korea were readymade to be heroes. These extraordinary families had set the example long before their sons joined E Company, 13th Infantry Battalion.

Afterward, they sealed their association by developing a unit of the Marine Corps League. For many, the league allowed them to maintain the bonds they had developed in the depths of combat in Korea, to fill the terrible holes created by those killed, and to mitigate the certain postwar trauma that many suffered. The veterans' spouses created auxiliaries and became the major organizers and movers in fundraising, community events, and charity that gave the league a community identity of service and assistance to those in need. Despite their shared trauma, they could join on Saturdays to have a beer or two, reminisce, and laugh uproariously—even at some of the wounded returned members. One of them in Korea had been bundled up and shipped out by helicopter, only to be shot down and wounded a second time, then put in a truck for evacuation only to be ambushed and wounded yet again. With the characteristic dark humor of veterans, the thrice-wounded member of the league was referred to as "el tres" (literally "the three" but in reality a recognition of his multiple wounds). Another of their band was awarded the Silver Star for heroism after running through knee-high machine-gun-bullet-grazing fire to save a wounded marine out in the open, shot in the behind doing so. His company members ribbed him for having a "culo alto" (high butt), for not having stayed close to the ground. But other times, when the humor left out the side door, some would choke up, others would stand to go to the bathroom, and others would stare out into space. Then their wives would intervene and gently move toward their husbands and ask them to dance if there was music playing. Some would be escorted out by their wives and bundled into their cars to be taken home to heal some more.

For some, grief dies hard and continues into the present moment as one tragedy is recalled and remembered. Los Chavalones began their own oral history project to ensure that they and following generations would know what they had done and suffered.

### El Bobby: Just Trading Souls

I was then a machine gunner perched up on Ammo Hill outside of Koto R on our way back from the Chosin. We were keeping the Chinese off the roads so that the other units could slip in behind us. We had just destroyed a bunker, our officers had all been killed, and our sergeant was in back of us and not available. Two guys were bringing up a Corpsman who had been hit trying to bring up a guy who had been shot beyond the slope of the hill. As I passed them in that direction, they told me not to go over there since the guy who had been shot was being used as bait. The Chinese had zeroed in on him and they were hitting anyone who tried to get him. He was yelling for us not to try to get him and to stay away. But hero me, I said, "fuck it" and crawled down to him, and it was damn hard work with all the snow and litter around. I got to him, and he still insisted on my leaving him. I couldn't, so I told him to crawl up on my back which he did with great pain since he had been hit in both legs and one of them was in really bad shape. But I grabbed a hold of him and stood up, and he was really heavy since he was a big guy by the name of Polaski, and he was soaked from the blood and wet snow. The rounds were going all around us but I didn't notice them much, and I managed to get us up and over the ridge and I tried to set him down but I had forgotten that his legs were broken so that one of them folded back under him and he used his foot as a pillow. I picked him up again and straightened him and gave him some morphine. Two guys dragged him down the hill and I never saw him again.

Just about then I decided to see if there were any other guys down where Polaski had been, and I asked some of the others that were around to go with me. Nobody volunteered, but just then "El Bobby" was coming up the hill. He had been held up spraying foxholes. He said, "Vamos," and I said no, don't go with me. I wanted to protect him. His wife was expecting their first.

But he said, "Vamos, para que sepan que los Mexicanos saben como morir donde quiera." (Let's go, so that they learn that Mexicans know how to die anywhere.) So we went down, and Bobby covered me by keeping the Chinese down. I collected some weapons but there was nobody else around.

We went up over the ridge again, when I looked back, Bobby was curled up on the ground shot in the chest. Another Machine Gunner was crying over him, and I couldn't quite figure out why since they had not been good friends, but I figured maybe he felt something for him. I picked up Bobby in my arms and tried to shake him awake, but it did do no good. By that time, we started getting hit pretty good with phosphorous shells and between the smoke and me crying I thought I saw Bobby going to heaven. But it was time to go and that was the end of Bobby. I grieved for Bobby; I still do.

Only years later did I find out the reason why the other Machine Gunner had been crying so much. He had killed Bobby by mistake. I guess "El Bobby" and Polaski just traded souls.[63]

Los Chavalones remembered and paid homage to all the Bobbys with a yearly commemoration at which those no longer present would be announced, honored, and mourned. Many, dressed in partial or whole uniforms, seemed to be able to bear things a little better than before they joined the League so that their losses of others and of their youth seems to have some reconciliation and peace. No one forgets, but perhaps this way of reliving the memories allows them to do so in safe places, with others present and not in the darkness of only themselves.

Where are they now, more than seventy years after that fateful day when they all boarded the train? Twelve did not return and are mourned and recalled to this day. For most members of E Company, life returned to normal despite physical and psychic wounds. They married, had children, became great-grandparents, and worked in occupations and professions: judges, doctors, policemen, city workers, and architects. Others quietly returned to what they had done before. Some even went back to high school. For some, Korea's trauma and psychological distress were not only debilitating but in fact very much defined their life paths. Some at this very moment still cannot hold an unshaking cup of coffee in its saucer. Others, upon entering a room, scan for exits or search for a place to sit with their backs to a wall.

Perhaps reunions are not only a reminder of the unselfish actions of the many, of their unselfish attention to duty to others, of comrades fallen and not returned, and of the unsung importance of their community to meet difficult and unbearable challenges. They also remind the Chavalones that with only a short time left now for this generation, that for some few left, the extraordinary event of war has not yet stopped and that somehow those few remaining lend them a hand to smooth their brows, to cool their foreheads, and to hold them close to their community's bosom. Those evenings of remembrances and annual commemorations for this dwindling generation and those following are not only for those extraordinary men of Company E but also for comrades of theirs and following generations. Such experiences constitute necrocitizenship at its most basic tragedy, thus providing ample support to Wars of Commission.

## The Díaz-Barriga and Dorsey Ethnographic Ritual Complex of Necrocitizenship

Among the richest ethnographic narratives of the processual and structural architectures of necrocitizenship are those articulated by Miguel Díaz-Barriga and Margaret Dorsey, in their exemplary work *Fencing in Democracy: Border Walls, Necrocitizenship, and the Security State.* Filled with "thick descriptions," one part of their narrative exemplifies the principles of necrocitizenship's powerful emotional and ritual dynamic. Annual rituals are important for many in southern Texas, according to Díaz-Barriga and Dorsey. This is especially visible in their analysis of the "El Veterano" Conjunto Festival in Robstown, Texas, in 2005. Robstown is a town of almost eleven thousand in Nueces County, Texas, and a western suburb of Corpus Christi, of which 92.41 percent of its residents are of Mexican origin.[64]

According to Díaz-Barriga and Dorsey, the festival was performed originally in memory of Eligio Escobar, a World War II veteran and conjunto musician, to raise money for the instruction of youngsters in the conjunto style of south Texas music.[65] Generally lasting twelve hours on a Sunday from noon to midnight, the process unfolds with a military ritual honoring each military branch. After the initial "Patriots Band" renditions, youth performances follow and, from my perspective, symbolically create clear cultural avenues of continuation to following generations. From then on, numerous invited conjunto bands play for the rest of the festival. This performance blends traditional Mexican musical expression with an accentuation of military-derived citizenship, thus integrating Mexican cultural expression with the broader cultural patterning of necrocitizenship.

Strikingly apparent and carefully narrated ethnographically is the venue in which the festival was staged and brings to bear the cultural patterning of the ritual processes of cultural necrocitizenship arrangements. These processes stitch together the meanings and symbols of sacrifice and citizenship-worthiness to Mexican cultural formats of familial representation and lineal descendances. As Díaz-Barriga and Dorsey show, the traditional Mexican Day of the Dead rituals are blended with citizenry obligations of death for nation and exhibited, performed, and rearticulated as a ritual process in which the eventual outcome is the integration of symbols, beliefs, and behaviors. This integration ties the knot between Mexican culture and the requirements of necrocitizenship, including death, sacrifice, and reinforcement for present and future generations.

As Díaz-Barriga and Dorsey describe it, upon entering the hall where the event was held, they paid an entrance fee collected by the matriarch of the event. Arnold van Gennep and Victor W. Turner in their theoretical works regard this as the separation aspect of the ritual process, or the initial process leading to eventual integration through liminality, which moves the person from a nonritual state of "normalcy" into the ritual place.[66] At the direction of one of the main organizers of the event, the matriarch ushered the anthropologists to four tables, behind which were twelve members of the Escobar extended family, including two veterans of the World War II generation, one of whom was a marine who had survived Iwo Jima—one of the bloodiest of the invasions of the Pacific theater.

> In front of the Escobar table . . . [was] a column of twelve similar tables that opened up to the dance floor. Two more columns of tables flanked theirs to the right and left. These tables also opened to the dance floor, which was peppered with approximately sixteen dancers. Organizers had erected a stage at the front of the dance hall with a large US flag as the only backdrop. Onstage, the vocalist wore a US flag shirt. To the right of the

BELONGING AND DYING

stage hung a banner announcing the "El Veterano" Conjunto Festival, also adorned with a US flag icon.[67]

The unmistakable symbols of necrocitizenry were embossed within the ritual space of the hall itself, supported by the physical presence of the Escobar family network and further emphasized by the veterans. A surviving marine who was present was a veteran of Iwo Jima, where eighteen thousand marines were wounded and seven thousand were killed (38 percent of the invasion force), and 99 percent of the twenty-one thousand Japanese soldiers died.[68] His was a kind of necropresence as one of the fortunate surviving while the rest lay in the volcanic ashes of that horrible site of destruction and awfulness of marines and Japanese.

The food at the event was a syncretic Tejano version of American fare: barbecue, rice, and charro beans, along with white bread, jalapeños, and pickles—and beer. Some visited the "veterans' memorial" near the dance hall entrance. Díaz-Barriga and Dorsey report being guided by Raul Escobar, who as a teenager was assigned as a Marine flamethrower. He provided a running account of combat as a marine and the poetry he composed during World War II. What became apparent to the ethnographers was that the setting itself was like the food, the celebration, and those present: a syncretism of necroartifacts integrated with a kind of Mexican Day of the Dead altar. Escobar's presentation induced a tortured liminality of enveloping human beings in flame while attentive to his poetic constructions as a penance for what he had had to do.

There was also a folding table, which created a memorial zone, featuring memorabilia from multiple wars. Díaz-Barriga and Dorsey observed and were shown young men in uniforms at military stations with correspondence from home surrounding their visages. These were representations creating days of the dead for those visiting, congruent with the memories of those dead, how their own lives were affected, and how the dead continue to be present. This was a liminal scene of death's stage, but leading to the permitted integration of a blood sacrifice as part and parcel of the willingness to be destroyed, to be able to join and call themselves "American."

In a peculiar way, these are rituals of marginality in which Mexicans—in Texas, with its long tradition of uncompromising racism—create ritual space and place for a temporary acceptance as citizens in death.[69] It is a kind of necrocitizenship that attracts those cast as "foreigners in their own land," racially inferior and linguistically deprived, as many Texans are wont to classify Tejanos. In other contexts, Mexicans are diminished in the public perception through racialized discourses about immigration, labeled rapists, murderers, and thieves and as "alien" beings. But the Veterano Conjunto and all its attending funerary practices and representations legitimize the presence of the participants. In this manner, a kind of necrocitizenship emerges that features elements of Mexican cultural expression and ritual tied to funerary displays emphasizing how they die to belong in the United States, countering that belittling traditional Texas racialized discourse and narrative they experience in the wider world.

## Conclusion: Tying the Knots

Mexicans and other Latinos have perennially fought, died, and remembered those who have passed in all American conflicts from the Civil War to the present. Each generation, by joining with the others in commemoration or special events, or in creating oral histories, seeks to set the record straight about having participated and been overrepresented in elite units and in the long casualty lists of every war, especially the most modern. They have furthermore come together to create an American Mexican Day of the Dead cultural complex, integrating their associations as civil societies to assist themselves and their surrounding communities, as exemplified by the Marine Corps League of Tucson, the Veterano Conjunto, and others like the American Legion not discussed here, each in their own way. But as commemoration and remembrance unfold, the underlying narratives of sacrifice of self and of others are held up as models of comportment so that they can feel that they belong to a national version of themselves, filtered through Mexican cultural prisms honoring their dead. Like all mortuary practices, however, they become practiced repetitions without question and buttress the emotive and cultural architectures of Wars of Commission and their underlying citizenship architecture.

# CHAPTER 4

## Dislocations, Corruption, Impunity, Murder, and the Normalization of Violence

*Genesis and Ethnographies of Narcocitizenship*

Narcocitizenship, like its counterpart necrocitizenship, is a developing and formative cultural complex that is distributed, multifaceted, covert, and overt. It is glued to strong emotional values and feelings of fear, acquiescence, and helplessness, and is a consequence of the Wars of Commission. Distributed by class, region, and context, its parameters range from beliefs in impunity from legal constraints, to the adherence to violence, to the objectification of women, to extravagant displays of wealth. Since the 1970s, a militarized mindset has solidified, relying on tactical and strategic use of arms, violence, threats, and "low-intensity" approaches to resolutions of conflict. To varying degrees, those affected by these phenomena become objects of influence and experience the following: the acceptance of passivity; an unwillingness to trust legal authorities for resolutions; generally cowing to numbness; objectification of tragedy and death; and finally, for many, dislocation to less onerous conditions in other regions or nations. Flight wins over fright.

Among many people who live in a narcostate and who are not engaged directly or indirectly in criminal actions, feelings of terror are widespread, while impunity, machismo, and aggressivity are commonplace among those who are. In part, narcocitizenship stems from the insatiable market for drugs in the United States and Europe, the development of the Mexican military, the parallel development of a paramilitary structure of drug cartels, drug politics and ensuing corruption, the integration of ideological and group identities, and long-term socialization effects over generations. All of these are expressed to one degree or another in public cultural and media venues that advertise and advocate elements of these cultural complex sources.

There is, of course, opposition to the cartels and offshoots by Mexicans in both institutional and noninstitutional settings. This opposition comes from honest judicial and political authorities and others like businessmen who must shell out part of their earnings to attached criminal gangs of cartels who demand a "deposit" to ensure products get to markets. They particularly resent the chokeholds of the gangs and fear traveling outside their base of operations without payouts.[1]

Thus, this chapter details the processes leading to the creation of aspects of a militarized narcostate and narcocitizenry, a reliance on the "low-intensity warfare" strategy by the military and cartels, the impact of this phenomena on various sectors of Mexican society, and the deep cultural and political issues that arise as consequences.

## The Militarization of the Mexican Military: An Essential Cultural Format

Ironically, until the rise of the drug cartels in Mexico, the Mexican military was largely ceremonial, a poorly equipped and trained body designed to support the ruling political party: the Partido Revolucionario Institucional (PRI).[2] Craig A. Deare describes the relationship between the state military and the PRI following the election of Miguel Alemán Valdés as president of Mexico in 1946, the first civilian to be elected to that office after a series of revolutionary generals. Basically, the Mexican military worked out a "deal" in which in exchange for autonomy and limited state control and oversight, nonmilitary presidents would be free of any political interference by the military. As well, Deare indicates that the president could rely on the military's total support of the president and especially exhibiting support at times of political stress. In fact, the military acted as a fifth estate, introducing its own legislative bills through the presidency. It was for all intents and purposes a seeming democratically elected presidency but guaranteed its political health by a military willing to defend its interests as it did during the various student uprisings in the 1960s and later more revolutionary activities by the Zapata movement.

For the next seventy years, from the end of World War II until the election of the National Action Party (Partido Acción Nacional, PAN) candidate Vicente Fox in 2000, this pact held. Over that long period of time and into the present to different degrees, the military's top leadership became corrupted by drug cartels, with the exception of its naval forces, including the Marine Corps. However, this exception does not absolve them since the Marines gained a reputation not only for effectiveness but also for civilian deaths and torture.[3] Both incorruptibility and civilian oppression marked their behavior.

The military's role as both benefactor and protector of the ruling political party changed during the presidency of Felipe Calderón, who held office from late 2006 through late 2012. Calderón not only tasked the miliary to undertake a "War on Drugs" at the behest of the United States but also initiated the militarization of the armed forces by the United States with millions of dollars in training and equipment.

The loss of military personnel is especially indicative of the "low-intensity" nature of this expanded military function, since prior to the drug wars the military had suffered few casualties. Afterward, 750 personnel have been killed from 2006 to 2019, and hundreds were wounded in a military in which the actual number of combat troops is forty-two thousand. Special operations forces are especially impacted by combat against the cartels in the past and present.[4] These military operations with high casualties included what might as well have been theater, in which known drug labs that had been previously closed were raided multiple times even though defunct. Also carried out were raids of drug areas controlled by opposition groups attempting to encroach a cartel that had bought off army officials, as well as raids and the destruction of drug labs and territory identified through electronic or human means by uncorrupted Special Forces or Marines.

There are, however, important developments to this militarization process that more closely resemble the American military industrial complex than what I have termed the "public works complex." Under this concept, public works are totally in control by the military via construction, implementation, control, and operations. Writing in May 2021, Stephanie Brewer noted, "This month marks the one-year anniversary of López

Obrador's Presidential Agreement assigning a range of policing tasks to the armed forces until 2024. Likewise, this month marks the second anniversary of the law that created the National Guard, the new federal security force proposed by López Obrador. Despite forming part of the civilian Ministry of Security and Citizen Protection, the National Guard is a militarized force that operates under the coordination of the Ministry of Defense (Secretaría de la Defensa Nacional, SEDENA)."[5] The "range of policing tasks" by the military then includes direct operational control, from establishing a new airport to overseeing construction projects to exercising oversight of customs and port facilities. The military retains budgetary control over all these projects, *without* oversight of the normal bureaucratic budgetary process. In a way, the original lack of oversight of the military by the government has been reversed, accompanying the military's greater access to, control of, and use of national and international resources.

Further, the expansion of the armed forces through a military national guard has made the army into a more formidable force but one that seems not to have been effectively used in combatting cartels; rather, it is used to engage as referees between cartels. But there is one other important function of this group. This same military force was used to interdict the movement of Central Americans in the south to placate the Trumpian threats of greater custom and tariff duties, to which López Obrador very quickly acquiesced. In all, militarization has now transformed the Mexican armed forces into a public works military complex with perhaps even greater desultory impacts on an extremely fragile civil infrastructure of judicial, legislative, and executive controls over the institutional frameworks of the state itself.

## Corruption and the Parallel Development of the Militarized Cartels

The genesis of the corruptive elements of the drug trade and the parallel growth of the militarized cartels that have expanded and spread like a carcinoma to enormous dimensions over the past forty years have been crucial in the formation of the narcostate. Both elements rely on the economic market of the United States and expansion to Europe. Corruption pervades geographies of the Mexican state, but it is transnational in scope. It is, in fact, part of the co-globalization process that accompanies transnational agriculture, manufacturing, and exportable goods and services. Its cultural and political dimensions permeate, to varying degrees, institutions that include banking, real estate, financial, educational, juridical, legislative, and each of the presidential offices since Luis Echeverría in the 1970s. According to the twenty-year investigatory efforts of Anabel Hernández—now exiled from Mexico due to extensive death threats—this permeation extends to include some figures in the present López Obrador presidency.[6]

In the narcostate, violence, or its possibility, is always present as the central means of enforcement in all matters and often without warning. The covert dimensions of this violence are often masked in invitations to aspiring politicians, bothersome academics, or journalists to be "interviewed" by cartel figures themselves or their political allies, followed by offers of support or veiled or unveiled threats.[7] Governorships are especially open to this process, depending on the strength of the cartels in the state, with all their economic and physical force. This kind of pressure may also be applied to presidential candidates. In this way, local, state, regional, and national offices from rural areas to urban areas may be influenced by cartel control, with opposition candidates snuffed out, compromised, and corrupted.

Likewise, successful businesses may also be approached by cartel associates requiring a slice of the business. Often, in response, businesses "dislocate" by moving to safer environments in the country or to the United States. Intermediaries undertake financial investments, especially in tourist-associated enterprises such as nightclubs, restaurants, and hotels. More recently they have made inroads into legitimate avocado farming businesses as well as developing their own, with attending international complications.[8] But the theft and illicit sale of fuel, known in Mexico as *huachicoleo*, was and continues to be under even greater scrutiny of the López Obrador administration as a source of millions of dollars to organized cartels and allied gangs. None of this could occur without the "collusion between state officials and organized crime," as the International Crisis Group asserts.[9]

Thus the "seepage" from illegitimate to legitimate enterprises of drug monies and cartel enterprises into legitimate enterprises creates the foundations of the narcocitizen cultural complex itself, commonly affecting entire regions—especially rural areas of Mexico. But the speed and strength of this process are increased by the large-scale militarization of the cartels themselves and in direct conflict with the state itself.

The seepage of the cartels into the civil and military structures of the state has been going on for at least seventy years, but civilian use of violence equal or sometimes superior to that of state and national agents has never been operationally as prominent as in the present. Parallel to the militarization of the Mexican military, the major cartels have been undergoing their own militarization, with sophisticated weaponry, intelligence networks, recruitment of former soldiers and special operations veterans, tactical and strategic planning, and a growing reliance on violence against the national, state, and local juridical and administrative structures normally associated with the civil control of populations.

This development is itself a consequence of American "low-intensity warfare" doctrine and training. By the late 1990s, according to Juan Camilo Castillo, Daniel Mejía, and Pascual Restrepo, the Gulf Cartel recruited thirty officers from the Special Air Mobile Force Group, which had been trained by the United States in low-intensity warfare tactics, as a special assassination cadre.[10] A shock troop known as "Los Zetas" eventually broke away from their cartel bosses and began competing with the Gulf Cartel, using a scale of violence more intense and murderous than had been used by other groups before their ascendency. This pattern of recruitment of former Mexican and Central American military members—the latter of whom were also trained by the American military and Israel—was used primarily to exterminate Mayan populations, facilitate the recruitment and training of members of the infamous Salvadoran Mara Salvatrucha (13th Street Gang or MS-13), and incorporate and train "off the street" marginalized youth, especially from rural areas, who became the sources of cartel paramilitary forces.[11] They recruited more than three hundred Zetas by 2003.[12] Guillermo Valdés Castellanos summarizes the impact of Los Zetas: "the creation and expansion of the Zetas at the end of the nineties and the beginning of the new century was a true inflection point that would initiate a new movement in the history of organized crime in Mexico: the organization of criminals in real mechanisms to kill."[13]

By the time Camilo Castillo, Mejía, and Restrepo's working paper was published in 2014, the militarization of the cartels arose dramatically with paramilitary capabilities including Los Zetas, of the Sinaloa Cartel, Juárez Cartel, Tijuana Cartel, Beltrán Leyva Cartel, and the Knights Templar Cartel.[14] In 2019, the Sinaloa Cartel had militarized to such an extent that it was able to defeat the Mexican National Guard in what has become known as the Battle of Culiacán, when the Mexican government attempted to capture Ovidio Guzmán López, the son of drug lord Joaquín "El Chapo" Guzmán. Such transformation to a militarized organization has enabled the cartel to pivot organizationally when its channels of drug markets become temporarily interrupted; for example, through the Caribbean by American militarized operations so that it is able to create extensive infrastructures "from sea to land, making Central America their principal transit route" for cocaine from Colombia.[15] With this strategic move, Guatemala and much of Central America and large swaths of Mexico have become permeated with drugs. As a result of this shift, these regions have transformed from simply transit countries into consumer countries, with all the attending social and cultural consequences.[16]

The reach of the Zetas and other cartel paramilitaries is based on the local control of small-scale criminal organizations and of police in many political districts, according to Séverine Durin.[17] The Zetas managed to expand the organizational infrastructure of the cartel to sell "protection" to local criminal gangs for the extraction of "social rent"—that is, extortion of entire neighborhoods and their attending businesses and from residents.[18] Thus Valdés Castellanos summarizes the process:

> The mode of operation was more or less like the following: in large or small cities with diverse transit routes . . . they would identify the automobile theft gangs, kidnappers, burglars, oil and petrol pipeline thieves, human traffickers of Central America, [and] narcotic dealers, and they would fix a rent or charge for a *piso* [territory] to let them work in exchange for protection; if they refused, the cartels would kill the leader or their bodyguards . . . and the following day they would submit to the cartel. In addition, the cartels would obligate the local criminals to open new lines of business: drug trafficking but controlled by them, extortion of small businesses, starting with forged or stolen checks and initially in bars, houses of prostitution, and table-dancing establishments and followed by pharmacies, restaurants and cafés, gasoline stations, hotels, garages, and

so on. Part of the earnings from these new sources went to them. So that the model would work, they would name a Zetas boss who would become the czar of all the crime in the city and military units called "estacas" [piles] that would oversee the rest of the criminal gangs and subdued them if they did not pay the rent for their pisos. An accountant completed the organizational makeup. In addition, they bought the entire municipal police force to prevent their operations from being disturbed, protected whoever worked under their tutelage, harassed or eliminated whomever did not comply, and provided information about the operations of federal authorities [as protection].[19]

This business model has been used in one form or another in towns and cities across the country, and it seeps into almost every aspect of life to one degree or another. Sometimes the model begins seemingly innocently, and then complexity settles in and becomes the quotidian reality, not only in urban settings but in the most rural and remote areas of swaths of the country.

## Transnational Process and the Local Ley Fuga

The seepage of violence into communities has effects that seem "traditional" but in fact are the result of transnational processes that mask the origin of the violent behavior. Mexico, especially in rural areas, is haunted by the specter of the "ley fuga," which was long practiced by Mexican Rurales (Federal Rural Police) in the late nineteenth and early twentieth centuries. Mexican Rurales often executed Mexican prisoners accused of "trying to escape," as did Texas Rangers in the same period, who executed especially Mexican-origin prisoners. Furthermore, the Arizona Rangers often cooperated without legal authority; while Colonel Emilio Kosterlitzky was head of the Mexican Rurales in Sonora, he and the Rangers crossed the border to capture citizen fugitives of each other's country and often executed the fugitives.[20] Localized versions of the ley fuga have long been practiced in Mexico, such as in the extrajudicial killing of suspected "witches," of those suspected of seeking to kidnap children, and the Canoa massacre in 1968, in which a priest, believing that five university employees who were in the area on a mountain-climbing trip were communists, convinced a mob of villagers to attack them, killing three and injuring the other two.[21]

Thus, localized versions of the ley fuga are not unknown, but there is an added wrinkle in the present: the application to "cholos" who have been deported to Mexico for drug-associated charges in the United States. Cholos are associated with gang membership and have a characteristic style of dress, tattoos, and counterculture hairstyles ranging from mohawks to buzz cuts.[22] They are mostly English speaking, often have been incarcerated more than once, have not completed formal education, and are often socially ostracized, both in Mexican neighborhoods in the United States and in their newly associated postdeported communities in Mexico.[23] In some rural areas, people have been willing to use localized versions of ley fuga to prevent theft or violence by returned cholos.

In early 2011, according to Mariángela Rodríguez Nicholls, a young cholo from Los Angeles was deported under the charge of sale and distribution of drugs to a small rural town in the Mexican state of Hidalgo. He settled in with his parents but without employment or the resources to sustain himself or buy the highs he needed. He burglarized neighboring homes and was relatively successful at it—until a neighbor-relative caught him and shot him with a double-barreled, 12-gauge shotgun, cutting him in half. The relative had warned the young man's parents that their son had been seen trespassing on his and others' property and that in doing so he placed himself in danger of being killed because in rural areas such as this, people are more apt to use violence as a way of dealing with such situations themselves rather than relying on authorities who are not trusted, available, or counted upon to intervene in a judicious manner.[24]

According to Rodríguez Nicholls, significant consequences ensued for the young man's family, the neighboring relative, and the density of relations within the town itself.[25] The alliances between confianza (mutual trust) kin that were necessary to survive on a daily basis in Mexican rural areas often impoverished by external sources were forever torn apart. Some neighboring kin were forced to dislocate from their residences and cultural origins for fear of retribution, not just by the relatives of the young man who was killed but by other cholos nearby. In this manner, a transnational process of drug sale, distribution, and use created chains of legal outcomes, shoved an ill-prepared young man across a boundary to a context of material and social disparity, and eventually led to parental anguish and loss, fractured and disabled familial relations, and the physical and emotive dislocation of parts of a long-established social network of kin.

## The Incipient Rural Example

The impact of drug-associated individuals on rural areas is well established by the ethnographies of James H. McDonald and Mariángela Rodríguez Nicholls.[26] McDonald's work is invaluable in that it provides an early example and a later example of this process. First, McDonald describes narcotics-associated young men returning from the United States to "Buenavista" Michoacán, who use their monies to buy land and farming areas that, for the most part, have been unproductive and unable to support traditional dairy production. Then he reanalyzes the town and its more narcotics-associated complex a few years later, when violence seems to be the overriding phenomenon taking over Buenavista and certainly the region. The first anecdote marks the initial penetration, establishment, and integration of a type of incipient narcocitizenship, which bears some positive functions such as more employment, rehabilitation of some of the largely ecologically damaged dairy lands, and the creation of small business enterprises. However, what seemed to have been beneficial economic functions in Buenavista were tragically integrated with a monster of a cartel—La Familia. McDonald describes it as being composed ideologically of a fundamentalist religious belief system coupled to alleged revolutionary intentions and supported by a violence-oriented transnational narcotic enterprise. The cartel has delocalized the initial crop of narcorancheros, declared civil war on the Mexican state, and recruited the poorest and most youthful of marginalized rural men. McDonald summarizes the tentative outcome for the present and future:

> The cultural changes going on there—founded on the cultural effects of the narcoeconomy—will eventually have an indelible impact on thought and practice.... *La Familia* has made some inroads by claiming divine and Revolutionary legitimacy, powerful forms of symbolic capital. They have further used their economic power to develop a parallel government and

a social base. In Buenavista, *narcos* have, to some extent, pulled together cultural and social capital in ways that have fortified their efforts. For the average citizen, confronting violence and its threat, new forms of cultural and economic domination, and the on-going erosion of state authority does not suggest any reconciliation of these various forms of capital in the near future, if it at all. What of a world in which there is a normalized abnormal and where regular citizens are relegated to the status of bystander to and consumer of the cultural spectacle of the narcoeconomy yet are otherwise rendered silent as they embody the tragedy of Mexico?[27]

As McDonald describes, fear, violence, and murder became part of what I would term *maturational seepage*, that is, the eventual use of murder as the major means of enforcement by gangs and cartels crucial to the narcocultural complex. Ordinary citizens may feel helplessness, resentment, and fear of complaining about any impunity observed or felt, and a kind of powerless objectification of circumstance. Since the legal authority structure itself is compromised, it would be useless to make complaints, and police and governmental and political authorities may very well be the agents of punishment for those complaining. Some may simply leave, migrating either to less problematic areas or to the United States, where they become transnational migrants.

From my point of view, these are the end states of uncertainty and unpredictability of a cultural pattern of one form of narcocitizenship coupled to a necrocitizenry patina in an ever-increasing process of maturation creepage. It is the certain accretion of deep cultural shift and change from civil to cartel authority, from police to gang authority, and from judicial institutions to the institutionalization of violence to "make things right." It is an emphasis on expectations to solutions, from civil society to weapons-dependent social solutions, actions based on highly militarized organizations and groups, and, most importantly, an emphasis on networks of influence undergird by AK-47s as final arbiters.

In her fine ethnography *Esclavitud posmoderna: Flexibilización, migración y cambio cultural*, Rodríguez Nicholls provides an example of how one aspect of narcocitizenship is displayed and its resulting cultural impact: the return of families and individuals from the United States to participate in the yearly ritual celebration of the patron saint of the small Purépecha pueblo of Acachuén.[28] As she explains, the town is one of ten pueblos of the Valley La Cañada, Michoacán, that has lost people to migration to the United States for the past fifty-six years, which has resulted in economic consequences similar to those of Buenavista. Like in Buenavista, obvious class and economic differences increased differentiation among a largely egalitarian Indigenous agricultural community suffering from the ecological and economic disparities linked to globalization. While men have been part of the half-century migratory process, Purepécha women who remain in the village, especially in the absence of men who have migrated, produce *megajón*, a type of white bread that is formed into almost infinite shapes, from dolls to ornaments, for the U.S. market. Through their involvement in the production assembly of megajón products, these women become part of the global market.

According to Rodríguez Nicholls, at this point, migrating spouses have been joined by their families and had children in the United States. Meanwhile, families return for various reasons. Some have returned voluntarily, with or without U.S. residency authorization; some have been deported. Others have gained authorized citizenship status that allows them to return without penalties and visit relatives. Many families return for the rituals and processions celebrating the annual saint's day of the Virgen de Guadalupe. Over time, ritual processes have been socially and culturally affected by migration and reinsertion back into the community after migration after deportations. In fact, the stability of the actual performance of rituals; the roles of processions, foods, and drinks; and attendance have acquired new symbolic and participatory impetus.

Rodríguez Nicholls narrates that traditionally, community support was often measured by the flowers that were contributed to surround the visage of the processual Guadalupe carried aloft by community members. The arrangement of flowers has largely been replaced by cash, contributed by drug-associated "northerners"—newly designated by their returned status—and those not-so-associated but still regarded as "northerners" because of their clothing and language that has been influenced by their stay in the United States. And it is here that the significant impact of drug-associated behaviors is most telling. Youths, both returning and resident, have been influenced by "cholo" culture that is strongly imbued by the use, sale, and distribution of narcotics. In fact, the author explains, the first murders by Purépechas were committed by cholo gang members and more than likely had to do with territorial disputes. Cholos are provided ritual space for their participation in the Virgen de Guadalupe ritual activities: for this short time, they become "Purépechas," according to community members. However, as it is a yearly event, it is likely that the young people in Acachuén, like the youth in Buenavista, will become more and more destructive and socially marginal to community norms and values as the drug culture seeps more and more into their daily lives.

In both Acachuén and Buenavista, economic migration and transnational drug elements have drastically changed the social and cultural dimensions of daily life in rural environments. Cultural dislocations and major community changes increasingly seem to be the short- and long-term futures of a narcostate, overwhelming and shifting the very basis of human relations, including ideological and ritual expressions and the physical well-being of entire rural communities. For narcocitizens acting to meet drug-initiated goals and to control the sale, distribution, and consumption of drugs, violence becomes normative.

## Murder as Business Control

Murder as a control mechanism that extends beyond rural contexts to maintain security among some criminal organizations is becoming a regular practice.[29] Groups will murder people who have provided service to them for some time. For example, in one of the Mexican coastal states, Enrique Maldonado owned a small construction company. His major piece of machinery was a mini excavator for creating flat surfaces on hillsides, digging sewage ditches, and excavating foundations for buildings. Through connections with his wife's aunt, who worked for one of the local cartels cutting and selling cocaine from coastal sources, Enrique was recruited to use his machine to excavate areas for the burial of numerous persons killed by the group and cover them up so that little evidence remained after a few years. After each job, he would find sizeable stacks of cash on the seat of his car. A year later, Enrique, accompanied by his youngest daughter, was bending over to unlock the hinges of the gates of his storefront one early morning when he was murdered by a single shot to the nape of his neck. The little girl was never the same afterward. After his funeral, Enrique's wife, Amapola, was informed by her aunt that she was next. Amapola fled with her daughters to the United States, was given asylum, and now lives in a northwestern state. Shortly afterward, Amapola's aunt was also killed, in the same manner as Enrique.

## Dislocations of Narcocitizenship

Avoiding violence can become real in the present only if the context of violence and insecurity is addressed by dislocating oneself from context and attempting to create an entirely *new* foundation from which future generations can emerge in a safer or neutral region, as is the case of thousands who have fled the specter of narcocitizenship in Mexico. Others move across the imposed bifurcation of the border to seek safe haven and continue their business in their original place of residence but live and survive outside in their new place of residence. They commute virtually or corporally, depending on circumstances, but on any given day, thousands of individuals and cars cross back and forth along the two-thousand-mile border to work, to school, or to visit relatives and friends.

Many thousands of others live on the southern side of the U.S.-Mexico border and commute to San Diego from Tijuana, or to Nogales, Arizona, from Nogales, Mexico, or to El Paso from Juárez, or any of the other crossing points along the two-thousand-mile boundary. In these circumstances, economy outweighs safety; these workers have dislocated themselves from their place of work and from their place of living, with the former imperative for the latter. Thus, dislocation takes myriad forms: physical, psychological, cultural, social, economic, and political. It is "distributed" by short- and long-term patterns of adjustments and negotiated spaces and places.

As well, because of the funneling along the Altar Valley in the Mexican state of Sonora created by the "Prevention Through Deterrence" policy, Indigenous O'odham communities of the Sonoran–Arizona border experience violent dislocation by the cartels. Their homes are burned down and entire communities are expelled, so that a "deterritorialization" process is forcibly imposed.[30]

Human dislocation often forces the best and the brightest to flee for their lives, as in the case of Clarissa Gómez (pseudonym), presented briefly in the introduction. As has been noted, Clarissa was a real estate developer and used her law degree to negotiate the often arcane and cloudy laws pertaining to foreign ownership of houses and property. After a divorce, Clarissa became involved with an American entrepreneur and builder; they married and started a development and real estate company and did extremely well, sharing homes in Mexico and the United States.

Things went awry when she began receiving repeated telephone calls demanding payment for keeping her business open. It seems that for many years she had been protected by a cousin deeply associated with one of the cartels—but that organization had been usurped by another. Clarissa left the country but not her business. After a second divorce, she now manages her business from a distant town in New Mexico. In the meantime, valuable property, which she held along some still pristine beach areas, was taken over by the reigning governor of the state—who was clearly involved with the new cartel masters on the corner—without payment, negotiation, or title. Clarissa still has her business, conducting it through a well-paid staff and occult communication mediums. She travels extensively but stays at arm's length from her former home. Yet the harassment has not ceased. Only a month prior to the writing of this very paragraph, in August 2022, Clarissa's office received further calls demanding that she show up at an address to sign notarization of her property, illegally obtained by members of the same group. Clarissa believed this was a ploy for her to be kidnapped.

She has not returned to her office; she avoids her apartment fronted by an expanse of beaches and emerald ocean and is severed from dozens of friends, remaining family members, and the cultural roots of her Mexican identity. Her travel to Mexico is limited to Mexico City, where, she asserts, "Nobody knows me."[31] Parts of her extended family have also moved to other cities in Mexico and one to South America. For the present, these arrangements have worked out. Clarissa and her two children, raised in the United States, became American citizens through her former husband. Both of her daughters have now graduated from prestigious American universities; neither wishes to return to Mexico.[32] Thus, this dislocation has far-reaching effects on both familial and economic networks. Not only have Clarissa and her family been forced out of the country but her successful business, which would have grown in Mexico and gone on to employ more young Mexicans, has been shifted to the United States. Most critical is the loss of a new generation of high-potential young Mexicans to the United States.

Manuel is another businessperson who has had to flee his original home. Manuel was more directly victimized than Clarissa but has relocated seemingly easily to another coastal area in Mexico, in a state infamous for its cartel.[33] In fact, "Port City," in which Manuel now lives, is part of a now-incarcerated criminal boss's territory, which Manuel made sure was "quiet" and relatively free from the ills of other areas of his own home state. Despite being infamous for the capture of one of the major cartel bosses, Port City is often the preferred vacation spot for other formidable criminal bosses, and therefore the cartels try to maintain some distance from protracted violence there. Nevertheless, there is occasional violent cartel activity, including gun battles between different cartels seeking to expand territory, as well as the death of one of the major cartel figures in a gunfight in which a policeman died as well.

The residences belonging to the boss "protected" the city and became so normalized that they are now part of "narcotours" in which taxi drivers take tourists and visitors for appreciation tours of places associated with notorious criminal persons who have been captured or killed.[34] When he was younger, Manuel would visit Port City with his family during the city's carnival in late winter; afterward, during Holy Week, he would visit various family residences—including the apartments where the state's major cartel boss was captured and was then later imprisoned and magically released.

Now, however, Manuel is not one for narco tours. Manuel's family had been master craftspeople in their home state for five generations before they were forced to close their precious metal shop. The dislocation of his family began with the usual phone calls requiring them to pay a percentage of their earnings, which they ignored for months. Then Manuel's sister was kidnapped in the Mexican city of Monterrey, where she was attending the university. The kidnapping demonstrates cartel-controlled gangs' unlimited tactical reach; Monterrey is in the state of Nuevo León and largely influenced by its own powerful cartel, separate and distinct from those that were influential in Manuel's home state. Nevertheless, some sort of tactical arrangement allowed for Manuel's sister to be kidnapped off the city street while on her way to class. She was held for thirteen days, until the family paid a one-million-peso ransom (approximately US$ 50,000). In response, Manuel's family kept their workshops in operation but moved their store to Port City, which they regarded as comparatively "safe" and "tranquil."

Manuel does fear discovery by the "bad guys," but they belong to a different set than those where he resides now. These new bad guys, in an unintended way, protect him—not directly by agreement but by the gossamer fabric holding together the narcocitizenship cultural complex of Port City and the control of the state's drug market. This fabric is negotiated through cartel agreements, threats of violence, murder, cohort relations of friendship, oral contracts, and contacts with judicial, juridical, and political authorities of the state.

Manuel is satisfied with his new location, but his roots as a Maya speaker remain in his home state. His entire family is also rooted in Indigenous traditions, and he regards himself as well-read in the culture of Indigenous Maya-speaking peoples (including their religious and mythic beliefs), from whom he is an uninterrupted descendant. Manuel's craft is very much associated with Indigenous symbols of water, fire, wind, and earth. The shop is walled with paintings and ceramics strongly evocative of Indigenous figures, motifs, and artifacts, and Manuel keeps a number of pre-Hispanic vessels that he has collected or inherited through his familial networks. He uses these to configure some of his more elaborate pendants, necklaces, and bracelets and he has successfully marketed these to both foreign and Mexican tourists. He is unequivocally successful.

Now in Port City, Manuel may marry, have children, and live a comfortable life. Yet his dislocation, while seemingly benign, has far-reaching consequences for himself and his family. His traumatized sister required intensive emotional and psychological treatment, his parents have left their homes of cultural origin, and his seven brothers and sisters have been forced to scatter to other parts of Mexico. They trust no one, remain rather private, and communicate with each other electronically but without the warmth of each other's touch. They see each other on holidays, and Manuel is largely responsible for maintaining his parents' finances and supporting his younger brothers and sisters. He communicates by subterfuge to his workshop in his state of origin to make special ornaments, jewelry, and artifacts of silver and gold and shares his designs with his artisans for further development.

Moreover, there is a long-term cultural disruption. The fragile comfort Manuel's family is able to keep up does not make up for the loss of their cultural and familial integrity or of Indigenous identity and respect. In his home state, Manuel was in a relationship with an Indigenous Maya-speaking woman who could or would not relocate to Port City with him. Over time after his move, he formed a new relationship with a woman who knows nothing of any Indigenous background or traditions but identifies strongly as a mestiza Mexican and not an *india* (Native person). Most certainly, if Manuel and his mestiza girlfriend tie the knot and raise a family in the largely northern mestizo state where they live now, future generations will not speak Maya, read about their ancestors, or respect those traditions. In a rather indelicate manner, narcocitizenship has trumped Indigenous network identity and future identities.

Among the most serious dislocations is that of the national citizenship into narcocitizenship, in which individuals and groups transfer their fidelity from the state to a new narco-cultural complex. The seepage of narcocitizenship includes citizens' disenchantment with the state, dissolution of any expectation of justice or fairness, and, most of all, loss of hope that any level of the state apparatus, from the local through the national, will protect them against bad actors operating with impunity. Although the state in this creeping process never was free from the influence of corruption, the present drug economy demands uninterrupted political, civil, and judicial control and allegiance to—or desperate avoidance of—a narcostate network.

Rubén Darío Ramírez-Sánchez narrates the disintegration of the efficacy of the state of Tabasco because of a failing economy and its violent displacement by organized criminals in its stead. He says:

> Between the State and the individual there is a process of dissolution of mechanisms of regulation, social integration, and the loss of cultural ties that guarantee a mediating function to contain social frustration. This favors the distancing between individuals and norms due to the devaluing of the belief in the State, with the fracturing of respect, and society ceases being a space of security. Thus, rupture of the social order reinforces the distrust of institutions—education and religion among others that once fulfilled the function of disseminating moral values.[35]

This dissolution, distancing, and rupture create the perfect storm for the establishment and displacement of citizenship with narcocitizenship.

Organized crime, then, displaces socially important spaces of learning and socialization and creates unpredictable spaces and places of violence whose sole objective is to induce "fear obedience" as an outcome for the further expansion of narcocitizenship. Fear obedience has nothing to do with learned moral values of growth and development of the human being; it deals with total physical, psychic, emotional, and cultural control of a guaranteed space of corporeal and virtual hegemony. For those not silent, fear obedience influences the quotidian reality of millions to varying degrees, from nominal sorts of dislocations to complete disenchantment and physical removal from their social, economic, political, and cultural contexts. Most significant is the loss of important cultural contexts of security and predictability that encompass the home, community, church, work, and school, all fonts of positive human tradition. In this scenario, the state and the church begin to wither away and are replaced with state-corrupted narcocitizenship that facilitates, partners, and benefits from an integration of local, state, and national entities with those of the cartels or their political surrogates. Indeed, this may become a normalized cultural expectation in the midst of this "global historical conjuncture."

## The Dislocation of the Press, Murder, and Exile

Great swaths of impoverished Mexicans, rural and urban, are upended by the violence accompanying the drug business that directly uncouples people civily from the state in its most basic core element of narcocitizenship and left without recourse of any sort. But it especially leads to the uncoupling and the silencing of the press, academic research, and civil reliance of any sort. This process creates a civil and informational vacuum and for many journalists, reporters, and academics the sphere of ideas that touch even the peripheries of the corruption of institutions by cartels and their associates causes their final elimination by assassination. Nonreporting by journalists on cartel activity has become a norm—except for those taking extraordinary chances, such as Miroslava

Breach and Jorge Armenta, who were both murdered in 2017. In the same year, Javier Valdez, an award-winning journalist and cofounder of news magazine *Ríodoce* and a correspondent in Sinaloa for *La Jornada* newspaper, was murdered in Culiacán on May 15 that same year. He was shot twelve times in front of his office, evidently for infuriating Sinaloa cartel members for his reporting of the dynamics of that organization and the imprisoned El Chapo Guzmán.[36] Journalist Lourdes Maldonado López, who had requested and been promised protection by President López Obrador during a news conference in 2019, was assassinated in Tijuana on January 18, 2022. Almost simultaneously in early 2022, three more journalists were murdered: Heber López Vásquez, director of Mexican online news site Noticias Web, killed in Oaxaca; freelance photographer Margarito Martínez Esquivel, assassinated in Tijuana; and Roberto Toledo, murdered in Michoacán. All three of them had been enrolled in a Mexican federal protection measure.

These assassinations are manifestations of militarization. Private citizens may be assassinated for labor disputes, personal vendettas, unwelcome information or protest, failure to pay for extortion demands, and, of course, cartel killings over competition from rivals. These murders directly reflect the impunity with which such acts can be carried out given the connivance, cooperation, and integration of legal police, juridical personnel, and political authorities. Major crimes are facilitated and often abetted by the military, police, civil authorities, and governmental offices. Their involvement ensures a rational approach to killing without consequences of any sort and has become much more of a normative dimension. Within this normative dimension, a "rational choice" model reigns prominent in the deliberations by planners and assassins.

In 2022, Juan de Dios García Davish and his spouse, Maria de Jesús Peters, both journalists in Tapachula, Chiapas, were forced to flee to Phoenix, Arizona, after six years of threats.[37] They would have joined the twelve murdered in 2022; in fleeing, they added two more to the twenty-one who had already fled the country between 2018 and 2022.[38] Again, militarization spreads into the narratives of intimidation. García Davish says that the caller to his home identified himself as "Commander Ramón Rocas Suárez" and asked whether he wished to be a friend or enemy of Los Zetas. As with most such calls—mirroring the experience of Clarissa and the experiences of individuals in thousands of other cases—the calls García Davish received included references and information about his family, work, and home that would be jeopardized if he did not acquiesce. Eventually, a chilling call made on May 13, 2022, by self-identified "Arturo Valenzuela Díaz," threatening to kill García Davish and his family, pushed them to leave Chiapas.

The threats García Davish and Peters received were either simple extortion or attempts to silence their intensive reporting on the abuse of migrants by federal, regional, state, and local authorities and partner criminal gangs and cartels. Threats against journalists such as these are used to obfuscate the latter's abusive activity. Extortion narratives are too frequently used by officials to rationalize inaction and judicial restraint. In doing so, these threatening actions are trivialized as simple extortion schemes rather than what they actually are: attempts to squash free inquiry into a massive range of criminality along the southern border. The same pattern holds for the northern border and forms many parts of the narcocitizenship nexus of the suppression of critical inquiry.

Between 1970—the initiation of the War on Drugs in Mexico—and 2022, approximately 230 journalists have "disappeared" or been assassinated, including some foreigners, who were likely not journalists but identified by drug associates as possible DEA agents.[39] Yet the reality of the murders mostly escapes notice unless it is made more present for us all. These murders have not, to date, been described in detail in English, so, to correct this imbalance, I present here a list of the journalists who were murdered between January and August 2022. Each person is identified with their picture, a headline from the news story reporting their death, a brief description of their work (my translations), and an explanation of the circumstances and methods of assassination in order to give their statistical reference a human face.[40]

## Journalists Assassinated in 2022 in Mexico

### Sixth Journalist Assassinated in Mexico in Less than a Month

Heber López Vásquez, age thirty-nine, director of the portal *RCP Noticias*, was assassinated by five shots inside his recording studio in the Port

FIGURE 17  Heber López Vásquez.

FIGURE 18  Roberto Toledo.

FIGURE 19  Margarito Martínez Esquivel.

of Salina Crus, state of Oaxaca, on January 11, 2022. He had received threats for his journalistic work in denouncing corruption among the local authorities.

### New Assassination of a Journalist in Michoacán, Mexico

Roberto Toledo, age fifty-five, lawyer and collaborator of *Monitor Michoacán*, was killed by eight bullets fired by three assassins in the locality of Zitácuaro, state of Michoacán. He had received threats for denouncing corruption in local politics. The threats had become violent a few days before he was killed.

### Photojournalist Assassinated in Tijuana, Mexico

Margarito Martínez Esquivel, age forty-nine, was a photojournalist of police and security themes for *El Semanario Zeta*. He collaborated with *La Jornada Baja California, Punto Norte, El Imparcial*, and the *San Diego Union-Tribune*, among other outlets. He was assassinated by a bullet to the head on January 17, 2022, in Tijuana. Martínez Esquivel was under the program protection for journalists of Baja California.

### Veteran Journalist Assassinated in Tijuana, Mexico

Lourdes Maldonado López, age sixty-eight, host of the program *Brebaje* on Sintoniza sin Fronteras, was assassinated with a bullet to the head inside her vehicle in front of her home in Tijuana, in the Sur de California. Her death came two days after winning a lawsuit against Primer Sistema de Noticias (PSN). During her long professional career, she covered political themes and corruption in the state of Baja California, and worked at Televisa, PSN, and the weekly *Séptimo Día*, among other media outlets. In 2018 she requested protection from President López Obrador: "I come here for your help and for labor justice because I fear for my life."

FIGURE 20  Lourdes Maldonado López.

## Fifth Journalist Assassinated in Mexico in Less than a Month

Marco Ernesto [Islas Flores], age [thirty], who founded the newspaper portal *Notiredesmx*, was assassinated on February [6], 2022, in Tijuana, state of Baja California, apparently, according to the marks on his corpse, by an assassin of the cartel. The presumed killer was captured shortly after.

FIGURE 21  Marco Ernesto Islas Flores.

## Stabbed Journalist Dies in Veracruz, Mexico

José Luis Gamboa Arenas, founder and editor of the news portal *Inforegio* of the digital medium *La Noticia*, was stabbed on February 10, 2022, in Veracruz and died five days later in a city hospital. "The reasons for the aggression are unknown or if they were related to informational activity."

## Journalist Assassinated in Sonora at the Beginning of a Most Dramatic Year in Mexico

Jorge Camero Zazueta, "El Choche," age twenty-eight, director of the digital portal *El Informativo*, was assassinated in Empalme, state of Sonora, on

FIGURE 22  José Luis Gamboa Arenas.

FIGURE 23  Jorge Camero Zazueta.

February 24, 2022, by eight shots when he was in a gym. Zazueta, until two weeks before, had been secretary to Mayor Luis Fuentes Aguilar. He resumed his work as a journalist after leaving his position from the municipality to defend himself against accusations that he had a relationship with organized crime.

**Journalist Assassinated in Zacatecas, Mexico**
Juan Carlos Muñiz, age thirty-six, digital media journalist of *Testigo Minero* and of Radio Zacatecas 97.9 FM, was assassinated by firearms on March 4, 2022, in Fresnedillo, state of Zacatecas.

**Assassinated in Michoacán, Mexico, for Demanding Justice for Another Journalist**
Armando Linares López, director of the digital media publication *Monitor Michoacán*, was shot in the municipality of Zitácuaro, state of Michoacán, on March 15, 2022. Linares had demanded justice for Roberto Toledo, of the *Monitor* Michoacán, assassinated on January 15, 2022. According to media personnel, he did not have any security or a protection protocol when he was attacked in his own home.

FIGURE 24  Juan Carlos Muñiz.

FIGURE 25  Armando Linares López.

Each of them, for the long term, will be missed by their families and fellow journalists; their murders cement death as a certainty with those who dare to report on the cartels as well as with their cooperating partners in the judicial, legislative, and executive systems from the local to the national level. Their loss is immeasurable, and the vacuum created only strengthens another aspect of narcocitizenship, replacing the civility of civil structures as weak as they have been traditionally.

## Tying the Knots of Narcocitizenship

How deeply the Mexican juridical and civil systems have been infiltrated by criminal actors is indicated by the most recent human rights report on the murder of forty-three students in the Mexican state of Guerrero as a "state crime."[41] According to the report, federal officials created a false narrative of findings, perpetuated the crime, and carried it out or assisted in its being carried out. The thirty-three officials named included a former attorney general, state officials of the state of Celaya, military authorities who had an embedded military member with the students as an informant (also killed), local and state police, and members of the cartels of the region.

Yet even when the government has taken stands against criminal networks, the results have been a public failure. The López Obrador administration adopted a message of "hugs, not bullets." This approach failed miserably in stopping homicides and criminal impunity. Almost 45,000 people were dislocated in 2020, hardly a resounding success, and continuing the 100,000 "disappeared" in the previous fifteen years.[42]

On October 17, 2019, members of the Mexican National Guard arrested Ovidio Guzmán López in the Battle of Culiacán between the military and militarized cartel forces. In the battle, hundreds of cartel members attacked civilian, government, and military targets across the city. They took several hostages as well as control of the unit where military family members were housed. Hours after his capture, Guzmán López was released. President López Obrador said that he ordered the release himself, in order to prevent additional violence. Since Guzmán López's release, cartels have killed civilians unaffiliated with the cartels, created roadblocks out of burning cars to prevent the movement of authorities, and threatened the general population—as in, for example, Ensenada, Ciudad Juárez, and Tijuana—as a strategy of violence to force the government to free arrested leaders and members of different cartels. This is the most recent indication of a change in strategy that directly challenges the civil authority of the Mexican republic.[43]

This direct challenge not only forces the Mexican government to further rely on military power to subdue or try to repress the cartels but offers few if any other tactical or strategic options. The state uses a combination of the newly formed National Guard, the Army, and the Navy to interrupt the steady stream of homicides and the transfer of enormous amounts of money from the United States to Mexico via cartel networks through the sale of tons of cocaine, amphetamines, pleasure drugs, and heroin to an America and European market. This effort broadens the incessant corruption of all sectors of Mexico to one degree or another, feeds the loss of political control of 30 percent of the country, and contributes to the increasing glorification of a fearsome ideological framework of drug cultures.

The dislocations of human populations resulting in losses of the best and the brightest, the killing of truth bearers, and the murders of civilians forced into working for cartels create a pandemic of fear. Ordinary people, without recourse from their elected officials, internalize hopelessness, while generations of youth from impoverished contexts internalize the ideological framework of drug culture and direct their futures into working for the cartels. Violence becomes normalized as an acceptable mode by which to solve interpersonal disputes and social and economic conditions. The result of these transformations is that the Republic of Mexico becomes a narcostate committing "state crimes" in which narcocitizenship is a certain outcome of Wars of Commission and emerging Wars of Omission.

# CHAPTER 5

## The Transborder Dynamics on Familial and Quotidian Realities of Everyday Life

### *Here and There and Here Again, the Cosalá Case*

NAYELI BURGUEÑO A.

Migratory dynamics between Mexico and the United States have historically been characterized by their dynamism and continuity. However, these dynamics have come to be driven or contained according to economic and political circumstances, which have translated into changes in U.S. immigration laws and a consequent increase in the military reinforcement of the border. The intensification of policies against the unauthorized migrant population with the consequent increase in deportations, together with the labor market crisis of 2008, had an impact on what became known as the "new migration phase" characterized by the increase in the return of Mexican migrants to their communities of origin in Mexico.[1] But pressures of insecurity in parts of rural Mexico—as has been suggested in chapter 1—have also led to many leaving their points of origin and dislocating north, only to be forced to return during this period of expulsion.

The anti-immigrant context, coupled with the economic crisis in the United States, impacted the forced return of thousands of undocumented migrants, mainly to rural areas of the country. One of the main characteristics of this return is that they are mainly families who, after having lived a migratory experience in the United States, return to their communities in Mexico, a forced and unplanned return. Hence, some authors have referred to them as *crisis returnees* or *forced returnees*.[2] Thus, during the

Obama and Trump administrations more than two million Mexicans were deported, coupled with the raids carried out by Sheriff Joe Arpaio against the migrant population of Mexican origin and the controversial SB 1070 law in the state of Arizona and its imitation versions in other states (as have been discussed in chapter 1 of this book). All resulted in an exodus of families leaving due to fear of deportations.

The return of migrant families deepened their conditions of vulnerability in economic, social, and even emotional terms, as it was an unexpected return with little or no preparation for change. These returns caused a series of social problems that are intensified by the absence of government programs to support their reinsertion into their places of origin. Families also face issues of physical insecurity because of encounters with drug-related conditions upon their return. It is estimated that the return of migrants to Mexico during the five-year period 2005–10 increased by 200 percent compared to the five-year period 2000–2005.[3] According to Ana Gonzáles-Barrera, the number of migrants returning to the country in the 2009–14 period alone reached one million people.[4]

One of the most important characteristics of the phenomenon of return to Mexico is that these are families whose members are composed of sons and daughters, born in the United States, who created new social and political features leading to their identification as "mixed" families.[5] It is estimated that by 2013, 600,000 minors born in the United States accompanied their parents to Mexico, and by 2015, they represented 92.7 percent of the total number of minors in the company of their parents.[6] These large numbers of U.S.-born children were subject to numerous serious challenges in the process of insertion to the parents' community of origin. Difficulties with the Spanish language and incorporation into schools present serious obstacles for minors and young U.S. students, exacerbated by initial issues of academic documentation and grade equivalences. These language difficulties are coupled with discriminatory ethnic differentiation as "pochos" or "gringos," social isolation, and physical and emotional violence that characterized the contexts to which they are forced to accompany their parents. This has resulted in the upheaval of domestic lives once protected by familial return but now stressed by internal conflict and social uncertainty.

The study of the phenomenon of contemporary remigration allows us not only to understand migration as a flow of people who come and go across national borders—as if it were only the result of economic processes or as a homogeneous mass without faces—but to actually understand the complexity of the processes involved more directly from the lives and experiences of the remigrating. It is a scenario very much characterized by adversity and violence, especially in the elementary and secondary school contexts. Thus, many of these "mixed" families faced very serious economic, social, cultural, linguistic, and educational issues that remain highly problematic even to this day.

## The Community of Cosalá: Livelihood Activities, Violence, and Migration

The research itself was carried out over a period of three years in the rural community of Cosalá, located in the highlands of the state of Sinaloa in northwestern Mexico. This research allows us to understand transnational family dynamics, survival, and adaptation strategies, using life history and ethnographic participant observation methods in a social context characterized by conditions of extreme violence.

The community of Cosalá represents the scenario of a complex reality in which hundreds of migrant families live; after having lived a migratory experience in the United States, these families have returned in recent years. Located in the Sierra Madre Occidental, the community of Cosalá is at an altitude of 1,250 feet above sea level, with a territorial extension of 2,164 kilometers in the north-central part of the state of Sinaloa. The community has jungle, forest, and pasture vegetation, with deep ravines—all characteristics of the mountainous zone. The ecology of Cosalá creates conditions so that only 15.74 percent of the land can be used for agricultural activities.

However, it was traditionally a source for gold and silver mining during the colonial period. Since its foundation in the sixteenth century, Cosalá was characterized by mining production, which created a great economic boom, becoming the main center of gold and silver extraction in the area and positioning itself as the capital of the state of Occidente in 1826.[7]

Economic development based on mining was interrupted by the crisis in the metals market and the subsequent decline of mining activity beginning in the 1940s. This led to the expulsion of the inhabitants of the highland areas to the productive valleys of the state within the framework of the new economic development model based on agricultural activities for export.[8]

However, in recent years there has been an upturn in mining activity in the community of Cosalá, with the reopening and exploitation of sixty-seven mines concessioned to the company Americas Gold and Silver Corporation, which was established and began exploiting the mines in 2016 and is supported by Canadian capital and investment. The reactivation of mining activity in the community has generated a demand for local workers for metal extraction and milling, which generates 232 jobs in the community.[9] Commercial activities represent another of Cosalá's main economic activities, followed by livestock and agricultural production. Since 2005, the town of Cosalá has also benefited from its designation as a "magical" town by the Ministry of Tourism because of its colonial architecture and history and physical ecology, which has led to the generation of jobs derived from tourism and recreational activities.

With a population of 6,577 inhabitants, the community of Cosalá has an index of marginalization and economic underdevelopment, categorizing the city as one of the poorest municipalities in the state of Sinaloa. The locality's level of economic instability is due to structural conditions because its activities are based mainly on primary agricultural production with very limited economic opportunities. According to a report of the National Council for the Evaluation of Social Development Policy (CONEVAL, Consejo Nacional de Evaluación de la Política de Desarrollo Social), 51.1 percent of the population in the municipality is in poverty, of which 12 percent are in extreme poverty conditions.[10] Productive activities based on agriculture and livestock are basically for self-consumption, where 70 percent of the population is in the informal sector without access to social services such as housing and health care.

Similarly, the educational attainment of the community reflects an average schooling of only the most basic elementary school level, regarded as a measure of a population where 43 percent live in communities with fewer than 249 inhabitants.[11] This indicates its unbalanced and asymmetrical educational attainment for the majority of its residents. Thus, migration has been a prominent mechanism to escape these present conditions. Historically, and especially after the decline of mining activity, migration of the Cosalá population to the agricultural valleys of the state of Sinaloa began in the 1990s with an increase in the flow of migration to the United States. This last migratory flow was the result of the crisis of the agro-export model initiated by the Carlos Salinas de Gortari administration through the privatization of cooperative farms and the reduction of agricultural supports. However, crucially important was the violence caused by the expansion of criminal organizations dedicated to drug cultivation and military operations that sought to contain them.[12] Together these migration movements contributed to the configuration of creating migratory corridors from the Sinaloa valley to the states of Sonora and Baja California, and later to the United States of America.[13]

According to Arturo Lizárraga-Hernández, the dynamics of migration in the community of Cosalá have gone through five phases.[14] The first phase began with the mining crisis in 1930, which led to the depopulation of the community in search of new employment alternatives. The second phase occurred between 1940 and 1949, motivated by the promotion and development of agricultural activities in the central valleys of the state. The emergence of these agricultural activities led to the demand for day labor and the migration of workers from the communities to the agricultural fields of the central valleys of Sinaloa. The third phase is identified as the period from 1950 to 1969, caused by the decline in the cultivation of narcotics that developed in the highlands after the mining crisis. This ensued violence marked by the rise of cartels and the initiation of Operation Condor in the 1970s, as the following explains.

According to Juan Antonio Fernández and Félix Brito Rodríguez, the scarce population that remained in the communities as a result of the crisis and abandonment of mining led to the development of complementary activities in agriculture and temporary livestock for subsistence.[15] Parallel to this was the emergence of the production of drugs based on the cultivation and processing of opium and marijuana and the consolidation of clandestine family-type commercial networks. In this regard, Fernández and Brito Rodríguez point out: "We reiterate that in its beginnings, drug cultivation in the highlands was a mere possibility through which the inhabitants sought to counteract the crisis that grew in the region after the closure of the metal mining companies and the migration of a large part of the population from the highlands to the valleys, since, as has been said, the economic momentum in the state was concentrated in the valleys of the region."[16] The boom in drug-production activities led to the consolidation of illegal organizations or cartels dedicated to the cultivation and sale of drugs, with the resulting violence and struggle for control of markets and military operations in response.

Thus, actions of the Mexican state led to the implementation of programs to combat drug cultivation and commercialization, such as Operation Condor, which initiated the fourth migratory phase, in the period 1970–79.[17] The objective of Operation Condor was the destruction of drug crops through the participation and action of the Mexican Army in the communities of the highlands and through a policy of cooperation imposed by the government of the United States, which supplied weapons, air and land equipment, and "low-intensity" warfare training.

The implementation of Operation Condor resulted in the displacement of hundreds of families from rural communities located in the highland areas, coupled with widespread violation of human rights of the inhabitants and a human toll of at least fifteen thousand dead.[18] Juan Antonio Fernández-Velázquez writes:

> In the militarized operation, the insecurity, delinquency and crime in the cities and towns of the north, center and south of Sinaloa and neighboring states was even more intense. More than ten thousand military, in addition to federal judicial police, also left thousands dead (conservative estimates speak of 15 thousand dead during the period), among innocent peasants, planters and distributors.[19]

The cultivation of narcotics and the Mexican state's struggle to eradicate them conditioned a scenario of violence in the community that characterized the fifth migratory phase of Cosalá's inhabitants, beginning in the 1980s, according to Lizárraga-Hernández:

> Indeed, examples of abuse and brutality abound in the mountain communities of the municipality of Cosalá, in the mineral of Nuestra Señora de Guadalupe, on repeated occasions the army, looking for weapons, after raiding the homes, tortured the men of the village according to the testimony of one of the inhabitants: "an army captain, after raping one of the nieces murdered her, and tortured her husband and one of her sons when they opposed such abuses."[20]

The prevailing conditions of economic disparity of the inhabitants of Cosalá, together with the presence of criminal organizations and military "low-intensity" warfare, created a scenario that worsened in the 1990s, subsequently increasing migration to the United States, to their main destinations of California, Arizona, and Nevada. Currently, Cosalá, along with the municipality of the state of Sinaloa, concentrates the highest levels of migration intensity in the state and is the municipality with the second-highest percentage of households with a family member living in the United States, accentuating it as a transnational community.[21]

The intensity of the migratory dynamics of Cosalá has led to the formation and consolidation of networks through social and family ties between both sides of the border. This has allowed for an important exchange of social, economic, emotional, and cultural resources between the migrant population settled in the United States and the community of Cosalá, through *transnational social fields*.[22] Through these cross-border fields or circuits, a series of cultural practices are developed, such as the sending of remittances, knowledge, information flows, mobility networks, communication, sending of material and symbolic resources, as well as affective ties and care practices, motivated by the sense of identity and belonging to the community.

The intensity of transnational practices is reflected in remittances, which migrants send to their families. In fact, Cosalá has the highest number of households receiving remittances in the state of Sinaloa (US$11 million from July 2022 to March 2023).[23] Thus, the presence of transnational corridors and networks explains the trajectories and dynamics of mobility, the main migration routes and destinations, and the exchange relationships that condition the coming and going of the migrant population of Cosalá.

## The Return of Migrant Families to Cosalá: Networks, Negotiations, and Adversity

From the increase in the flow of returned migrants to Cosalá during the first decade of the twenty-first century, it is imperative to understand not only the causes and impacts but also the challenges and conditions experienced by the migrants themselves as part of their trajectories. Important to understand as well are the underlying strategies that they use as a result of their experience as a returned community, in a context that perpetuates their conditions of exclusion and economic distress.

According to my study conducted with the returned families in Cosalá, 84 percent of the families that returned did so after 2008, and their main motive was deportation or fear of being deported. The risk of being deported, especially when there has been the expulsion of a family member, increases and the return is presented as a self-deportation for the rest of the family members except for those born in the United States. With the passage of the Illegal Immigration Reform and Immigrant Responsibility Act (IIRIRA) in 1996, the criminalization of immigration law violations was established, with the consequent increase in detentions and apprehensions of unauthorized migrants by U.S. immigration authorities. The increase of Enforcement and Removal Operations (ERO) of Immigration and Customs Enforcement (ICE), aimed at the detention of unauthorized migrants inside the United States, allows the detention and removal of persons living in the country, reaching up to four hundred arrests per day under the Trump administration.[24]

For undocumented parents with children born in the United States, the fear of deportation and separation influenced their decision to return to Cosalá as a strategy to maintain family cohesion. According to the Institute for Women in Migration (Instituto para las Mujeres en la Migración, IMUMI), it is estimated that in 2012 there were 5,100 minors in the custody of the U.S. government's Child Protective Services (CPS) due to parental deportation, which implies a difficult legal process to be returned with their families to Mexico so that their own children would not suffer this ignominy.[25]

In this sense, the persecution against unauthorized migration and the family separation policies prevailing in the United States had an impact on the relocation processes of migrant families, as a survival and reproduction strategy through forced return to Mexico. Given the transborder networks created and the frequent interactions by especially electronic media, these families continued to have a sense of belonging to the community and cherished the existence of social and family ties, which came to represent survival resources for the returned families. However, the return presents a series of challenges, which define and influence the process of reinsertion in all areas of social life.

## The Returning Context

The conditions of economic disparity and consistently occurring violence by drug-related conflicts in the town of Cosalá have created a complex scenario for returnee families, in which community and family social networks are the only support resources available to them upon their return to Cosalá. The extended family has become the most important source of social capital, and through family ties the process of incorporation is somewhat facilitated, mainly in the labor market—the main challenge they face given the precariousness of employment opportunities in the community.

The main economic activities in which parents participate upon their return to Cosalá are agricultural and livestock work made possible through family networks based on domestic production and collective family property. Although the migrants have occupational capital given their work experience—mainly in the construction industry and the service sector in the United States—this knowledge cannot be applied upon their return due to the impoverished state of the economic structure of Cosalá. According to the data obtained from the returning families interviewed, 68 percent of them earn less than two minimum wages per month and 30 percent do not have basic education. Likewise, health-care conditions are precarious, since only 11 percent have medical coverage and social protection. This places families in highly stratified and unequal economic positions with little relief.

The condition of economic disparity imposes a situation of vulnerability on the families, 87 percent of whom indicate that their income is not sufficient to cover the costs of food needs. They perceive this as a more unfavorable scenario than the one that existed before they began their migratory experience to the United States and reflects worsening opportunities for gainful employment coupled with the insecurity and increased violence present in the community.

According to the State Public Security Council (Consejo Estatal de Seguridad Pública, CESP), Cosalá is the municipality with the highest number of culpable homicides in the state of Sinaloa.[26] Although manslaughter is classified as a reckless, unintentional murder, it shows the intensity of these acts attributed as "accidental," which is noteworthy because it surpasses even the municipality of Culiacán, the state capital, which was famously sequestered twice, as previous discussions in this text presented.

The presence of illegal drug cultivation and production has an impact on the levels of violence and insecurity in the region, along with the active presence of military forces dedicated to the seizure and destruction of crops and laboratories used for the processing and manufacture of drugs.[27] The National Survey of Victimization and Perception of Public Security 2022 indicates that 50.5 percent of the population feels insecure and afraid of the possibility of being a victim of a crime. According to the results of the survey, public safety is conceived as the most important problem, even more urgent than economic problems or the fight against corruption.[28]

Returned families then face a process not conducive to either stability or to a healthy adjustment, which implies not only geographic relocation and displacement but also severe social and cultural conditions that would tax even the healthiest of familial relations and support. This context then has repercussions on their dreams, goals, attempted adjustments, and their own forms of adaptation.[29] The social and cultural resources that allow them to negotiate and design strategies are used as support tools related to the social and cultural capital they have, mainly the use of kinship networks.

Transnational relations allow the migrant families settled at the destination to get closer to and be present in the community with members of the community and extended family in the places of origin, consolidating the links and negotiations used in the return. Kinship relationships are constituted as facilitators in the reinsertion process of the families returning to Cosalá, who provide housing and employment through productive activities and who act as providers of immediate food and health needs. However, these relationships place great stress on available social resources given the limitations of economy and ecology. Nevertheless, the networks available to the members of the extended family make up an assemblage of resources, limited as they may be, which are present and active in providing measured support through solidarity ties with the returning families.

The relocation of migrant families to Cosalá represents a major challenge for the U.S. citizen-accompanying minors since 83 percent of the families interviewed have sons and daughters born in the United States. I refer to these children as "accompanying" minors because although the family unit may be referred to as "returned," the children themselves are not returnees but accompanying their parents, many for the first time. The mixed composition of the families, determined by different migratory statuses and cultural and linguistic issues, conditions and complicates the processes facing the returned families and problematizes their adjustments. This reconfigures new dynamics of returning migrant families, who suffer difficult processes of negotiation, relocation, and ruptures.

## Returnees and Their Characteristics: Accompanied U.S.-Born "Illegal" Dual Citizens and New Identities

The main characteristic of the contemporary return phenomenon is that it is a family-type return accompanied by minors born in the United States. The presence of minors with U.S. citizenship residing in Mexico registered an increase starting in 2000, doubling the figure by 2015 with approximately 500,000 children and young people under eighteen years of age residing in the country.[30] For these minors, their arrival in Mexico represents facing an unknown scenario to which they are migrating for the first time and with great challenges for their cultural and social adaptation. Thus, because of American-language policies in most border states, there is little formal instruction in Spanish. This leads to language vacuums, except for the Spanish that is spoken at home. Children having undergone bilingual instruction seem to adjust more readily than those without, but they are not in the majority.

In my survey of Cosalá, sixty-three minors were identified as returnees in the company of their parents, 73 percent of whom were born in the United States and whose ages fluctuate mainly between eleven and fifteen years of age. Although the Mexican Constitution guarantees the right to nationality to the children of Mexican parents born abroad, this right requires an administrative procedure and documentation that in many cases the returned families do not have, so that of the accompanying minors from these returned families in Cosalá, 83 percent of them are not formally recognized as Mexican nationals.

Importantly, lack of legal identity as Mexican nationals hinders access to social benefits for minors, such as health care, school scholarships, or even educational enrollments. This is aggravated in rural areas due to the family's unfamiliarity with educational rights for their children as well as by the often cultural, linguistic, and social barriers created by the schools themselves in not recognizing the children's English knowledge as a resource rather than an impediment. In addition, by not having Mexican citizenship, minors are left out of the state's health system, of which only 7 percent of minors have medical coverage and social security. This places them in a condition of vulnerability, as demonstrated during the COVID-19 pandemic, when access to vaccines required citizen identification with the registration of the Unique Population Registry Code (Clave Única de Registro de Población, CURP) for their application.[31]

Illegal status as a characteristic of the accompanying minors has repercussions for their access to federal student support programs such as scholarships or financial support, leaving them out of these benefits and eliminating opportunities for their academic and personal development. The inability and lack of knowledge of government institutions to understand the conditions and dynamics of transnational families is expressed in the obstacles and limitations facing these families.

Although access to education is a fundamental right established by the country's Constitution, it has been hindered and even denied in the case of accompanying minors. This is compounded by the schools' lack of support for the teaching of the Spanish language and for ignoring limited English literacy as a resource as well. What results is a demanding process of academic equivalencies—which means, in most cases, that these children are returned to previous grades or are left out of the educational institution. Many of the families left their former homes without necessary documents of registration, enrollments, and educational standing because of the severe legal pressures of state laws regarding immigration and the roundups by Immigration and Customs Enforcement (ICE) agents at places of work, worship, recreation, and even neighborhoods.

The Mexican government has made some progress in terms of the right to education of the accompanying children through the 2015 modification of the General Education Law, which eliminates the administrative procedures of authentication of documents and translations in schools to facilitate their access. Additionally, the reform of 2017 established the revalidation of studies process as well. However, in the case of Cosalá, there is still a lack of updating and knowledge about these processes, continuing with the requirement of documentation for the permanence and validation of their studies. Regarding this issue, a returning mother says:

> I would like them to explain to people what they are going to encounter here when they arrive. For example, over there [in the United States], no matter when you arrive, no matter what time you arrive, no matter what day you arrive, they accept your children in school. They don't put any obstacles in their way. I struggled a lot with her here. She lost the school year because I had no support from the school authorities for her to follow the course of her year. That's how I see it, maybe I'm wrong. . . . She took the exams, she took them in Spanish, and she studied all her life in English and passed them. I had to get the certificates from here and even then they didn't accept her in school [high school]. She had to do the whole year and they made me do a lot of rounds in Culiacán. I went to the Language Center to get her grades and report cards translated and even then, they didn't accept her.

Further, the children who remain longer in the U.S. school system are more vulnerable when they return to the rural Mexican educational context, where the administrative, cultural, and pedagogical aspects appear to be obstacles. We even see that some students find themselves at constant risk of not being able to continue in school because they are frequently reminded to deliver what the school regards as necessary documents. Samuel, a high school student returning to Cosalá, expresses, "They said I could be here and study but after a certain limit if I didn't turn in the papers, I would have to go out."

The invisibility shown by educational institutions to transnational children hinders the development of their potential and capabilities, which is also one of the main concerns of returning families. The Mexican state does not pay attention to returned migrant families; it does not recognize that this is an existing and recurrent phenomenon in the checkered history of migration between Mexico and the United States. Rather than regarded as migratory flows of departure and return as part of the unequal economic and labor dynamics of a global transnational stage of economic decline, returning families are merely regarded as the price to be paid for "illegal" status. The transnational status of these minors is not recognized or taken advantage of by the country's educational institutions.

Yet the youth and minors present a great cultural richness that has to do with the configuration of a transnational identity, made up of cultural elements from both nations. These identities are constructed through the social and cultural contexts they have lived through their own experiences and biographies, in both the United States and Mexico, which translate into cultural practices of belonging to both. For accompanying minors, transnational identities represent a resource that includes skills, abilities, information, and knowledge, including social networks of exchange.[32] These identities are translated into a series of practices that children and young people develop, such as the mastery of the English language, the celebration of traditions and rituals, and the permanence of affective and social ties with their parents' networks from their country of origin. This has allowed the maintenance of social networks during the re-emigration of minors to become a survival strategy for the returned families in the face of marginalization and violence. Thus the children experience layered identities placed into question by traditional Mexican pedagogical and administrative approaches and cultural premise—not unlike those of traditional American schools regarding migrating Mexican students arriving in the United States.

## Violence, Ruptures, and Relocations

The context of the returned families is complicated by the scenarios of violence in the region, characterized by the development of illicit drug production and cultivation activities.[33] Given the scenario of insecurity present in the community, among the only consistent resources for migrant families is the possibility of sending their children to the United States, one of the main reasons for the re-emigration of minors.

Focus groups with young high school returnees in the Cosalá community were conducted to gather their experiences of the situation of violence and the design of strategies or readjustments that they carry out in their daily lives. The fear of violent scenarios was masked by one returnee, who indicates, "Nothing bad happens here; there are no robberies because they 'don't let' anyone misbehave." This demonstrates the naturalization of the environment of violence and the recognition of the parallel judicial and legal system beyond the state in the control of the population, an issue that is not openly addressed by anyone. How-

THE TRANSBORDER DYNAMICS ON FAMILIAL AND QUOTIDIAN REALITIES

ever, there are certain measures that they tell us about, such as the risk of going out at night; group accompaniment in the streets, especially for women; and being on the fringes of drug-trafficking activities. When we asked about their expectations or future plans, we found that 82 percent of these young people intend to return to the United States.

Young people are the most vulnerable population to be co-opted by drug-trafficking organizations. The lack of educational expectations and the economic reality characterized by the scarcity of the families' incomes increase the risk of young people being recruited to participate in the illicit production of drugs. Returnee families live in fear that their children will be co-opted into these activities or become victims of crime, which is the most important factor in relocating their sons and daughters.

One of the parents interviewed told us that after living in the state of California for more than eighteen years, he returned to Cosalá with his wife and four children born in the United States. Faced with the difficulties in the school insertion of the minors due to administrative obstacles required, such as the demand for documents, he said:

> The older ones who were going to high school [United States] had a lot of trouble to be allowed to enter school here [Cosalá]. They asked us to arrange their dual nationality and we had to go to Culiacán and pay a lawyer and all of that was very expensive. . . . My boys liked school, the oldest one even played basketball. . . . The oldest one is no longer here with me. I lost him. He went to the mountains and you know that whoever goes there is not doing any good.

The level of insecurity and violence therefore plays a disruptive role in the trajectories of returnee families. This is true in the case of Gladys and her family, who returned to Cosalá with her husband and three daughters from the city of Glendale, Arizona, due to her husband's deportation.[34] Gladys tells us about the feeling of vulnerability and fear they experienced due to the harassment of her seventeen-year-old daughter by a member of a criminal organization.

In the conversation with Gladys, she expressed her fear that her daughter might be stolen or that her daughter herself might decide to become romantically involved with this person. Upon my return to the community in the following fifteen days, the family had left Cosalá without notifying or informing anyone in town about their plans to leave. After a couple of months of still not knowing about the situation of Gladys and her family, we got news that they had returned to the United States. The children had managed to enter the country without any problems—as they all had U.S. citizenship—while the undocumented parents had been helped to enter the country clandestinely by a coyote from the neighboring town. This was the only way around the impact of "fear obedience" (see chapter 4).

In the same vein, Flor tragically relates how after the murder of her son and trying to prevent the involvement of her grandchildren and the risk they were running, she decided to send them back to the United States to be with her sister, who lives in the state of California. The children—thirteen, fifteen, and nineteen years old—left in 2022; two of them now study and the oldest works in the agricultural fields. This illustrates how re-emigration due to violence is the only strategy that is efficacious for these minors—but for a high price, since it leads to separation from the family and in some cases perpetuates the conditions of economic inequality and social disparity, especially given their fragile reconnections in the point of origin without the support of their parents.

Of the minors returned with their parents to Cosalá, 67 percent have re-emigrated to the United States, mainly to the state of California between thirteen and nineteen years of age. The egregious consequence is the transnational fracturing of an intact family, and with it, the emotional and psychological price paid by the youngsters. This is a subject that will have to be further investigated in depth in the study of these families.

What was observed in the community of Cosalá reconstructs the narrative of return as the final phase of the mobility of migrant families. The structural factor of violence comes to modify the dynamics of insertion and settlement in the community and plays as an expelling and dividing factor of the returned families. The transnational family does not remain static and immovable in the face of complex scenarios; family members develop limited strategies that allow them to respond modestly to the different contexts and challenges of which they have no control, where the return represents a stage of reproduction of the migrant family in the space of mobility that characterizes them. Therefore, the transnationality of the families not only remains but simultaneously expands and shrinks tridirectionally—from the networks created prior to the original migration to the United States, from those while in residence in the United States, and finally from the relocation networks of their U.S.-born children who try to keep alive their shrunk relations with parents left in Cosalá.

The violence present in the community is a reality that is repeated in most rural areas of the state of Sinaloa. Its impact has modified not only the relocation and displacement of people but also the abandonment of localities by their inhabitants. It is estimated that 3,316 people have been displaced by violence in rural areas.[35] However, drug-trafficking activity has had an impact on the normalization of the activity and the construction of a narcocitizenship in which values, practices, and meanings are reproduced, leading to an apology of violence and an exaltation of power, money, and transgression.

This scenario, as a result of the structural crisis that accompanies the rural areas of the country, had an impact on the lack of economic and labor opportunities and prepared a breeding ground for participation in drug-trafficking activities. Thus, returning migrant families face not only great economic, social, and cultural challenges upon their return to the community but also a scenario of fear generated by violence. This is compounded by the lack of public policies and programs in favor of these communities, given the invisibility of both governments to recognize the coming and going of transnational families and their needs, challenges, and potential.

## Final Reflections

The economic conditions and the presence of drug trafficking in the community of Cosalá represent the conjunction of necro-narco citizenship, where the impacts of the phenomenon of global capitalism can be observed at the local level. The necropolitics exercised from the conformation of the control networks of the superstate are translated into the reinforcement and militarization of the borders in the United States and its policies of expulsion of migrant families, conceived as "illegal." These policies and militarization aggressively led to a relocation of the migrant population of Mexican origin and their return to a context destined to greater conditions of exclusion and death. The necrocitizenship present in the community of Cosalá and in the returned migrant families is the result of the existence of an economic model based on primary production, the export of raw materials, and the presence of foreign companies extracting natural resources. This conditions a subsistence economy based on agricultural and livestock activities for self-consumption and conditions of precariousness and poverty.

The necro-narco structure is present through the high levels of social marginalization, which has favored the development of drug-trafficking activities and its machinery of terror. The normalization of the drug-trafficking culture has impacted a whole system of values, norms, and beliefs, which end up introducing young people and minors to illicit activities in the search for economic survival accompanied by a culture of power and transgression. Narcocitizens legitimize a policy of death in which disappearances and assassinations become a daily occurrence. The presence of the military in the community further increases the risk of confrontations and acts of violence generated by the fight against the cartels in the region. The intersection of necro- and narcocitizenship is perpetuated in a web of violence that is intertwined with legal and illegal violence. Hence, transnational families are faced with a reality in which the scenario of fear acts as a relocation factor directly impacting family disintegration, as we have pointed out.

The implications in the region result in a further deepening of the conditions of insecurity in the face of the growing activity and strengthening of drug-trafficking activities and the increase in economic disparities as well as the creation of parallel non-state institutions. Necro-narco citizenship, as a phenomenon present in the rural populations of the state, demands a series of changes and structural measures that go beyond national borders. The responsibility of the policy of control, exploitation, and violence that is exercised as part of the control network of the states implies the necessity of a joint review of regional policies of Mexico and the United States. Migration control policies, the drug consumption market, and the logic of economic development imposed through the agro-export extractivist model, including drugs, that prevails in Mexico are essential issues that should be on the political agenda of both countries to build new forms of economic and social organization in the search for more just and violence-free societies. But at its most profound emotional level, the absolute necessity is supporting populations not having to succumb to "fear obedience."

# CHAPTER 6

# Casualties of Wars of Commission and Omission

## *Youth at the Crossroads*

Drugs have become almost a normative expectation in the day-to-day lives of many youths, especially in rural areas of the Southwest North American Region (SWNAR) and beyond. Sectors of the Mexican-origin population region, especially in rural areas of the northern side, suffer from the extreme impacts of drug deaths in the daily lives of youth. Mexican youth in rural areas of the southern side of the region are becoming assimilated into the universe of drug users instead of being only observers of drugs passing through. It is no wonder that thousands of youths, surrounded by a dearth of opportunities and by structural dimensions partially defined by rejection and multiple depressions that have been caused and propagated by economic and ecological conditions and contexts with little to no respite, are drawn into the violence and hopelessness of the narcostate.

These circumstances—part of a regional version of a globalizing process beyond necrocitizenship and narcocitizenship—influence entire generations of youths who ingest, consume, and die from products of destruction. Moreover, generations of Mexican-origin youth on both sides of the border enter the commercial transborder drug market as supporters and employees of cartels, cartel-controlled gangs, or politically associated cartel-influenced groups now prevalent in Mexico, buttressed by gang networks in the United States. While most of the Mexican youth of the region go to school, work, and sacrifice to build stable lives, too many others become the casualties of the drug wars. The casualties themselves are of different kinds. Many have died or been killed as part of the operational costs of doing business or combatting against the business: members of cartels or criminal groups and members of the armed forces of both sides of the region. Many die from overdoses; we will refer to these as KIAs. In Mexico, between January 2006 and May 2021, 350,000 people have been killed; more than 100,000 have been "disappeared."[1] In the short six-year span between 2015 and 2021, the homicide rate increased by 76.3 percent at 26.6 deaths per 100,000 people, or more than 34,000 victims; according to the Institute for Economics and Peace's *Mexico Peace Index 2022*, that equates to approximately 94 homicides per day.[2]

Illustrating the deadliness of cartel-associated casualties is a tragic and chilling report by Michael Marizco from 2010. Near the colonial town of Tubutama, Sonora, sixty miles south of the Arizona–Sonora border (a town originally founded by missionary Eusebio Kino in 1691, and where droves of my paternal grandmother's ancestors were born), more than twenty-one young men were killed in an ambush. An examination of sixteen bodies by authorities concluded that the young men were between the ages of eighteen and forty.[3] A Sinaloa Cartel associate told Marizco that at about 9 p.m. on July 1, a convoy affiliated with the Sinaloa Cartel consisting of about twenty-five vehicles—SUVs, pickup trucks, and station wagons—left the nearby towns of Altar and Caborca and headed toward Tubutama to ambush the Leyva Cartel group. In addition to the sixteen people killed, another nine were wounded, and from the pictures provided by this report, young men in bloodied battle fatigues lay strewn next to their vehicles.[4]

The lessons of low-intensity warfare by gangs and cartels were well learned and executed, as on other occasions, and such warfare continues to this moment, with some border towns almost vacated by residents by a kind of declaration of a "dead zone" in which all present are either killed or forced to flee.[5] Cartels have taken to shutting down entire regions by killing innocent people. This was the case in Baja California in August 2022, when cartel leaders ordered the burning of two dozen vehicles, put up roadblocks around the state, and placed a curfew on Tijuana. They warned residents to stay home or be attacked, and in fact they did attack some stores with Molotov cocktails. In the process they killed a young

CASUALTIES OF WARS OF COMMISSION AND OMISSION                                131

woman who had been seeking employment in a drugstore that was firebombed. All of this was done as a counter to the reported unhappiness of cartel leaders facing possible arrest.[6]

As I wrote this portion on January 5, 2023, the city of Culiacán and parts of the state of Sinaloa had been shut down for a second time. There were burning truck blockades and street closures, and even a commercial jet with passengers on board in the Culiacán airport was shot at. Authorities had also blocked highways leading to the seaport city of Mazatlán, and highway toll booths were taken over in different towns by the Sinaloa Cartel. The reason for all this violence was the second arrest of young Ovidio Guzmán López, alias "El Ratón."

Even the very young seemed to have been recruited in his defense. In figure 26, two young boys in a car hold weapons; the one at the forefront is armed with an AR-15 hidden by the door. Eventually, they too will be belonging and dying by becoming narcocitizens.

In assessing the events at Culiacán, one narcocitizen and cartel member expressed a full recognition of narcocitizenship in defense of the drug trade and its leadership. "We felt bad that we were not able to rescue [Ovidio Guzmán] because one is here, we are here for them, according to their orders and to defend them with our lives if necessary, but our chiefs will continue; it will affect us that they have taken him, but the business of the bosses has to continue," said the gang member.[7] Like their counterparts in the military who also died that day serving God and country, the gang member was willing to die for drugs and dollars and became a fully enrolled narcocitizen, with all its adjoining rights and duties, including belonging to die in its cause. In this manner he also became enrolled as a necrocitizen soldier of the cartel.

FIGURE 26  Baby-faced Sinaloa Cartel recruits awaiting orders during the second Culiacán takeover, January 5, 2023. Video still from anonymous source present during the event.

As has occurred dozens of times in Mexico, people in Culiacán not involved in the fighting were basically imprisoned in their homes and moreover had to keep close to the ground even within their own homes to ensure their safety.[8] The casualty toll amounted to ten military and nineteen gang or cartel members dead, plus thirty-five military personnel and an untold number of cartel or gang members wounded.[9] Add to these losses the deep psychological trauma visited on the civilian population, and what results are huge costs to the families of the dead and the living and a deadly impact on the already weakened civil and social fabrics of the region and nation.[10] Innocent children are too often witnesses to the crimes of adults—whether present in a kidnapping or holdup by criminal gangs or subject to the sight of dumped bodies of young people along a freeway, children suffer severe psychological trauma from their experiences.[11] They sometimes become targets as well as victims.

Thus, between the deaths of cartel members in their battles for territory, military killings of the guilty *and* the innocent, the growing number of innocent people murdered to serve as a lesson, to induce obedience and silence, or as a business practice, for the foreseeable future social decay will progress and youths will become the sources and the victims of all these conditions. These are the most obvious casualties of the Wars of Commission.

Representing casualties of the Wars of Omission, and no less tragic than the casualties of the Wars of Commission, are those who die from overdoses. Their number is increasing, a trend anticipated by those who saw Mexico transitioning from a mostly drug-producing and transporting country to a drug-consuming one as well. This is attested by Stacy de la Torre, coordinator of programs of the United Nations Office on Drugs and Crime (UNODC) in Mexico, who reported that the number of persons in treatment due to consumption of methamphetamines in Mexico increased by 218 percent between 2013 and 2020. Mexico is now the only country in the world in which the consumption of methamphetamines is the principal reason for drug treatment.[12] Considering all categories of drug-related casualties in combination, it seems clear that in the near future Mexico's fragile civic fabric will be further eroded.

Without rigorous intervention, additional casualties due to opioid consumption, following the U.S. pattern, will also ensue. In a 2019 article, David Goodman-Meza and his co-authors have warned:

Mexico faces unique vulnerabilities given its geographic location, changing population demographics, and population disease burden, all of which place it at great risk of a widespread opioid use epidemic similar to that of the United States and Canada. The intersection of a fragile emerging social structure as a result of nationals returning through deportation from the United States; structural challenges in the treatment of pain; lobbying from pharmaceutical companies; increasing local production, distribution, and availability of heroin; and a lack of infrastructure to support evidence-based treatment of opioid use disorder are likely to increase the risk of a generalized Mexican opioid use epidemic. However, a range of cultural and social factors . . . may heighten the country's resistance to the widespread misuse of opioids. Nevertheless, previous examples of increased usage in settings with increased domestic availability as a result of international drug trafficking suggest that a grave risk exists that the combination of expanded access to prescribed opioids and local heroin production may lead Mexico past the threshold for an opioid use epidemic.[13]

Mexico is considered the key country in the manufacturing and trafficking of methamphetamines and opioids.[14] From 1999 to 2020, almost a million people have died from drug overdoses in the United States alone.[15] Another 100,000 died in 2021 from fentanyl overdoses. But as American authorities admitted only recently,

The Centers for Disease Control and Prevention is unable to track overdose deaths in real-time. Its published data is one year behind, obscuring the picture of what is happening on the ground in 2022. The agency continues to count the death toll for 2021—in a provisional tally seven months ago, it calculated the overall number of drug overdoses at 107,622. Two-thirds were due to fentanyl . . . with the leading cause of death of those between 19–49.[16]

According to the California Department of Public Health, fentanyl-related overdose deaths in California youth ages ten to nineteen increased from 36 in 2018 to 261 in 2020, a 625 percent increase.[17] If that growth remains constant, within ten years for California alone the overdose deaths for this age cohort would number in the thousands, not hundreds. The same source's preliminary 2021 data indicate that there were

6,843 opioid-related overdose deaths in California, of which 5,722 were attributed to fentanyl.

A comparison of the urban and the rural shows that "recent studies suggest that the geography of mass incarceration in general, and the drug war in particular, are shifting. For example, jails expanded far more rapidly in small- and medium-sized counties than in large urban counties in recent decades."[18] Thus, the rural environment has its own structural issues that do not mitigate but initiate and exacerbate drug use of multiple sorts, as will be shown; these include rural populations racially typed by melanin, such as in more Indigenous areas of Mexico and the United States. Katherine Beckett and Marco Brydolf-Horwitz explain: "Although the scale and impact of the most recent war on drugs has been unique, the centrality of race to it is hardly novel. . . . In fact, scholars have shown that anti-drug campaigns are often bound up with, and reinforce, efforts to control and/or denigrate non-white populations."[19] The war on addiction in rural areas is filled with casualties that seem to have been "rescued" multiple times, only to fall again—or, even worse, to die intentionally or by pushing the needle too far. Mass and periodic incarcerations also cause significant damage.[20] When frail rural contexts characterized by poverty and poor institutional frameworks—especially poor or weakly supported schools and the most basic access to health and nutritional support—are glued to historical racism and ethnocentrism, anxieties and stressors compromise the emotional and mental health of entire communities, especially its younger generations. Relief is only a pill or needle away.

## Dying to Live in New Mexico

Although there will necessarily be more deaths in urban than in rural areas, the impacts are as egregious in the social fabric of smaller rural communities. In 2020, New Mexico, which has only the thirty-seventh-largest state population in the United States, nevertheless was the eleventh-highest in drug-overdose deaths, of which almost 40 percent were fentanyl related.[21] In *The Pastoral Clinic: Addiction and Dispossession Along the Rio Grande*, Angela Garcia shows how deeply tragic heroin addiction is in a small rural area of New Mexico. Eloquently narrating the shadow place between life and death for those addicted to heroin and fentanyl, Garcia shows that in the rural Española Valley, New Mexico, dying may become the only way to live in a specially defined manner.[22]

Garcia tells the story of Alma Gallegos, who, just before turning twenty-nine, was found in the parking lot of a hospital, near death from an overdose of heroin. After being treated with naloxone in the emergency room, Alma recovered; she "remained in the hospital until the local drug court mandated that she be transferred to Nuevo Día, the very drug treatment facility from which she had recently discharged herself." The ethnographer reports that in a clinical treatment session, "Alma turned to me in exasperation and, in a language the counselor couldn't understand, said, 'Es que lo que tengo no termina.'" *It's just that what I have has no end.* Alma's story ends sadly: "Two years later Alma was again rushed to the same hospital emergency room, where she was pronounced dead after overdosing on heroin."[23] This tale does more than relate a tragically too frequent event not only for Alma but for so many others who cycle in and out of the process of addiction, treatment, remission, arrest, release, treatment, and readdiction. Alma's story reflects a repeated pattern for too many youths. By her quinceañera, she had already been set for her too-soon demise by conditions and contexts in one ancient part of New Mexico.

New Mexico is a beautiful state, a land with a long history of populations of Native people, more recent colonial populations of Spanish Mexicans, and even more recent Anglo-Americans, following the Mexican-American War of 1846. It is majestic in many ways, ecologically nourished by the Rio Grande and runoff from the mountain ranges surrounding its valleys. Yet New Mexico is hardly the "land of enchantment," as much of its tourism literature would describe it. This abundant land of deserts and fertile grounds is not a rich place for many of the people who have lived and continue to live there, and a poor place for more. It has been this way certainly since the Spanish colonial period of three hundred years ago, and not greatly different from the American period to today.

In terms of income equality, New Mexicans do not fare well. The average weekly earnings relative to ethnicity of workers is:

Anglo-American: $1,010.98
Asian American and Pacific Islander: $937.03
African American: $836.39

Hispanic Mexican: $729.83

Native American: $703.16

This income disparity is even more striking when one considers that of the 892,903 workers of New Mexico, a combined 55 percent are of Native American and Hispanic Mexican heritage.[24] With a poverty rate of 50.17 percent for the former and 35.23 percent for the latter, the two populations are in structural conditions that can lead to emotional trauma spurred by poor housing, poor health, poor medical care, poor transportation, poor education, poor social networks of support, and negative feelings of self-worth.[25]

In a rural environment, these elements are built structurally. George I. Sánchez's classic 1940s treatise *Forgotten People: A Study of New Mexicans* revealed these elements honestly, and he laid out the egregious economic and social conditions that plagued New Mexico for centuries.[26] In many ways, these conditions persist today—including second-class citizenship, linguistic erasures, political inequalities, economic disparities, and vestiges and realities of colonial dimensions, especially of land use and disenfranchisement from land. These variables create the emotional and psychological anxieties and distresses that are conducive to drug and alcohol use.[27] It is a perfect site for a War of Omission. This process was set in motion in this period by the globalization of the drug trade; localities became the targets of a distribution and export, impacting local communities like those of New Mexico.

Furthermore, the scale of drug distribution and consumption is much greater in urban environments. The central agents are newly formed global versions of gangs lacking territoriality as the locus of identity, who generate mostly prison-gestated global versions of violence, extortion, and penetrating drug cultures, accompanied by militarized policing and group and neighborhood suppression. All are in fact the created phenomena of Wars of Omission.

## From the Local to the Global: The Evolution of the Nonterritorial Drug Gang in Los Angeles

In his overview of the origins of Southern California Latino gangs, Al Valdez explores the establishment of the first mostly Mexican-origin gangs in the early 1940s.[28] These gangs were made up mostly of what James Diego Vigil describes as youths suffering from "multiple marginality" of culture, class, context, and color seeking redemption through local gang identity and territorial control.[29] A hundred years later, this is still the case for many; however, they are not located locally but are globally spread and very different from the traditional locally identified gangs like the Mexican Mafia or the Salvadoran Mara Salvatrucha (MS-13) that have arisen, mostly nurtured by prison experience and socialization. These new globally oriented gangs are glued to a transborder process of drug importation and networks "organized by a vertical command structure" very much like their cartel counterparts.[30] The consequences of the development of these networks affect neighborhoods and institutions and include the counterweight of heavy policing and militarized roundups, imprisonments, and—especially in the case of Salvadorans—deportation. Equivalent impacts manifest in the major cities of El Salvador and certainly in rural areas with many of the same attending consequences, especially of large-scale imprisonment. This cycle of drug selling and drug consumption leads to prison time and greater incorporation between prisoners and their affiliated gangs of the Mara Salvatrucha.

According to Valdez, the Mara itself began as largely a defense mechanism by newly arrived migrants from Central America and especially El Salvador.[31] Valdez describes the urban ecology of the protective mantle Mexican gangs spread over their neighborhoods, but in time Central Americans formed their own gangs. Both Mexican and Central American gangs morphed into "Latino" gangs and shook off local cultural and place identities. Eventually, according to Valdez, the Salvadoran gangs transformed into the infamous La Mara and 18th Street Gangs, and their organization and attending criminal activities were transnationalized by their deportation and contributed to the civil and state discord in Central America.[32] Valdez thus establishes an underlying pattern of young people, especially boys and young men, seeking out others in similar circumstances to find sources of protection, social exchange, and intragenerational connections and communication.

The extortion of small businesses became a major method used by the gangs to support new members and integrate them into gang networks and establish social control and community-level fear. But it was the introduction of drug trafficking that became most lucrative and simultaneously changed any "normal" expectations. Drug trafficking directly tied prison gangs to community participation, which exerted powerful forces of violence and repression throughout many barrios in Los Angles and into Southern California, urban and rural. Valdez provides an account of this process and its source for the enormous growth of gang enterprises now infused by the drug market: "In 1988, Los Angeles County reported 452 gang-related murders and had approximately 50,000 gang members in 450 different gangs. In 1990 the county reported approximately 690 gangs operating within its borders. By 1991 there were estimated to be 100,000 gang members and 750 different street gangs in L.A. County."[33] As of 2020, Los Angeles County possessed a gang population of approximately 120,000 members associated with 1,300 street gangs. These gangs occupy many counties in Southern California and have migrated to other regions of the United States; they currently account for 40 percent of all homicides.[34]

Among the most globally well known of these gangs were the MS, which later became known as MS-13, and the 18th Street Gang. Both developed into a cartel- and prison gang–associated group to different degrees and extended their reach to many parts of the United States, Mexico, El Salvador, and other Central American states such as Honduras. And like their cartel counterparts, the gangs also segmented with police suppression, deportations, and arrests of entire groups on the grounds of association, not necessarily commission of crimes. This all continued to affect both local and international communities.

During the Trump administration, the U.S. Department of Justice contributed to their segmentation by prosecuting cartel leaders, as Valdez explains.[35] For almost 750 MS-13 gang members arrested, 500 were convicted, with 37 receiving life sentences. Its membership was prosecuted internationally, with hundreds arrested in Central America and a number extradited to the United States. Thus, the jails and prisons of El Salvador continue to be filled with MS members. In addition, many innocent people have been caught up in an emergency regime created to deal with the aftermath of a failed truce between the Salvadoran government and the MS-13 and 18th Street Gangs. The truce, formed in 2020, broke down in March 2022, sparking "a violent response from the gangs that left at least 87 dead in one weekend." The government created a "state of exception" based on massive human rights violations, in which thousands of innocent people remain in jails without trial or judicial procedures.[36]

None of these circumstances could continue without the earnings from extortion, kidnapping, murder, and, at an international scale, the distribution and consumption of drugs upheld by generations of youth becoming "old" before their time—or dead.

## Age-Graded Aspects of Crime in Tepito

If we were to surmise that moving the equivalent structural conditions to urban contexts in Mexico would somehow differ, we would be in error. The disturbing pattern of youth recruitment—with the additional awful patina of violence and criminality—reigns like a death's-head in the trauma-ridden life course of those in the most dangerous barrios in Mexico City. There, the sequence of addiction and imprisonment becomes glued to the life course of children living in "age-graded" aspects of trajectories.[37] One such barrio is Tepito, a neighborhood famous for two things: it is the place where some famous world-class boxers are born, and it is where illicit goods ranging from jewelry to AK-47s can be purchased.[38] In the past twenty years or so, drugs and all their attending ills have penetrated what was once a tight-knit community known as the "barrio bravo" for its defiance of public authorities. Today, violence and criminal gangs have taken over the daily life course of many in Tepito, especially youth.

G. H. Elder's concept of the age-graded trajectory is defined as long-term patterns and behavioral sequences that are developmental pathways to maturity originating from multiple sources.[39] These sources consistently create patterns of behavioral expectations and actions.

In their ethnographic studies in Tepito, Piotr Chomczyński and Timothy Clark describe what they see as the underlying architecture of emergence for vulnerable youth:

> In these highly impoverished, DTO-controlled (Drug Trafficking Organization), central Mexican communities . . . DTO associates or members target youths for recruitment from families with problems. . . . For example, Pavel (a 17-year-old at the time of our interview) from a violent home was recruited at age 11 into the Millenio Cartel when the DTO moved him into a house with seven adults: "My job was to kidnap a victim from

the street (using) a car (lavantone) and execute them. They [the adults] chose the people, and I complied with what they told me to do. I did many executions and 'lavantones.' . . . Each month, they paid me at least 15,000 pesos, and after each job, they gave me some amount—once it was 50,000 pesos." Our field notes on the Tepito neighborhood from May 2016 further elucidate an early immersion into drug trafficking, demonstrating that age structure exerted little apparent effect, as all ages either were in the vicinity or part of the drug trafficking process.[40]

During a visit by the researchers to one of the drug dealer's nondescript homes, people moved in and out. Women were present, and little children were crawling on the floor while nearby, bags of cocaine rested on a table, readied for sale. A sense of normalcy seemed to mark the scene, with men and women carrying on lively conversations and joking.[41] Chomczyński and Clark describe such normalization in the following way: "In settings like this, where drug production occurs, community members ranged from babies to seniors. Children are raised in an environment in which their families earn their living from drugs, and drugs are viewed as normative" and thus are introduced early into a possible life course.[42]

As Chomczyński and Clark summarize, DTO-controlled communities leave few options. According to one informant, the DTOs observe people in the street carefully, note all their behavioral characteristics, and decide whom to recruit for different roles like assassin or enforcer. Those who do not accept the invitation are placed in a liminal situation and have to regard the failed recruitment as problematic—such requests and refusals are not forgotten.[43] Another way of expressing the dynamic is that these are bounded and "total institutions" without much leeway for oppositional or recalcitrant behavior. Traditional social and cultural referents of mutuality and positive human exchange are replaced by patterns of behavioral control and immersion in personal and social destruction. Thus, entire communities and their underlying patterns of narcocitizenry become introduced, reinforced, and learned. Entire communities who are highly exploited and marginalized become narcocitizens, socialized and enculturated from very young ages until, usually, they come to their end in prison or death.

# From Hope to Despair in Ciudad Nezahualcóyotl

Other central Mexican areas near Mexico City have been taken over by the cartels not only in Tepito but in many parts of Mexico.[44] How this occurs can very well be understood through the case of Ciudad Nezahualcóyotl, where I conducted fieldwork over three years in the 1970s.[45] Fifty years later, Ciudad Nezahualcóyotl has been taken over by one of the major cartels. In the 1970s, "Neza" had a perennially negative reputation as a place of gangs, crime, police corruption, and high rates of illnesses. Ecologically, it was unenviable; during the winter months rain would wash in fecal matter, mounds of toilet paper, and trash from the *aguas negras*—the sewage lake that borders the city—and in the summer, *tolvaneras* (windstorms) would pick up matter from the drying lakebed and blow it into the city, to be ingested and aspirated by the residents. Thus, intestinal, respiratory, and skin issues were endemic, including for myself.

During pre-Hispanic times, this same area of Lake Texcoco was the source of life and culture among the great Mesoamerican cities and empires. In the 1970s, even though the immigrant movement of populations averaged ten thousand people per month (with more than seventeen thousand people per square kilometer), the available water was largely contaminated by poor pipelines and sewage flowing out from broken pipes. Endemic conflict prevailed over legal tenure of household lots, with the same lot sold up to sixteen times to different families by land developers. Furthermore, a large number of youngsters belonged to gangs like the Girafos (the Giraffes), who had been trained by the military to beat up students during the late 1960s during marches and demonstrations.

Yet what I found in my three years of work in Ciudad Nezahualcóyotl were many households of hope dealing with the existing economic, political, social, and ecological conditions.[46] For the most part, households were composed of multigenerational families, many within the households working one or more jobs, kids going to school daily, ritual activities adhered to by the faithful of many sorts, and economic transactions termed *tandas*, or rotating credit associations. Thousands attended Mass on Sunday mornings and many frequented the wrestling matches in the afternoon or played soccer out in the often muddy fields, while people gathered to eat carne asada cooked outside, freshly made corn tortillas from the comal (flat griddle), and cold bottles of Negro Modelo beer or aguas of lemonade or passion fruit. Aunts, uncles, cousins, brothers, and sisters—some freshly migrated from Oaxaca or the urban barrios of Mexico City—gathered in familial celebrations, often associated with the ritual cycles of baptism, confirmation, communion, marriage, and even death. Other gatherings included birthdays, saints' days, Days of the Dead, and the Virgen de Guadalupe (originating from the ancient source known as Tonantzin, goddess of fertility).

But this was not a wealthy population, and like most of urban Mexico, 40 percent were underemployed—even though working two jobs— and many were unemployed, mostly temporarily given their work ethic. When I first conducted my fieldwork in the 1970s, migrants to this less-than-welcoming place of 62.5 square kilometers populated by 500,000 people were also heavily engaged in political activities of mass demonstrations and a refusal to give in to the political corruption of authorities and land developers. They also rose against the occasional holdup by local police when going home on one of the many buses that moved people to their jobs in Mexico City.

Larger furniture stores lined Avenida Chimalhuacan, the main thoroughfare, but the heart of the city was in the hundreds of small stores— tortillerías, sewing and dress shops, grocery stores, vulcanizing tire shops, and carpentry stores. There were stands selling religious figurines of many sorts—but not of the Santa Muerte, the female figure of death venerated especially by those associated with criminality and later the icon of those connected to drug and human trafficking. The shoe repair man moved his portable shop through the streets, announcing "Zapaterilla," avoiding puddles and holes and the trenches made by the city when replacing wrong-sized sewer pipes, while the *paletera*, seller of ice cream bars and *raspados*, maneuvered next to the knife and scissor sharpener.

This was a hopeful place for those who lived and worked in Ciudad Nezahualcóyotl. Over the next forty years, the chaos seemed to subside, and even university campuses and business schools sprouted. The authorities became less grafty and contributed more to the well-being of the city's growing population and small businesses. Neza became known as a mecca for street parties and nightclubbing. Cohorts of children

CASUALTIES OF WARS OF COMMISSION AND OMISSION

were born in Neza, as it in time also became a stepping-stone migration source to New York City. Beginning in the late 1980s, these cohorts, by this time young adults, migrated and formed a distinct cultural presence known to some as "Neza York" in the Queens and Washington Heights neighborhoods.[47] Now, an incipient retirement back to Nezahualcóyotl has begun in the first decade of the twenty-first century.

But a poison has now spread in the city, introduced by one of the major cartels. What has occurred in Tepito is now taking place in Neza: the creation of the underlying architecture of a life's course very different from that of the past fifty years of generations of Neza and Neza York. Hope has begun to turn to despair and helplessness and death.[48] In his final piece for the Committee to Protect Journalists (CPJ), published posthumously in 2014, journalist Mike O'Connor explores how the press in Nezahualcóyotl has been forced to go mute by the dangers posed in reporting the activities of La Familia Michoacana cartel.[49] This silencing is an example of the way an entire city adjoining Mexico City can be taken over by force and violence penetrating all levels of the social spectrum and juridical system. At the same time, city authorities claim that there are no cartel activities, nor is the press prevented from freely reporting. Cops on the street are forced to acquiesce simultaneously. Thus, two important civil and juridical institutions, the press and law enforcement, are removed as possible impediments to criminality and subornation. Both bodies are institutionally imperative to a democratic society; in the long term, they become casualties as violent as those killed, kidnapped, or overdosed.

O'Connor says, "Neza, about 10 miles southeast of the center of Mexico City, which has a little over one million people, is part of metropolitan Mexico City, where the politicians keep saying there are no organized crime cartels. Miguel Ángel Mancera, Mexico City's mayor, forcefully told an interviewer that in his city, 'There is not a single cartel. Nothing like the names of cartels you find in the states.'" Yet the police, O'Connor reports, admit that cartel members on patrol in various areas of the city are armed with assault weapons and are statements of control and possession of the streets and neighborhoods, so a police car entering such a situation quickly makes a U-turn and leaves the area. According to the police, the criminal neighborhood guardians are themselves known assassins. A police officer told O'Connor that about four years prior— around 2009—"Neza's leaders simply 'turned over' the city to the Familia

# 144

Michoacana, one of the country's top cartels, to let it run wild with drug sales, kidnapping and wholesale extortion of businesses. Interestingly, that's the same way journalists describe it. They use the same term[,] 'turned over,' or sometimes 'handed over,' or maybe 'sold.' The journalists say they can't write about that because they would be killed."[50]

All the tell-tale signs are present, including the burning of businesses that refuse to pay their *plazas* (contributions) and the press reduced by threats. In terms of the press, O'Connor's interviews provide chilling examples:

> Mireya Cuellar, the national editor of *La Jornada* newspaper, said it has been extraordinarily frustrating to see the cartels march through much of Mexico and not be able to report it. "They aren't knocking on the door of the capital any longer," she said. "They are in the kitchen now, and we can't tell anyone they're here." *La Jornada* no longer reports on organized crime in Neza. "The tragedy is that you can't say what you know is happening. Just like you can't say in so many of the states," Cuellar said. "Your correspondent may be at least abducted or beaten or even killed. Apparently there is no government that can protect you."
>
> "The tendency in Neza," said Carlos Benavides, assistant managing editor of the national newspaper *El Universal*, "is the same as in the states where cartels have taken power. Reporters have to step back and not do what we all would like them to be able to do."
>
> To stay alive in Neza journalists simply stop telling the public what the cartel doesn't want the public to know. All of the journalists CPJ spoke with who cover Neza said they stay away from organized crime stories or play it very cautiously. For the most part, they don't investigate or look for the big picture. They crank out today's limited story and hope the cartel doesn't get angry.[51]

But the greatest casualty is civil society. O'Connor narrates how narcotization seeps into every aspect of society by way of cartels communicating with business leaders and heads of commercial organizations of the city. By detailing their family relations and their daily habits, callers intimidate these leaders into paying and collecting contributions from their association members. O'Connor reports myriad examples of businesses encountering cartel aggression, such as bus drivers' associations forced to pay plazas after two of their fellows were killed and another kidnapped (later released) as examples to dissuade resistance.

Thus, the cartel has expanded to infiltrate all levels of society, deeply and consistently, civilly and juridically. But although their other activities like kidnapping, extortion, and prostitution are important segments, the attempted sale and distribution of drugs—and ensuing addiction—to about a million residents and their children is their main commercial object of sale. The Familia Michoacana, according to O'Connor at that time, sold drugs in Neza only to Mexicans.

This shift from transit to consumer functions bodes very ill not only for Nezahualcóyotl but for the Central Valley. Formerly this area was the site of ancient and complex Mexican cultures: the imperial Toltecs and Aztecs, the Spanish colonial inundation, the War of Independence, the emergence of the Mexican state, the revolutionary political cauldron of Mexican identity, and the center of great artistic and literary inventions. Now, it's becoming a wobbly, national entity interconnected to the violent web of cartels, gangs, impunity, political corruption, subornation, and a transborder network of militarized yet useless oppression in the face of a large-scale market of drug consumption and billions of dollars. It is bound to create unknown and unforgiving social processes that strike at the very foundations of what we may regard as the cognitive and moral basis of being human: mutuality, interdependence, and the ability to freely think and act without coercion, violence, or oppression of expression and thought.

## Casualties of War and Omission: Quotidian Realities

Both necro- and narcocitizens must live out their daily lives even in cartel-dominated Mexican cities. The fact is that in places like Sinaloa or Guerrero, where the long history of drug enterprises has influenced cohorts of "normals," police or military agents, and los mafiosos, differences are put aside for the time being, since everyone knows or is related to someone in their respective categories. Social pacts are made.

In 2023, I conducted interviews with informants who grew up in one of the major cities in Sinaloa known for the heavy presence of drug-related kinship groups, families, and longtime residents associated or involved with others in the production, sale, and distribution of a variety of drugs. They constitute a trigenerational cluster of kin beginning with the eldest man, who grew up with one of the major cartel bosses and whose own children and grandchildren have attended the same schools and participated in a dense relation of kinship, friendship, co-godparenthoods, visitations, gift exchange, and rituals like baptisms, communions, confirmations, weddings, quinceañeras, and funerals. But importantly, especially when visiting their rural towns of origin, their paths will cross, greetings ensue, and tables and chairs are arranged in front of homes or a local store where they tell stories of their youth, remembrances of things past, and things of the present.

Groups of people living together in myriad and familiar circumstances at approximately the same time will become somewhat identified with a group identity. For Mexicans, cohort identities are made up of networks with densities not unlike those exhibited by "intentional" communities like the local territorial gang; the kibbutz in Israel; religious sects like the Church of the Latter-Day Saints, or Catholic or Buddhist seminarians; or elite military units like the Marine Corps. In Mexico and in Mexican or Latina/o/x neighborhoods and settings in the Southwest North American Region, like Española, such cohorts create an intimacy based on remembrances of things past that glue them together, regardless of individuals' professions and crafts. Theirs is an easy familiarity of mischief, loves lost, tragic deaths, amazing successes, and expectations fulfilled and failed, and may very well develop over generations.

So, when a class reunion or wedding or baptism or funeral is held, and a coterie of mafiosos arrives dressed in their finery of custom-made cowboy boots, tailored jeans, silk shirts open at the chest to reveal gold chains and 24-karat-gold miniature AK-47s, and gold-rimmed black Stetsons, those "normals" already present will greet the incoming guests with open arms. For those who are in the same cohort group, the respective crafts of the male "normals" and the mafiosos are unimportant. Easy recollections are mimed, stories are told, and raucous laughter fills the room to tales of romances gone wrong, military service and the stupidity of officers and sergeants, and certainly the deaths of others mentioned— but not their circumstances, if they are drug connected.

At times within such cohorts, little favors may be done without too many compromises, but the boundaries are there and not trespassed. If a home invasion by a local gang occurs to a "normal" and an heirloom or something very personal has been taken, then a favor might be asked for its return. It will be given, but the perpetrator will not be identified or penalized. At times the normal might push to find who was responsible and told gently that it will reach others who should not be disturbed or too involved in both juridical and mafia affairs. Even within cohorts of fellowship and admiration, then, eventually the non-state solution wins.

There are also daily circumstances in which the paths of the normals, police or military agents, and los mafiosos might cross, but then the underlying arrangements might be revealed, as one of my informants, Emilio, related to me. This was the case for a restaurant where Emilio worked in one of the major cities, where the mafiosos occupy the back, the judicial police the front, and the normals in the middle. The restaurant's atmosphere fostered a *let it be* attitude, but once in a while, the boundaries of the unstated borders are broken. In one case, one of the *sicarios* (gang members) who had been drinking and snorting cocaine began to make loud remarks about how weak and powerless the judicial police were, characterizing them as *mamones* (suckling babies). This caught the attention of the police present, who began to rise out of their seats, taking their weapons from their holsters, while the mafiosos did the same. The normals ducked underneath the tables, shattering glasses and dishes, while waiters quickly shuffled out of the room. Fortunately, one of the gang members shouted to the judicial police that they were arranged and named their leader, at which time one of the judicial chiefs phoned his supervisor, who confirmed that they were in fact arranged. And to make sure that things would return to normality, one of the gang chiefs slapped the original sicario responsible and told him to stop being a mamon. Everyone holstered their weapons, dishes and glasses were picked up by nervous waiters—including Emilio—and all returned to their respective places to finish their meals and beer.

Normalcy in this case and others like it is not built on understandings of mutuality and trust and civil authority but rather on enforced relations made by arrangements by a stratified architecture in which what is legal or illegal has little relevance. In this case, the judicial police and the mafiosos are playing with their own deck of cards supported and made possible by institutional and extra-institutional arrangements in which the normal have to hide underneath, out of the way, in non-contention and unimportance. The abnormal has become normalized and the normals become powerless and insignificant as citizens with rights, duties, and obligations, with few options but to acquiesce. Thus inadvertently and without their permission they become true narcocitizens, where the state is meaningless and civil authority an aberration and the civil casualty of a lost war. Or normals can live in the quotidian reality of protection from cohorts whose well-being is entirely based on imperfect security. It touches all, while political resistance is difficult to create; a muted existence and slow but certain acceptance ensue. The Wars of Commission and Omission become distributed among the guilty and the innocent. And in the long run, civic death among those directly and indirectly affected ensues.

More importantly, it is the cohorts of youth who witness, experience, and too often join in the process to create more *palomias* (cohorts) of their children and their children's children, so that a deeply flawed system of cultural expectations and relations moves socially and is reinforced culturally. There are situations where relatives refuse to be engaged in the business itself but take advantage of their kinship by taking money or "favors" from relatives who are so involved, but it is a tricky business avoiding eventually having to reciprocate in kind. And at the same time, others to whom they are related try to resist the process by not engaging—or, more likely, move north to escape and live something akin to normalcy. Yet many times in going north they must contend with the abnormality of racialized and commoditized identities in their escape, compounding their already painful dislocation.

Emilio graduated from law school in Sonora but found he was unable to support his family without becoming connected to the networks of possible employers who were "tainted" to some degree.[52] He made a moral decision to cross the border and earn a living any way he could. Eventually, after a great deal of trial and error, Emilio settled in Las Cruces, New Mexico. He worked an assortment of jobs; since his father had been a highly skilled craftsman and carpenter, he learned from an early age to design, plan, and build homes alongside his father. He put these skills to good use in a local building company and was quickly promoted by the owner. Like Emilio, she had learned early on the intricacies of owning a construction business, from planning a job to its fruition. Between the two of them, they hired only the best craftspeople and acquired a reputation for excellence and attention to detail.

Eventually, Emilio brought his wife and two children to Las Cruces from a large city in Sonora, where the entire family had been born. He established his legal residency in the United States through his boss. His wife and two children, ages six and twelve, had been in the United States under an expired visitor's visa during this period. His wife attended community college classes in accounting and his children were model students, with all three functionally bilingual in Spanish and English. The family decided that Emilio's wife and children would return to Sonora to re-establish a six-month record of residency in Mexico, in order to apply for residency in the United States under an immigration rule that gives a second preference to spouses and children of lawful permanent residents.

But the return was not without risks; the city that they would be returning to had a long reputation as being under the control of criminal elements and had suffered a number of major battles between the Mexican military and cartel gangs and groups as well as disappearances and homicides of major citizens in the city. How might this reality of violence and uncertainty be balanced by Emilio's wife and children for at least six months? All were in harm's way, and the children's security was at risk even in a private school.

Emilio was very much aware of the networks of people who were part of or members of cartels in the major city where he was from originally and to which his wife and children would be returning. People with whom he had gone to elementary, preparatory, high school, and university and who belonged to the same soccer leagues were now involved in cartels. Emilio asserted that these people did not harm anyone who was not involved in the "business" and that in fact one of the leaders was known for building schools, hospitals, and recreation halls and supporting local churches and youth clubs of different kinds. This leader was, in Emilio's view, a Robin Hood who helped the very poor in rural areas, often lending farmers money for seed, fertilizers, and mechanical tools as well as providing loans for their children to attend out-of-area schools and training schools. But more importantly, they eliminated petty theft, rape, and burglaries and prohibited the local municipal police from extorting citizens.

And as a further measure of moral commitment, the leader forbade the sale of fentanyl in the state and region his organization controlled while they exported tons of pills north at the same time.

The organization became the parallel judicial body. Yet the organization would neither brook opposition to nor discuss their "right" to execute those trying to enter their business plaza, and demanded obedience without objections of its underlings. Emilio described how such control is also manifested when conflicts arise between cartels over territorial control: social media, such as Facebook, is often used to warn parts of the populace, especially in rural areas, to stay in their homes when the cartel will be "limpiando" (cleaning out) opposition cartel assassins and members of the opposition.

The children of cartel members would be attending the private school that Emilio and his wife had attended, and they knew that some of the parents whose children would be attending the same school were nominally or fully engaged in the organization. Thus, for Emilio, his children would be protected by the knowledge that part of his own generational cohort would be present and of confianza, and that it was in his *palomia*'s own interest to ensure that the school was safe and untouched by cartel-associated violence.

There was also a spatial protection, in that the family would be living with Emilio's mother and aunts in the same neighborhood where he was raised, ensconced within generational networks of relatives and cohorts of known quantities. So, in a sense, being close to these families associated with the cartels in the same neighborhoods where they lived offered added protection—unless, of course, the military decided to raid one or more of these households, or an opposing cartel sought to eliminate the leader and shoot up the household while children hid inside. However, Emilio stated, the children are very happy, and from the very first day they were greeted by all their new classmates and given an applause of welcome.

It is in such circumstances then that people like Emilio make decisions for the futures of their children, not in Mexico but across the border. From Emilio's point of view, they have exchanged short-term discomfort for long-term security, although unstated and not without uncertainties. Those who seek to escape from the persistent Wars of Commission and Omission are made of such grit.

# CHAPTER 7

## Journaling in Sinaloa

*Between Uncertainty and Fear*

ARTURO SANTAMARÍA GÓMEZ

*Dr. Santamaría Gómez is a highly regarded social scientist and writer. Like many other Latin American academics, he combines scholarly careers with journalism. He produced numerous academic publications while teaching at the Autonomous University of Sinaloa and while serving as a critic and editorial writer for some of the major newspapers and periodicals of the state of Sinaloa and across Mexico. I asked Dr. Santamaría, as a longtime colleague and friend, to consider writing a piece for this book concerning the manner in which intellectuals in Mexico handle the double duty of scholarship and public communication. I hoped his piece could speak to this context of institutional frailty and the present and real dangers of violent suppression aided by impunity, corruption, and political uncertainty. All these features are part of the daily dynamics of living in Sinaloa and other parts of Mexico. Santamaría describes his journey from activist student to public professional and from revolutionary to one quieted now because of real dangers to life and limb. His is not a narrative that is unique except in detail; instead, the pattern of his unfolding journey has many similarities to other journeys of biologists, social scientists of many shapes, and intellectuals in general.*

*His narrative unfolds in the 1960s, when, as a teenager, Santamaría joined with others from secondary schools to create guerrilla protest and demonstration groups. They were attempting a social revolution in a na-*

*tion already beset by institutional frailties contemporaneous with the rise of organized networks devoted to growing poppies and marijuana for export to the United States. Underlying weaknesses began to manifest from existing conditions due to the enveloping one-party state of the Institutional Revolutionary Party (Partido Revolucionario Institucional, PRI) which had held power since the rise of the Mexican revolutionary state. It functioned on the basis of the vertical stratification of party influence, ensuring control over the major public, private, and governmental segments of society while doling out some social benefits in agriculture, education, and health. Like most centralized institutional forms, it depended on networks of governmental, educational, labor, and public elites and their constituent cohorts of influential vertical networks of exchange for the system to function—with it attending favors and corruption. For example, in the late 1940s the Mexican senate claimed to have bought a French railroad engine and cars for ten million pesos. They did not actually purchase it but instead doled out the money to senate members so that the engine and cars still sat in France when the story was told.[1] Many years later, in the late 1990s, a governmental agency sold back huge oil pipes to the original seller in Texas at half the cost and repurchased them at full cost—all while a former high official sat on the governing board of that company and more than likely benefited in this transaction.[2] In many ways, this pattern can only become even more influential through the billions in narcotic funds made available through the rise of the corporate-oriented cartel. Political processes are both directly and indirectly influenced—if not defined—by extra-institutional actors, with some in the guise of benevolent politicians and others simply using the old "pan o palo" (bread or stick) approach to take over entire institutions.*

*Dr. Santamaría provides us with a historical and biographical narrative of how over a period of years this process of control eventually led to further muting of any real participatory political process. This hindering enabled the creation of parallel and sometimes integrated bodies of political power completely outside possible institutional control so that external agents heavily influenced many institutions that eventually became the power holders within institutions. These influenced institutions then promoted a type of political participation based not on civil responsibility but controlled through a corruptible one-party state. What Dr. Santamaría details is the tragic hijacking of democratic processes in the guise of political participation, aided and abetted by unsavory elements with the eventual impressive oppression of the free expression of ideas and issues of representation and the imprinting of "fear obedience."*

*The original Spanish version is provided following the English translation for two academic reasons. First, it is closer in style and structure to the original representation. This provides an opportunity to recognize emotive elements difficult to duplicate in a translation, and thus these emotional aspects of the political ventures in which Santamaría participated come closer to their origins. Second, few translations can duplicate the original authenticity of the untranslated narrative—in this case, of a style closer to Mexican journalism than to only an ethnobiography. It is a kind of a journal narrative within a journal narrative.*

*—Carlos G. Vélez-Ibáñez*

\* \* \*

## Beginnings in Sinaloa

After a brief month and a half in Culiacán, I arrived in Mazatlán at the beginning of October 1982 at the age of twenty-eight, from Mexico City and single. I was an activist in a university political group, founded at UNAM in 1977, that wanted to build a national revolutionary organization. Some of us were very young; I was fifteen years old during the rebellious era, democratic and righteous, that began with the Student Movement of 1968, which shook our minds and hearts like no other contemporary historical event in Mexican history. The massacre of October 2, 1968, and later the massacre on June 10, 1971, of other student protestors in Mexico City were the events that demanded that, as young university students, we morally commit ourselves to fight for a more just, democratic country. We believed that the revolutionary socialist way was the answer. The Mexican revolutionary tradition of 1910 and the recent Cuban Revolution of 1959 led by Fidel Castro and Che Guevara also had a great ideological influence on us and we were encouraged to imitate them.

On October 18, 1982, I gave my first class at the School of Social Sciences (ECS) at the Autonomous University of Sinaloa (UAS), thanks to the fact that there was an unfilled chair in sociology and communication sciences called Social Economic Structure of Latin America. At that time, I had a master's degree in Latin American studies from the School of Political and Social Sciences of UNAM. That year no other ECS professor had a master's degree, so I was hired. The UAS in Mazatlán was very new; the ECS had been founded in 1975 and its professors were very young—I was twenty-eight in 1982—so a UNAM professor with a postgraduate degree was welcome.

I was hired to teach twenty hours of class a week in two shifts. Outside of working time, including hours to prepare for classes, my energies were devoted to political work outside the university. My political organization—the Spartacus Revolutionary Left Group—had asked me to concentrate on the creation of movements and struggles of proletarian social groups, and that was what I did for almost three years, taking advantage of the fact that I had no family to support and put at risk. It was an intense period of participating in strikes, marches, occupations of urban and rural properties, supporting homeless people and landless peasants, intense propaganda work, and endless political meetings in different parts of the country.

By early 1985 I abandoned revolutionary activism after twelve years of actively participating in student and union struggles even in the United States. I did not abandon my socialist ideology, but I did abandon party militancy and activism. Teaching, reading, academic research, and the impulse to write called to me more and I returned to UNAM, already married to a Mazatleca woman, and enrolled in the Doctorate in Political Science Program with the financial support of a generous scholarship from the Autonomous University of Sinaloa. At the age of thirty-one, I decided that my fundamental tasks were going to be academic and journalistic writing about the political, social, and cultural issues of Mexico, but I never thought that my journalistic criticism would be riskier than my leftist militancy.

## The University as a Political Party

Beginning with the early 1970s, the UAS had been run from the president's office and the directors of all the schools by different leftist groups, mainly the Mexican Communist Party (PCM). In December 1981, the

PCM merged with other parties and became the Unified Socialist Party of Mexico (PSUM). The university union included academic, administrative, and maintenance workers, and was also led by the PCM-PSUM and other leftist organizations. The collective bargaining agreement was very generous: all workers without exception had the right to scholarships from the UAS for postgraduate studies. Therefore, I was able to return to Mexico City, where I was born and previously studied, to study for two and a half years for my doctorate. I returned in 1987 to Sinaloa, where months later—in an election where all the members of the school, including office workers, cleaning staff, professors, and students each had one vote—I was elected director of the School of Social Sciences, a position I held for two years. In actuality, like a democratic republic, the participants of the university voted and each individual's vote counted to elect the authorities of the institution.

I believe that two factors contributed to winning the election of director: (1) I had earned a PhD in political science, the first in social sciences in the entire UAS, and (2) I had been awarded a prestigious scholarship in 1987 by the Fulbright Foundation, months before returning to Sinaloa, supported by Dr. Juan Gómez-Quiñonez, a prominent Chicano historian at UCLA, to conduct research on the participation of undocumented workers in the sewing industry and the International Ladies Garment Workers Union (ILGWU), in New York, Chicago, and Los Angeles. I used these facts for publicity in my campaign for the director. In the end, voters, especially students, considered academic merit to elect me director in 1987.

Even with the degree of Doctor of Political Science, upon returning to the School of Social Sciences I did not obtain my appointment as a full-time professor and researcher. This was not obtained, in fact, by academic merits but by commitments or political pacts with the university president. When the campaign to elect the next president began in 1989, the negotiations for appointments for full-time professors and researchers were also taking place. I asked Mr. Audómar Ahumada Quintero, then president and member of the Unified Socialist Party of Mexico (PSUM), for three full-time faculty appointments that the School of Social Sciences needed to begin its research tasks, which didn't exist until then. The president accepted on the condition that we support his candidacy for president. I told him that I, personally, could not accept that condition

(I no longer believed in political criteria for electing authorities) but that I would talk to the other two professors. They accepted. Mr. Audómar Ahumada Quintero, despite my refusal, granted me full-time status and did not force me to do anything (for that I will always be grateful). At the beginning of the term of the next president, David Moreno Lizárraga, the three appointments and better conditions for my research appeared, although my research began back with my thesis as an undergraduate for my B.A. degree in sociology.

Despite having entered the School of Political and Social Sciences (FCPyS) at UNAM in 1972, I did not graduate until 1980. I should have finished in 1977, according to the programmed five-year curriculum, but my degree was delayed by the social and union activism that took me first to Arizona and New York in 1974, where I began to know the Chicano social struggles and the American left. Then in 1976 I participated as a volunteer with the United Farmworkers Union (UFWU). That last year, my childhood friend and UNAM colleague, Eduardo Espinoza Pérez, and I worked as volunteers translating contracts and other documents for the unforgettable United Farm Workers Union of America, led by the historic César Chávez. From that experience, my bachelor's thesis was born. Subsequently, my bachelor of science in sociology was further delayed by my involvement in the workers' struggles in Ecatepec, state of Mexico, between 1977 and 1982, with a new interval in California in 1979, when I finished my research on UFWU, "The Cause and Movement of Agricultural Workers in California," thanks to the archives of the Department of Chicano Studies at the University of California at Berkeley. Consequently, I began a long friendship that has been maintained for more than four decades with activists of the American left, Chicano, Afro-, and Anglo-American academics.

My master's thesis in Latin American studies, which was published in a co-edition by Ediciones de Cultura Popular and the UAS in 1988, "The North American Left and the Organization of Undocumented Workers," was the result of constant research in Los Angeles, San José, San Francisco, Chicago, New York, Albuquerque, and several towns in South Texas.

Six years later, in 1994, I defended my PhD dissertation in political science while at FCPyS of the UNAM, titled "The Politics Between Mexico and Aztlán: Mexican Chicano Relations from '68 to Chiapas 94." It was published at the end of that year as a co-edition by UAS and EOP of California State University, Los Angeles.

This publication encompasses twenty years of being in close work with Chicano academics, trade unionists, political activists, and Mexican immigrants in the United States, which has continued to this day, although with less intensity.

Several more books followed on the involvement of Mexican immigrants in different spheres of American society: *México en los mass media Hispanos de Estados Unidos* [*Mexico in the Hispanic Mass Media of the United States*] (co-publication UAS-CSULA, 1996); *Mexicanos en Estados Unidos: La nación, la política y el voto sin fronteras* [*Mexicans in the United States: The Nation, the Politics, and the Borderless Vote*] (co-publication UAS-PRD, 2001); *El consumo de la nostalgia: Los inmigrantes latinoamericanos y la creación del mercado hispano en estados Unidos* [*Nostalgia Consumption: Latin American Immigrants and the Creation of the Hispanic Market in the United States*] (co-authored with Juan Manuel Mendoza, ed. UAS, 2008); *2006, Emigrantes mexicanos: Movimientos y elecciones transterritoriales* [*2006, Mexican Emigrants: Transterritorial Movements and Elections*] (ed. UAS, 2007); *Futbol, emigrantes y neonacionalismo* [*Football, Emigrants, and Neonationalism*] (ed. UAS, 2011). In addition to these texts, I contributed chapters in collective books about Mexican emigration to the United States.

While still investigating Mexican immigration north of the border, I began writing a weekly article in the diario *Noroeste* in 1988 on political and organized crime issues. The Sinaloan reality was imposed in the selection of my journalistic and academic topics. However, doing so in such a widely read and influential media meant venturing into dangerous terrain.

I had been to Sinaloa in 1965 on a trip with my father, who was a journalist and occasionally toured different parts of the country. My family had several Sinaloan student friends who studied in Mexico City. That had given me the opportunity to get to know a little about the people of northwestern Mexico. However, only after I came to live and work in Sinaloa did I realize how culturally diverse Mexico was.

Although both UAS and UNAM are public universities with long histories, and both experienced the 1968 student and teacher upheavals, they evolved from radically different sources. Also, its institutional presence, human resources, financial support, and the social and cultural environment that surrounds it are markedly different from that of the UAS and continue to be so in 2023 because the National University receives many more public resources than any other university in the country. UNAM is based in the capital of a country with a centennial history. Founded in 1323, Tenochtitlán is a pre-Hispanic city, with a population in the Valley of Mexico that includes Mexico City and dozens of surrounding cities, of more than 20 million inhabitants in 2023, with more cultural, financial, and political resources than any other Mexican city. Culiacán, founded in 1531 but with a sparse population until the early twentieth century, had 300,000 inhabitants in 1980 and Mazatlán had just under 200,000 that same year. In 1980, Sinaloa had a total of 1.85 million inhabitants and just over 3 million in 2023.

UNAM is a continuation of the Royal Pontifical University of Mexico, founded in 1551; UAS is a continuation of the Liceo Rosales, created in 1873. Although both universities are centenarians, there is a big temporal gap between them, which translates into profound institutional differences and academic and cultural traditions.

When I arrived in Sinaloa in 1982 and started working at the UAS, there was still intense political turmoil that had been ongoing since 1967 when a student movement broke out that successfully sought to modify the Organic Law of the University. With that law, students and professors could participate in the elections of president and directors of the schools that lasted until 2006. Unions, academic or administrative, declared strikes every year along with numerous student organizations, usually led by various Mexican leftist groups, inside and outside the university, and supported practically every social and political struggle that was brewing in Sinaloa. In these conditions of permanent turmoil, the academic and research life of the university was unstable and precarious.

In the 1980s and 1990s, there were no postgraduate degrees offered in either Mazatlán or Culiacán campuses. The master's in social sciences (Mazatlán Campus) was created in 2008; the doctorate in social sciences (Culiacán Campus) in 1995. The lag in postgraduate studies and scientific research was evident.

The years of greatest ideological and political radicalism at the UAS were the early 1970s, when a student political group baptized "The Sick"—because, they said, they were infected with the "infantile disease of leftism" of which Lenin spoke—exerted an enormous influence on the institution and kept it in a precarious academic life, especially when they joined a guerrilla group called the September 23 Communist League in 1973.

Simultaneously with these events, the drug-trafficking groups of Sinaloa unleashed intense criminal violence in the cities, particularly in Culiacán, which led the federal government to launch "Operation Condor" in the Sinaloan mountains against several populations. Therefore, in the seventies, the UAS went through a decade shaken by incessant political turmoil and criminal violence that left deep scars. The most surprising thing for me was to learn that there were professors and students who were linked to drug trafficking. It was not uncommon for Mexican university students from Sinaloa to integrate with different guerrillas who emerged in Mexico during the late sixties, but that they were also members of organized crime was unusual. There were not many university students involved in the drug business, but there were students and teachers in the different schools who sold drugs or who formed groups that traded them, acquiring them in the mountains and moving them into the cities of Sinaloa and other parts of the country, especially on the border with the United States. By the 1980s and 1990s, there were professors who were in positions of leadership in criminal groups.

In fact, in the early 1980s, criminal activity penetrated Sinaloa to the extent that Félix Gallardo, one of the most powerful drug traffickers in the history of Mexico, was the biggest contributor to financing the construction of the UAS Culiacán Central Library. This fact is publicly known in Sinaloa and is confirmed by the inauguration plaque in its facilities.

Despite the above, the UAS—in a slow process that lasted throughout the 1980s and early 1990s—was shedding the influence of parties and political agitation, stabilizing school and administrative life. During the presidency of Dr. Rubén Rocha Moya, the first graduate programs were created for students with scholarships from the National Council of Science and Technology (CONACYT), and dozens of his graduates and professors began to study in master's and doctoral programs both in Mexico and abroad.

## Crisis of Socialism, Criminal Violence, and the Ideological Conversion of the UAS

Hundreds of university students—who previously as students or young professors and civil servants were imbued with ideological radicalism and experienced institutional instability in the 1970s and early 1980s—continued to participate in the university and had not completely shed their previous conceptions of the world.

Some joined the Party of the Democratic Revolution (PRD), a moderate left party founded in 1989, very different from ideological and analytical Marxism, and most were limited to disputing the presidency of the university every four years or, every three, the directors of the schools. The political mobilization for the election of university authorities did not cease, but the 1970s–1980s leftist University-Party model had practically disappeared except for a few variants. After 1968, the Mexican Communist Party decided to act within Mexican universities to direct a political, ideological, and cultural criticism of the government and capitalism. But more radical organizations proposed to use the resources of the university to support all kinds of worker, peasant, and student struggles against the established system. The public university was to act as a Revolutionary Party. This experiment, with some variants, was also implemented both at the Autonomous University of Puebla and the Autonomous University of Guerrero.

The [University-Party] idea, believed extinct with the disappearance of the left in the university at the end of the eighties, emerged again unexpectedly in the first decade of the new century but as a right-wing University-Party, the Sinaloan Party (PAS)—fiercely corporate and in the hands of a [political] boss, authoritarian, sole, and permanent leader: Héctor Melesio Cuén Ojeda.

The Mexican political tradition of an individual tightly controlling a community, social, union, educational, political, or other organization for personal benefit has not been totally eradicated. In some regions, such as Sinaloa, social institutions, such as unions, especially teachers, and surprisingly in the UAS, have resurfaced powerfully. Why this anachronism?

It is evident that the old leftist project of utilizing the university as a political party was returned—in a context of leftist world Marxist ideological crisis after the fall of the Berlin wall in 1989 and the disappearance of the USSR in 1991—by repentant socialists and other individuals who filled minor roles in the university and perceived in the old model, now disgraced, the opportunity to empower themselves of the university to convert it again into a patrimonial and political instrument. In another cultural and political context this would sound impossible—although this model is similar to that of the University of Guadalajara. But in Sinaloa that is possible by a scenario of great criminal violence and a stretched social medium.

At the end of the 1970s, the September 23 Communist League had been defeated throughout the country. Sinaloa had been one of its strongholds; the survivors turned in their weapons and transitioned into legal political work. During that same decade, Pedro Avilés became the first major drug trafficker in Sinaloa. He was the main exporter of marijuana and heroin to the United States, but he was killed by the police in 1978, two years after Operation Condor. This was a police-military campaign by the Mexican government throughout the whole state. However, the weapons of organized crime increased in quantity and firepower despite the military operation, so within a few years organized crime began to grow, strengthened by its foray into cocaine trafficking once Colombian cartels were forced to transport their drugs to the United States using Mexican territory. By the late eighties and early nineties, the different groups of Sinaloan narcos would unite in Guadalajara—under the leadership of Miguel Ángel Félix Gallardo—to found the Guadalajara Cartel from which, years later, the Sinaloa Cartel would be born with El Mayo Zambada and El Chapo Guzmán at the head.

Thus, guerrilla violence and university radicalism were extinguished, but the power and presence of drug traffickers in Sinaloan society and Mexican society, in general, increased substantially.

That increase in narco power became very visible: the increase in violence and fear already existing in the seventies in Sinaloa, particularly in the city of Culiacán, began to spiral in the eighties.

The perception of insecurity in Sinaloa and the ideological and organizational crisis of the left in the UAS resulted in fear of expressing or demonstrating dissatisfaction with authorities, previously done in excess. University students went from being radically critical to being extremely passive. Student organizations, left-wing parties, political activism within the university, and even student activities for social and cultural purposes disappeared.

By the beginning of the new century, the transition to student depoliticization and the passivity of the old generations of professors and administrative employees encountered a new version of the University-Party with the arrival of a new president: Héctor Melesio Cuén Ojeda, who was never more than a third-level university official. He had not been a leading academic or high-level administrator; however, the electoral system allowed everyone to vote, and after an intense campaign with abundant money to buy votes, he won the election and became president in 2005.

Cuén Ojeda, a chemist by profession, very quickly began to organize his absolute and personal control over the university. The State Congress, at the proposal of Cuén Ojeda and in agreement with Governor Jesús Aguilar Padilla (PRI), modified the Organic Law of the University on July 27, 2006, by which authorities were elected through the vote of the entire university community, where whoever obtained student support automatically won the election. This mechanism, proper for a republic but not for a university [sic], was absurd because it permanently politicized and destabilized the university, although it seemed democratic. However, the mechanism proposed by Cuén Ojeda was the total opposite: a mechanism in which he, unconditionally, would choose presidents and directors from then on. The objective was to turn the university into a political instrument not only to control the university but to govern Sinaloa.

Few of us realized what the new group consolidating UAS was proposing, and fewer of us publicly pointed out this danger.

## *Caciquism* Emerges in the UAS

In 2006, when the members of the Academic Commission were elected to select the candidates for university authorities, I pointed out through my newspaper column in the *Noroeste* that this ensured all the directors were Cuén Ojeda "yes-men." His response was furious; he himself, along with several journalists at his service, wanted to disqualify me as an academic, as a columnist, and as a person. The article that bothered Cuén Ojeda most was "I Am UAS?" ["¿La UAS soy yo?"], in obvious reference to a phrase attributed to King Louis XIV: "I am the State."

As I pointed out Cuén Ojeda's growing patrimonialism, he and his family began monitoring my activities and pressuring professors and students not to support my opinions.

*Espejo Magazine*, a Sinaloa media source, documented an example of Cuén Ojeda and his family's unexplained patrimonial enrichment from UAS:

From documentation provided by the **Public Property Registry** and the **Public Commerce Registry**, the former president, his wife, his children, and a daughter-in-law, from 2009 on, have considerably increased their real estate investments and various businesses, as owners and shareholders.

Although Cuén Ojeda registered his first company in 1983, 89 percent of his wealth came later from patrimonial disbursements in his name, that of his wife and daughters **Angélica and Mónica Cuén Díaz**, and his son **Melesio Jr.** and his wife, **Belinda Portugal Domínguez**. Héctor Melesio Cuén Ojeda's son to date has added at least six companies, the first two created in 2008 when he was 24 years old:

- **Smart Advertising Solutions [Soluciones Inteligentes Publicitarias]** and
- **MC Multimedia [MC Multimedios]**
- **HB Operations [HB Operaciones]**, 2011
- **Real Estate Luis XV [Inmobiliaria Luis XV]**, 2015, two more in 2017
- **Administration Tres Ríos [Administradora Tres Ríos]** and
- **Wenchos**.

Belinda Portugal and one of her sisters, meanwhile, set out to create a gift company named **Kolach**, registered at the same address as **HB Operations**.

Among all these family businesses, two stand out, **HB Operations** and **Real Estate Luis XV**, since acquisition of houses and land have been promoted through them. Records of the Public Property Registry clearly show that the Cuén family owns 30 properties among which houses, apartments, land, commercial premises, donations, and trusts stand out.

With respect to **Real Estate Luis XV**, it should be noted that its legal domicile was registered on Francisco Labastida Ochoa Street 1675, in the Tres Ríos Urban Development that currently operates from a branch, where the Cuén family restaurant, **Casa María**, is located on the corner of Benito Juárez and Ramón Corona streets.

According to *Noroeste/Indaga*, Héctor Melesio Cuén Ojeda and his family have invested just over 64 million pesos in these properties, 47 percent by check.[3]

This report confirmed what was loudly said in the corridors of the university; however, when this information was taken to the authorities of the state government as a sign of inexplicable enrichment and corruption, it was dismissed. The official response was as expected because Governor Aguilar Padilla supported Cuén Ojeda.

In addition to the exponential growth of his wealth since assuming the non-re-electable four-year presidency of the UAS, after his four-year limit Cuén Ojeda began to build a preparty political group that he called "Count on Me" [Cuenta Conmigo]. When it was created in 2009, I denounced in my newspaper column how almost all its members were officials, professors, administrative employees, and students at the university. But, in addition, I said that the name of the political association reflected the megalomania of its leader because he used his surname to identify it with him.

Although he had ceased to be president, he retained maximum and absolute authority. He had imposed his successor and converted the UAS back into a political party, through his civil association "Count on Me." It was allied with the PRI, which in 2011 won the municipal presidency of Culiacán, the capital of Sinaloa. I criticized this in my column and the response of the university cacique was unprecedented in the history of the university, such that it elicited the reaction of four former UAS presidents, published in the newspaper *Noroeste* on December 29, 2011:

> Concerned for the safety and physical integrity of the distinguished Dr. Arturo Santamaría Gómez and his family, by the serious threats made against them in an anonymous publication that appeared on December 9 in a Culiacán newspaper, as well as in other media, we undersigned, former presidents of the Autonomous University of Sinaloa, express our committed solidarity with Dr. Santamaría while deploring any action or attempt to limit the right of any citizen to criticism and freedom of expression.
>
> During our presidencies, without surrendering his critical attitude, Dr. Santamaría always demonstrated his highly qualified willingness to contribute to the academic, progressive, and autonomous development of the highest institution of learning in Sinaloa.
>
> We consider the fascist expressions, spewed against it in the publication signed by an alleged "groups of university students," constitutes an attack against the university and its liberal and democratic traditions, and warn of the ominous climate of intolerance suffered by the Autonomous

University of Sinaloa, that Sinaloan public opinion and the country cannot ignore.

To Dr. Santamaría we reiterate our solidarity and support, and we call on university students and public opinion in Sinaloa and the country to condemn this, and to be alert to the siege and threat to him who knows how to exercise with responsibility and civic courage the right to criticism.[4]

To this statement, former president Jorge Medina Viedas declared in an interview with *Noroeste* on November 9, 2011:

The aggression against columnist and university professor Arturo Santamaría Gómez, who was called "hitman of journalism" in an anonymous publication, is unprecedented within the UAS, said former president Jorge Medina Viedas.

"We decided to do this out of a duty of solidarity with those who are the object of an aggression that has no precedent in the history of university life, except in those years 66, 65, when there were some anonymous but innocuous flyers," he said.

"That someone can go to a newspaper to deliver a document, with ideas that in my view are fascist, we could not remain silent as former presidents, because Santamaría is a prestigious academic, a very respectable person, but above all because he is a citizen, and we cannot allow a precedent of that nature to occur in Sinaloa. Because then no one will be able to speak; it would be the beginning of a stage of authoritarianism and intolerance, which we cannot allow."

Those who signed a letter published yesterday in this medium, in support of the columnist and former defender of Noroeste readers, along with former presidents Audómar Ahumada Quintero, Rubén Rocha Moya, and David Moreno Lizárraga, considered that the attack, like others directed against the university students such as Teresa Guerra Ochoa, Ana Luz Ruelas, and Marco Antonio Medrano, has the "fingerprint" of the Mayor of Culiacán, Héctor Melesio Cuén Ojeda.

"The origin of the authorship is the same, it has the same fingerprints of the Mayor of Culiacán, Héctor Cuén, the former President of the University, the same one who wants to impose an iron hand on the University, and what he did with Arturo Santamaría is what he tried to do with Ana Luz, and Tere, precisely with the intent of silencing other voices."

He added that Cuén Ojeda pointed out that the offensive against Santamaría puts him in "total war," as he exercises a regime of terror, and authoritarianism, where President Víctor Antonio Corrales does not "play any role."

"His statements paint him as a total cacique, that is him, that paints him exactly as he is, as an intolerant person . . . he is like a little Napoleon, 'autonomy is me,' I would say; he is a sort of little king: 'the University c'est moi.'"[5]

In effect, Cuén Ojeda had ordered his subordinates to publish an implicit death threat against me because they considered me "a hitman of the pen" due to my constant criticism of the political manipulation he exercised over the UAS, said Cuén Ojeda, thereby creating an atmosphere of violence to which I could fall victim. To add insult to injury, the document published in the newspaper *El Debate* was anonymous and therefore illegal.

After I denounced the anonymous unsigned text as illegal, a UAS professor in Mazatlán, Miguel Ángel Díaz Quintero, formerly my student in 1982, claimed it was his—which was not true because the libelous text was written and published in Culiacán. Cuén Ojeda rewarded him in 2014 with the vice presidency of the UAS South Zone of Sinaloa. After Díaz Quintero assumed responsibility, in an interview with *Noreste* reporter Roxana Vivanco, the former president Cuén Ojeda said that my opinions about him were offensive; therefore, it was justified to call me a "hitman."[6] "You have seen recently in the press," Cuén Ojeda told reporters, that "some people even call them hitmen, because not only can you kill physically, but you can also kill in the media, destroy lives, destroy families. . . . I think that if you review Santamaria's writings, they are frequently offensive toward me. Many times, declare me an authoritarian and egomaniacal person, but you, who are here, know me, and you know that I am not like that."

Eight days later, on December 31 of the same year, eight directors and professors of the four UAS campuses in the state, including the director of my School of Social Sciences in Mazatlán, in another article published in the same *El Debate*, came out in support of Cuén Ojeda, saying that they were the authors of the questionable document—which was not true—and fully vindicated calling me a "hitman."[7] However, the most relevant thing about this new attack is that they tried to discredit and refute four former presidents who had published in my defense and freedom of expression within the UAS, recalling the old political militancy of the three men, Medina, Ahumada, and Rocha, in the Mexican Communist Party (disbanded in 1981) and David Moreno in another leftist group, Socialist Current, as well as their new participation in PRI governments. "Do you really believe that because the 'signers' who wrote this new libelous attack were former presidents, we, Sinaloans, are blind to the evidence of their links with those who in the past were enemies of the UAS?"

It was surprising since at least two of those professors, Díaz Quintero and Jorge Figueroa Cansino, had also been militants of the PCM and the People's Revolutionary Movement, both members of Cuenta Conmigo, which allied with the PRI and Nueva Alianza to give Cuén Ojeda the municipal presidency of Culiacán. It was absurd that they tried to disqualify three former presidents for being members of the same leftist parties they had also participated in, and it was absurd because the three were now working with PRI governments, while their leader Cuén Ojeda was elected at the hands of the PRI, the party they previously criticized. What they sought with their gibberish was to shield Cuén Ojeda and continue with the absolute domination they exercised over the university.

Rubén Rocha Moya, president of UAS (1993–97) and governor of Sinaloa (2021–27), wrote an article in *El Debate* on the same theme, referring to the serious situation within UAS under the rule of Héctor Melesio Cuén Ojeda:

For a long time, UAS was an example of democracy and the exercise of criticism. When authoritarianism and intolerance back in the 60s and 70s suffocated identity, elections were, in fact, mere simulations, inequitable and fraudulent, and challenges and conflicts abounded.

Quite the opposite was UAS; from 1972 to 2005, its electoral system never admitted any electoral fraud in direct or indirect elections by the University Council, weighted or individual votes by teachers, employees, and students.

Consequently, since 1966, and even before, respect for university legality, diversity, differences, and the free expression of ideas and critical opinions flourished at UAS. These values survived even the intolerance of the ultra-left of the early seventies. And they prevailed until six years ago. That is, until the arrival of Melesio Cuén to the presidency.

Since then, a process of involution has been taking place. The authorities began to be bothered by the freedom to, if anything, tell officials what they do not want to hear.

And they proceeded against their critics through recurring censorship, intimidation, the discrediting of people, persecuting them, and even expulsion. Criticizing officials is now tantamount to attacking the university itself. "I am the University" (they believe). That is why the University Council itself established an ominous "gag law" to sanction critics.

The last two university administrations (those of Melesio Cuén and Corrales Montaño, the two main leaders of PAS since it was founded in 2013), in their eagerness to control everything, with submission have usurped the place [UAS] of intelligence, criticism, and freedom.[8]

A month earlier, on December 10, 2011, in *Noroeste*, Dr. Tere Guerra, a prominent UAS academic and persecuted by Cuén Ojeda, wrote a letter to the editor of the newspaper where she comments on the libel they wrote against me:

> On December 3, Dr. Arturo Santamaría published in *Noroeste* a forceful criticism of the interference by former president Héctor Melesio Cuén Ojeda in UAS, and the undue subordination to him of the governing bodies of the institution, questioning the behavior of President Antonio Corrales and his statement regarding the case of the administrative union, refusing to recognize and respect a court judgment for protection, claiming "university autonomy" crudely and daily violated by Héctor Melesio Cuén Ojeda.
>
> It is regrettable that the inquisition is re-established at UAS, that dissidents of former president Héctor Melesio Cuén Ojeda are persecuted and dismissed, and that the elementary constitutional right of free expression by university students is violated. They want only praise, and above all, they seek subordination to the political project of the mayor of the capital [of Sinaloa].[9]

That letter was followed by several more published in the newspaper *Noroeste*, including academics from Europe and South America, as well as other cities in Mexico, who showed their surprise and indignation that a professor was harassed for his criticism of a former president now turned mayor of the state capital who continues to pull all the strings at UAS.

On December 23, 2011, I went to both the State Human Rights Commission and the State Attorney General's Office, based in the city of Culiacán, to sue Héctor Melesio Cuén Ojeda for death threats. That same day, Cuén Ojeda's statements had appeared in *Noroeste* and other media, wherein he confirmed he was the intellectual author of the threats and what was said in the libel of December 9.[10] The president of the State Human Rights Commission, Juan José Ríos Estavillo, declared that a "serious statement (would be made before the Sinaloan media and published that same day) this week by the Mayor of Culiacán regarding the case of Arturo Santamaría," and added: "At the outset, we are finding and circumscribing an alleged, near violation of human rights, hence the need to establish precautionary measures to prevent them from repeating themselves."[11]

In an interview with journalist Francisco Cuamea on December 29, 2011, I defined the power of Héctor Melesio Cuén Ojeda as "illiterate despotism" because, in effect, this character had no relevant academic background except that of having taught before being an administrative official of the university.[12] In my opinion, Cuén Ojeda's lack of intellectual training decisively influenced his despotic vision of university leadership and government policy. But undoubtedly surrounding the idea of the power he cultivated was his family formation; his grandfather had been a cacique in Badiraguato. Cuén Ojeda has repeated in numerous interviews all his life that he has emulated his grandfather, who precisely exercised absolute power in his town, according to the historian Froylán Enciso in his book *Our Narcotic History* (2017):

> "Is there an authoritarian shadow hanging over the country?" asked Cuamea, and I replied:
>
> "In this atmosphere of violence in Mexico, created by organized crime, it is easy for authoritarian tendencies and instincts to emerge among political and power actors; it suits those with those inclinations because the population is afraid and citizens are intimidated; this permits imposing their interests more easily."
>
> "Is it true that UAS is plunged into silence?"
>
> "That's right, even in the face of major social and economic issues. Unlike what one sees in other universities, such as UNAM, which has been

an example of social sensitivity headed by the president, at UAS we see the opposite; absent is that type of discussion and its community remains subordinate, crouched, afraid to comment on the problems of the university because they know they can be fired, they can take away working hours or be physically punished. Yes, there is great fear. Few, very few, dare to speak, and those of us who do are labeled hitmen."[13]

The demands and criticisms I made, as well as the numerous demonstrations of support from journalists and academics, reduced the intimidation and implicit death threats by Cuén Ojeda, but the lies discrediting me by numerous columnists and commentators of Radio UAS at the service of the former president continued for a long time, at least until 2023. For almost twenty years there have been dozens of articles that journalists in the pay of Cuén Ojeda have written against me. Although I retired from UAS, the governing bodies of UAS continue to try to discredit me academically; this also confirms these sources are at the service of this character. It is unbelievable that they invent student evaluations of my performance as a professor of subjects I never taught, in years when I no longer taught at the School of Social Sciences.[14] The intent was to discredit my journalistic opinions regarding the interference of Cuén Ojeda's Sinaloan Party in UAS.

## The Power of the Narcos and the Critical Limits of the Academy

The issues of violence and the power of organized crime have been growing in Sinaloa; I could not ignore them in my journalistic opinions, the subject of my three books, and several academic articles. I never imagined that the issue of drug trafficking—without ever mentioning names of politicians who have been linked to organized crime leaders, nor mentioning specific companies associated with drug traffickers—was going to generate any direct threat. Indeed, it did once through a person close to me. They sent me a warning not to talk about the power of the narcos in Sinaloa. They sent me the following message: "Tone it down." And, indeed, I "toned it down." I had to.

I didn't stop writing about it in the newspaper; I started writing in more academic and general terms. However, in four academic books, I did mention specific names and situations without any problem. There were no threats or problems of any kind.

The first was a book written by three colleagues from the university—Pedro Brito Osuna, Luis Antonio Martínez Peña, and me—where we collected texts previously published in newspapers and magazines. The title was *Morir en Sinaloa: Violencia, narco y cultura* [*Dying in Sinaloa: Violence, Narco, and Culture*] (2009). The second was a book that I edited, and for which I wrote the introduction, called *Las jefas del Narco: El ascenso de las mujeres en el crimen organizado* [*The Female Bosses of Narcotics: The Rise of Women in Organized Crime*] (first ed. 2012, second ed. 2013). In it, nine of my students wrote parts of their postgraduate theses in social sciences and journalism reports. The third was *Carnival, reinas y narco* [*Carnival, Queens, and Narco: The Terrible Power of Beauty*] (2014). I was the sole author. The book was republished by Grijalbo–Random House–Mondadori in 2014. One more, "Culiacán, Global City of Organized Crime," remained in the pipeline because it was never published.

The three published books were well received by readers. The first only circulated in Sinaloa and the print run was only five hundred copies. The second, due to the novelty of the subject and the fact that the publisher is very important, had a print run in two editions of approximately fifteen thousand copies. The third was less lucky; about five thousand books were printed.

There was no intimidation or threats for writing about women drug traffickers, but publications financed by Cuenta Conmigo (which later morphed into the Sinaloa Party) intended to discredit me for having written those books by saying I had ties with drug traffickers, when, according to a number of political commentators of Sinaloa and the rest of the country, PAS has been identified as having connections with organized crime.

The work "Culiacán, Global City of Organized Crime," a strictly academic text, was not accepted by Random House: it was not commercially attractive. This convinced me not to investigate the issue of drug trafficking again. In those years they murdered the Sinaloan journalist Javier Valdez, who wrote several books—authentic best sellers in Mexico—about the violence of organized crime. That tragedy ended up convincing me to no longer address the issue in-depth and to only talk about the subject in *Noroeste*, but choosing my words carefully without using the information that abounds in Sinaloa and the whole country.

The power of organized crime has grown so much in Mexico and more specifically in Sinaloa, where there is practically no social area that is exempt; emphasizing this impact on politics and business with precise data is extremely risky.

Academic freedom and investigative journalism have clear limits in contemporary Mexico; they are imposed not by the government but by organized crime, a kind of power parallel to the state.

I end by reproducing my newspaper article published on February 18, 2023, in *Noroeste*.[15]

## If Mexico Is a Narcostate, Since When?

They can arrest dozens of capos, in fact, dozens of them have been arrested for at least four decades, but the Mexican state has not been able to end, or even diminish, the narcos. On the contrary, their organizations are increasingly powerful not only in our own territory but in many other countries; in the case of the Sinaloa Cartel in around eighty countries.

It is evident that the government of the Fourth Transformation, as López Obrador likes to call his administration, has failed to defeat drug trafficking, as have all the presidential six-year terms since 1975 if we date the beginning with Operation Condor launched in Sinaloa between 1975 and 1976. This means that, if nine governments have failed in their strategies against drug trafficking, it is evident that means a prolonged defeat of the state in the face of organized crime.

The most serious thing is that this prolonged failure is large because the narco has penetrated deeply into strategic areas of the state and corrupted many of its security forces, and key men and women within its apparatuses. Otherwise, how can we explain the geometric expansion of organized crime? This begs the question, "Is Mexico a narcostate?"

In turn, a narcostate, if there is one, is not viable without important sectors of society, including the legal community and political parties, having been penetrated by criminal organizations. If the state is weak, or at least incompetent, in the face of organized crime, it is because the whole of political and civil society, including government and political parties, business and civil society, that is, nonprofit institutions, are also weak before criminal organizations. A state is not abstract but is integral to its society, or at least to parts of it.

This is relevant looking at the trial of the former secretary of security of the government of Felipe Calderón, García Luna. When his lawyer asked "El Rey" Zambada if in 2013 he had given money to Gabriel Regino, López Obrador's undersecretary of security at the time, numerous newspaper and other platform commentators reaffirmed their conviction that AMLO has had agreements with the Sinaloa Cartel not just now but for several years and therefore, the Fourth Transformation heads up a narco government.

Indeed, AMLO made very suspicious statements, until the arrest and imprisonment of Ovidio Guzmán and the arrest of Lupe Tapia—lieutenant of El Mayo Zambada—about having a kind of pact with Sinaloan drug traffickers. That no longer seems to be the case; in addition to imprisoning two strategic capos, there have been constant millionaire seizures of fentanyl and methamphetamines produced by the Sinaloa Cartel.

Well-read and influential journalists such as Carlos Marín, Fernández Menéndez, Héctor de Mauleón, Pablo Hiriart, or Raymundo Rivapalacio, among many others, do not hesitate to maintain that López Obrador protects the Sinaloa Cartel; simultaneously, they doubt that Genaro García Luna and, therefore, Felipe Calderón, did. The opinions of these columnists obviously seem very unbalanced. Their conclusion is markedly influenced by official United States government investigations into drug penetration of the Calderón administration extensively reviewed by Mexican journalist David Aponte in his book *The Infiltrators: Narco Inside Governments* (2011). Héctor de Mauleón, one of AMLO's harshest critics, writes in the prologue:

> DEA's "Operation Cleanup" showed that drug traffickers had full command within the Undersecretariat for Specialized Investigation into Organized Crime (SIEDO) and in main management levels of the Federal Ministry of Public Security. In addition to buying-off top-level officials, among them, Deputy Attorney General Noé Ramírez Mandujano and SIEDO director Miguel Colorado González, the narco had commanders and agents in

the operations of the Attorney General of the Republic, Eduardo Medina Mora, under his control.

> Organized crime named, removed, high police officials, directed intelligence work whose purpose was aimed at capturing leaders and hitmen of rival cartels. . . . In the initial years of the war against drug trafficking by the government of Felipe Calderón, the triumphs of the SIEDO were actually victories the Sinaloa group obtained over its adversaries.[16]

If this has happened during the government of López Obrador, it will not take long for it to be demonstrated with proof in hand, to assert that the journalists mentioned, while also openly defending García Luna and Calderón, are not professional or ethical. They take sides against a government they vehemently abhor.

It must be said that if there is a narcostate in Mexico, it has been present for several governments—not only in that of Andrés Manuel López Obrador. In reality, no party is spared from having had affairs with organized crime. Nor are the powerful so immune. On July 25, 2024, Héctor Melesio Cuén Ojeda was assassinated by unknown assailants when he was about to take office as a plurinominal federal legislator of Sinaloa. Curiously, this was on the same day that Israel "El Mayo" Zambada García and one of El Chapo's sons were arrested in El Paso, Texas, by U.S. federal authorities.[17]

* * *

## Escribir en Sinaloa: Entre la incertidumbre y el miedo

### Empezar a vivir en Sinaloa

Después de una breve estancia de mes y medio en Culiacán llegué a Mazatlán a principios de octubre de 1982 a los veintiocho años, en soltería y procedente de la Ciudad de México. Era militante de una agrupación política universitaria, fundada en la UNAM en 1977, que quería construir una organización nacional de corte revolucionario. Algunos de nosotros, siendo muy jóvenes, yo de quince años, veníamos de la ola rebelde, democrática y justiciera que se inició con el Movimiento Estudiantil de 1968, el cual sacudió nuestras mentes y corazones como ningún otro hecho histórico contemporáneo en la historia mexicana. La matanza del 2 de octubre de 1968 y posteriormente la masacre del 10 de junio de 1971 de otros estudiantes manifestantes en la Ciudad de México fueron los sucesos que nos exigieron que, como jóvenes universitarios, moralmente nos comprometiéramos a luchar por un país más justo y democrático. Creíamos que la vía revolucionaria socialista lo era. La tradición revolucionaria mexicana de 1910 y la cercana revolución cubana de 1959 encabezada por Fidel Castro y El Che Guevara también tenía una gran influencia ideológica sobre la juventud rebelde que nos animaban a imitarlos.

El 18 de octubre de 1982 di mi primera clase en la Escuela de Ciencias Sociales (ECS) de la Universidad Autónoma de Sinaloa, gracias a que había una cátedra para estudiantes de sociología y ciencias de la comunicación llamada Estructura Económico Social de América Latina. En ese momento yo contaba con una maestría en estudios Latinoamericanos cursada en la Facultad de Ciencias Políticas y Sociales de la UNAM. En ese año ningún otro profesor de la ECS poseía un título de maestría y el yo tenerlo contó para que me contrataran. La UAS en Mazatlán era muy joven, la ECS había sido fundada en 1975, y también sus profesores eran muy jóvenes—yo tenía veintiocho en 1982—así que un profesor con postgrado y de la UNAM era bienvenido.

Fui contratado para impartir veinte horas de clase a la semana en los dos turnos. Fuera de tiempo laboral, incluyendo las horas para preparar las clases, mis energías las dedicaba al trabajo político fuera de la universidad. Mi organización política—el Grupo de Izquierda Revolucionaria Espartaco—me había pedido que me concentrara en la creación de movimientos y luchas de grupos sociales proletarios y fue lo que hice durante casi tres años, aprovechando que no tenía familia que mantener y arriesgar. Fue un intenso periodo de participar en huelgas, marchas, ocupaciones de predios urbanos y rurales, apoyando a gente sin casa y a campesinos sin tierra, intenso trabajo propagandístico e inagotables reuniones políticas en diferentes partes del país.

Para principios de 1985 abandoné el activismo revolucionario después de doce años de participar activamente en luchas estudiantiles y sindicales incluso en Estados Unidos. No abandonaba mi ideología socialista pero sí la militancia y activismo partidarios. La enseñanza, la lectura, la investigación académica y el impulso a escribir me llamaban más y regresé a la UNAM, ya casado con una mujer mazatleca, e inscribirme en el Doctorado en Ciencia Política con el soporte económico de una beca de la generosa Universidad Autónoma de Sinaloa. A los treinta y uno años decidí que mis tareas fundamentales iban a ser la labor académica y la opinión periodística de los temas políticos, sociales y culturales de México, pero nunca pensé que mi crítica periodística iba a ser más riesgosa que mi militancia izquierdista.

## La universidad como partido

La UAS desde principios de los años 70 había sido dirigida tanto desde la Rectoría como de las direcciones de todas las escuelas por miembros de los diferentes grupos de izquierda que actuaban en la institución, principalmente el Partido Comunista Mexicano (PCM); en diciembre de 1981, cuando se fusionó con otros partidos, adoptó el nombre de Partido Socialista Unificado de México (PSUM). Debido a que el sindicato de la universidad, tanto de académicos como de administrativos y mantenimiento, también estaba dirigido por el PCM-PSUM y otras organizaciones de izquierda, el contrato colectivo de trabajo fue desde inicio muy generoso, el cual incluía que todos sus trabajadores sin excepción tenían el derecho de ser becados por la UAS para estudios de postgrado. Así fue que yo pude regresar a la Ciudad de México—donde nací y estudié—durante dos años y medio para llevar a cabo el programa de doctorado y regresar en 1987 a Sinaloa, donde meses después, a través de una elección donde votaban paritariamente todos los integrantes de la escuela—profesores, estudiantes, oficinistas y empleados de limpieza— gané la dirección de la Escuela de Ciencias Sociales, de la que fui titular durante dos años. En efecto, tal y como en una república democrática, el conjunto de los integrantes de la universidad votaba y cada individuo valía un voto para elegir a las autoridades de la institución.

Creo que dos de los factores que contribuyeron para que yo ganara la elección de director fueron: (1) el que hubiese adquirido el grado de Doctor en Ciencia Política—el primero en ciencias sociales en toda la UAS—y (2) que yo hubiese sido becado en 1987 por la Fundación Fulbright, meses antes de regresar a Sinaloa, respaldado por el Dr. Juan Gómez Quiñonez, destacado historiador Chicano de la UCLA, para realizar una investigación sobre la participación de los trabajadores indocumentados en la industria de la costura y el International Ladies Garment Workers Union (ILGWU), en Nueva York, Chicago y Los Ángeles. Este hecho lo aproveché como recurso propagandístico en mi campaña para director, gracias al prestigio de la Beca Fulbright y de la UCLA. Es decir, a final de cuentas, los votantes, sobre todo los estudiantes porque eran gran mayoría, tomaron en cuenta los méritos académicos para elegirme director en 1987.

Aun con el grado de Doctor en Ciencia Política al regresar a la Escuela de Ciencias Sociales no obtuve mi nombramiento de profesor e investigador de tiempo completo. Este no se obtenía, en los hechos, por méritos académicos sino por compromisos o pactos políticos con la rectoría de la UAS. Cuando en 1989 se inició la campaña para elegir al siguiente rector, momento en el que generalmente se daban las negociaciones para obtener los nombramientos de profesores e investigadores de tiempo completo, le solicité al Lic. Audómar Ahumada Quintero, el entonces rector y miembro del Partido Socialista Unificado de México (PSUM), que la escuela de Ciencias Sociales necesitaba tres nombramientos de profesores de tiempo completo para iniciar sus tareas de investigación, las cuales no existían hasta entonces. El rector aceptó con la condición de que apoyáramos a su candidato a rectoría. Yo le dije que personalmente no podía aceptar esa condición (ya no creía en los criterios políticos para elegir autoridades) pero que hablaría con los otros dos profesores. Ellos aceptaron. El Lic. Audómar Ahumada Quintero a pesar de mi negativa me concedió el TC y no me obligó a nada (ese hecho siempre se lo agradeceré). Al iniciar el periodo del siguiente rector, David Moreno Lizárraga, aparecieron los tres nombramientos y ya encontré mejores condiciones para mi labor de investigador, aunque esta no empezó en esas circunstancias sino desde mis estudios de licenciatura en sociología cuando escribí la tesis para obtener el grado.

A pesar de haber ingresado a la Facultad de Ciencias Políticas y Sociales (FCPyS) de la UNAM en 1972, me gradué en 1980. Debería haberlo hecho en 1977, después de cinco años del Plan de Estudios de la carrera, pero el activismo social y sindical que me llevó primeramente a Arizona y a Nueva York en 1974, donde empecé a conocer las luchas sociales chicanas y a la izquierda norteamericana, y después en 1976 a participar como voluntario en el Sindicato de trabajadores agrícolas unidos (UFWU), retrasó mi titulación. Este último año, mi gran amigo de la infancia y después compañero en la UNAM, Eduardo Espinoza Pérez, y yo trabajamos como voluntarios haciendo traducciones de contratos y otros documentos del inolvidable United Farm Workers Union of America, que dirigía el histórico César Chávez. De esa experiencia nació mi tesis de licenciatura. Posteriormente, mi involucramiento en las luchas obreras en Ecatepec, Estado de México, entre 1977 y 1982—con un nuevo intervalo en California en 1979, cuando terminé mi investigación sobre la UFWU, intitulada "La Causa y el Movimiento de los Trabajadores Agrícolas en California," gracias a los archivos del Departamento de Estudios Chicanos de la Universidad de California en Berkeley—retrasé aún más mi titulación como licenciado en sociología. Desde entonces inicié una larga amistad que se ha mantenido por más de cuatro décadas con militantes de la izquierda estadounidense y académicos chicanos, afro y angloamericanos.

Mi tesis de Maestría en Estudios Latinoamericanos, la cual fue publicada en una coedición por Ediciones de Cultura Popular y la UAS en 1988, con el nombre de "La izquierda norteamericana y la organización de los trabajadores indocumentados," fue resultado de constantes visitas de investigación tanto a Los Ángeles, San José, San Francisco, Chicago, Nueva York, Alburquerque, y varias poblaciones del sur de Texas.

Seis años después, en 1994, defendí mi tesis de Doctorado en Ciencia Política, también cursado en la FCPyS de la UNAM, que lleva el título de "La Política entre México y Aztlán. Relaciones Chicano Mexicanas del 68 a Chiapas 94." A finales de ese año este trabajo se publicó en una coedición de la UAS y la EOP de la California State University, Los Ángeles.

Este texto de alguna manera era la culminación de 20 años de estar en estrecha relación con académicos, sindicalistas y militantes políticos chicanos e inmigrantes mexicanos en Estados Unidos, la cual ha continuado hasta la fecha, aunque con menor intensidad.

A esa obra continuaron varios libros más sobre el involucramiento de los inmigrantes mexicanos en diferentes esferas de la sociedad norteamericana: *México en los mass media Hispanos de Estados Unidos* (coedición UAS-CSTU-LA, 1996); *Mexicanos en Estados Unidos: La nación, la política y el voto sin fronteras* (coedición UAS-PRD, 2001); *El consumo de la nostalgia: Los inmigrantes latinoamericanos y la creación del mercado hispano en estados Unidos* (en coautoría con Juan Manuel Mendoza, ed. UAS, 2008); *2006, Emigrantes Mexicanos: Movimientos y Elecciones Transterritoriales* (ed. UAS, 2007); *Futbol, emigrantes y neonacionalismo* (ed. UAS, 2011). Sumado a esos textos, escribí capítulos en libros colectivos que hablaban de la emigración mexicana a Estados Unidos.

Al mismo tiempo que seguía investigando la inmigración mexicana al norte de la frontera, empecé a escribir a partir de 1988 un artículo semanal en el diario *Noroeste* sobre temas políticos y del crimen organizado. La contundente realidad sinaloense se iba imponiendo en la selección de mis tópicos periodísticos y académicos. Sin embargo, hacerlo en un medio de comunicación tan leído e influyente implicaba incursionar en terrenos peligrosos.

Yo había conocido Sinaloa en 1965 en un viaje con mi padre, quien era periodista y de vez en cuando emprendía giras por diferentes partes del país. También desde temprana edad mi familia tuvo lazos de amistad con jóvenes estudiantes sinaloenses que estudiaban en la Ciudad de México, lo cual me había dado la oportunidad de conocer un poco lo que era la gente del noroeste mexicano. No obstante, al llegar a vivir y trabajar a Sinaloa, sin saber que aquí iba a echar raíces por el resto de mi vida, me di cuenta de lo culturalmente diverso que era México.

Para empezar, la Universidad Autónoma de Sinaloa era radicalmente distinta a la UNAM en muchos aspectos, a pesar de que las dos eran universidades públicas con largas raíces históricas y que desde 1968 pasaban por una intensa agitación estudiantil y magisterial. Obviamente sus instalaciones y medios financieros y académicos eran enormemente diferentes—y lo siguen siendo en 2023—porque la Universidad Nacional recibe muchos más recursos públicos que cualquier otra universidad del país, pero también su institucionalidad, recursos humanos y el medio social y cultural que lo rodea es marcadamente diferente al de la UAS, simplemente porque la UNAM está asentada en la capital del país con una centenaria historia, si tomamos en cuenta la fundación de la ciudad prehispánica, Tenochtitlán, en 1323, y con una población en el Valle de México, que incluye la Ciudad de México y decenas de ciudad conurbadas, de más de 20 millones de habitantes en 2023, además de recursos culturales, financieros y políticos que no tiene ninguna otra ciudad mexicana. Culiacán, fundada en 1531 pero con una escasa población hasta principios del siglo veinte, tenía poco más de 300,000 habitantes en 1980 y Mazatlán poco menos de 200,000 en ese mismo año. Sinaloa tenía en su totalidad 1.85 millón habitantes en 1980 y poco más de 3 millones en 2023.

La UNAM es continuación de la Real Universidad Pontificia de México, fundada en 1551, y la UAS es continuación del Liceo Rosales, creado en 1873; así que, aun siendo centenarias ambas universidades, hay una marcada distancia en el tiempo, la cual se traduce en profundas diferencias institucionales y tradiciones académicas y culturales.

En 1982, cuando llegué a Sinaloa e ingresé a trabajar a la UAS, todavía se experimentaba una intensa agitación política que procedía desde 1967, cuando estalló un movimiento estudiantil que buscaba modificar la Ley Orgánica de la Universidad con la cual los estudiantes y profesores pudieran participar en las elecciones de rector y directores de las escuelas, lo cual se logró y perduró hasta 2006. Los sindicatos, ya sea de académicos y/o administrativos, estallaban huelgas cada año y habían numerosas organizaciones estudiantiles, generalmente dirigidas por partidos o grupos de la variada izquierda mexicana, que dentro y fuera de la universidad estallaban movimientos y apoyaban prácticamente toda lucha social y política que se gestaba en Sinaloa. En estas condiciones de agitación permanente la vida académica de la universidad era muy inestable y la investigación muy precaria.

En los años 80 y 90 no existía ningún postgrado en el campus de la UAS en Mazatlán. La Maestría en Ciencias Sociales (Campus Mazatlán) se creó en 2008 y el Doctorado en Ciencias Sociales (Campus Culiacán) en 1995. El rezago en estudios de postgrado y en investigación científica en la UAS era evidente.

Los años de mayor radicalidad ideológica y política en la UAS sucedieron a principios de los 70, cuando un grupo político estudiantil bautizado como "Los Enfermos"—debido a que, decían ellos, estaban inoculados con el virus de la "enfermedad infantil del izquierdismo" del que hablaba Lenin—ejercía una enorme influencia en la institución y la mantenía en una vida académica precaria, sobre todo cuando se vincularon en 1973 a un grupo guerrillero llamado Liga Comunista 23 de septiembre.

De manera simultánea a esos hechos, los grupos de narcotraficantes de Sinaloa habían desatado una intensa violencia criminal en las ciudades del estado, particularmente en Culiacán, lo cual llevó al gobierno federal a lanzar en 1975 mediante el Ejército Mexicano la "Operación Cóndor" tanto en la sierra sinaloense con varias de sus poblaciones. Es decir, en los años setenta la UAS pasó por una década sacudida por una agitación política y violencia criminal incesantes que dejó profundas huellas. Lo más sorprendente para mí fue saber que en ese contexto hubo profesores y estudiantes de la UAS que estaban vinculados al narcotráfico. No era raro que universitarios mexicanos, como los de Sinaloa, formaron parte de las diferentes guerrillas que surgieron en México desde fines de los sesenta, pero que fueran integrantes del crimen organizado sí era inusual. No eran muchos los universitarios inmiscuidos en el negocio de las drogas, pero sí había en las diferentes escuelas estudiantes y profesores quienes vendieran drogas o quienes formaran grupos que comerciaran con ellas adquiriéndolas en la sierra y trasladándolas a las ciudades de Sinaloa y de otras partes del país, sobre todo de la frontera con Estados Unidos. Ya en los 80 y 90 hubo profesores que ocuparon lugares relevantes en los mandos de las estructuras criminales.

El anterior hecho revelaba hasta dónde había penetrado la alternativa de vida criminal en Sinaloa, al grado de que Félix Gallardo, uno de los narcotraficantes más poderosos en la historia de México, fue el principal contribuyente para financiar a principios de los 80 la edificación de la Biblioteca Central de la UAS en Culiacán. Tal hecho es conocido públicamente en Sinaloa y lo constata la placa de inauguración en sus instalaciones.

A pesar de lo anterior, la UAS en un proceso lento, que le llevó toda la década de los 80 y principios de los 90, fue despojándose de la influencia de partidos y de la agitación política institucionalizando su vida escolar y administrativa. En ese proceso creó sus primeros programas de postgrado durante la Rectoría del Dr. Rubén Rocha Moya con estudiantes becados por el Consejo Nacional de Ciencia y Tecnología (CONACYT), y también decenas de sus egresados y de profesores empezaron a cursar programas de maestría y doctorado tanto en México como el extranjero.

## Crisis del socialismo, la violencia criminal y la conversión ideológica de la UAS

Cientos de universitarios que, como estudiantes o jóvenes profesores y funcionarios fueron actores del radicalismo ideológico e inestabilidad institucional de los 70 y principios de los 80, continuaban actuando en la universidad y no se habían despojado del todo de sus anteriores concepciones del mundo.

Algunos de ellos se habían incorporado al Partido de la Revolución Democrática (PRD), un partido de izquierda moderada fundado en 1989, muy distante de los planteamientos ideológicos y analíticos del marxismo, y la mayoría se limitaba a disputar la rectoría de la universidad cada cuatro años o cada tres las direcciones de las escuelas. No cesaba la movilización política en la elección de autoridades universitarias, pero prácticamente había desaparecido el modelo de Universidad-Partido concebido así, aunque con variantes, por todas las agrupaciones políticas de izquierda que participaban en la UAS a lo largo de los setenta y ochenta. El Partido Comunista Mexicano después de 1968 había definido actuar en el seno de las universidades mexicanas y llegar a dirigirlas a través de sus cuadros académicos para desde ahí ejercer una crítica política, ideológica y cultural al gobierno y al capitalismo; pero otras organizaciones más radicales planteaban utilizar los recursos de la universidad para apoyar todo tipo de lucha obrera, campesina y estudiantil contra el sistema establecido. Es decir, la universidad pública debía actuar como Partido Revolucionario. Este experimento también se concretó con algunas variantes, tanto en la Universidad Autónoma de Puebla como en la Universidad Autónoma de Guerrero en la misma época.

Esa idea que se creía extinguida con la transfiguración y/o desaparición de las izquierdas en la universidad a finales de los ochenta, emergió nuevamente, de manera inesperada, en la primera década del nuevo siglo, pero ahora como Universidad-Partido de derecha (el Partido Sinaloense, PAS), férreamente corporativo y en manos de un dirigente de corte caciquil; es decir, autoritario, quien es el líder único y permanente: Héctor Melesio Cuén Ojeda.

La tradición política mexicana de que un individuo controle férreamente a una comunidad, organización social, sindical, educativa, política o de otra índole para beneficio propio no ha podido erradicarse totalmente. En algunas regiones, como Sinaloa, instituciones sociales, como los sindicatos, sobre todo los magisteriales, y sorprendentemente en la UAS, han resurgido poderosamente. ¿Por qué este anacronismo?

Es evidente que el viejo proyecto izquierdista de utilizar a la universidad como partido político fue retomado—en un contexto de crisis ideológica de la izquierda marxista mundial después de la caída del Muro de Berlín en 1989 y la desaparición de la URSS en 1991—por socialistas arrepentidos y otros individuos que en la universidad en esos años jugaban un papel secundario y vieron en ese viejo modelo, ahora derechizado, la oportunidad de apoderarse de la universidad para convertirlo nuevamente en un instrumento patrimonialista y político. En otro contexto cultural y político esto suena inconcebible—aunque existe un modelo similar en la Universidad de Guadalajara—pero en Sinaloa esto ha sido posible en un escenario de alta violencia criminal y miedo social ampliamente extendido.

A finales de los setenta del siglo anterior la Liga Comunista 23 de septiembre, organización guerrillera, había sido derrotada en todo el país, Sinaloa había sido uno de sus bastiones, pero, aun con sobrevivientes que transitaron a la lucha política legal, levantaron totalmente las armas. En esa misma década, Pedro Avilés se había convertido en el primer gran narcotraficante de Sinaloa; él era el principal exportador de mariguana y heroína a Estados Unidos, pero fue abatido por la policía en 1978, dos años después de la Operación Cóndor—campaña policiaco-militar del gobierno mexicano que se extendió a todo el estado. Sin embargo, las armas del crimen organizado aumentaron en cantidad y poder de fuego porque, a pesar de la operación militar, en pocos años el crimen organizado empezó a crecer cada vez más, ahora fortalecido con su incursión en el tráfico de cocaína una vez que los carteles colombianos se vieron obligados a transportar su droga a Estados Unidos utilizando el territorio mexicano. Para finales de los ochenta y principios de los noventa, los diferentes grupos de narcos sinaloenses se unirían en Guadalajara, bajo el liderazgo de Miguel Ángel Félix Gallardo, para fundar el Cártel de Guadalajara del que, años después, nacería el Cártel de Sinaloa con El Mayo Zambada y El Chapo Guzmán a la cabeza.

Así pues, se extinguió la violencia guerrillera y la radicalidad universitaria, pero aumentó sustancialmente el poder y presencia del narco en la sociedad sinaloense, en particular, y la mexicana, en general.

Ese aumento del poder narco se tradujo en algo muy visible: el incremento de la violencia y el miedo en Sinaloa, particularmente en la ciudad de Culiacán, ya existente en los setenta pero que empezó a crecer en espiral a partir de los ochenta.

La percepción de inseguridad en Sinaloa y la crisis ideológica y organizativa de las izquierdas se tradujo en la UAS en temor a expresarse, a manifestarse e inconformarse frente a las autoridades, lo que anteriormente se hacía en exceso. Los universitarios pasaron de ser radicalmente críticos a ser extremadamente pasivos. Desaparecieron las organizaciones estudiantiles, los partidos de izquierda, el activismo político dentro de la universidad e incluso las actividades estudiantiles colectivas con fines sociales y culturales.

Para inicios del nuevo siglo el tránsito a la despolitización estudiantil y la pasividad de las viejas generaciones de profesores y empleados administrativos encontró una nueva versión de la Universidad-Partido con el arribo de un nuevo rector: Héctor Melesio Cuén Ojeda, quien antes de serlo había sido un funcionario universitario de tercer nivel; no había sido un académico destacado ni administrador de alto nivel; sin embargo, el sistema de elección de rector de la universidad a través del voto de todos los integrantes de la institución le permitió, mediante una intensa campaña, donde abundó el dinero que permitió tener compradores de votos, ganar la elección y convertirse en rector de la UAS en 2005.

Cuén Ojeda, de profesión químico, muy rápidamente empezó a construir mecanismos de control absoluto y personal sobre la universidad. El Congreso del Estado modificó, a propuesta de Cuén Ojeda y de acuerdo con el Gobernador Jesús Aguilar Padilla (PRI), la Ley Orgánica de la Universidad el 27 de julio de 2006 con la que se elegían autoridades mediante el voto de toda la comunidad universitaria, donde quien obtuviera el respaldo estudiantil ganaba automáticamente la elección. Ese mecanismo, propio para una república pero no para una universidad, era absurdo porque politizaba y desestabilizaba permanentemente a la universidad por más radicalmente democrático que pareciera; sin embargo, el que proponía Cuén Ojeda era totalmente lo opuesto: una mecanismo en el que incondicionales de él escogerían a rectores y directores de entonces en adelante. El objetivo era convertir a la universidad en un instrumento político no tan solo para controlar y usufructuar a la universidad sino para llegar a gobernar a Sinaloa.

Pocos fuimos los que nos dimos cuenta de lo que se proponía el nuevo grupo que hegemonizaba la UAS y menos los que señalamos públicamente este peligro.

## Emerge el *caciquismo* en la UAS

En 2006, cuando se eligieron a los integrantes de la Comisión Académica para seleccionar a los candidatos a autoridades universitarias, señalé, a través de mi columna en el diario *Noroeste*, que con ese paso se aseguraba que todos los directores fueran incondicionales de Cuén Ojeda. La respuesta de este personaje fue furibunda; él mismo y varios periodistas a su servicio quisieron descalificarme como académico, como columnista y como persona. El artículo que más molestó a Cuén Ojeda fue uno que intitulé "¿La UAS soy yo?," en obvia referencia al rey absolutista Luis XIV, a quien en Francia se le atribuye la frase "El Estado soy yo."

Señalar el creciente autoritarismo y el uso patrimonialista de la UAS por parte de Héctor Melesio Cuén Ojeda y su familia provocó que empezaran a vigilar mis actividades y a presionar a profesores y estudiantes de la universidad para que no apoyaran mis opiniones.

Una muestra del uso patrimonialista de la UAS se reflejó en un enriquecimiento inexplicable de Cuén Ojeda y su familia, tal y como lo demostraron los medios periodísticos de Sinaloa:

A partir de la documentación proporcionada por el **Registro Público de la Propiedad** y el **Registro Público de Comercio**, se da cuenta de cómo del 2009 en adelante se registra un ascenso considerable en inversiones de bienes raíces y la creación de empresas, donde tanto el ex rector y su esposa, así como todos sus hijos y una nuera son propietarios y accionistas de diversos negocios.

Si bien Cuén Ojeda registró su primera empresa desde 1983, el 89 por ciento de su riqueza en bienes patrimoniales llegó posteriormente con erogaciones a su nombre, de su esposa y de sus hijas **Angélica y Mónica Cuén Díaz**, además de **Melesio hijo** y la esposa de éste, **Belinda Portugal Domínguez**.

Por su parte, Héctor Melesio Cuén Ojeda hijo suma a la fecha por lo menos seis empresas, las primeras dos creadas en 2008 cuando contaba con 24 años de edad:
- **Soluciones Inteligentes Publicitarias** y
- **MC Multimedios**.
- Le continúan **HB Operaciones** en 2011,

- **Inmobiliaria Luis XV** en el 2015 y dos más en 2017:
- **Administradora Tres Ríos** y
- **Wenchos**.

Belinda Portugal y una de sus hermanas, mientras tanto, emprendieron para crear una empresa de regalos del nombre **Kolach**, que a su vez se ubica en el mismo domicilio con el que fue dada de alta la empresa **HB Operaciones**.

De entre todas estas empresas familiares destacan dos—**HB Operaciones e Inmobiliaria Luis XV**—ya que a través de ellas es cómo se ha propiciado la adquisición de casas y terrenos. De acuerdo a la consulta del Registro Público de la Propiedad, visiblemente, la familia Cuén es propietaria de 30 propiedades entre las que destacan casas, departamentos, terrenos, locales comerciales, donaciones y fideicomisos.

Con respecto a **Inmobiliaria Luis XV** cabe destacar que su domicilio legal fue registrado sobre la calle Francisco Labastida Ochoa 1675, en el Desarrollo Urbano Tres Ríos que actualmente opera desde una sucursal, donde se encuentra el restaurante **Casa María, también de la familia Cuén**, en la esquina de las calles Benito Juárez y Ramón Corona.

De acuerdo con **Noroeste/InnDaga** Héctor Melesio Cuen Ojeda y su familia han invertido poco más de 64 millones de pesos entre todas estas propiedades, 47 por ciento de ellos comprados con cheque.[18]

Este reportaje confirmaba lo que a voces se decía en los corredores de la universidad; sin embargo, cuando esta información fue llevada a las autoridades del gobierno estatal fue desechada como una muestra de enriquecimiento inexplicable y corrupción. La respuesta oficial era la esperada porque el Gobernador Aguilar Padilla apoyaba a Cuén Ojeda.

Aunado a un crecimiento exponencial de su riqueza, a partir de que asumió la rectoría de la UAS, Cuén Ojeda, al dejar su cargo, porque el periodo de rector era tan solo de cuatro años sin posibilidad de reelección, empezó a construir una agrupación política prepartidaria que llamó "Cuenta Conmigo." Cuando esta se crea en 2009, en mi columna periodística denuncié como casi la totalidad de sus miembros estaba constituida por una gran mayoría de funcionarios, profesores, empleados administrativos y estudiantes de la universidad. Pero, además, yo decía que el nombre de la asociación política reflejaba la megalomanía de su líder, porque utilizaba su apellido para identificarla con él.

Cuén Ojeda había dejado de ser rector, pero seguía siendo su poder máximo, único y absoluto. Había impuesto a su sucesor y con la UAS convertida nuevamente en partido, mediante su asociación civil llamada "Cuenta Conmigo" y aliada al PRI ganó en 2011 la presidencia municipal de Culiacán, la capital de Sinaloa. Esto lo critiqué en mi columna y la respuesta de cacique de la universidad adquirió un tono sin precedentes en la historia de la universidad que mereció la reacción de cuatro ex rectores de la UAS, publicada en el periódico *Noroeste* el 29 de diciembre de 2011:

> Preocupados por la seguridad e integridad física del distinguido universitario, Doctor Arturo Santamaría Gómez y de su familia, por las graves amenaza proferidas en su contra en un desplegado anónimo aparecido el 9 de diciembre en un diario de Culiacán, así como por otros medios, los abajo firmantes, ex rectores de la Universidad Autónoma de Sinaloa, manifestamos nuestra comprometida solidaridad con el doctor Santamaría, a la vez que deploramos toda acción o intento de limitar el derecho de cualquier ciudadano a la crítica y libertad de expresión.
>
> En nuestros periodos rectorales, sin renunciar a su actitud crítica, el doctor Santamaría demostró siempre su disposición altamente calificada para contribuir al desarrollo académico, progresista y autónomo de la máxima casa de estudios de Sinaloa.
>
> Consideramos que las expresiones de corte fascista, vertidas en su contra en el desplegado firmado por un supuesto "grupos de universitarios," constituye un atentado en contra de la universidad y sus tradiciones liberales y democráticas, y advierten el clima ominoso y de intolerancia que sufre la Universidad Autónoma de Sinaloa, todo lo cual la opinión pública sinaloense y del país no pueden pasar por alto.
>
> Al doctor Santamaría le reiteramos nuestro apoyo solidario y llamamos a los universitarios y a la opinión pública sinaloense y del país a condenar este hecho, y a que estén alertas ante el asedio y la amenaza de que es objeto quien ha sabido ejercer con responsabilidad y valor cívico el derecho a la crítica.[19]

A lo anterior, uno de ellos, el ex Rector Jorge Medina Viedas, declaró en entrevista a Noroeste, el 9 de noviembre de 2011:

> La agresión contra el columnista y catedrático universitario Arturo Santamaría Gómez, a quien se le llamó "sicario del periodismo" en un desple-

gado anónimo, no tiene precedente dentro de la UAS, expresó el ex rector Jorge Medina Viedas.

"Decidimos hacer esto por un deber de solidaridad con quien es objeto de una agresión que no tiene precedente en la historia de la vida universitaria, salvo en aquellos años 66, 65, que había algunos volantes anónimos, pero inocuos para esto," señaló.

"Que alguien sea capaz de ir a un periódico a entregar un documento, por unos conceptos que a mi modo de ver tienen rasgos fascistas, no podíamos quedarnos callados como ex rectores, porque Santamaría es un académico de prestigio, una gente muy respetable, y sobre todo porque es un ciudadano, y no podemos permitir que se dé un precedente de esa naturaleza en Sinaloa, porque entonces ya nadie va a poder hablar, sería la instalación de una etapa de autoritarismo y de intolerancia, que no podemos permitir."

Quien firmó un escrito publicado ayer en este medio, en apoyo al articulista y ex defensor de lector de *Noroeste*, junto con los ex rectores Audómar Ahumada Quintero, Rubén Rocha Moya y David Moreno Lizárraga, consideró que el ataque, al igual que otros dirigidos contra universitarios como Teresa Guerra Ochoa, Ana Luz Ruelas y Marco Antonio Medrano, tiene la "huella digital" del Alcalde de Culiacán, Héctor Melesio Cuén Ojeda.

"El origen de la autoría es la misma, tiene las mismas huellas digitales del Alcalde de Culiacán, Héctor Cuén, el ex Rector de la Universidad, el mismo que quiere imponer una ley de hierro sobre la Universidad, y lo que hizo con Arturo Santamaría, es lo que se intentó hacer con Ana Luz, Tere, justamente con la idea de acallar otras voces."

Añadió que Cuén Ojeda, quien señaló que el desplegado contra Santamaría "lo pone de cuerpo entero," ejerce en la UAS un régimen de terror, autoritarismo, y donde el rector Víctor Antonio Corrales no "juega ningún papel."

"Sus declaraciones a él lo pintan de cuerpo entero como un cacique, eso es él, eso lo pinta a él exactamente como es, como una persona intolerante . . . él es como un pequeño Napoleón, la autonomía soy yo," diría; es como una especie de pequeño reyecito: "la Universidad c'est moi."[20]

En efecto, Cuén Ojeda había ordenado a sus subordinados que publicaran una implícita amenaza de muerte contra mi persona porque me consideraban "un sicario de la pluma" debido a mis constantes críticas a él por la manipulación política que ejercía sobre la UAS, y porque, debido a lo mismo, decía Cuén Ojeda, yo contribuía a crear una atmósfera de violencia de la que podía caer víctima. Para colmo de la cobardía, el documento publicado a media plana por el diario *EL Debate* era anónimo y, por lo tanto, ilegal.

Al yo denunciar la ilegalidad de ese texto por no estar firmado, pocos días después, un profesor de la UAS en Mazatlán, Miguel Ángel Díaz Quintero, quien por cierto había sido alumno mío en 1982, se adjudicó su redacción—lo cual no era cierto porque el libelo fue escrito y publicado en Culiacán. En recompensa a sus servicios, Cuén Ojeda lo convirtió en 2014 en vicerrector de la UAS–Zona Sur de Sinaloa. Después de que Díaz Quintero se responsabilizó del libelo, en una entrevista que le hizo la reportera Roxana Vivanco al ex rector (*Noroeste*, 23 de diciembre,-2011), Cuén Ojeda decía que mis opiniones sobre él eran ofensivas y por tal motivo era correcto que me llamaran "sicario."[21] "Ustedes han visto en los últimos tiempos en la prensa," les decía Cuén Ojeda a los reporteros, que "algunas gentes que inclusive les dicen sicarios, porque no únicamente se mata físicamente sino que también se puede matar mediáticamente, destruir vidas, destruir familias . . . Creo que si ustedes revisan los escritos de él [Santamaría], muchas veces son ofensivos en torno a mi persona. Muchas veces me pone como una persona autoritaria,ególatra, y ustedes, los que están aquí me conocen, y saben que yo no soy así."

Ocho días después, el 31 de diciembre de ese mismo año, ocho directores y profesores de los cuatro campus de la UAS en el estado, incluyendo al director de mi propia Facultad de Ciencias Sociales en Mazatlán, en otro desplegado publicado nuevamente en el periódico *El Debate*, salían en apoyo a Cuén Ojeda, diciendo que ellos eran los autores del documento de marras—lo que no era cierto—y reivindicaban plenamente el calificativo de "sicario" hacia mi persona.[22] Sin embargo, lo más relevante de ese nuevo libelo es que trataban de desacreditar y refutar el documento que los cuatro ex rectores habían publicado en mi defensa y de la libertad de expresión al interior de la UAS, al recordar la vieja militancia política de tres de ellos, Medina, Ahumada y Rocha, en el Partido Comunista Mexicano (desparecido en 1981) y de David Moreno en la Corriente Socialista, otra agrupación de izquierda, así como por sus nuevos trabajos en gobiernos del PRI. ¿O es que creen que como ex rectores "firmantes"—escribieron los responsables de este nuevo libelo—los sinaloenses estamos ciegos ante las evidencias de sus nexos con aquellos que en el pasado fueron enemigos de la UAS?

No dejaba de sorprender que, al menos dos de esos profesores, Díaz Quintero y Jorge Figueroa Cansino, también habían sido militantes del PCM y del Movimiento Revolucionario del Pueblo, y también ambos miembros de Cuenta Conmigo, que se había aliado con el PRI y Nueva Alianza para que Cuén Ojeda ganara la presidencia municipal de Culiacán. Era absurdo que trataran de descalificar a tres ex rectores por haber sido miembros de los partidos de izquierda en los que ellos también habían participado y era absurdo porque tres ex rectores trabajaran ahora con gobiernos priistas, cuando su líder Cuén Ojeda había ganado la alcaldía de Culiacán de la mano del PRI, el partido que criticaban. En realidad, lo que buscaban con sus galimatías era escudar a toda costa a Cuén Ojeda y continuar con el dominio absoluto que ejercían sobre la universidad.

En este mismo contexto, Rubén Rocha Moya, quien fuera rector de la UAS (1993–97) y gobernador de Sinaloa (2021–27), escribió un artículo en el diario *El Debate* donde se refería la grave situación por la que transitaba la UAS bajo el dominio caciquil de Héctor Melesio Cuén Ojeda:

> Por mucho tiempo la UAS fue un ejemplo de democracia y de ejercicio de la crítica. Lo fue cuando el autoritarismo y la intolerancia (60 y 70s) sofocaban a la identidad, y los comicios de hecho eran una simulación, inequitativos y fraudulentos. Abundaban las impugnaciones y los conflictos.
>
> Por el contrario, en la UAS, de 1972 a 2005, ya fuera por elección indirecta, a través del Consejo Universitario, o por voto directo, ponderado o unitario de maestros, empleados y estudiantes, su sistema electoral jamás admitió fraude electoral alguno.
>
> De igual manera, desde 1966, y aún antes, en la UAS floreció el respeto a la legalidad universitaria, a la diversidad, a las diferencias, a la libre expresión de las ideas y a las opiniones críticas. Estos valores sobrevivieron incluso a la intolerancia de la ultraizquierda de principios de los setenta. Y prevalecieron hasta hace seis años. (Es decir, hasta el arribo de Melesio Cuén a la rectoría).
>
> Desde entonces se ha observado un proceso de involución. A las autoridades empezó a molestarles la libertad que, si algo significa, es poder decirles a los funcionarios lo que no desean oír.

Y procedieron contra los críticos con los recursos de la censura, la intimidación, la descalificación de las personas, hasta perseguirlas y aun expulsarlas. Criticar a los funcionarios es ahora equivalente a atacar a la universidad. "Yo soy la Universidad" (creen). Por eso, en el propio Consejo Universitario dejaron establecido una ominosa "ley mordaza" para sancionar a los críticos.

Las dos últimas administraciones universitarias (la de Melesio Cuén y Corrales Montaño, los dos principales líderes del PAS desde que se fundó en 2013), en su afán de controlar todo, con la sumisión y sumisión han usurpado el lugar de la inteligencia, de la crítica y la libertad.[23]

Un mes antes, el 10 de diciembre de 2011, en el diario *Noroeste*, la Dra. Teresa Guerra Ochoa, destacada académica de la UAS y también perseguida por Cuén Ojeda, escribió una carta al director del periódico donde comenta el libelo que escribieron contra mí:

> El Dr. Arturo Santamaría (publicó) el pasado 3 de diciembre en *Noroeste* una contundente crítica a la intromisión del ex Rector Héctor Melesio Cuén Ojeda en la UAS, y a la subordinación indebida hacia él de las instancias directivas de la institución, cuestionando el proceder del Rector Antonio Corrales y su declaración en el caso del sindicato de administrativos, ya que el Rector se niega a reconocer y respetar la decisión de un tribunal de amparo, escudándose en el argumento de la "autonomía (de la universidad) que burda y cotidianamente es vulnerada por el Alcalde de la capital" (Héctor Melesio Cuén Ojeda).
>
> Es lamentable que en la UAS vuelva a instaurarse la inquisición, que se persiga y despida a los disidentes de ex Rector Héctor Melesio Cuén Ojeda, que se vulnere el elemental derecho constitucional de la libre expresión de los universitarios. La única opinión que quieren es la alabanza, y sobre todo, buscan la subordinación al proyecto político del Alcalde de la capital.[24]

A esa carta siguieron varias más publicadas en el diario *Noroeste*, incluso de académicos de Europa y Sudamérica, así como de otras ciudades de México, que mostraban su sorpresa e indignación porque se acosara a un profesor por sus críticas al ex Rector ya convertido en alcalde de la capital del estado, pero que seguía controlando todos los hilos de la UAS.

El 23 de diciembre de 2011 acudí tanto a la Comisión estatal de Derechos Humanos como a la Procuraduría General de Justicia del Estado, con sitio en la ciudad de Culiacán, para demandar a Héctor Melesio Cuén Ojeda por amenazas de muerte. Ese mismo día, habían aparecido en *Noroeste* y otros medios las declaraciones de Cuén Ojeda, donde al mostrar su pleno acuerdo con lo dicho en el libelo del 9 de diciembre confirmaba que él era el autor intelectual de las amenazas. Así lo entendía también el presidente de la Comisión estatal de Derechos Humanos, Juan José Ríos Estavillo, cuando declaró que era "sería la declaración (hecha ante los medios sinaloenses y publicada ese mismo día) emitida esta semana por el Alcalde de Culiacán, en torno al caso de Arturo Santamaría," y agregó: "En un principio, como estamos encontrando y circunscribiendo una presunta, casi violación a los derechos humanos, de ahí la necesidad de establecer medidas cautelares para evitar que se sigan repitiendo."[25]

En una entrevista que me hizo el periodista Francisco Cuamea en diciembre de 2011, definí como "Despotismo Iletrado" el poder de Héctor Melesio Cuén Ojeda porque, en efecto, este personaje no tenía ningún antecedente académico relevante salvo el de haber impartido clases antes de ser funcionario administrativo de la universidad.[26] A mi juicio, la ausencia de formación intelectual de Cuén Ojeda influía decididamente en su visión despótica de la conducción universitaria y la política de gobierno, pero sin suda lo que más gravitaba en la concepción del poder que cultivaba era su formación familiar, donde su abuelo había sido cacique en Badiraguato. Cuén ha repetido en numerosas entrevistas que su ejemplo de vida ha sido el abuelo, quien, precisamente, ejercía un poder omnímodo en su pueblo, según nos narra el historiador Froylán Enciso en su libro *Nuestra Historia Narcótica* (2017):

> "¿Hay una sombra autoritaria que esté rondando por el país?," me preguntó Cuamea, y le respondí:
>
> "En esta atmósfera de violencia (que ha creado el crimen organizado) es fácil que emerjan entre los actores políticos o de poder en México esos instintos o tendencias autoritarias, porque hay quienes tienen inclinaciones por poderes absolutistas y les convienen atmósferas violentas porque a la población le da miedo y los ciudadanos se intimidan, de esta manera aquellos pueden imponer sus intereses más fácilmente."
>
> "¿Es cierto que la UAS está sumida en el silencio?"

"Así es, incluso ante los grandes temas sociales y económicos. A diferencia de lo que ve uno en otras universidades, como en la UNAM, que ha dado un ejemplo de sensibilidad social encabezada por el Rector, en la UAS vemos todo lo contrario, está ausente de ese tipo de discusiones y su comunidad permanece subordinada, agachada, con temor a opinar sobre los problemas de la universidad porque saben que los pueden despedir, que les pueden quitar horas de trabajo o los pueden castigar físicamente. Sí, hay un gran temor. Pocos se atreven a hablar, muy pocos, y los que lo hacemos, nos dicen que somos sicarios."[27]

Las demandas y denuncias que hice, así como las numerosas muestras de apoyo de periodistas y académicos sirvieron para contener las intimidaciones e implícitas amenazas de muerte por parte de Melesio Cuén, pero los infundios y descalificaciones contra mí persona de numerosos columnistas y comentaristas de Radio UAS al servicio del ex rector continuaron por mucho tiempo, por lo menos hasta 2023. A lo largo de casi veinte años han sido decenas de artículos los que periodistas a sueldo de Cuén Ojeda han escrito contra mí, pero lo inconcebible, y que a la vez confirma el uso de la UAS al servicio de este personaje, es que, aún yo jubilado de la universidad, las instancias de la institución se sigan utilizando para buscar desacreditarme académicamente cuando inventan evaluaciones estudiantiles de mi desempeño como profesor de materias que jamás impartí y, ¡el colmo!, en años en los que yo ya no impartía clases en la Facultad de Ciencias Sociales de la UAS.[28] La intención era devaluarme como profesor para que mis opiniones periodísticas sobre la injerencia del Partido Sinaloense—el partido de Cuén Ojeda—en la UAS, también fueran desacreditadas.

## El poder del narco y los límites críticos de la academia

El tema de la violencia y el poder del crimen organizado han sido crecientes en Sinaloa; no podía yo dejarlos de lado en mis opiniones periodísticas, en tres libros sobre el tema y en varios algunos artículos académicos. Nunca me imaginé que el tema del narcotráfico—aun sin mencionar nunca nombres de políticos a los que se les ha relacionado con líderes del crimen organizado, ni tampoco mencionar empresas específicas asociadas a los narcotraficantes—iban a generar alguna amenaza directa. En efecto, aunque fue una sola vez mediante una persona cercana a mi. Me hicieron llegar una advertencia de que ya no hablara del poder de los narcos en Sinaloa. Me enviaron el siguiente mensaje: "Ya bájale." Y, efecto, "le bajé." No era para menos.

No dejé de escribir en el periódico sobre el tema, pero lo empecé a hacerlo en términos más académicos y generales. Sin embargo, en cuatro libros de corte académico sí mencioné nombres y situaciones específicas sin que hubiese ningún problema. No hubo amenazas ni problemas de ningún tipo.

El primero fue un libro escrito entre tres colegas de la universidad— Pedro Brito Osuna, Luis Antonio Martínez Peña y yo mismo—donde recopilamos textos publicados anteriormente en periódicos y revistas. El título fue *Morir en Sinaloa: Violencia, narco y cultura* (Editorial UAS, 2009). El segundo fue un libro que coordiné y donde escribí la introducción de un libro que se llamó *Las jefas del narco: El ascenso de las mujeres en el crimen organizado* (Grijalbo–Random House–Mondadori, primera edición 2012, segunda edición 2013). En él escribían nueve alumnos míos partes de sus tesis de postgrado en ciencias sociales y también reportajes periodísticos. El tercero llevó el título de *De carnaval, reinas y narco: El terrible poder de la belleza* (2014), donde fui el único autor. El libro fue publicado nuevamente por Grijalbo–Random House–Mondadori en 2014. Uno más, "Culiacán ciudad, global del crimen organizado," se quedó en el tintero porque nunca fue publicado.

Los tres libros publicados tuvieron una buena acogida entre los lectores. El primero solo circuló en Sinaloa y el tiraje fue de tan solo quinientosejemplares. El segundo, debido a la novedad del tema y a que la editorial es muy importante, tuvo un tiraje en dos ediciones de aproximadamente quince ejemplares. El tercero tuvo menos suerte y se imprimieron alrededor de cinco mil libros.

No hubo ninguna intimidación ni amenazas por escribir sobre mujeres narcotraficantes, pero publicaciones financiadas por la organización política Cuenta Conmigo (posteriormente convertida en el Partido Sinaloense) intentando desacreditarme decían, por haber escrito esos libros, que yo tenía nexos con los narcotraficantes, cuando, según numerosos comentaristas políticos de Sinaloa y del resto del país, precisamente el PAS ha sido señalado de tener vínculos con el crimen organizado.

El texto "Culiacán ciudad, global del crimen organizado" era un texto estrictamente académico y por esa razón no fue aceptado por Random House. Su dictamen fue: "no es comercialmente atractivo." Esta respuesta me sirvió para ya no volver a investigar sobre el tema del narcotráfico. En esos años asesinaron al periodista sinaloense Javier Valdez, quien escribió varios libros—auténticos best sellers en México—sobre la violencia del crimen organizado. Esa tragedia terminó de convencerme de ya no abordar más el tema a profundidad y solo sigo hablando del tema en el periódico *Noroeste*, pero cuidando mucho mis palabras y sin utilizar la información que abunda en Sinaloa y el conjunto del país.

El poder del crimen organizado ha crecido tanto en México y más específicamente en Sinaloa, donde no hay prácticamente campo societario que ignore; destacando el impacto sobre el político y empresarial que decirlo con datos precisos es sumamente riesgoso.

Los límites de la libertad académica y del periodismo de análisis tienen claros límites en el México contemporáneo; no los establece el gobierno sino el crimen organizado, una especie de poder paralelo al del estado.

Termino reproduciendo un artículo periodístico publicado el 18 de febrero de 2023 en el periódico *Noroeste*.[29]

## ¿Si México es un narco estado, desde cuándo?

Pueden detener a decenas de capos, de hecho, se han detenido a decenas de ellos desde hace por lo menos cuatro décadas, pero el estado mexicano no ha podido acabar ni siquiera disminuir al narco. Al contrario, sus organizaciones son cada vez más poderosas no tan solo en nuestro propio territorio sino en muchos otros países; en el caso del Cártel de Sinaloa en alrededor de ochenta espacios nacionales.

Es evidente que el gobierno de la Cuarta Transformación, como le gusta llamar López Obrador a su administración, ha fracasado en su combate, al igual que todos los sexenios presidenciales de 1975 en adelante, si es que tomamos como fecha de referencia de inicio a la Operación Cóndor lanzada en Sinaloa entre 1975 y 1976. Esto quiere decir que, si nueve gobiernos han fallado en sus estrategias contra el narco, es evidente que hay una derrota prolongada del estado ante el crimen organizado.

Lo más grave es que ese fracaso prolongado en gran medida se debe a que el narco ha penetrado profundamente a zonas estratégicas del estado y corrompido a muchos de sus cuerpos de seguridad, y a hombres y mujeres claves de sus aparatos. De otra manera no se explicaría la expansión geométrica del crimen organizado y la constante pregunta de ¿México es un narco estado?

A su vez, un narco estado, si es que lo hay, no es viable sin que sectores y espacios importantes de la empresa legal y otros campos de la sociedad, incluyendo partidos políticos, hayan sido fuertemente penetrados por las organizaciones criminales. Si el estado es débil, o por lo menos incompetente ante el crimen organizado, lo es porque el conjunto de la sociedad política, que incluye gobierno y partidos políticos, la empresa y la sociedad civil, es decir la sociedad organizada sin fines de lucro, también son débiles ante las organizaciones del crimen. Un Estado no flota en el aire sino asido a su sociedad, o al menos a partes de ella.

Este comentario viene al caso porque con el juicio al ex secretario de seguridad del gobierno de Felipe Calderón, García Luna, numerosos comentaristas en los diarios y plataformas—sobre todo cuando el abogado del acusado le preguntó a "El Rey" Zambada si había entregado dinero a Gabriel Regino, subsecretario de Seguridad de López Obrador en 2013, siendo este Jefe de Gobierno de la Ciudad de México—reafirman su convencimiento de que AMLO ha tenido acuerdos con el Cártel de Sinaloa no ahora sino desde hace varios años y que, por lo tanto, la 4T encabeza un narco gobierno.

En efecto, AMLO dio muestras muy sospechosas, hasta la detención y encarcelamiento de Ovidio Guzmán y la también detención de Lupe Tapia, lugarteniente de El Mayo Zambada, de tener una especie de pacto con los narcotraficantes sinaloenses, pero si lo hubo ya no parece haberlo porque; además de hacer presos a dos capos estratégicos, ha habido constantes millonarios decomisos de fentanilo y metafentaminas, drogas que produce el Cártel de Sinaloa.

Periodistas muy leídos e influyentes como Carlos Marín, Fernández Menéndez, Héctor de Mauleón, Pablo Hiriart o Raymundo Rivapalacio, entre muchos otros, no titubean al sostener que López Obrador protege al Cártel de Sinaloa, pero a la vez ponen en duda de que Genaro García Luna y, por lo tanto, Felipe Calderón, lo hayan hecho. La balanza analítica de estos columnistas evidentemente se ve muy desequilibrada. Su óptica está marcadamente politizada e ideologizada porque investigaciones oficiales del gobierno de Estados Unidos sobre la penetración del narco en la administración de Calderón fueron reseñadas con amplitud por el periodista mexicano David Aponte en su libro *Los infiltrados: El narco dentro de los gobiernos* (2011). Escribe en el prólogo Héctor de Mauleón, uno de los más severos críticos de AMLO:

> La ["Operación Limpieza" de la DEA] mostró que los narcotraficantes tenían mando pleno en el interior de la Subsecretaría de Investigación Especializada en la Delincuencia organizada (SIEDO) y se habían introducido también en los principales circuitos directivos de la Secretaría de Seguridad Pública federal. Además de efectuar la compra de funcionarios de primer lugar (entre ellos, el subprocurador Noé Ramírez Mandujano y el director de la SIEDO, Miguel Colorado González), el narco mantenía bajo su dominio a comandantes y agentes integrados al círculo de trabajo del procurador general de la República, Eduardo Medina Mora.
>
> El crimen nombraba, removía, a los altos funcionarios policiacos. Dirigía trabajos de inteligencia cuyo fin estaba encaminado a lograr la captura de líderes y sicarios de cárteles rivales. . . . En los años iniciales de la guerra decretada en contra del narcotráfico por el gobierno de Felipe Calderón, los grandes triunfos de la SIEDO fueron en realidad victorias que el grupo de Sinaloa obtuvo sobre sus adversarios.[30]

Si esto mismo ha sucedido durante el gobierno de López Obrador, no pasará mucho tiempo para que se demuestre con pelos en la mano, pero sostenerlo, como lo hacen los periodistas mencionados, y al mismo tiempo defender velada o abiertamente a García Luna y a Calderón, no es nada profesional ni ético. En realidad, se toma partido abierto contra un gobierno al que desnudamente aborrecen.

Habrá que decir que, si en México hay un narco estado, lo es desde hace varios gobiernos y no tan solo con el de Andrés Manuel López Obrador. En realidad, ningún partido se salva de haber tenido amoríos con el crimen organizado. Tampoco son tan inmunes los poderosos. En el 25 de julio de 2024, Héctor Melesio Cuén Ojeda fue asesinado por desconocidos cuando se disponía a tomar posesión de su cargo como legislador federal plurinominal de Sinaloa. Curiosamente esto el mismo día que "El Mayo" Zambada y uno de los hijos de El Chapo eran detenidos en El Paso, Texas, por autoridades federales norteamericanas.[31]

CHAPTER 8

# Landing on Souls of Young Folks

## *The Deterritorialization of the Narcocorrido*

*What, for example, is a young boy to think, seeing adult members of his family riding the bus to work in the early morning and returning late every day, but earning barely enough to get by, living in a colonia with no electricity or perhaps no running water? Compare that to a narcotrafficker who speaks like they do and comes from a similar background, yet commands attention and respect, and can parade around in a motorcade of shiny black SUVs accompanied by bodyguards. It is a compelling fantasy.*

—MARK C. EDBERG, "NARCOCORRIDOS"

In the introduction, I referenced Michael Kearney's assertion in 1991 that in this late stage of global capitalism, "the unitedstatesian empire" is "experiencing a . . . dissolution in the spatial, and symbolic distinction between itself and its dependencies."[1] The sites of the purchase and expenditure of labor have become spatially separated as well, and thus there has been a national separation of the sites of production and reproduction. An "elastic" supply of labor is recruited and expelled—documented or not. Like any commodity of accumulation, elastic labor is underproduced or overproduced. It is elaborately rationalized by national and international "regulations" that make the violation of these regulations a cottage industry guaranteed by an imposed bifurcation termed the "border." Recently, Hector Amaya contributed greatly to this understanding of capitalism by articulating the "deterritorialization" of commodities (investigating, in particular, those of the narcocorridos).[2] As Mexicans would phrase it, "No tiene madre el capitalismo" (Capitalism has no mother). Of such stuff is made an aspect of the War of Omission.

This process of globalization accentuates the structural necessity of a global inclination to have no allegiance to place, territory, or persons.

Instead, people and things move from place to place, migrating to scrape value of commodities and labor. In his seminal review of the study of the border region, Robert R. Alvarez Jr. discusses the notion of migration states: "The global political-economic context has been a necessary complement to the study of local-level behavior. Migrants are engaged in a global capitalism that at one level obliterates the border distinction but that, at another level, is a mechanism of border control through the hegemonic state apparatus. Migrants, as labor, are enticed by and allowed into the U.S. labor markets, yet are regulated and controlled as commodities without a legitimate bilateral accommodation in the market."[3] This dynamic certainly guarantees inequality and touches almost everyone to one degree or other, and is driven by the enormous movements across borders for work, play, and trade. The border region is a space and place as well for winking at rules, bending them, having influence to make them work in one's favor, creating regulations to provide an edge, and, more than anything else, forging "connections" to shake the heights of the severe inequality between and among thousands of persons on both sides of the bifurcation.[4] As Alvarez asserts, given its hegemonic state apparatus, such practices are part of the contradictions created by the state's regulatory insistence but countered by the flexibility of human conduct in negotiating it.[5]

In the social and economic dynamics of the border region, drug trafficking is normalized, years' worth of contraband passes in both directions, and thousands of weapons are exported south and tons of drugs north. The impact of the narcotics plague on the Southwest North American Region has been treated by numerous Mexican and American sources. There is a wealth of Mexican sources on youth, especially in the Mexican state of Sinaloa, according to Héctor Gabriel Zazueta Beltrán, César Omar Sepúlveda Moreno, and Nora Teresa Millán López.[6] The more psychologically oriented clinical and educational literatures provide academic studies on drug addiction and cultural- and class-influenced factors on both sides of the border.[7] The Mexican literature also addresses the cultural production of the anthems of narcoculture—the hardnosed narcocorridos—and their purported influences on the southern region. Even though these songs are produced predominantly in California and Texas, little about them appears in the literature of the northern region. These anthems require a theoretical context for their emergence and transnational characteristics of what I call "American Mexican Triangle" narcocorridos.

Narcocorridos are a case study in how changing demographics, legal restrictions, and global media technology follow the same consumptive pattern as any other commodity. These transnational anthems are largely produced in the northern side of the Southwest North American Region and move from Mexico to especially California and elsewhere. Thus, the transnational global process of production extends to narcocorridos. Their mobility as commodities and narcocultural expressions is strongly embedded in the cultural production of the broader narcocultural complex. These musical forms are referred to as "expressive culture," that is, a cultural complex made up of many mediums of narration that emerge out of the historical realities of populations. These are often regarded as folklore, or the telling about events, people, and things from the ground up rather than from privileged status positions. Yet they may eventually become part of the professionalization process by others and eventually perhaps be used by wordsmiths as part of a market venture.[8] The narcocorridos are little different in this regard; Miguel A. Cabañas describes them as transnational phenomena linked to transnational migration and deterritorialization processes of origins.[9]

The consequences of the transnational global "American Mexican Triangle" narcocorrido emerge from the basic architectures of the songs' content and their exhibition and performance via multimedia platforms. In this chapter, I first provide a reading of the literature of a cognitive and behavioral sort that may appear to differ from the "Robin Hood" and localized rags-to-riches corrido narratives and performances. I then examine the content and configurations of the now globalized narcocorrido, generated mostly by North American producers, and the pedagogical formats intrinsic to their formulations. Finally, I explore what audiences are the narcocorrido's greatest consumers and identify what portents may be derived from such economic and social circumstances to those most susceptible to the narcocorrido's underlying architectural design.

## The Narcocorrido: From Abject Lesson to Narcogangsta Emergence

Narcocorridos are a version of the traditional Mexican corrido, made most notable in the late nineteenth century and during the Mexican Revolution. The traditional genre was created by local observers of the struggles against the dictator Porfirio Díaz and celebrated revolutionaries such as Pancho Villa, Emiliano Zapata, and the unconquerable "Soldaderas"—the revolutionary women soldiers such as Petra Herrera, for whom a corrido was composed for her participation in the battle of Torreón.[10] Over time, this heroic ballad form transformed to accentuate themes of lost loves and treacherous partners (mostly men if sung by women, and mostly women if sung by men), and of course immigration and migration themes by the 1960s and 1970s. These were the central nostalgic sort of corridos about battles, heroic men and women, and lost loves.

Corridos played on many radio stations early on both sides of the border in the Southwest North American Region, beginning in the twentieth century and continuing to this day. For the most part, they began as the specialties of radio transmitters broadcasting from Mexico and carried by stations on both sides. During the heyday of vinyl records, millions were sold throughout Latin America, the SWNAR, and in the Midwest, where sizeable Mexican-origin populations lived, such as in Chicago. Certainly, on Sundays in Tucson in my household in the late forties and fifties, the corridos, ballads, mariachi, huapangos, norteños, and "musica tropical" from Cuba and Puerto Rico were celebrated. We woke up to *corridistas* Pedro Infante, Lola Beltrán, or Jorge Negrete on Don Jacinto Orozco's morning show, put on loudly by my Sonorense father for all to arise to get ready for Sunday nine o'clock Mass at the Santa Cruz Church, a few miles north of south Tucson's Government Heights area. Afterward, we would take a short walk across Sixth Avenue to Le Cave's Bakery for their glazed doughnuts or go by car to La Panadería de Ronquillo for pan de huevo and a half-dozen "birotes" (French sourdough rolls). At that time, Mexican corridos were produced south of the border bifurcation, even though some of the first narcocorridos were recorded north. Other corrido-like songs such as the "Cuando" originated in New Mexico.[11]

The beginnings of the narcorrido arise in one form or another along the border. According to Juan Carlos Ramírez-Pimienta, the earliest, "El Pablote," was written by José Rosales and recorded on September 8, 1931, by the Brunswick Radio Corporation, a subsidiary of Warner Bros. Pictures in El Paso, Texas.[12] "El Pablote" is about Pablo Gonzalez, an important drug trafficker of Ciudad Juárez; however, Ramírez-Pimienta notes that the song does not mention the drug trade, nor is it an accolade per se. Instead, it is a narrative of Gonzalez's death in a bar gunfight at the hands of a police officer who shot him with no other choice, but primarily due to the moral and character failings of Gonzalez himself.[13]

This original narcocorrido and others that followed were specifically written and performed for what we now "regard as a kind of a hemp king with great influence."[14] Yet until the 1980s, the "heroic" narcocorridos for the most part condemned narcotrafficking and narcotraffickers as abject lessons to avoid, according to Ramírez-Pimienta.[15] From the 1980s onward, corrido audiences moved north via large-scale Mexican migration to the United States in response to large-scale economic global recessions. In addition, various state governments in Mexico implemented prohibitions against playing the music. Then the music became highly commoditized by the digital revolution involving YouTube and social media. From the 1980s to what I have termed the "American Mexican Triangle," narcocorridos became regarded as only a commercial product in the United States, extolling violence, highly objectified women's roles, and lavish expenditures through the transnational sale of drugs. This was quite different from the traditional nostalgic corridos. Protagonists became users and abusers who are especially featured in electronic media visual representations. Although some narcocorridos question the underlying values of violence, they are mostly inept attempts to regulate an expression of economic disparities and acute inequalities of late-stage capitalism and waste of physical and human ecologies.

California, especially, became the mecca of narcocorrido production and dissemination as well as the hub for many other Mexican groups and entertainers. In 2012, music journalist Omar Shamout reported that "in Los Angeles, *narcocorridos* can be heard daily on mainstream Spanish-language radio stations such as KBUE 94.3FM, one of the top 10 Spanish-language radio stations in the nation and averages over 30,000 listeners every 15 minutes."[16] In 2023, an advertisement for Prajin Music Group, based in Newport Beach, stated that they attracted 1.5 million views of their artists' videos, of which an important segment are the narcocorridos.[17] The narrators of this cultural expression became part of the transnational culturally "Mexican" market emanating from Newport Beach, one of the richest and most conservative Republican cities in California. This music would, ironically, constitute an "American narcocorrido" in Mexican guise.

Thus, I partly agree with Juan Carlos Ramírez-Pimienta that locality or place in Mexico is especially of great importance to the content, meaning, and themes of narcocorridos.[18] Yet highlighting the transnationality of narcocorridos known as *movimientos alterados* (altered movements), *alterados* (altered), *duros* (hard ones), or the American Mexican Triangle is the creation of the production company Twiins Culiacán, based in Los Angeles. Emiliano Villareal points out that this company was "branded as originating in Culiacán" by its founders, who further "applied this same type of branding to at least two of the bands they produce: 'Los Bukanas de Culiacán' and 'Los Buchones de Culiacán.'" The irony, as Villareal points out, is that both bands are based in Los Angeles and made up of U.S.-born Chicanos.[19]

These versions north of the border are transnational in character but extremely commoditized, exemplifying and simplifying their basic architecture to violence, objectification of women, and the American dream of assembling hoards of cash on hand. This is the American Mexican Triangle of values. On the other hand, there is no doubt that the triangle is shaped in part by an extreme Mexican macho position (*machista*) extolling the control, use, and discarding of women as a tool for buttressing an otherwise fragile male ego.[20] This attitude toward women is especially manifested by leaders of cartel organizations who have categories for women whom they control and "doll up" with plastic surgery, apartments, travel, and designer clothes. They differentiate these women from wives whom they term *catedrales* (cathedrals), and girlfriends called *capillas* (chapels) who are to be available according to whim.[21] Their wives are to be respected for their motherhood and the "capillas" to be treated as objects of convenience, use, abuse, and discard.[22] But at the other end of the spectrum of these imaginaries are the reality of the numerous killings of young women, especially in urban areas like Ciudad Juárez, Chihuahua, where femicide has plagued young women workers from the maquiladoras. Ciudad Juárez made Mexico an international reference point for gender-based violence in the 1990s, following the murder of more than 370 women and girls in the city.[23]

The movimiento alterado, or American Mexican narcocorrido, is culturally equivalent to commoditized gangsta rap and hip-hop. The latter genre unfolded as the consequence of commercialization and cultural hybridity of what originally emerged as localized cultural comments from African American youth expressing the smothering social realities of class and racial oppression. As Edberg notes, "Some early gangsta rap (e.g., Ice T, Public Enemy) combined political critique and the discourse of hardcore urban life, before the genre became dominated by artifice and exaggeration for marketing purposes."[24] Gangsta rap and narcocorridos emerge out of the same structural maladies of poverty, discrimination, and ethnocentrism. In South Los Angeles, South Phoenix, and South Chicago, Mexicans and Central Americans now occupy what were formerly all–African American neighborhoods. Listeners and performers of narcocorridos listen and play music next to equally economically disenfranchised African Americans—often in contexts in which life is always uphill and a deep struggle to excel and achieve when everything is stacked against them. Alterado narcocorridos and hardcore rap blend as transitional forms of overexpression in landscapes that usually omit their cultural presence—or, at best, denigrate their presence by ignoring their realities. These hybrid "altered" songs took off among Mexican Americans, especially after the death of Chalino Sánchez, the Long Beach–produced narcocorridista killed in Culiácan, Sinaloa, in 1992.[25] These "altered" works are buttressed by narco reggaeton played everywhere, from bars and dance halls to junior high and high school grounds and parks and recreation areas.

I would also term the latest version of the altered corridos as an American Mexican Triangle. Amaya insists: "North of the Rio Grande . . . narcocorridos are economic and ideological artifacts central to mainstream cultural industries and the Mexican American experience. Hugely popular among 35 [37.2 in 2021] million Latinas/os with Mexican roots, narcocorridos are cultural tools that nostalgically connect audiences back to Mexico."[26] While I largely agree with Amaya's assertion, I disagree with his final claim about the nostalgic connection. In reality, narcocorridos have little to with cultural nostalgia. Instead, they are produced by youngsters experimenting with music closer to their reality of being Mexicans and Americans.

## How to Think About Narcocorridos from Cognitive Perspectives

Violence and machista notions of impunity and aggressivity, in the trappings of a Mexicanized cultural vehicle, are central to the narcocorrido genre. Violence and its adherence to narcocitizenship define the triangular complex and dig into its historical American cultural gestalt, which has been traditionally used to create interventions, execute invasions of various sorts, subordinate women, and carry out the conquest of Mexicans and Native peoples and the forced enslavement of Africans.

The American Mexican Triangle of the narcocorrido is especially visible on YouTube. Performers of the genre such as Peso Pluma (the stage name of Hassan Emilio Kabande Laija, who has a Lebanese father and a Sinaloan mother, with family in Culiacán) and others extoll repressive, sexist, and violent values in their lyrics and accompanying music videos. To take one example, in the music video for "Delivery," by Peso Pluma and Alemán, Pluma appears surrounded by cakes of drugs and women in revealing attire with the prospect of violence around the corner. Yet in their success and popularity, these performers also model how some poor Mexican youth can become other than just an "other."

South of the border, in the context of Mexican narcocitizenship—expressed to an extreme in the brutal violence of American-trained Special Forces members of the cartels—the narcocorrido becomes a kind of youthful transborder anthem acquiring mythical standing and appreciation of a wishful fantasy for wealth, status, and power. It tells expansive and mythologized narratives while exposing kernels of truths about class, compressed self, identity, sexism, poverty, force and aggression, borders, migration, backbreaking labor, and capo heroes. Simultaneously, it undermines regulations, laws of convenience, authorities, and the privileges of the wealthy responsible for it all. And finally, these narratives support the entire ailing and fragile late-stage capitalism by their commoditization and allegiance owed to no one, no locality, and no group except themselves.

To different degrees, these transnational commoditized versions of narcocorridos promote new formats for murder, material gain without conscience, and the terrorization of opposition. The psychological or anthropological impacts of narcocorridos have to be understood within the larger public cultural complex of narcoculture. This includes not only musical representations but also social media, television and films, YouTube videos, and the clothing, ornamentations, material objects, and linguistic expressions projected daily by media, physical appearances, oral and written discourse, and commercial representations of myriad sorts. These expressions of narcoculture are configured with exaggerated posing and overdetermined figures and materials and accentuate the underlying materialistic and aggressively expressed violent stacks of marijuana and coke bags and piles of money. Some versions accentuate the physical forms of women aiming an M-16 back to the viewer, as depicted in a probably fan-made narcocorrido album cover with the title *Quien dijo que las mujeres no podían.*[27]

Providing insights on the operational side of these forms of the corridos, Helena Simonett divides their creation along two dimensions: those produced by transnational and national commercial enterprises and those developed privately as charter songs written on both sides of the border at the behest of those involved in the drug enterprise.[28] The latter are often written by Mexican Americans in California and Texas for a client who is entering the drug business and wants to create a reputation of note. Charter songs are frequently a private rendering, usually sung or played in private clubs, saloons, and bars on both sides of the border bifurcation.

A YouTube video focusing on one such writer in El Paso, Texas, begins with an interview with the composer, then progresses through some scenes of his experimenting with different lyrics.[29] When the songwriter completes the ballad, he goes to a meeting in a parking lot with the client, who arrives in a truck with tinted windows. After entering the truck, the composer gives the written text to the driver and requestor, who asks him to sing. Accompanied by two others, one in the front seat next to the driver and another in the back seat with the composer, he strums a guitar in the truck. After a number of refrains, those present begin to nod affirmatively and smile, and the driver accepts the song after the composer has stopped. He then hands over a wad of dollar bills, and, without counting it, the composer thanks the driver, stuffs the money in his pocket, exits the truck, gets into his own car with the cameraman and the interviewer, and happily drives off. The last scene shows the composer on a bicycle, pulling a stroller in which a little boy is seated. The boy looks up with big, brown, oval innocent eyes at his father, who sings and hums the song he composed. For one refrain, he prods his child to sing along with him while he rides away from the camera. It is a seemingly innocuous scene of a father humming to his child, happily content being serenaded in the bright of day. But the song is one of dark celebration of an armed machista, and a crass materialistic line of celebration of impunity, from which arises "hard" new formats and hybrids of narcocorridos.[30]

What impacts, if any, do these new narcocorridos have on youth? To answer this question, we will examine the research that accentuates the American Mexican Triangle. From Victor Horacio Esparza Bernal's review of research, several salient themes emerge that I perceive.[31] First, Esparza Bernal examines Lilian Paola Ovalle's work (my translation and paraphrasing). In a study of four hundred university students and youths in diverse public settings in Tijuana, one of the major fronts of the narcotics enterprise and its quotidian features, Ovalle asked participants to provide their categorical descriptions of the social representations of the narcotics enterprise.[32] In more than 90 percent of their responses, the students said that they regarded narcotics trafficking as risky, profitable, and affecting public safety, yet the study concluded that the sample regarded narcotic trafficking between indifference and satanization (the author's term), with an emphasis on its danger and profitability. When asked what narcotics trafficking meant to them, a third of the sample thought it illegal, another third considered it socially destructive, and the rest considered it a signal of wealth and power, with only 14 percent considering it violent and criminal.[33]

An analogous work cited by Esparza Bernal is research conducted by David Moreno Candil, César Burgos Dávila, and Jairo Valdez Batiz in Culiacán, Sinaloa, a central city influenced by the Sinaloa Cartel, and Apatzingán, Michoacán, also a city with a heavy cartel presence. Both cities are known for high incidences of violence, which strongly affect public health, education, public security, economy, and government. Moreno, Burgos, and Valdez asked study participants to complete a questionnaire on the objectification and valorization of narcotics trafficking.[34] They focused on two questions, the first on the cultural manifestations of the enterprise and the second on social ills. In Culiacán, 51 percent of the respondents regarded drug culture as ostentatious—specifically the narcocorridos, expressive expensive accessories, dress, and luxury cars.[35] On the other hand, in Michoacán, 60 percent of participants regarded narcotrafficking as a social ill. They focused on the assassinations, governmental corruption, insecurity, fear, violence, and people carrying guns, among other indicators. The researchers concluded that for Culiacán, narcotrafficking is an aspect of public culture that is heard, worn, purchased, and used, while in Michoacán it is the opposite, expressed as a rejection of such displays.[36]

Among the most salient studies to our current line of inquiry is one conducted by David Moreno Candil and Fátima Flores Palacios (my translation and paraphrasing), who sought to ascertain the acceptance or rejection of narcoculture, according to social distance scaling and level of contact with narcotraffickers within generational cohorts. The study had 228 participants divided into two age cohorts, one consisting of people less than thirty years of age and one consisting of those more than fifty years old.[37] The majority of the older cohort rejected contact with narcotraffickers, while less than 40 percent of the younger cohort did the same. Conversely, more than 60 percent of youth did not reject narcotraffickers, while 45 percent of the older cohort did not reject narcotraffickers. Moreno and Flores concluded that the youthful cohort significantly rejected less and less social distance than the older grouping and had significantly greater contact with narcotraffickers.[38]

Another study useful for ferreting out the possible influences of the complex narcoculture enterprise is one undertaken by Ariagor Manuel Almanza Avendaño et al. in the Mexican state of Tamaulipas, a northern border state abutting Texas and an important transit point to the United States from South America and Yucatán.[39] In addition to cartel conflicts, kidnappings, and murders, the state is particularly important as a place in which to gauge narco influence on youth. In their study, Almanza Avendaño et al. assess the way the enterprise is perceived socially and its level of acceptance, values, and perceptions by interviewing ten secondary school students between fourteen and fifteen years old.[40] For the most part, the students regarded trafficking as a drug enterprise made up of "bad" persons committing violence against communities. The young subjects used specific negative categories to describe those involved in the enterprise, such as drug mules, falcons, bad people, assassins, or capos. However, these youths also indicated that the central motive of those involved was not one of moral failing but instead a result of economic need and a lack of state interest in their well-being. These youths emphasized unfulfilled familial needs and the failure of state educational and labor institutions to remedy them as the primary rationale for engaging in narcotrafficking. Secondarily, they identified the quest for power, luxury items, and the need for social mobility as additional rationales.

Finally, this youth sample fully realized the potential dangers of death and high risk, especially from untrustworthy companions.[41] Therefore, it is not "narcoculture" per se that is the culprit but rather sheer poverty of opportunity as the causal value.

Almanza Avendaño et al.'s findings are supported by a subsequent study by Anel Hortensia Gómez San Luis and Almanza Avendaño.[42] The study's focus groups reinforce the crucial element of economic fulfillment as the central stimulus used by cartels to recruit youth as well as its acceptance among economically depressed families and especially their children. Such recruitment is sold by cartels as a small-risk enterprise. At the same time, respondents were fully cognizant of the risk involved if they were to be arrested by military or police forces, who usually use violence to find out their sources of drugs. They were also realistic in assessing that death was just around the corner, as one might be killed by authorities or cartel members for allegedly providing information or killed by the former for not doing so.[43]

But these works that Esparza Bernal reviews do not empirically address the psychocultural impact of narcoculture on youth. A few studies find that the effect of daily diets of narco film series and the "alterado" narocorridos is significant.[44] There is sufficient evidence that youngsters perceive drug trafficking as a possible way out from extreme poverty and as a shortcut to needed resources. There is also plenty of evidence that once engaged in the social densities of gang or group identities, these young people become members of highly ritualized, dense social networks glued to identifying markers like tattoos, clothing, behavioral cues, and language. However, as Vigil argues, to consider external influences on actual behaviors without understanding underlying emotional, social, and economic detriments is less than efficacious.[45]

Works on the southern side of the bifurcate border region provide more specific analysis of possible effects of a steady diet of both film and the "alterados" narcorrido—or the American Mexican Triangle, as I have termed it.[46] Héctor Gabriel Zazueta Beltrán, César Omar Sepúlveda Moreno, and Nora Teresa Millán López posit that viewing narco *novela* films or listening to narcocorridos by adolescents at their most formative life cycle affects them negatively but do not differentiate the types of narcocorridos as sources.[47] From this perspective, there is a tendency to editorialize while reviewing the literature as well as to draw up hypotheses that seem more like moral judgments than crafted empirical statements seeking discovery. Zazueta Beltrán, Sepúlveda Moreno, and Millán López generally consider that, like the narco novelas, the "alterados" are disseminated through different mediums like the internet. Focusing on youth's relationships with alterados, the authors argue that the alterados dictate violence, emphasize money as the supreme value, and devalue those who are poor—which, from the authors' point of view, should be debated by different but unstated scientific disciplines.[48] They posit that developing youths are often filled with self-esteem issues and insecurities about the present and future, since adolescence is the prime stage for emerging adult identities.

They also echo a premise from another work that Zazueta Beltrán coauthored, with José Carlos Pardini Moss, which states that such young people are pressured by materialistic culture of wants rather than needs gained by certain social groups.[49] In the process, they may lose interest in formal education, and instead their aspirations shift to developing criminal associations, supported by the argument that major credit is given to external personal appearances and possessions instead of the recognition and merit of educated and informed persons.[50]

With this understanding, Zazueta Beltrán, Sepúlveda Moreno, and Millán López identify a stratified sample of 983 secondary school students according to four variables in response to whether they (1) see narco series and would rather be wealthy than poor in spite of danger, (2) see narco series and consider it a primary mechanism to acquire wealth, (3) listen to alterado narcocorridos and would rather be wealthy than poor in spite of danger, (4) listen to alterado narcocorridos and consider it an achievement to be in narcotic activities to be wealthy. The researchers administered a questionnaire with eight items concerning the frequency of seeing and listening to narco series and narcocorridos as well as their perception of opportunities to overcome social barriers and achieve personal success among other variables.[51] The authors conclude from these results that the development of cultural hegemony around narcotrafficking values creates a dominant subculture that introduces a functional code into society itself that rationalizes values that are usually unacceptable. Furthermore, they conclude that both narco series and narcocorridos are created as the cutting edge of commercial links that have emerged on the internet that target juveniles and their principal consumers.[52] Thus, from the authors' point of view, it is incumbent upon institutions and families to organize a coordinated strategy that contributes to developing in children a major curiosity for experience, a tendency to experiment vicariously, and a desire to have major trust in their self-development.[53] It is questionable from my point of view that these recommendations follow their findings.

More importantly, these recommendations do not address the structural conditions responsible for the narcocorrido phenomenon and its draw of interest to youth in the first place, nor does it really address the need for rigorous research among those most vulnerable, like the young people in Tepito whose life courses are overtaken by violence and criminal gangs.[54] Zazueta Beltrán, Sepúlveda Moreno, and Millán López's sample, which would ideally represent the diversity of the youth population, is in fact made up mostly of students in an elite educational institution associated closely with a university and its supportive institutions. What is sorely missing in the sample is representation across class, locality, health, and advantages and disadvantages according to income, resources, material capital, health, and familial support. A more socio-economically diverse sample set could have provided a more revealing gauge of probable vulnerabilities, thereby allowing for interventions closer to young people's lived experiences rather than to a generalized "see and listen" and not "see and *not* listen" differentiation by avoiding the structural conditions that give rise to their interests in "altered" narcocorridos.

## The Chicano / Mexican American Scene and African American "Hard Rap" as an Analog

There has been no comparable study of this scale in the social sciences, nor with the same premises as that just presented, among Chicano / Mexican American youth populations who see narco films or listen to narcocorridos. Nor have empirical studies investigated the possible effect of narcocorridos and their subvariants like the "alterado" or "duro" types on adolescents. However, the literature on the possible impact of "hard" rap may stand as an analog, given the similarity between the structural conditions of African Americans and Chicanos / Mexican Americans. Where these conditions differ fundamentally is the crucial variable of historical enslavement of African Americans, which profoundly influences and shapes institutionalized racism against African Americans.

Since "hard" gangsta rap is a worldwide phenomenon, the literature on its possible impact is extensive, extending to many continents.[55] In a recent review of this literature, Pilar Fernandez Salgado states there does seem to be a causal link between rap music consumption and aggressive outcomes.[56] However, Salgado questions this connection, especially given the stage of adolescence that involves experimentation and exploration and not necessarily aggressivity but sensation seeking.

For the most part, the studies are several steps away theoretically and methodologically from what possible effects might ensue from steady consumption of any variant of the narcocorridos among vulnerable African American populations, and studies do not exist concerning Chicano / Mexican American vulnerable populations. However, useful to arriving at a kind of understanding is James Diego Vigil's and Vigil and S. C. Yun's category of the structural disadvantage of "multiple marginality" as central mechanisms for why young people seek gang membership.[57] Multiple marginality can be used as an underlying premise for analysis; and, by analogy between gang membership and narcocorridos, we can consider possible ramifications of the consumption of narcocorridos. This premise must be coupled analytically to our broader theoretical orientation of focusing on structural economic and ecological issues of late-stage global capitalism. Such a theoretical foundation then lends a more complete understanding of the effects of heavy diets of narcocorridos on young Chicanos/as, where narcocorridos are reinforcers and expressions of underlying structural contexts rather than causative.

Whether south or north of the border bifurcation, "multiple marginality" is a condition of structural inequality I would define by the following variables of disparity:

- underfunded educational institutions
- pedagogical cultural and linguistic erasure
- familial life beset with economic and ecological disparities
- informal labor participation of households
- lack of recreational areas and consistent spatial degradation of streets, parks, and neighborhoods
- poor health access and treatment
- dietary imbalances

- insecure economic support
- fractured household relations
- overpressured single-adult earners
- social familial vacuums created by deportations and incarcerations
- having multiple mouths to feed within a household

All these variables contribute to emotional and psychological distress on families and communities and certainly their adolescent members. These conditions have especially egregious effects on the developmental and cognitive health of youngsters, especially in their pre- and middle-teen period, even though families and youngsters in some of these contexts not only survive but excel. Which and how many of these conditions are necessary and sufficient to create the underlying structures of uncertainty and indeterminacy is an empirical and "distributional" question and not a certainty.

Following Erik H. Erikson, Vigil hypothesizes that the emergent period of adolescence is a "psychosocial moratorium," or a time of uncertain identities and contradictions in which a person seeks approval and emotional support daily.[58] Gang membership especially attracts those in this developmental stage who suffer under the conditions of structural inequality.[59] A machista approach smooths the insecurities and uncertainties for adolescent boys that surround their needs for emotional recognition. Gang integration provides the uncertain young men stuck in unrewarding economic and ecological circumstances some social stability and reduces their indeterminacy. (This was evident in the Tepito case as well in Mexico City, where few ritual markers operate.)

So, given such fragility of context and certain emotional and psychological ramifications, what can be deduced from empirically derived studies to ascertain the probable impact of the alterado or "duro" narcocorridos on adolescent Chicanos and Mexican Americans? Among the most qualitatively focused studies on the consumption of narcocorridos of Chicano youth is that of Cati V. de los Rios. This study is a valuable analysis of the translanguaging and transnational functions of youthful compositions expressing many of the discontents and creativities of a transborder economic and ecological reality. However, Rios's sample of four young musicians does not provide the range or discussion of possible impact on more randomly selected samples of vulnerable youth, and any findings would be pertinent only to this very limited sample and therefore questionable.[60]

While a great deal of the border literature on the narcocorrido considers it as a mediator between self and reality and as a kind of coping mechanism that forms the underlying architecture of youthful identity, most youth of the transborder region are not dependent on narcocorridos as musical guides for identity or as resistance mechanisms against economic and ecological oppression. We lack empirical literature that unpacks the demographics to consider and test whether in fact the more egregious American Mexican Triangle sort of music is influential or has any impact on this vulnerable population. As of now, the literature is scanty and at best possibly an indicator of real structural conditions. This does not obviate the most obvious: that most of the narcocorridos are part of the transborder commercial enterprise that uses all mediums to sell violence, sex, and conspicuous consumption—a not un-American value set.

Thus, the Wars of Commission and Omission have transnational anthems of observation and listening through multimedia sources and mechanisms of the quotidian realities of daily struggles. The latest versions of narcocorridos—which I have regarded as the American Mexican Triangle of violence, objectification of women, and consumptive accumulation of money and things—are transnational and commercialized, promulgated to sell self-absorbed narratives of late-stage global capitalism. They are the expressions of self-consumption focused on the most vulnerable developmentally to assuage their discontent in expressive ways. Like the opiates they represent, they also dull the expressive details of the realities of the drug traffic itself. In so doing they dull the underlying mode of human caring and sacrifice for the well-being of self and others, and with this dullness so too is dulled the need for human social exchange that is not coupled to exploitive extraction of some sort.

Thus, these anthems of and for the poor are the opiates of mostly poor youth on both sides of the bifurcation we call the border. Too often, these young people are interrupted by too-early deaths or lulled into sucked-out shapes of addiction by the array of old and new pills and needles by a ready market created to fill in the spaces of real social and economic equity, replaced by the sounds of guns, slow deaths, and the fracturing of souls. From such circumstances rise Wars of Omission that seep into Wars of Commission and advance necro/narco citizenships.

# Commentary and Conclusions

This work has no real conclusion but a disturbed commentary. The irreparable, incessantly engaged, global late-stage economic process of penetration makes drawing conclusions difficult. Among its handiworks are the worldwide drug markets, highly focused in the United States and unabated. Millions are engaged by Wars of Omission and Commission enabled by climatic implosion, world migrations, and extreme economic disparities, and labor and structural financial frailties abound; late-stage global capitalism and market penetrations are not subject to long-term abatements. In this discussion, I have sought to reveal the hidden dimensions of global capitalism and the quotidian dimensions of its creation of structural circumstances that are almost irresolvable.

Objects of interdiction such as the cartels splinter by intentional and unintentional violence into smaller segments that operate at reduced scales, only to bud anew and grow due to the insatiable market for drugs in the United States and the deep and continuing poverty in Mexico and throughout the Americas. These circumstances were made grievous in this historical twentieth- and twenty-first-century stage by the world pandemic, violent droughts and floods exacerbated by a warming climate, dislocations of millions of people, political upheavals regurgitating authoritarian regimes, and creating ecological fractures through mining technologies—all contributing to great demographic displacements of populations, especially from south to north, as well as civil oppression along the U.S. border region of mostly "othered" Mexican-origin populations, and of Indigenous populations such as the Tohono O'odham and Yaqui peoples.

Mexican-origin populations, especially, attempt to "unother" themselves by adhering to ideologies of sacrifice and death through ritualized participation in militarized processes and events categorized in this work as "necrocitizenship." This is especially manifested as overrepresented casualties in myriad wars as well as in remembrances and joining in associations and auxiliary memberships. At times, these are also reminders of the deepest of tragedies of the young interrupted before their time and of those who have never been able to come home. They are both remembrances and homages to ritually glue the complexities of dying to belong against the historical "othering" of the population.

These circumstances unfolded in the last years of the late twentieth century and became much more fully fleshed out in the early twenty-first, marking a "global historical conjuncture."[1] Both the original ethnographic details—my own in chapter 3, by Nayeli Burgueño A. in chapter 5, and the autoethnobiography by Arturo Santamaría Gómez in chapter 7—and the many ethnographic citations of Mexican-origin and Mexican populations cited in this work accentuate Eric R. Wolf's dictum that ethnography must reveal people's histories. Without these histories, they are ignored as nonexistent, especially by contemporary economic globalized processes and research approaches.[2] The distributional patterns of heterogeneous populations must be assessed to be able to concentrate analytically on the impact of the Wars of Commission and Omission, especially on youths, and to understand the edifices and technologies buttressing the wars. Any such understanding must include the enormous influence of "necrocitizenship" and its attending ritual, symbolic, and behavioral cues that guarantee an uncritical acceptance of "belonging and dying" in order to shed the imposition of otherness.

The Wars of Commission data and specificities underlying necrocitizenship reveal the structures and policies designed to implement interdiction strategies and tactics. These strategies include funding in the billions of dollars for robot dogs, walls, electronic surveillance and intelligence networks, military razor wire, thousands of personnel, and observational and military hardware, and their public cultural renditions in video games replaying the major themes of border walls as necessary protection for home and hearth. The United States' training investments and the equipment of the Mexican military radically changed its traditional role, from "gatekeeper" to low-intensity warring capacities, which has often gone awry via its impact on civilian deaths and interdictions.

Coupled and emergent in "narcocitizenship" are the many militarized cartels using the same "low-intensity warfare" approaches, personnel, and organizational strategies as parallel enterprises. Many are manned by former Mexican Special Forces members trained by the United States and Israel, trained veterans who then took over the organizations in which they were hired to serve as assassins. The actions of the cartels are accompanied by their dominance of civil, educational, and political institutions and capitalist enterprises, especially in the penetration of local, municipal, and state elections. The cartels possess seemingly unlimited access to federal, judicial, and military institutions and have created business models of "vertical integration" of suborned local gangs, politicians, military, and police. Entire regions, cities, neighborhoods, municipalities, and towns are subject to almost institutionalized cartel-controlled dictums and curfews. Blackmailed service-associated enterprises are often penetrated and over time controlled. Important agricultural products like avocados, natural resources of lumber, and trade goods may be subject to "transportation taxes," while thousands of liters of state-transported gasoline are siphoned off and sold in two-liter jugs on city streets.

Combined, these destructive practices have led to large displacements and dislocations of Mexican populations and migrations north, especially from the states of Michoacán, Guerrero, and Sinaloa. The casualty rates of both Mexico and the United States, and particularly of the Southwest North American Region, are in the hundreds of thousands—people killed and wounded in cartel and military conflicts as well as those who have been murdered and "disappeared." Compounding these casualties are the deaths of the young from overdoses of the usual cast of addictive drugs, now expanded by the flood of fentanyl and amphetamines that bring great wealth to cartels and misery to many families. During the 2022 fiscal year, the U.S. Drug Enforcement Administration confiscated 22,000 pounds of fentanyl, 175,000 pounds of methamphetamine, and more than 70,000 pounds of cocaine.[3] However, these amounts are probably overshadowed by what is not discovered and sold. Mexico will soon follow in the footsteps of the United States in becoming a site for the consumption, not just production and transportation, of drugs. In both regions it is mostly the young, especially those in poverty created by the Wars of Omission, who are particularly the objects of possible addiction and drug business recruitment. The Wars of Omission provide the impetus to subsequent generations becoming trapped in the syndrome of addiction, incarceration, treatment, release, and recidivism as well as early deaths.

But the impact of these wars on civic life, especially in Mexico, is visible in political and informational institutions like mayoralties at the most local level. Entire parts of cities and institutions are turned over to criminal associations and their political allies in government, education, banking, business, the military, courts, and police. This ceding of civic institutions, combined with the ongoing murders of writers, journalists, and judges and the suppression of academic analyses, all suck the life out of the body politic and all result in the impunity of leaders from democratic pressures and legal restraints. Thus, Santamaría's autoethnobiography narrates the attempt to fight against these conditions and the inherent dangers involved. This narrative itself had to be carefully crafted using publicly published sources to ensure the safety of its author; and in fact, Santamaría had to leave out some aspects considered too risky to be included. The outcomes for the social fabric of the society are those of quiet desperation, exceeded only by the silence of nonprotest. All members of society are therefore corrupted to some degree or another, so that narcocitizenship becomes the normative civic status, with or without permission or legal authority.

Often the best and the brightest are forced to flee to the north, where too often they must join the lowest rung of the economic ladder with a new label and load of "illegal" or "Mexican" to bear. Clarissa was exceptional because of circumstances. Yet, for the most part, many would rather choose the uncertainty of dislocation to provide better futures for their families and certainly for their children. Still, they are frequently forced to return to even worse circumstances by the incessant deportation chant of extremist policies promulgated by American policies and dictums. The result, as Burgueño shows, is the fracturing of families once more after their return, as they are forced to send their U.S.-born chil-

## COMMENTARY AND CONCLUSIONS

dren back to the United States to avoid their recruitment or kidnapping by drug associates, as well as rejected by Mexican schools for having been erased linguistically in American schools. In such circumstances, to avoid "fear obedience," they become uprooted from context to travel back to a situation of living in fear by once again becoming "illegal" culturally as an "other" despite citizenship.

Meanwhile, the young (but also the not-so-young) compose anthems to express contexts, influences, assumptions, feelings, and desires in the shorthand of narcocorridos. Narcocorridos tell of the ingredients of the "life" of the corrupt: the capos, the stashes, the murders, the molls, and the tragedies of dying before their time. Now produced primarily in California, these transnational anthems extoll the virtues of violence, the objectification of women, and the numbing of self by the promise of luxury—the American Mexican Triangle. These anthems of the necro/narco networks are but the full expression of self-consumption in this very late stage of species self-consumption. On both sides of the bifurcation, death becomes the raison d'être for living. But if new narcocorridos begin to take up the new policy of the "Chapitos"—the sons of El Chapo Guzmán—outlawing the manufacturing of fentanyl, such a self-imposed remedy may be a welcome change to authorities and a twist to the American market.[4] As well, like many other Mexican musical genres, even the narcocorridos are subject to being undermined by countercultural musical expression as promulgated by the "Reinas Chulas." Their Banda de las Recodas takes on the narcocorrido with "Lo Hecho en México" by using its format to create an unsparing critique of the genre and especially undermining its triangular architecture with a focused commentary of femicide and a sharp and unyielding critique of Mexican society.[5]

Finally, between climate destruction and an ever-poisoned atmosphere, the catastrophic aftermaths of ecological disasters, accompanied by quasi-wars, and the structural economic demise of aspects of global capitalism in various guises, including so-called socialist countries and regions, there does not seem to be either the willingness or the vision for real substantial mediations on the horizon. And for the political structures that guide policies of many sorts, greater and greater emphasis on authoritarian Trumpian narratives calling to invade the "other" side have entered the American political script anew. In the Mexican government, the López Obrador administration has advocated turning over public works to the military as the only recourse against probable corruption of already partially corrupt institutions. But the fact is that with the unyielding American drug market, no palliative can remedy this malady at this historical juncture.

So the dead continue to pile up; the addicted continue to swallow, snort, and needle their way to shortened lives; generations are left out and exploited while making even more skewed and tortured mirrors of themselves. Many flee, dislocated from their ancestral homes to join millions of others for surcease and relief for the lucky few, while the rest join maquiladora-like jobs on both sides of the bifurcation of the Southwest North American Region and beyond. Regardless of where they land, they quest for the same condition of security and determinacy as do all humans and for some even in death.

# NOTES

## Introduction

1. Carlos G. Vélez-Ibáñez, "Continuity and Contiguity of the Southwest North American Region: The Dynamics of a Common Political Ecology," in *The U.S. Mexico Transborder Region*, ed. Carlos G. Vélez-Ibañez and Josiah Heyman (Tucson: University of Arizona Press, 2017), 11–43.

2. For a fuller rendering of the impact of nineteenth-century industrialization of the SWNAR, see Vélez-Ibáñez, "Continuity and Contiguity." Also, for great historical human movements, see Julian Lim, *Porous Borders: Multiracial Migrations and the Law* (Chapel Hill: University of North Carolina Press, 2017); and Thomas E. Sheridan, *Arizona: A History* (Tucson: University of Arizona Press, 2013).

3. Paul Ashby, "How Canada and Mexico Have Become Part of the U.S. Policing Regime," NACLA, December 12, 2014, https://nacla.org/blog/2014/12/01/how-canada-and-mexico-have-become-part-us-policing-regime.

4. Michael Kearney, "Borders and Boundaries of State and Self at the End of Empire," *Journal of Historical Sociology* 4, no. 1 (March 1991): 52–74.

5. Kearney, "Borders and Boundaries," 57.

6. John D. Waghelstein, "Low-Intensity Conflict in the Post-Vietnam Period" (transcript of presentation at American Enterprise Institute, Washington, D.C., January 17, 1985), 1.

7. Asa Cristina Laurell, "Three Decades of Neoliberalism in Mexico: The Destruction of Society," *International Journal of Health Services* 45, no. 2 (2015): 247.

8. Laurell, "Three Decades," 250.

9. Laurell, "Three Decades," 250.

10. Laurell, "Three Decades," 250.

11. See especially Dawn McCarty, "The Impact of the North American Free Trade Agreement (NAFTA) on Rural Children and Families in Mexico: Transnational Policy and Practice Implications," *Journal of Public Child Welfare* 1, no. 4 (2007): 105–23.

12. Laurell, "Three Decades," 252.

13. Josiah Heyman, personal communication, 2024.

14. Carlos Illades and Teresa Santiago, *Estado de guerra: De la guerra sucia a la narcoguerra* (Mexico City: Ediciones Era, 2014); Guillermo Trejo and Sandra Ley, *Votes, Drugs, and Violence: The Political Logic of Criminal Wars in Mexico* (Cambridge: Cambridge University Press, 2020); Laurell, "Three Decades."

15. On media representation, see especially Leo R. Chavez, *The Latino Threat: Constructing Immigrants, Citizens, and the Nation* (Stanford: Stanford University Press, 2008).

16. See Howard Campbell and Josiah Heyman, "Slantwise: Beyond Domination and Resistance on the Border," *Journal of Contemporary Ethnography* 36, no. 1 (February 2007): 3–30; and Carlos G. Vélez-Ibáñez, *An Impossible Living in a Transborder World: Culture, Confianza, and Economy of Mexican-Origin Populations* (Tucson: University of Arizona Press, 2017), with the latter extending the former's more politically focused concept to the latter's more economic foci in which populations of diverse sorts avoid direct competition with powerful economic structures, nor do they struggle directly against them, but rather they create miniature versions such as rotating savings and credit associations to deal with scarcity of resources and investment opportunities.

17. Nina Glick-Schiller, "Explanatory Frameworks in Transnational Migration Studies: The Missing Multi-scalar Global Perspective," *Ethnic and Racial Studies* 38, no. 13 (2015): 2278.

18. Nayeli Burgueño, *Retorno a la comunidad: Migración y los fondos de identidad trasnacional* (Culiacán: Universidad Autónoma de Sinaloa, 2023).

19. Eric Wolf, *Europe and the People Without a History* (Berkeley: University of California Press, 1997), xxii–xxiii.

## Chapter 1

1. Glick-Schiller, "Explanatory Frameworks in Transnational Migration Studies," 2278. See also Alison Elizabeth Lee, "US-Mexico Border Militarization and Violence: Dispossession of Undocumented Laboring Classes from Puebla, Mexico," *Migraciones Internacionales* 9, no. 4 (September 2018): 216.

2. The United States-Mexico-Canada Agreement entered into force on July 1, 2020, as the USMCA, prompted and designed by the Donald Trump administration by holding tariffs on Mexico, especially as the instruments of aggressive agreement. Its basic tenets include:

- Creating a more level playing field for American workers, including improved rules of origin for automobiles, trucks, and other products, and disciplines on currency manipulation.

- Benefiting American farmers, ranchers, and agribusinesses by modernizing and strengthening food and agriculture trade in North America.
- Supporting a twenty-first-century economy through new protections for U.S. intellectual property, and ensuring opportunities for trade in U.S. services.
- New chapters covering digital trade, anticorruption, and good regulatory practices, as well as a chapter devoted to ensuring that small- and medium-sized enterprises benefit from the agreement.

"United States-Mexico-Canada Agreement," Office of the United States Trade Representative, Executive Office of the President, accessed June 9, 2022, https://ustr.gov/trade-agreements/free-trade-agreements/united-states-mexico-canada-agreement.

Thus, to qualify for preferential treatment, 75 percent of a car must be region-made, up from 62.5 percent under NAFTA, so that suppliers from Asia would be affected and replaced by parts originating in the United States or Canada, which would induce higher costs in wages. See "United States-Mexico-Canada Agreement (USMCA) Impacts on Sourcing and Production Investment Decisions," PWC, accessed November 18, 2022, https://www.pwc.com/us/en/services/consulting/cyber security-risk-regulatory/library/united-states-mexico-canada-agreement.html.

3. Özlem Onaran, *Wage Share, Globalization, and Crisis: The Case of the Manufacturing Industry in Korea, Mexico, and Turkey*, Working Paper 132, Political Economy Research Institute, University of Massachusetts, Amherst, March 2007, 38.

4. Chapter 3 provides the essential data and examples supporting this assertion.

5. Josiah Heyman, personal communication, 2024. See also Peter Andreas, *Border Games: The Politics of Policing the U.S.–Mexico Divide* (Ithaca, N.Y.: Cornell University Press, 1998); Josiah Heyman, "Constructing a Perfect Wall: Race, Class, and Citizenship in US-Mexico Border Policing," in *Migration in the Twenty-First Century*, ed. Pauline Gardiner Barber and Winnie Lem (New York: Routledge, 2012), 153–74.

6. See Juanita Sundberg, "The State of Exception and the Imperial Way of Life in the United States–Mexico Borderlands," *Environment and Planning D: Society and Space* 33, no. 2 (2015): 210.

7. The encomienda and repartimiento institutions were legal rationales. Although they are complex, the former may be summed up as a "labor and resource tribute from the 'Indios' in gold, in kind, or in labour and was required to protect them and instruct them in the Christian faith." *Encyclopaedia Britannica*, s.v. "Encomienda," accessed November 18, 2022, https://www.britannica.com/topic/encomienda. The latter was an earlier version termed "repartimiento," a system by which the crown allowed certain colonists to recruit Indigenous peoples for forced labor, especially for mining and agriculture. See *Encyclopaedia Britannica*, s.v. "Repartimiento," accessed November 18, 2022, https://www.britannica.com/topic/repartimiento. The other practices of vassalage and rights of discovery were part of the civil architecture that gave control over all land, peoples, and natural resources granted to colonizers by the crown or its agents, and, importantly, their right to use violence and force. The

Act of Possession (Requerimiento) was part of the "seeing man" repertoire, and it was a statement announced by the Spanish colonizing authorities and other European powers from the fifteenth to eighteenth centuries proclaiming complete control over an area of land for their sovereign. See Manuel P. Servín, "The Legal Basis for the Establishment of Spanish Colonial Sovereignty: The Act of Possession," *New Mexico Historical Review* 53, no. 4 (1978): 295.

8. Carlos G. Vélez-Ibáñez, *Hegemonies of Language and Their Discontents: The Southwest North American Region Since 1540* (Tucson: University of Arizona Press, 2017).

9. As has been stated elsewhere (Vélez-Ibáñez, *Hegemonies of Language*), discontent ranged from passive acquiescence to rebellion over the three-hundred-year span of attempted hegemony. Incessant discontent was expressed by many, ranging from not relating Indigenous "sins" to confessors in Spanish to taking up arms, such as in the Pueblo Revolt of 1689 and hundreds of uprisings throughout the Southwest North American Region against the colonial empire.

10. David Montejano, *Anglos and Mexicans in the Making of Texas, 1836–1986* (Austin: University of Texas Press, 1987); Marta Menchaca, *Recovering History, Constructing Race: The Indian, Black, and White Roots of Mexican Americans* (Austin: University of Texas Press, 2001).

11. For a discussion on this subject, see Joseph E. Park, "The History of Mexican Labor in Arizona During the Territorial Period" (master's thesis, University of Arizona, 1961). The Treaty of the Mesilla was the result of the Gadsden Purchase pursued by James Gadsden, the chief envoy for the United States and a South Carolinian railroad speculator, who threatened Mexican negotiators with American armed force if they did not agree to the $10 million purchase price of Mexican territory. During the negotiations, Gadsden laid down an ultimatum, stating, "It is now time to recognize that the Valley of Mesilla must belong to the United States [either] for a stipulated indemnity, or because we shall take it." See Park, "History of Mexican Labor," 27.

12. For an excellent discussion of this process of "elasticity" and its premises as well as its use for centuries, see Luis F. B. Plascencia and Gloria Cuadras, *Mexican Workers and the Making of Arizona* (Tucson: University of Arizona Press, 2018).

13. The Arizona State Legislature passed the "Support Our Law Enforcement and Safe Neighborhoods Act" (Arizona SB 1070) in 2010; Governor Jan Brewer signed the bill on April 23 the same year. According to BallotPedia, "The law created new state immigration-related crimes and broadened the authority of state and local law enforcement to enforce immigration laws." However, the U.S. Supreme Court struck down three bill provisions in 2012, while other opponents challenged the legislation by citing constitutional and civil rights violations. For more information, see "Arizona SB 1070," Immigration Policy, Ballotpedia, accessed January 3, 2023, https://ballot pedia.org/Arizona_SB_1070.

14. Leo R. Chavez, *Anchor Babies and the Challenge of Birthright Citizenship* (Stanford: Stanford University Press, 2017); Leo R. Chavez, *Covering Immigration: Popular Images and the Politics of the Nation* (Berkeley: University of California Press, 2001); Chavez, *Latino Threat*.

15. For some foundational works on state capture and the rise of transnational trafficking networks in general, see Luis Astorga, *Drogas sin fronteras* (Mexico City: Grijalbo Mondadori, S.A.-Junior, 2003); Luis Jorge Garay y Salamanca and Eduardo Salcedo-Albarán, eds., *Narcotráfico, corrupción y estados* (Mexico City: Penguin Random House Grupo Editorial México, 2012); John Bailey and Roy Godson, eds., *Organized Crime and Democratic Governability* (Pittsburgh: University of Pittsburgh Press, 2000); and Wil G. Pansters, ed., *Violence, Coercion, and State-Making in Twentieth-Century Mexico* (Stanford: Stanford University Press, 2012).

16. Petra Molnar, "Robo Dogs and Refugees: The Future of the Global Border Industrial Complex," *Border Chronicle*, February 17, 2022, https://www.theborder chronicle.com/p/robo-dogs-and-refugees-the-future; Catherine E. Shoichet, "Robot Dogs Could Patrol the U.S.-Mexico Border," CNN, February 9, 2022, https:// www.cnn.com/2022/02/19/us/robot-dogs-us-mexico-border-patrol-cec/index .html. There are myriad other technologies like infrared sensors, seismic sensors, pole-mounted cameras, unmanned aerial drones, hydrostatic blimps, and generator-powered klieg lights. Josiah Heyman offers exhaustive lists of bordering surveillance and interdiction technologies in "Who Is Watched? Racialization of Surveillance Technologies and Practices in the US-Mexico Borderlands," *Information & Culture* 57, no. 2 (May 2022): 123–49.

17. Department of Homeland Security, "Department of Homeland Security (DHS): Strategic Outlook for 2021–2022," GovWin, Washington, D.C., 2021, https://info .deltek.com/DHS-Strategic-Outlook-2021-2022-GovWin-Deltek.

18. "Border Patrol Agents," U.S.A. Facts, Homeland Security, accessed November 18, 2022, https://usafacts.org/data/topics/security-safety/crime-and-justice/home land-security/border-patrol-agents/.

19. "Veterans," U.S. Customs and Border Protection, accessed November 18, 2022, https://www.cbp.gov/careers/veterans.

## Chapter 2

1. Vélez-Ibáñez, *Hegemonies of Language*, 19–20.

2. See Otto Santa Ana, *Brown Tide Rising: Metaphors of Latinos in Contemporary American Public Discourse* (Austin: University of Texas Press, 2000).

3. Chavez, *Covering Immigration*.

4. Chavez, *Covering Immigration*; Chavez, *Latino Threat*; Chavez, *Anchor Babies*.

5. Achille Mbembe, *Necropolitics*, trans. Steve Corcoran (Durham, N.C.: Duke University Press, 2019), 78.

6. Mbembe, *Necropolitics*, 79.

7. Mbembe, *Necropolitics*, 79.

8. Miguel Díaz-Barriga and Margaret E. Dorsey, *Fencing in Democracy: Border Walls, Necrocitizenship, and the Security State* (Durham, N.C.: Duke University Press, 2020).

9. Office of Border Patrol, "Message from the Commissioner," in *National Border Patrol Strategy* (Washington, D.C.: U.S. Customs and Border Protection, 2004), n.p.

10. "CBP Snapshot" (based on Fiscal Year 2021 data), U.S. Customs and Border Protection, accessed November 15, 2023, https://www.cbp.gov/document/stats/cbp-snapshot.

11. Erin Duffin, "Enacted Border Patrol Program Budget in the United States from 1990–2020," Statista, accessed January 4, 2023, https://www.statista.com/statistics/455587/enacted-border-patrol-program-budget-in-the-us/#statisticContainer.

12. Thomas E. Sheridan and Randall H. McGuire, "Introduction: The Border and Its Bodies: The Embodiment of Risk Along the U.S. Mexico Line," in *The Border and Its Bodies: The Embodiment of Risk Along the U.S.-Mexico Line*, ed. Thomas E. Sheridan and Randall H. McGuire (Tucson: University of Arizona Press), 16–17.

13. Caitlin Dickerson, "A Rare Look Inside Trump's Immigration Crackdown Draws Legal Threats," *New York Times*, July 23, 2020.

14. Reece Jones, *Nobody Is Protected: How the Border Patrol Became the Most Dangerous Police Force in the United States* (Berkeley: Counterpoint, 2022). Jones cites the Police Executive Research Forum that was charged with reviewing Border Patrol use of deadly force policies and their use against unarmed Mexicans across the border between 2010 and 2012. There were twenty-nine cases of Border Patrol agents firing their weapons against people who allegedly threw rocks. In one case, it was found that the eighteen-year-old who was alleged to be playing basketball on church property could not have thrown a rock; additionally, agents were found to have fired their weapons at cars that were not a danger and to have deliberately stepped in front of vehicles to initiate confrontations. Jones, *Nobody Is Protected*, 175. In spite of repeated trials of agents in two cases, neither were found culpable, and in one civil case, the Supreme Court ruled that a killing of a Mexican in Mexico by an agent is not legally subject to American law. As well, *Nogales International* reported extensively on the trial of former USBP agent Lonnie Swartz, who shot and killed José Antonio Elena Rodríguez in 2012 after firing sixteen times at José Antonio through the border slats. See Kendal Blust, "Five Years Later, Still No Peace for Family of Slain Teen," *Nogales International*, October 12, 2017, https://www.nogalesinternational.com/news/five-years-later-still-no-peace-for-family-of-slain-teen/article_3fbbe8ae-af89-11e7-b509-db4a32183492.html.

15. Gustavo Solis and Matthew Bowler, "Officials Doing Little as More Migrants Drown in Imperial County Canal," KPBS, February 8, 2022, https://www.kpbs.org/news/local/2022/02/08/officials-doing-little-as-more-migrants-drown-in-imperial-county-canal.

16. See Christopher Woody, "Mexicans in the World's Most Violent City Are Taking Barbed Wire Right Off the Border Wall to Protect Their Own Homes," Business Insider, March 20, 2019, https://www.businessinsider.com/tijuana-residents-stealing-concertina-barbed-wire-on-border-for-homes-2019-3.

17. "Border Security Wall Construction Mod APK v1.3 [Unlocked]," 100APKDL, accessed January 5, 2023, https://www.100apkdl.com/border-security-wall-construction-mod/com.twotwentygames.home.security.wall.borderwall.construction.builder.simulator2/.

NOTES TO PAGES 34–40

18. Rachael Marchbanks, "The Borderline: Indigenous Communities on the International Frontier," *Journal of American Indian Tribal Education* 26, no. 3 (February 2015), https://tribalcollegejournal.org/borderline-indigenous-communities-international-frontier/. The Tohono O'odham have been especially affected by such separation due to wall construction and barriers, as indicated by the depth of their tribal affiliations on both sides of the border, as the map from Marchbanks indicates.

19. Nick Alexandrov, "Prevention Through Deterrence: The Strategy Shared by the El Paso Shooter and the U.S. Border Patrol," *Counter Punch*, August 16, 2019, https://www.counterpunch.org/2019/08/16/prevention-through-deterrence-the-strategy-shared-by-the-el-paso-shooter-and-the-u-s-border-patrol/.

20. U.S. General Accounting Office, *Illegal Immigration: Southwest Border Strategy Results Inconclusive; More Evaluation Needed*, Report to the Committee on the Judiciary, US Senate and the Committee on the Judiciary, House of Representatives (Washington, D.C.: Government Printing Office, 1997), 84.

21. "Pop-Up Installation Synopsis," Undocumented Migration Project, accessed November 10, 2022, https://www.undocumentedmigrationproject.org/installation.

22. James Verini, "Death in the Desert: How U.S. Policy Turned the Sonoran Desert into a Graveyard for Migrants," *New York Times Magazine*, August 23, 2020, 30.

23. Verini, "Death in the Desert." The actual narrative of how Roberto was found would be especially sensitive to his parents and loved ones and therefore I have amended that description.

24. Ieva Jusionyte, *Threshold: Emergency Responders on the U.S.-Mexico Border* (Berkeley: University of California Press, 2018), 9.

25. See discussion by Santamaría Gómez in chapter 7 of this work.

26. Howard Campbell, *Downtown Juarez: Underworlds of Violence and Abuse* (Austin: University of Texas Press, 2021), 158–72.

27. "Mexico Missing Students: Remains of Third Victim Identified," BBC News, June 16, 2021, https://www.bbc.com/news/world-latin-america-57498250.

28. BBC News, "Mexico Missing Students."

29. Recent fieldwork by the author in Culiacán is detailing a plethora of familial adaptations, including those mentioned, but central is the normalization of living in fear, avoiding possible sources of injury or death, careful monitoring of children, and dealing with the impunity of cartel members' behaviors.

30. Manuel Lazcano y Ochoa and Nery Córdova, *Una vida en la vida sinaloense* (Sinaloa: Universidad de Occidente, 1992), 203.

31. Héctor R. Olea, *Badiraguato: Visión Panorámica de su historia* (Mexico City: DIFOCUR-Ayuntamiento de Badiraguato, 1988). According to Evelyn Hu-DeHart,

> In 1893, after several false starts, Mexico and China signed a Treaty of Amity and Commerce which included a "most favored nation" clause. Since the United States had virtually terminated Chinese immigration by the Exclusion Act of 1882, Mexico became an attractive alternative. Actually, by the time the treaty was signed in 1893, Chinese colonies

were already established in several northern states: Baja California (then a Territory), Sinaloa, Chihuahua, Tamaulipas, Coahuila and Sonora. In 1890, Governor Ramón Corral of Sonora reported in a name-by-name census that of all foreign residents in his state 229 were Chinese, second only to the 337 North Americans and well ahead of the Germans, English and Spanish in the state. The total population for the state at that time was about 56,000. From that early date on, the Chinese in Sonora would rank as the first or second most populous foreign group.

Evelyn Hu-DeHart, "Immigrants to a Developing Society: The Chinese in Northern Mexico, 1875–1932," *Journal of Arizona History* 21 (Autumn 1980): 2.

32. See Lazcanoy Ochoa and Córdova, *Una vida en la vida sinaloense.*

33. Benjamin T. Smith, *The Dope: The Real History of the Mexican Drug Trade* (New York: W. W. Norton, 2021), 7.

34. Smith, *Dope*, 8.

35. There are contending points of view as to whether the American military initiated opium production through Camacho's office or if it was the Mafia–presidential office that created the connection for self-serving reasons or for the war effort. The Mafia may have been the intermediary connection to U.S. military authorities in Sinaloa. See Arturo Santamaria, *Las jefas del narco: El ascenso de las mujeres en el crimen organizado* (Mexico City: Random House Mondradon, 2012).

36. Antonio Hass, "Comentario," *Revista Siempre*, March 23, 1988.

37. See Arturo Santamaría Gómez, Luis Antonio Martínez Peña, and Pedro Brito Osuna, *Morir en Sinaloa: Violencia, narco y cultura* (Culiacán: Universidad de Sinaloa, 2012).

38. BBC News, "Mexico Arrests 30 Marines over Disappearances in Tamaulipas," April 13, 2021, https://www.bbc.com/news/world-latin-america-56524191.

39. Patrick Timmons, "Trump's Wall at Nixon's Border: How Richard Nixon's Operation Intercept Laid the Foundation for Decades of U.S.-Mexico Border Policy, Including Trump's Wall," *NACLA Report on the Americas* 49, no. 1 (2017): 15–24; Luis F. B. Plascencia, "Where Is 'the Border'? The Fourth Amendment, Boundary Enforcement and the Making of an Inherently Suspect Class," in *The U.S.-Mexico Transborder Region: Cultural Dynamics and Historical Interactions*, ed. Carlos G. Vélez-Ibáñez and Josiah Heyman (Tucson: University of Arizona Press, 2017), 244–80.

40. Arturo Lizárraga-Hernández, *Nos llevó la ventolera: El proceso de la emigración rural al extranjero en Sinaloa* (Culiacán: Universidad Autónoma de Sinaloa, 2004).

41. Nery Córdova Solís, "La narcocultura: Poder, realidad, iconografía y 'mito,'" *Cultura y representaciones sociales* 6, no. 12 (March 2012): 212.

42. Glen Van Herk, "Organized Crime Controls 35% of Mexico," *Yucatan Times*, March 23, 2021.

43. Gregory Midgette, Steven Davenport, Jonathan P. Caulkins, and Beau Kilmer, *What America's Users Spend on Illegal Drugs, 2006–2016* (Santa Monica: RAND Corporation, 2019).

NOTES TO PAGES 43–52

44. Jane Esberg, "More Than Cartels: Counting Mexico's Crime Rings," International Crisis Group, May 8, 2020, https://www.crisisgroup.org/latin-america-caribbean/mexico/more-cartels-counting-mexicos-crime-rings.

45. Congressional Research Service, *Mexico: Organized Crime and Drug Trafficking Organizations* (Washington, D.C.: Congressional Research Service [CRS], 2020), 2, https://crsreports.congress.gov.

46. See Eduardo Guerrero Gutiérrez's articles in *Nexos* and elsewhere for longitudinal data and analysis of violence in regions throughout Mexico. On the splintering of organized crime groups from the 1980s to 2015, see "Maps and Data," Mexico Violence Resource Project, accessed May 14, 2024, https://www.mexicocrimemaps.org/maps-and-data. See also Ricardo Ravelo, *Herencia Maldita: El reto de Calderón y el nuevo mapa del narcotráfio* (Mexico City: Grijalbo, 2007).

47. LaLiszt (@Liz_Baray), "me vale que critiquen por subir este video, pero así estan las cosas," Twitter, July 24, 2021, https://twitter.com/i/status/141910415583 1001093.

48. Ciro Gomez Leyva (@CiroGomezL), "Un grupo armado de al menos 20 camionetas entró a #Caborca, #Sonora, y tomaron la ciudad durante seis horas," Twitter, February 16, 2022, https://twitter.com/CiroGomezL/status/1494170301361532930.

49. Yuri Neves, "What's Behind the Killings of Mexico's Mayors?," InSight Crime, May 28, 2019, https://www.insightcrime.org/news/analysis/killings-of-mexico-mayors/.

50. U.S. General Accountability Office, "Firearms Trafficking: U.S. Efforts to Disrupt Gun Smuggling into Mexico: Would Benefit from Additional Data and Analysis," *GAO 100 Highlights*, February 2021, https://www.gao.gov/assets/d21322high.pdf.

51. BBC News, "Mexico Arrests 30 Marines over Disappearances in Tamaulipas."

52. Laura Gottesdiener, "Mexican Navy Offers Rare Apology over Missing People in Border Town," Reuters, July 13, 2021, https://www.reuters.com/world/americas/mexican-navy-offers-rare-apology-over-missing-people-border-town-2021-07-13/.

53. Michael Lettieri, "U.S. Military Training of Mexican Armed Forces and Law Enforcement," Mexico Violence Resource Project, 2022, https://www.mexicoviolence.org/military-training.

54. Juan Montes and David Luhnow, "Mexico's Leader Has Answer for All His Needs: The Army," *Washington Post*, May 28, 2020.

55. Mariano Sánchez-Talanquer and Kenneth F. Greene, "Is Mexico Falling into the Authoritarian Trap?," *Journal of Democracy* 32, no. 4 (2021): 68–69.

56. "Corruption Perceptions Index: Mexico," Transparency International, accessed January 3, 2023, https://www.transparency.org/en/cpi/2021/index/mex.

57. For a representation of violence of the drug war, see CNN Editorial Research, "Mexico Drug War Fast Fact," CNN, April 12, 2021, https://www.cnn.com/2013/09/02/world/americas/mexico-drug-war-fast-facts/index.html.

58. CNN Editorial Research, "Mexico Drug War."

59. Walter A. Ewing, "'Enemy Territory': Immigration Enforcement in the US-Mexico Borderlands," *Journal on Migration and Human Security* 2, no. 3 (2014): 198–99.

60. Teresa Mares, *Life on the Other Border: Farmworkers and Food Justice in Vermont* (Berkeley: University of California Press, 2020).

61. Maria L. Cruz-Torres, *Pink Gold: Women, Shrimp, and Work in Mexico* (Austin: University of Texas Press, 2023).

62. Jeremy Slack and Daniel E. Martínez, "Postremoval Geographies: Immigration Enforcement and Organized Crime on the U.S.-Mexico Border," *Annals of the American Association of Geographers* 111, no. 4 (2020): 1062–78.

## Chapter 3

1. Díaz-Barriga and Dorsey, *Fencing in Democracy*, 12.

2. Lauren Berlant, *The Queen of America Goes to Washington* (Durham, N.C.: Duke University Press 1997), 27.

3. A notable exception is the case of Felix Longoria, who was killed in World War II in Europe and denied burial by a funeral home in Three Rivers, Texas. He was interred four years after his death in Arlington National Cemetery through the intercession of then senator Lyndon B. Johnson, after heavy Mexican American protests, illustrating the power of the quest for legitimacy and death in one sequence of events. Iván Román, "When a Fallen Mexican American War Hero Was Denied a Wake, a Civil Rights Push Began," History, October 9, 2020, https://www.history.com/news/mexican-american-rights-longoria-lyndon-johnson-hector-garcia.

4. Wikipedia, s.v. "Naturalization Act of 1790," last modified December 16, 2023, 16:30, https://en.wikipedia.org/wiki/Naturalization_Act_of_1790; Andrew Glass, "U.S. Enacts First Immigration Law, March 26, 1790," Politico, March 26, 2012, https://www.politico.com/story/2012/03/the-united-states-enacts-first-immigration-law-074438.

5. Glass, "U.S. Enacts First Immigration Law."

6. Vélez-Ibáñez, *Hegemonies of Language*, 146–56.

7. Miguel Antonio Levario, *Militarizing the Border: When Mexicans Became the Enemy* (College Station: Texas A&M University Press, 2012).

8. Texas, prior to its incorporation as a slave state to the United States, was a poster child for colonization in the southern part of the United States from 1835 to 1880 and onward.

9. The Taos Revolt of 1847 was a Mexican-led uprising, which—although defeated by occupying American forces—resulted in the assassination of Charles Bent, appointed governor by military authorities. Twenty-eight rebels were hanged by a mostly kangaroo court with the foreman of the jury being George Bent, Charles's brother. For more information, see Mark Boardman, "The Assassination of Charles Bent," *True West*, January 30, 2020, https://truewestmagazine.com/article/the-assassination-of-charles-bent/. Furthermore, the famous Cortina Revolt of 1859 resulted in the use of Texas Rangers, U.S. Army troops, and Texas Irregulars to suppress Juan Cortina while destroying entire Mexican towns on both sides of the border having nothing to do with Cortina's revolt. See Doug J. Swanson, *Cult of Glory: The Bold and Brutal History of the Texas Rangers* (New York: Viking, 2020). The conquest

NOTES TO PAGES 62-65

of California by American troops was not an easy venture and a number of battles were fought against Californio volunteers, ending with the Cahuenga Treaty of 1846. Their resistance to invasion was appreciated by American authorities and a series of forts were installed to ensure the population was suppressed. See Patricia Campos Scheiner, "Californio Resistance to the U.S. Invasion of 1846" (master's thesis, California State University, East Bay, 2009).

10. Levario, *Militarizing the Border*, 2. Levario is drawing from Timothy J. Dunn, *The Militarization of the U.S.-Mexico Border, 1998–1972: Low-Intensity Conflict Doctrine Comes Home* (Austin: CMAS Books, 1996).

11. Drishti Pillai and Samantha Artiga, "Title 42 and Its Impact on Migrant Families," KFF, May 26, 2022, https://www.kff.org/racial-equity-and-health-policy/issue -brief/title-42-and-its-impact-on-migrant-families/.

12. ACLU, "Supreme Court Keeps Title 42 Policy in Place for Now," December 27, 2022, https://www.aclu.org/press-releases/supreme-court-keeps-title-42-policy -place-now.

13. It may be suggested that the initial military participation of Latinas/os is marked by the use of Mexican, Puerto Rican, and Cuban troops by Governor Bernardo de Galvez of Florida and the Spanish Imperial Army against the English Crown during the American Revolutionary War between 1777 and 1781. See Erick Trickey, "The Little-Remembered Ally Who Helped America Win the Revolution," *Smithsonian Magazine*, January 13, 2017, https://www.smithsonianmag.com/history/little -remembered-ally-who-helped-america-win-revolution-180961782/. However, this argument of inclusion stretches the fundamental relations between Mexican-origin and Puerto Rican populations and the U.S. military and the national state. This work departs from this assumption and concentrates solely on the relationship initiated between these populations and the U.S. military and the national society via conquest and invasions.

14. In the United States this war is referred to as the "Mexican-American War" or the "Mexican War," while in Mexico it is called the "American Intervention." See Griswold del Castillo, *The Treaty of Guadalupe Hidalgo* (Norman: University of Oklahoma Press, 1990), 4–6; and Ulysses S. Grant, *The Personal Memoirs of Ulysses S. Grant* (Old Saybrook: Konecky & Konecky, 1992), 37–38.

15. For a map representing white southern origins of most of east Texas and from whence progeny settled in the western half, I consulted the Texas Slavery Project, accessed 2019, http://www.texasslaveryproject.org/maps/hb/ (site discontinued).

16. A regiment of Mexican Texans commanded by Col. Juan Seguín fought on the side of Sam Houston. Seguín later fought against the invading Americans as an officer in the Mexican army.

17. John O'Donnell-Rosales, *Hispanic Confederates from the Gulf Coast States* (Baltimore: Clearfield, 2009).

18. F. Stanley, *The Civil War in New Mexico* (Santa Fe: Sunstone, 2011).

19. Loreta Janeta Velazquez, *The Woman in Battle: A Narrative of the Exploits, Adventures, and Travels of Madame Loreta Janeta Velazquez, Otherwise Known as*

*Lieutenant Harry T. Buford, Confederate States Army*, edited by C. J. Worthington (Richmond, Va.: Dustin, Gilman & Co., 1876).

20. Theodore Roosevelt, "Appendix A. Muster-Out Roll," in *The Rough Riders* (New York: P. F. Collier & Son, 1899), 233–81; "Puerto Ricans Become U.S. Citizens, Are Recruited for War Effort," History, November 16, 2009, https://www.history.com/this-day-in-history/puerto-ricans-become-u-s-citizens-are-recruited-for-war-effort.

21. The mythic version is supported by the following: History, "Puerto Ricans Become U.S. Citizens, Are Recruited for War Effort," History.com, https://www.history.com/this-day-in-history/puerto-ricans-become-u-s-citizens-are-recruited-for-war-effort. At the turn of the twentieth century, among the few Medal of Honor recipients during the Boxer Rebellion (1901) was France Silva of Hayward. See "France Silva," The Hall of Valor Project, accessed March 5, 2023, https://valor.militarytimes.com/hero/858. Its mythic opposite is supported by Harry Franqui-Rivera, "Mitología nacional: Ciudadanía norteamericana para la gente de Puerto Rico y Servicio Militar," *Memorias: Revista digital de Historia y Arqueología desde el Caribe colombiano*, accessed November 18, 2024.

22. Col. Gilberto Villahermosa, "America's Hispanics in America's Wars," *Army Magazine*, September 2002, https://www.valerosos.com/HispanicsMilitary.html.

23. Congressional Medal of Honor Society, "David B. Barclay," Stories of Sacrifice, accessed March 1, 2023, https://www.cmohs.org/recipients/david-b-barkeley.

24. Tony Santiago, "Major Oscar Francis Perdomo," *Aviation Online Magazine*, accessed March 5, 2023, http://www.avstop.com/history/hispanic_aviators/major_oscar_francis_perdomo.htm.

25. J. Luz Saenz, *Los mexico-americanos en la Gran Guerra: Y su contingente en pro de la democracia, la humanidad y la justicia* (San Antonio: Artes Gráficas, 1933).

26. American Battle Monuments Commission, "Jose C. Salazar," World War I Honor Roll, accessed March 1, 2023, https://www.abmc.gov/decedent-search/salazar%3Djose-0.

27. Mario T. García, *The Latino Generation: Voices of the New America* (Chapel Hill: University of North Carolina Press, 2018).

28. Brooke West, "Despite Anti-Hispanic Bias Staff Sergeant Led a Dozen Men," *Narratives: Stories of U.S. Latinos and Latinas in World War II* 4, no. 1 (Spring 2003): 31.

29. Carlos G. Vélez-Ibáñez, *Border Visions: Mexican Cultures of the Southwest United States* (Tucson: University of Arizona Press, 1996), 203; Office of Deputy Assistant Secretary of Defense for Equal Opportunity and Safety Policy, *Hispanics in America's Defense* (Washington, D.C.: Department of Defense), 71–90.

30. Personal interview with Antonio Alcaraz, Tucson, Arizona, 1973. The "repatriation" movement was a program of expulsion of Mexicans from the United States between 1930 and 1935 in which more than a million Mexicans were "expatriated," of which 150,000 were U.S.-born American citizens.

31. Yvonne Lim, "Boyhood Dream Led to Career as Fighter Ace," *Narratives: Stories of U.S. Latinos and Latinas in World War II* 4, no. 1 (Spring 2003): 72.

32. Elizabeth Egeland, "Marine Survived War by 'Grace of God,'" *Narratives: Stories of U.S. Latinos and Latinas in World War II* 4, no. 1 (Spring 2003): 23.

NOTES TO PAGES 68-69     235

33. "Statistics & FAQs," Congressional Medal of Honor Society, accessed 2023, https://www.cmohs.org/medal/faqs.

34. Vélez-Ibáñez, *Border Visions*, 119–21.

35. "Statistics & FAQs," Congressional Medal of Honor Society, accessed 2023, https://www.cmohs.org/medal/faqs.

36. Villahermosa, "America's Hispanics in America's Wars."

37. See Silvia Álvarez Curbelo, "The Color of War: Puerto Rican Soldiers and Discrimination During World War II," in *Beyond the Latino World War II Hero*, ed. Maggie Rivas-Rodriguez and Emilio Zamora (Austin: University of Texas Press), 110–124. This test is reminiscent of another method that was practiced in this period: the "brown paper bag" test conducted especially by African American sororities and fraternities in universities and other private "societies," in which candidates' skin color was compared to a brown paper bag. Those with skin tones lighter than the bag were admitted as members while those who were darker were rejected. See Audrey Elisa Kerr, *The Paper Bag Principle: Class, Complexion, and Community in Black Washington, D.C.* (Knoxville: University of Tennessee Press, 2006).

38. Pedro A. del Valle, *Semper Fidelis: An Autobiography* (Hawthorne: Christian Book Club of America, 1976).

39. Accolades include the Presidential Unit Citation, Guadalcanal, 1942, and Okinawa, 1945; Expeditionary Medal with Bronze Star, Haiti, 1916; Dominican Campaign Medal, Dominican Republic, 1916; Victory Medal, 1918; Second Nicaraguan Campaign Medal, Nicaragua, 1930; American Defense Service Medal; Asiatic-Pacific Campaign Medal with five Bronze Stars; American Campaign Medal; World War II Victory Medal; Order of the Crown of Italy, Italy, 1936; East African Medal, Ethiopia, 1936; Colonial Order of the Star of Italy, Ethiopia, 1936; Italian Bronze Medal for Military Valor, Ethiopia, 1936; Cuban Naval Order of Merit, Second Class, Cuba, 1936; Ecuadorian Decoration of Abdon Calderon Star, First Class, with Diploma, Ecuador, 1942. "Who's Who in Marine Corps History," Marine Corps University, accessed March 7, 2023, https://www.usmcu.edu/Research/Marine-Corps-History-Division/People/Whos-Who-in-Marine-Corps-History/.

40. Henry A. J. Ramos, *The American G.I. Forum: In Pursuit of the Dream, 1948–1983* (Houston: Arte Público Press, 1998), 2–3. Ramos writes, "Private Felix Longoria, a Mexican-American solider whose remains had been returned from overseas nearly four years after he was killed in action in the Philippines," was the case in point. The owner of the Rice Funeral Home in Three Rivers, Texas, explained to Longoria's widow that he would arrange for the soldier's burial in the town's segregated "Mexican" cemetery but would not, as requested, allow use of the chapel for the wake because local "whites" would not like it (9).

41. Peter Dimas, dir., *Los Veteranos of World War II* (Phoenix: Braun-Sacred Heart Center, 2007).

42. Guillermo X. Garcia, "War Gave Soldier Confidence to Strive for More," *Narratives: Stories of U.S. Latinos and Latinas in World War II* 3, no. 1 (Fall 2001): 15.

43. Kristin Stanford, "Sixth Brother in Uniform," *Narratives: Stories of U.S. Latinos and Latinas in World War II* 3, no. 2 (Spring 2002): 10.

44. Amanda Traphagan, "Young Woman Found Freedom as Navy Nurse," *Narratives: Stories of U.S. Latinos and Latinas in World War II* 4, no. 1 (Spring 2003): 34. See also Rachel Howell, "High Grades Landed Nurse a Job Working in Operating Room," *Narratives: Stories of U.S. Latinos and Latinas in World War II* 4, no. 1 (Spring 2003): 35.

45. National Archives at College Park, Md., Records of the Adjunct General's Office, 1905–1981, World War II Honor List of Dead and Missing Army and Army Air Forces Personnel from Arizona, 1946, RG 407.

46. Alfonso Lara, "The Other Soldiers," *Narratives: Stories of U.S. Latinos and Latinas in World War II* 3, no. 2 (Spring 2002): 32–33.

47. Herbert Oxnam (Major, USMCR retired) in discussion with the author, Tucson, Arizona, October 12, 1992.

48. Tom Beal, "12 Local Marines: From Barrio to Korea to Graves," *Arizona Daily Star*, May 27, 2002.

49. Vélez-Ibáñez, *Border Visions*, 119–21.

50. Eugene Suarez was born in Tucson, Arizona, on March 5, 1931, and served in the Marine Corps between 1948 and 1949. He was called up again to serve in Korea in 1950. He returned shaken and shocked with hundreds of feet of now-lost combat motion picture film and still photographs. He went on to become the chief of police of the National Indian Police of the Department of the Interior and is now a partner with his son of S&K Tortilla Products of Manassas Park, Virginia.

51. Bill Abbott states: "The 1970 census which is being used as our Vietnam era population base did not list an Hispanic count but gave an estimate of 4.5 percent of the American population. In a massive sampling of the database, it was established that between 5 and 6 percent of Vietnam dead had identifiable Hispanic surnames. These were Mexican, Puerto Rican, Cuban and other Latino-Americans with ancestries based in Central and South America. They came largely from California and Texas, with lesser numbers from Colorado, New Mexico, Arizona, Florida, New York and a few from many other states across the country. Thus it is safe to say that Hispanic-Americans were over-represented among Vietnam casualties—an estimated 5.5 percent of the dead against 4.5 percent of the 1970 population." Bill Abbott, "Names on the Wall: A Closer Look at Those Who Died in Vietnam," History Net, June 12, 2006, https://www.historynet.com/names-on-the-wall-a-closer-look -at-those-who-died-in-vietnam/. However, these statistics are misleading since the 4.5 percent are of all ages and genders and in reality would be reduced by half to truly represent the correct statistic of those eligible to serve between eighteen and twenty-five years old; nor do they include wounded.

52. Robert Lecke, *The March to Glory* (New York: Bantam Books, 1990), 132.

53. Vélez-Ibáñez, *Border Visions*, 204–5.

54. Richard A. Kulka et al., *Contractual Report of Findings from the National Vietnam Veterans Readjustment Study*, vol. 1, *Executive Summary, Description of Findings, and Technical Appendices* (Research Triangle Park: Research Triangle Institute, 1988).

NOTES TO PAGES 73-86

55. Richard A. Kulka et al., *Trauma and the Vietnam War Generation: Report of Findings from the National Vietnam Veteran's Readjustment Study* (New York: Brunner Mazel, 1990).

56. Corporal Jose Angel Garibay, Corporal Jorge A. Gonzalez, and Corporal Jesus Alberto Suarez.

57. Joe V. Aldaz Jr., "Latino Veterans Fight for Victory," D'Aniello Institute for Veterans and Military Families, Syracuse University, September 14, 2020, https://ivmf.syracuse.edu/2020/09/14/latino-veterans-fight-for-victory.

58. George W. Bush, "Satellite Remarks to the League of United Latin American Citizens Convention," July 8, 2004, in *Public Papers of the Presidents of the United States: George W. Bush, 2004*, book 2, *July 1–September 30, 2004* (Washington, D.C.: US Government Printing Office, 2007), 1250.

59. "Hispanics in the United States Marine Corps," Somos Primos, accessed March 6, 2023, http://www.somosprimos.com/tony/tonymarines/hispanicmarines.htm#Gulf_War_and_Operation_Restore_Hope.

60. Somos Primos, "Hispanics in the United States Marine Corps."

61. This section was partially taken from my 1990 commemorative speech given to the 40th reunion of E Company, Tucson, Arizona, July 28, 1990.

62. Lecke, *The March to Glory*, 132. Portions of the description of the winter conditions and the major Chinese figure mentioned were excerpted from this source.

63. Vélez-Ibáñez, *Border Visions*, 203–4.

64. "Explore Census Data," United States Census Bureau, accessed March 6, 2023, https://data.census.gov/.

65. Díaz-Barriga and Dorsey, *Fencing in Democracy*, 65–77.

66. Arnold van Gennep, *Rites of Passage*, trans. M. B. Vizedom and G. L. Caffee (Chicago: University of Chicago Press, 1960); Victor W. Turner, *Dramas, Fields, and Metaphors: Symbolic Action in Human Society* (Ithaca, N.Y.: Cornell University Press, 1974).

67. Díaz-Barriga and Dorsey, *Fencing in Democracy*, 68.

68. See "Iwo Jima," History, February 16, 2021, https://www.history.com/topics/world-war-ii/battle-of-iwo-jima.

69. Marta Menchaca, *The Mexican American Experience in Texas* (Austin: University of Texas Press, 2022).

## Chapter 4

1. In a May 7, 2023, conversation at a funeral home, a businessman in Las Vegas, Nevada, who is an agricultural producer in the Mexican state of San Luis Potosí related that between the large-scale taxation of the present administration and the payoffs necessary to stay in business, he felt squeezed without hope of anything changing and was very concerned about the future of civil life in Mexico.

2. Craig A. Deare, *Militarization "a la AMLO": How Bad Can It Get?* (Washington, D.C.: Wilson Center, Mexico Institute, 2021), 1–22, https://www.wilsoncenter.org/sites/default/files/media/uploads/documents/Militarization_a_la_AMLO_Deare%20.pdf.

3. The Mexican Marine Corps since the Mérida Initiative especially has been very much associated with the U.S. Marine Corps in low-intensity warfare, training as elite troops of intervention and civilian protections against unwarranted "collateral" damage or torture and unnecessary killing of civilians. This follows the basic doctrine of the Marine Corps of "Civic Action" in combination with combat arms from the Vietnam War, in contrast to the U.S. Army's doctrine of "body counts" as the basic metric of success. See William D. Parker, *U.S. Marine Corps Civil Affairs in I Corps: Republic of South Vietnam, April 1966–April 1967* (Washington, D.C.: Historical Division Headquarters, U.S. Marine Corps, 1970). However, recently thirty Mexican marines were arrested and put on trial for the disappearance of a number of young men in the Mexican state of Tamaulipas as well as the murder of one U.S. citizen. See "Mexico Detains 30 Marines Accused of Disappearances," France 24, March 14, 2021, https://www.france24.com/en/live-news/20210413-mexico-detains -30-marines-accused-of-disppearances.

4. See John Daniel Davidson, "A Drug Cartel Just Defeated the Mexican Military in Battle," *The Federalist*, October 21, 2019, https://thefederalist.com/2019/10/21/a -drug-cartel-just-defeated-the-mexican-military-in-battle/.

5. Stephanie Brewer, "Militarized Mexico: A Lost War That Has Not Brought Peace," Washington Office on Latin America, May 12, 2021, https://www.wola.org /analysis/militarized-mexico-a-lost-war/.

6. DW Documentary, "Uncovering Crime and Corruption—Anabel Hernández Takes on Mexico's Drug Cartels," May 3, 2022, video, 51:54, https://www.youtube .com/watch?v=HYm7aJqXK8A&ab_channel=DWDocumentary.

7. I cannot provide sources for these ethnographic narratives since it would place those "interviewed" in jeopardy.

8. Most recently, Michoacán avocado orchards were infiltrated to the extent that the cartel threatened American inspectors without whose certification export to the United States is impossible. There were attempts to export uninspected avocados, but these failed, which set off countermeasures by the cartels. See Gabriela Miranda, "US Suspends Avocado Imports from Mexico after Inspector Receives Threats," *USA Today*, February 16, 2022. In the Mexican state of Jalisco, avocado production and distribution are very much affected by forced "taxes" by cartel enforcers. Field notes and interviews, September 5, 2023, of a former high-ranking state official.

9. International Crisis Group, "Keeping Oil from the Fire: Tackling Mexico's Fuel Theft Bracket," Briefing No. 46, March 25, 2022, https://www.crisisgroup.org/latin -america-caribbean/mexico/keeping-oil-fire-tackling-mexicos-fuel-theft-racket.

10. Juan Camilo Castillo, Daniel Mejía, and Pascual Restrepo, *Scarcity Without Leviathan: The Violent Effects of Cocaine Supply Shortages in the Mexican Drug War*, Working Paper No. 356 (Washington, D.C.: Center for Global Development, 2014), https://www.cgdev.org/publication/scarcity-without-leviathan-violent-effects -cocaine-supply-shortages-mexican-drug-war. The Special Forces Airmobile Group is a special commando unit trained in and by the United States and detailed by the Mexican Army to different commands and serves as a rapid deployment force. "Special Forces Airmobile Group [Grupos Aeromóviles de Fuerzas Especiales]," Global

Security.org, accessed December 20, 2023, https://www.globalsecurity.org/military/world/mexico/army-orbat-gafe.htm.

11. On Mayan exterminations, see Séverine Durin, *¡Salvese quien pueda! Violencia generalizada y desplazamiento forzado en el noreste de México* (Mexico City: CIESAS, 2019), 145.

12. Durin, *¡Salvese quien pueda!*, 145.

13. Guillermo Valdés Castellanos, "El nacimiento de un ejército criminal," *Nexos*, September 1, 2013, https://www.nexos.com.mx/?p=15460.

14. Castillo, Mejía, and Restrepo, *Scarcity Without Leviathan*, 30.

15. Kevin Lewis O'Neill, "Moral Failure: A Jeremiad of the War on Drugs in Guatemala," *Journal of the Royal Anthropological Institute* 28 (2021): 55.

16. O'Neill, "Moral Failure," 55.

17. Durin, *¡Salvese quien pueda!*, 145.

18. Durin, *¡Salvese quien pueda!*, 145.

19. Castellanos, "El nacimiento," 12.

20. For Arizona, see D. L. Turner, "Arizona's Twenty-Four Hour War: The Arizona Rangers and the Cananea Copper Strike of 1906," *Journal of Arizona History* 48, no. 3 (Autumn 2007): 257–88; for Texas, see Swanson, *Cult of Glory*.

21. "Police Seize Elderly Mexican Man over 'Witch' Killing," CNN, November 13, 2009, https://www.cnn.com/2009/WORLD/americas/11/13/mexico.witchcraft.killing/; Leigh Binford and Nancy Churchhill, "Lynching and States of Fear in Urban Mexico," *Anthropologica* 51, no. 2 (2009): 301–12. Additionally, an 1874 *New York Times* article is among the earliest to report witch killings in American newspapers: "Mexico: Four Witches Burned in Sinaloa, the Alcalde's Report of the Trial and Execution," *New York Times*, May 25, 1874.

22. Beside *cholo*, the use of *pocho* is less negative but refers to Americanized Mexicans who are translingual but not bilingual, speak Spanish with an American accent, and suffer great anxiety when attempting to converse with dominant Spanish speakers. See Vélez-Ibáñez, *Hegemonies of Language*.

23. Cholos' association with drugs extends back to early in the 1940s, with some referred to not only as *cholos* but also as *pachucos* and *homies*, and spawned a generational hierarchy of "pee wees" "gangsters," and "veteranos"—the latter having left gang life. See James Diego Vigil's numerous works on the subject of gangs, especially *Gang Redux: A Balanced Anti-gang Strategy* (Long Grove: Waveland, 2010).

24. Mariángela Rodríguez Nicholls, *Esclavitud posmoderna: Flexibilización, migración y cambio cultural* (Mexico City: CIESAS, 2011).

25. Rodríguez Nicholls, *Esclavitud posmoderna*.

26. James H. McDonald, "Reconfiguring the Countryside: Power, Control, and the (Re)organization of Farmers in West Mexico," *Human Organization* 60, no. 3 (2001): 247–58; James H. McDonald, "The Narcoeconomy and Small-Town, Rural Mexico," *Human Organization* 64, no. 2 (Summer 2005): 115–24; James H. McDonald, "The Cultural Effects of the Narcoeconomy in Rural Mexico," *Journal of International and Global Studies* 1, no. 1 (2009): 1–23; Rodríguez Nicholls, *Esclavitud posmoderna*.

27. McDonald, "Cultural Effects," 20.

28. Rodríguez Nicholls, *Esclavitud posmoderna.*

29. These data were based on a series of fieldwork interviews with informants in a southwestern state whose identities must be kept anonymous since some of the families involved may still be followed by their former employers.

30. See Blake Gentry, Geoffrey Alan Boyce, Jose M. Garcia, and Samuel N. Chambers, "Indigenous Survival and Settler Colonial Dispossession on the Mexican Frontier? The Case of Cedagi Whaia and Wo'oson O'oDham Indigenous Communities," *Journal of Latin American Geography* 18, no. 1 (2019): 65–93.

31. Personal interview with the author, July 30, 2023.

32. Both narratives are the consequence of intensive interviews over a period of two years of fieldwork.

33. All sites, names, and locations are pseudonyms and entirely masked due to security issues.

34. This is an example like that mentioned in the Oaxacan Port City case. "Los narco-tours de Mazatlán: Conoce las casas de los capos," Univision, February 4, 2016, video, 4:38, https://www.youtube.com/watch?v=mGizQ7Oc56Q; "La Mansion del Capo en Mazatlán," Omar Piña, April 12, 2021, video, 19:00, https://www.youtube.com/watch?v=9G0sVqGecoc.

35. Rubén Darío Ramírez-Sánchez, "Del edén al infierno: Inseguridad y construcción estatal en Tabasco," *LiminaR: Estudios Sociales y Humanísticos* 17, no. 2 (July–December 2019): 199.

36. See "Murderer of Mexican Journalist Javier Valdez Sentenced to 32 Years in Prison," Committee to Protect Journalists, June 18, 2021, https://cpj.org/2021/06/murderer-of-mexican-journalist-javier-valdez-sentenced-to-32-years-in-prison/.

37. Javier Arce and Joanna Jacobo Rivera, "Journalists Flee Violence in Mexico," *Arizona Republic*, August 8, 2022, 1–16A.

38. Noemí Piñeda, quoted in Arce and Rivera, "Journalists Flee Violence," 16A.

39. Piñeda, quoted in Arce and Rivera, "Journalists Flee Violence," 16A.

40. "Observatorio de la Libertad de Prensa, Atentados contra periodistas," infoamérica, 2022, https://www.infoamerica.org/libex/libex_portada.htm. All details about the murdered journalists, including photos, are from this source. I have reproduced the photo and text about each individual as they appeared in August 2022.

41. See *Informe de la Presidencia de la Comision para la Verdad y Acceso a la Justicia del Caso* (Mexico City: Gobierno de México, Ayotzinapa, 2022), https://comisionayotzinapa.segob.gob.mx/es/Comision_para_la_Verdad/Segundo_Informe.

42. Maria Abi-Habib, "In Mexico, One Cartel Is Cleared, but Others Storm," *New York Times*, May 4, 2022; Jim Cavallaro, "Transnational Litigation and Corporate Accountability: Mexico's Case Against Arms Traffickers, Keynote Speech," University of Arizona, May 24, 2023, video, 4:15:50, https://www.youtube.com/watch?v=qga_ext341w.

43. Analy Nuño, "Mexico's Citizens Caught in Crossfire as Cartels Launch Attacks Across the Country," *The Guardian*, August 18, 2022.

## Chapter 5

1. Douglas Massey, Jorge Durand, and Karen A. Pren, "Border Enforcement and Return Migration by Documented and Undocumented Mexicans," *Journal of Ethnic and Migration Studies* 41, no. 7 (2015): 1015–40.

2. María Eugenia D'Aubeterre and María Leticia Rivermar, "Migración de retorno en la sierra norte de Puebla a raíz de la crisis económica estadounidense," in *Nuevas experiencias de la migración de retorno*, ed. Elaine Levine, Silvia Nuñez García, and Mónica Verea (Mexico City: Universidad Nacional Autónoma de México, Instituto Matías Romero, 2016), 159–80; Silvia Molina y Vedia and Rubén Hernández Duarte, "Aportaciones de la transmigración: Mexicanos en Estados Unidos, mexicanos en tránsito y en sus comunidades de origen," in *Migración, organizaciones civiles y transmigración: Redes e interdependencia*, ed. Alejandro Méndez Rodríguez, Jeanette de Rosas Quintero, Miguel Ángel Márquez Zárate, Silvia Molina y Vedia, and Virgiña Castillo (Mexico City: UNAM, 2014), 143–80.

3. Secretaría de Gobernación, "Índices de intensidad migratoria México-Estados Unidos," Consejo Nacional de Población, Gobierno de México, 2010, https://www .gob.mx/conapo/documentos/indices-de-intensidad-migratoria-mexico-estados -unidos-2010.

4. Ana Gonzales-Barrera, "More Mexicans Leaving than Coming to the U.S.," Pew Research Center, November 19, 2015, https://www.pewresearch.org/hispanic/2015 /11/19/more-mexicans-leaving-than-coming-to-the-u-s/.

5. A mixed family is defined as a family whose members have different migration statuses as a result of the place of birth of its members. Jeffrey S. Passel and Paul Taylor, "Unauthorized Immigrants and Their U.S.-Born Children," Pew Research Center, August 11, 2010, https://www.pewresearch.org/hispanic/2010/08/11/unauthorized -immigrants-and-their-us-born-children/.

6. Victoria Kline, "And Now Where Do We Go? The Challenges Faced by Transnational Migrant Families Between the United States and Mexico," in *Nuevas experiencias de la migración de retorno*, ed. Elaine Levine, Silvia Núñez, and Mónica Verea (Mexico City: UNAM, Instituto Matías Romero, 2016), 45–58; Bryant Jensen, Rebeca Mejía Arauz, and Rodrigo Aguilar Zepeda, "La enseñanza equitativa para los niños retornados a México," *Sinéctica*, no. 48 (2017), https://www.redalyc.org/journal/998 /99856084005/html/.

7. A. Beltrán, *Cosalá in the Context of Regional History* (Mexico City: Instituto Sinaloense de Cultura, Government of the State of Sinaloa, 2010).

8. Arturo Lizárraga-Hernández, *Nos llevó la ventolera: El proceso de la emigración rural al extranjero en Sinaloa* (Culiacán: Universidad Autónoma de Sinaloa, 2004); Guillermo Eduardo Ibarra, *Ensayos sobre el desarrollo económico regional de Sinaloa, México* (Culiacán: Universidad Autónoma de Sinaloa, Instituto Sinaloense de Cultura, 2009).

9. "Cosalá Operations," Americas Gold and Silver, accessed July 20, 2023, https:// www.americas-gold.com/operations/cosala-operations/.

10. CONEVAL, *Poverty Indicators by Municipality* (Mexico City: Consejo Nacional de Evaluación de la Política de Desarrollo Social, 2022).

11. Instituto Nacional de Estadística, Geografía e Informática (INEGI), *Population and Housing Census 2020* (Mexico City: INEGI, Government of Mexico, 2020).

12. Lizárraga-Hernández, *Nos llevó la ventolera*; Ibarra, *Ensayos sobre el desarrollo económico regional*.

13. Arturo Lizárraga-Hernández, ed., *Procesos y efectos de la emigración sinaloense al extranjero* (Mexico City: Universidad Autónoma de Sinaloa, 2010); Erika Montoya and Arturo Santamaría, "De ida y de regreso: Migración Sinaloa-Arizona en medio de las políticas antimigrantes, violencia y desempleo," in *Visiones de aquí y de allá: Implicaciones de la apolítica antiinmigrante en las comunidades de origen mexicano en Estados Unidos y México*, ed. Carlos G. Vélez-Ibáñez, Roberto Sánchez Benítez, and M. Maríangela Rodríguez (Mexico City: Universidad Nacional Autónoma de México, Tempe: Arizona State University; Ciudad Juárez: Universidad Autónoma de Ciudad Juárez, 2015).

14. Lizárraga-Hernández, *Nos llevó la ventolera*.

15. Juan Antonio Fernández-Velázquez and Félix Brito Rodríguez, "Pistolerismo y narcotráfico: Escenarios de la violencia cotidiana en Sinaloa, 1940–1980," *Escripta* 2, no. 4 (July–December 2020): 125–58.

16. Fernández-Velázquez and Brito Rodríguez, "Pistolerismo y narcotráfico," 137.

17. Lizárraga-Hernández, *Nos llevó la ventolera*.

18. Juan Antonio Fernández-Velázquez, "La operación Cóndor en los Altos de Sinaloa: La labora del estado durante los primeros años de la Campaña antidroga," *Ra Ximhai* 14, no. 1 (2018): 63–84.

19. Fernández-Velázquez, "La operación Cóndor en los Altos de Sinaloa," 76.

20. Fernández-Velázquez, "La operación Cóndor en los Altos de Sinaloa," 77, citing Arturo Lizárraga-Hernández, Ernestine Lizárraga, and Jorge Abel Guerrero Velasco, "Sinaloa: Migración, pobreza, narcotráfico y crisis económica," in *De aquí, de allá: Migración y desarrollo local*, ed Eduardo Meza Ramos and Lourdes Pacheco Ladrón de Guevara (Mexico City: Unidad Académica de Economía, Universidad Autónoma de Nayarit, 2010), 59–80. See also Lizárraga-Hernández, *Nos llevó la ventolera*.

21. Unidad de Política Migratoria, Registros e Identidad de Personas, *Diagnóstico de la movilidad humana en Sinaloa* (Mexico City: Secretaría de Gobernación, 2020); Lizárraga-Hernández, *Nos llevó la ventolera*.

22. Renato Pintor-Sandoval, "The Habitus and Transnational Fields in the Process of Migrant Transnationalism," *International Migrations* 6, no. 2 (2011): 159–92.

23. Bank of Mexico, "Income from Remittances, Distribution by Municipality," Economic Information System, accessed July 20, 2023, https://www.banxico.org.mx/.

24. U.S. Immigration and Customs Enforcement, Department of Homeland Security, "Arrestos migratorios de ERO ICE aumentan casi un 40 por ciento en comparación con el año pasado," Comunicados de Prensa, May 17, 2017, https://www.ice.gov/es/news/releases/arrestos-migratorios-de-ero-ice-aumentan-casi-un-40-por-ciento-en-comparacion-con-el.

25. Institute for Women in Migration / Instituto para las Mujeres en la Migración (IMUMI), *Now Where To? The Challenges Facing Transnational Migrant Families Between the United States and Mexico* (Mexico City: IMUMI, 2013); Seth Freed

Wessler, "Thousands of Kids Lost from Parents in U.S. Deportation System," Colorlines, November 2, 2011, https://colorlines.com/article/thousands-kids-lost-parents-us-deportation-system/.

26. State Public Security Council, *Diagnóstico Febrero 2021* (Culiacán: Coordinación General del Consejo Estatal de Seguridad Pública del Estado de Sinaloa, 2021).

27. "Desmantelan narco-laboratorio en Cosalá: Este es el botín para droga sintética asegurado por SEDENA," *El Debate*, February 28, 2023, https://www.debate.com.mx/sinaloa/policiaca/Desmantelan-narcolaboratorio-en-Cosala-Este-es-el-botin-para-droga-sintetica-asegurado-por-Sedena-20230228-0044.html; Agustín Rodríguez, "Ejército asegura a 6 laboratorios clandestinos de droga en Sinaloa," TV Azteca, June 7, 2022, https://www.tvazteca.com/aztecanoticias/ejercito-laboratorios-sinaloa-jvgl; Eduardo Murillo, "Asegura SEDENA 6 laboratorios clandestinos del Cártel de Sinaloa," *La Jornada*, July 6, 2022, https://www.jornada.com.mx/notas/2022/06/07/politica/asegura-sedena-seis-laboratorios-clandestinos-del-cartel-de-sinaloa/.

28. Instituto Nacional de Estadística, Geografía e Informática (INEGI), *Encuesta Nacional de Victimización y Percepción sobre Seguridad Pública 2022* (Mexico City: INEGI, Government of Mexico, 2022).

29. L. Rivera-Sánchez, "Sujetos móviles y pertenencías urbanas: Notas en torno a una investigación sobre prácticas y experiencias de reinserción social de migrantes retornados a espacios urbanos," *Estudios sociológicos* 33, no. 97 (2015): 169–96.

30. Jensen, Mejía Arauz, and Aguilar Zepeda, "La enseñanza equitativa para los niños retornados"; Claudia Masferrer, Erin R. Hamilton, and Nicole Denier, "Half a Million American Minors Now Live in Mexico," The Conversation, July 1, 2019, https://theconversation.com/half-a-million-american-minors-now-live-in-mexico-119057.

31. CURP is an identity code that verifies citizenship or residence in Mexico.

32. Carlos G. Vélez-Ibáñez and James B. Greenberg, "Formation and Transformation of Funds of Knowledge Among US-Mexican Households," *Anthropology and Education Quarterly* 23, no. 4 (December 1992): 313–35.

33. Fernández-Velázquez and Brito Rodríguez, "Pistolerismo y narcotráfico"; Lizárraga-Hernández, *Nos llevó la ventolera*; Beltrán, *Cosalá in the Context of Regional History*; Ronaldo González-Valdes, *Sinaloa, una sociedad demediada* (Culiacán: H. Ayuntamiento de Culiacán, Dirección de Cultura, 2007).

34. For the safety of the subject, "Gladys" is a pseudonym.

35. Manuela Bustamante, "Tiene Sinaloa registro de más de 3 mil personas desplazadas por la violencia," *El Sol de Sinaloa*, June 14, 2023, https://www.elsoldesinaloa.com.mx/local/tiene-sinaloa-registro-de-mas-de-3-mil-personas-desplazadas-por-la-violencia-10219281.html.

## Chapter 6

1. "Mexico's Official 'Disappeared' List Grows to More Than 100,000," Reuters, May 16, 2022, https://www.reuters.com/world/americas/mexicos-official-disappeared-list-grows-more-than-100000-2022-05-17. According to the report, "Over

the past two years, it has risen from about 73,000 people to more than 100,000, most of them men." See also Pardo Veiras and José Luis y Íñigo Arredondo, "Opinión: Una guerra inventada y 350,000 muertos en México," *Washington Post,* June 14, 2021.

2. Institute for Economics and Peace, *Mexico Peace Index 2022: Identifying and Measuring the Factors That Drive Peace* (Sydney: Institute for Economics and Peace, 2022).

3. Michael Marizco, "Was Sonora Shootout a First Act?," *Nogales International,* July 8, 2010, https://www.nogalesinternational.com/news/was-sonora-shootout-a -first-act/article_eeae9ae1-6132-557a-92fa-9a75e4b6802d.html.

4. Marizco, "Was Sonora Shootout a First Act?" On October 21, 2023, rival criminal gangs in Sasabe, Sonora, seventy-two miles south of Tucson, Arizona, fought for control and began burning down residents' homes and taking up residence in abandoned houses. The outcome is that only fifteen families remain from a total of 2,500 residents, all of whom have fled, especially seeking humanitarian aid in the United States. See José Igancio Castañeda Perez, "Families in Sasabe Seek Refuge from Gangs," *Arizona Republic,* November 26, 2023, 1B.

5. In another state nearby, in 2018, an anthropology fieldwork class in a small rural agricultural town heard, from some kilometers distant, rapid gunfire. The gunfire was from an ambush on a dirt curve similar to that of Tubutama and was directed toward an army convoy escorting an ambulance carrying a wounded captured assassin. A rocket-propelled round struck the lead truck, the ambulance was unscathed, and the following two army trucks were destroyed. Sixteen soldiers were killed. The ambulance detoured around the destroyed truck and joined the ambushers, who escorted the assassin to medical care in a cartel-controlled nearby town. Such an ambush normally using an L-shaped arrangement was used by Viet Cong forces in Vietnam; cartels trained by former Mexican special forces like the Zetas or Sinaloa cartels were instructed many times using Vietnam scenarios by Special Forces trainers.

6. Jessica Garrison, Wendy Fry, and Alexandra Mendoza, "Baja California Tries to Return to Normal After a Weekend of Cartel Violence," *Los Angeles Times,* August 14, 2022.

7. Miguel Ángel Vega, "Cuando Jesus Maria se convertido en zona de guerras," *Río Doce,* January 15, 2023, https://riodoce.mx/2023/01/17/cuando-jesus-maria-se -convirtio-en-zona-de-guerra/.

8. "Se extiende narcoterrorismo a todo Sinaloa por detención de Ovidio Guzmán," *Noroeste/Redacción,* January 5, 2023. Additionally, one of the contributors to a chapter in this work contacted me through social messaging and related the fearsome events and contexts in which gunfire could be heard in the next colonia in their upper-middle-class neighborhood. The contributor and a sixteen-year-old daughter huddled underneath their beds; both relived the trauma for the second time from that exact same event in 2019 when young Guzmán was similarly captured and released. This time, however, he was quickly flown out to Mexico City aboard a military jet, which led to some cartel members shooting at a departing plane to Mexico City from Culiacán.

NOTES TO PAGES 132–134

9. According to one of my informants, medical doctors were taken from one of the central medical hospitals by cartel and gang members, either to care for their wounded or to be used as human capital for negotiations.

10. "Los detalles de la captura de Ovidio Guzmán: 29 muertos, un black hawk y armas de alto poder," Infobae, January 6, 2023, https://www.infobae.com/america /mexico/2023/01/06/los-detalles-de-la-captura-de-ovidio-guzman-9-militares -muertos-un-black-hawk-y-armas-de-alto-poder.

11. On June 26, 2023, one of my informants from a northern Mexican state told me that he had been informed that morning by his wife that while driving their children and two of their cousins to school, she had to distract them from looking out at the prone bodies of six young men dumped by the side of the freeway. The cousins had already been undergoing therapy for an assault and robbery at their home in which the children had been threatened with death unless their parents opened their safe in their home.

12. United Nations Office on Drugs and Crime (UNODC), "¿Qué dice el Informe mundial sobre las drogas 2022 de las tendencias de América Latina y el Caribe?," Centro de Excelencia UNODC-INEGI, July 8, 2022, https://www.cdeunodc.inegi.org .mx/index.php/2022/07/08/dice-informe-mundial-las-drogas-2022-las-tendencias -america-latina-caribe.

13. David Goodman-Meza et al., "Where Is the Opioid Use Epidemic in Mexico? A Cautionary Tale for Policymakers South of the US–Mexico Border," *American Journal of Public Health* 109, no. 1 (January 1, 2019): 79.

14. Josue Ángel González Torres, "México y el mercado mundial de drogas en 2022," *Diario Contra Replica*, June 29, 2022.

15. Christine L. Mattson et al., "Trends and Geographic Patterns in Drug and Synthetic Opioid Overdose Deaths—United States, 2013–2019," *Morbidity and Mortality Weekly Report* 70, no. 6 (February 2021): 202–7.

16. Nick Miroff et al., "Cause of Death: Washington Faltered as Fentanyl Gripped America," *Washington Post*, December 12, 2022.

17. "Fentanyl & Opioid Overdose Prevention," California Department of Public Health, accessed September 14, 2023, https://www.cdph.ca.gov/Programs/OPA /Pages/Communications-Toolkits/Fentanyl-Overdose-Prevention.aspx.

18. Karin A. Mack, Christopher M. Jones, and Michael F. Ballesteros, "Illicit Drug Use, Illicit Drug Use Disorders, and Drug Overdose Deaths in Metropolitan and Nonmetropolitan Areas—United States," *Morbidity and Mortality Weekly Report* 66, no. 19 (October 2017): 4.

19. Katherine Beckett and Marco Brydolf-Horwitz, "A Kinder, Gentler Drug War? Race, Drugs, and Punishment in 21st Century America," *Punishment & Society* 22, no. 4 (May 2020): 510.

20. Yet there is a social casualty writ large that is not only cyclical but exponential and has created a private source for public imprisonment mostly due to drugs: the incarceration of thousands, especially of African Americans nationwide and of Latino-origin populations in the Southwest North American Region. Entire generations of

youth graduate from nonviolent and non-gang-related rationales through the use of drugs to full-blown participation, earning graduate degrees in the sale, distribution, and use of multitudes of drugs as part of gangs associated with both the diminished Mafia and Mexican and Colombian cartels of a transnational sort. In this process, thousands of individuals are incarcerated in local, county, state, and federal jails in which gradual and intense socialization into the "vida loca" (crazy life) is most certain and accentuated by degrees of violence and certain death by conflicts over territorial control and inherent social conflicts over ascendancy and power.

21. "Drug Overdose in New Mexico," New Mexico Department of Public Health, last updated May 2022, https://www.nmhealth.org/publication/view/marketing/2117/; "New Mexico Population," PopulationU.com, United States Population, accessed July 1, 2023, https://www.populationu.com/us/new-mexico-population#:~:text=New%20 Mexico%20population%20in%202022,largest%20state%20in%20the%20US.

22. Angela Garcia, *The Pastoral Clinic: Addiction and Dispossession Along the Rio Grande* (Berkeley: University of California Press, 2010).

23. Garcia, *Pastoral Clinic*, 57–58.

24. U.S. Department of Labor, "Earnings Disparities by Race and Ethnicity," Office of Federal Contract Compliance Programs, accessed July 4, 2023, https://www.dol .gov/agencies/ofccp/about/data/earnings/race-and-ethnicity.

25. "How Does Poverty Impact Substance Abuse?," Substance Abuse, accessed July 4, 2023, https://substanceabuse.org/how-does-poverty-impact-substance-abuse .html.

26. George I. Sánchez, *Forgotten People: A Study of New Mexicans* (Albuquerque: University of New Mexico Press, 1967).

27. World Population Review, "New Mexico Poverty by Race," New Mexico Population 2023, accessed July 4, 2023, https://worldpopulationreview.com/states/new -mexico-population.

28. Al Valdez, "The Origins of Southern California Latino Gangs," in *Maras: Gang Violence and Security in Central America*, ed. Thomas Bruneau, Lucía Dammert, and Elizabeth Skinner (Austin: University of Texas Press, 2011), 23–42. See also Chris Blatchford, *The Black Hand: The Story of Rene "Boxer" Enriquez and His Life in the Mexican Mafia* (New York: William Morrow, 2009).

29. James Diego Vigil, *Chicano High Schoolers in a Changing Los Angeles* (Columbus, Ohio: Biblio, 2020).

30. See John P. Sullivan, "Maras Morphing: Revisiting Third Generation Gangs," *Global Crime* 7, no. 3–4 (August–November 2006): 487–504; and John P. Sullivan, "Transnational Gangs: The Impact of Third Generation Gangs in Central America," *Air and Space Power Journal*, July 2008.

31. Valdez, "Origins of Southern California Latino Gangs."

32. According to Valdez:

> To date, there are still approximately one million Salvadoran immigrants who have resettled permanently in the United States.

In Los Angeles, most of the newly arrived Salvadoran immigrants, a large number of whom were undocumented, settled in the Rampart area west of downtown. Unfortunately, many of them suffered from a type of culture shock as they tried to integrate into L.A. city life. . . . Of those Salvadorans who got involved in street gangs in the early days, most joined the 18th Street Gang, one of the largest and most active street gangs present in the area during this time.

In a pattern that has become familiar, the predatory and dynamic Los Angeles Street environment in which immigrant Salvadoran youths found themselves became the catalyst that compelled the first Mara Salvatrucha (MS) cliques to form, between 1985 and 1988, and encouraged those few Salvadorans who had joined the 18th Street Gang to leave it. It has been reported that the founders of MS were originally members of an L.A.-based heavy-metal "stoner" group who used music and drugs as a basis for socializing, and that their gang was first known as MSS, or Mara Salvatrucha Stoners. Stoner groups were popular during this period in Los Angeles because they offered many Latino youths an alternative affiliation, particularly to the 18th Street Gang.

The MSS gang later shortened its name to "MS," or "Mara Salvatrucha" (the number "13" had not yet been added to the name). ("Origins of Southern California Latino Gangs," 25–26)

33. Valdez, "Origins of Southern California Latino Gangs," 26–27.

34. Los Angeles Almanac, "Gang-Related Crime Los Angeles County," Crime and Justice, accessed July 7, 2023, https://www.laalmanac.com/crime/cr03x.php#homicides.

35. Valdez, "Origins of Southern California Latino Gangs."

36. Héctor Silva Avalos, "States of Exception: The New Security Model in Central America," Washington Office on Latin America, February 23, 2023, https://www.wola.org/analysis/states-of-exception-new-security-model-central-america.

37. G. H. Elder, "Perspectives on the Life Course," in *Life Course Dynamics*, ed. G. H. Elder (Ithaca, N.Y.: Cornell University Press, 1985), 23–49.

38. William Brandt, "Tepito: Mexico City's Fierce Neighborhood," *Lensculture*, 2023, https://www.lensculture.com/articles/adriana-zehbrauskas-tepito-mexico-city-s-fierce-neighborhood.

39. Elder, "Perspectives on the Life Course."

40. Piotr A. Chomczyński and Timothy W. Clark, "Crime and the Life Course in Another America: Collective Trajectory in Mexican Drug Cartel Dominated Communities," *Justice Quarterly* 40, no. 2 (2023): 298.

41. Chomczyński and Clark, field notes, May 14, 2016.

42. Chomczyński and Clark, "Crime and the Life Course," 299. See also Elena Azaola, *Diagnóstico de las y los adolescentes que cometen delitos graves en México* (Mexico City: UNICEF, 2015); Piotr Chomczyński and Roger Guy, "'Our Biographies

Are the Same': Juvenile Work in Mexican Drug Trafficking Organizations from the Perspective of a Collective Trajectory," *British Journal of Criminology* 61, no. 4 (July 2021): 946–64; and Falko Ernst, "The Life and Death of a Mexican Hitman," InSight Crime, February 18, 2019, https://www.insightcrime.org/news/analysis/the-life-and -death-of-a-mexican-hitman/.

43. Azaola, *Diagnóstico de las y los adolescentes*; Chomczyński and Guy, "'Our Biographies Are the Same'"; Ernst, "The Life and Death of a Mexican Hitman."

44. See José Antonio Caporal, *El cártel de Neza* (Mexico City: Debolsillo, 2012).

45. The description of Ciudad Nezahualcóyotl has been adapted from Carlos G. Vélez-Ibáñez, *Rituals of Marginality: Politics, Process, and Cultural Change in Urban Mexico, 1969–1974* (Berkeley: University of California Press, 1983).

46. Vélez-Ibáñez, *Rituals of Marginality.*

47. Judith Matloff, "The Tale of New York and Neza York," Al Jazeera, January 18, 2014, http://america.aljazeera.com/features/2014/1/the-tale-of-new-yorkandneza york.html.

48. Field notes, 2023, from an informant now in the United States. The informant is a trained professional who now owns a gardening business and employs numerous undocumented cousins. He overstayed his visa and remained in Arizona. He previously lived on the border between Sinaloa and Nayarit and his extended family was heavily involved with a cartel in its production of fentanyl. One relative died from indirect inhalation by going to sleep soon after "cutting" it with cocaine. The relative fell asleep at work and stopped breathing. A popular belief holds that anyone who works with the drug and goes to sleep without waiting four hours will die; however, it is more likely that the accumulation of indirect ingestion caused his demise.

49. Mike O'Connor, "Gunmen Rule Neza and the Press on Outskirts of Mexico City," Committee to Protect Journalists, February 2014, https://cpj.org/2014/02 /attacks-on-the-press-mexico-analysis.

50. O'Connor, "Gunmen Rule Neza."

51. O'Connor, "Gunmen Rule Neza."

52. Emilio (pseudonym), author's field notes, February and May 2023. All places and names have been changed for the sake of anonymity.

## Chapter 7

1. The story of the Mexican senate appropriation of a French railway engine and cars was related to my father by a Mexican politician who was also a high-ranking officer in the Mexican army and had married one of my mother's sisters. He had arranged to drop off a daughter and son to my home in 1948 for them to learn English. Among the many conversations that I overheard as a preteen between he and my father was the related story of the railroad and how Mexican politicians basically suborned the Mexican appropriation system. My father could only shake his head in disbelief in our conversations about this in following discussions.

2. The story of the sale and resale of the oil pipes was related to me by a close relative who had been in an executive position in one of the major Mexican governmental

NOTES TO PAGES 152–172

financial bodies and in charge of keeping track of all expenditures. After he found these transactions and reported them to his superior, he was told to forget about it, since obviously arrangements had been made. The relative soon resigned from the position, unwilling to continue the charade of accountability.

3. "Unidad de Inteligencia de la Fiscalía investiga a la familia Cuén, por presunto enriquecimiento inexplicable," *Espejo*, April 17, 2023, https://revistaespejo.com/2023/04/17/unidad-de-inteligencia-cuen/.

4. Rubén Rocha Moya et al., "Nuestra solidaridad con el Doctor Arturo Santamaría Gómez," *Noroeste*, December 29, 2011.

5. Roxana Vivanco, "'Sin precedente en la UAS agresión contra Santamaría,'" *Noroeste*, November 9, 2015.

6. Roxana Vivanco, "El texto pone a Santamaría de cuerpo entero: Cuén," *Noroeste*, December 23, 2011.

7. "Nuestra solidaridad con la Universidad Autónoma de Sinaloa," *El Debate*, December 31, 2011.

8. Rubén Rocha Moya, "UAS: De la libertad a la censura," *El Debate*, January 10, 2012.

9. Tere Guerra, "Palabra de lector: Crítica desde la crítica," *Noroeste*, December 10, 2011.

10. Vivanco, "El texto pone a Santamaría de cuerpo entero."

11. Janneth Aldecoa, "Declaraciones del alcalde son serias: CEDH," *Noroeste*, December 24, 2011.

12. Francisco Cuamea, "Amenazan mi integridad: Arturo Santamaría," *Reporteros*, December 21, 2011, http://reporteroscom.blogspot.com/2011/12/amenazan-mi-integridad-arturo.html.

13. Froylán Enciso Higuera, *Nuestra historia narcótica: Pasajes para (re) legalizar las drogas en México* (Mexico City: Debate, 2017), 162.

14. See Arturo Santamaría Gómez, Universidad Autónoma de Sinaloa, evaluations from 2016 to July 6, 2021 (years I no longer worked at UAS), https://www.misprofesores.com/profesores/Arturo-Santamaria-Gomez_41071.

15. Arturo Santamaría Gómez, "¿Si México es un narco estado, desde cuándo?," *Noroeste*, February 18, 2023.

16. Quoted in David Aponte, *Los infiltrados: El narco dentro de los gobiernos* (Mexico City: Grijalbo, 2011), 57.

17. Carlos Velázquez, "Asesinan a Héctor Melesio Cuén, diputado electo del PAN-PRI-PRD, en Sinaloa," *El Financiero*, July 26, 2024, https://www.elfinanciero.com.mx/estados/2024/07/26/asesinan-a-hector-melesio-cuen-diputado-electo-del-pan-pri-prd-en-sinaloa/. However, a different narrative is told by a major figure in the Sinaloa Cartel:

> El Mayo's letter, released by his lawyer Frank Perez on Saturday, forced Governor Rubén Rocha Moya, President Andrés Manuel López Obrador and president-elect Claudia Sheinbaum to take a stand just hours after its

publication. At the center of the scandal is the murder of Héctor Melesio Cuén Ojeda, Rocha's political rival, made public on the same day as the arrest of the 76-year-old drug lord and Joaquín Guzmán López, one of the sons of Joaquín "El Chapo" Guzmán. Zambada claims that he was going to meet with both men on the day of his surprise arrest, that the Sinaloa Cartel leadership was going to settle a conflict at the state's main public university, and that one of his bodyguards was a commander in the state Judicial Police. His uncorroborated statements have sparked controversy over the influence of organized crime in Mexico's public affairs and have provided a first warning of the scope of a potential deal between El Mayo and U.S. authorities.

El Mayo says the meeting was scheduled for 11:00 a.m. on July 25 at Huertos del Pedregal, a luxurious event hall on the outskirts of Culiacán, the state capital and stronghold of the Sinaloa Cartel. In addition to the politicians, Iván Archivaldo Guzmán, leader of Los Chapitos, the cartel faction commanded by El Chapo's sons, was scheduled to attend. Zambada greeted Cuén, "a longtime friend of mine," moments before meeting Guzmán López, "whom I have known since he was a child," and who asked El Mayo to follow him. "A group of men assaulted me, threw me to the ground and put a dark-colored hood over my head," said the drug lord of the alleged ambush. (Elías Camhaji, "The Letter from 'El Mayo' Zambada That Widens the Scandal in Mexico: A Murder, a Capture and a Secret Meeting," *El Pais*, August 13, 2024, https://english.elpais.com/international/2024-08 -13/the-letter-from-el-mayo-zambada-that-widens-the-scandal-in-mexico -a-murder-a-capture-and-a-secret-meeting.html)

What followed in September 2024 as I write this on October 1, 2024, was an all-out war between "Los Chapitos" and Zambada's heirs, which resulted in the deaths of over one hundred, road closures between Culiacan and Mazatlan, the closing of schools in Culiacan, and people no longer strolling the malecon at dusk in Mazatlan. Residents in Culiacan for the most part stay indoors in fear, and limited traffic is allowed through army checkpoints. These circumstances are reported to the author by informants in Culiacan and Mazatlan as well as by more than a dozen articles and YouTube videos from Mexico on the internet.

18. "Unidad de Inteligencia de la Fiscalía."

19. Rocha Moya et al., "Nuestra solidaridad con el Doctor Arturo Santamaría Gómez."

20. Vivanco, "'Sin precedente en la UAS agresión contra Santamaría.'"

21. Vivanco, "El texto pone a Santamaría de cuerpo entero: Cuén."

22. "Nuestra solidaridad con la Universidad Autónoma de Sinaloa."

23. Rocha Moya, "UAS."

24. Guerra, "Palabra de lector."

25. Aldecoa, "Declaraciones del alcalde son serias."

26. Cuamea, "Amenazan mi integridad."

NOTES TO PAGES 192–200

27. Enciso Higuera, *Nuestra historia narcótica*, 162.

28. En efecto, en la dirección MisProfesores.com aparecen evaluaciones a partir de 2016 y hasta el 6 de julio de 2021, años en los que yo ya no trabajaba en la UAS. Arturo Santamaría Gómez, Universidad Autónoma de Sinaloa, https://www.misprofesores.com/profesores/Arturo-Santamaria-Gomez_41071.

29. Santamaría Gómez, "¿Si México es un narco estado, desde cuándo?"

30. Aponte, *Los infiltrados*, 57.

31. Carlos Velázquez, "Asesinan a Héctor Melesio Cuén, diputado electo del PAN-PRI-PRD, en Sinaloa," *El Financiero*, July 26, 2024, https://www.elfinanciero.com.mx/estados/2024/07/26/asesinan-a-hector-melesio-cuen-diputado-electo-del-pan-pri-prd-en-sinaloa/. Vean la nota 17 para la explicación en inglés.

## Chapter 8

1. Kearney, "Borders and Boundaries," 57.

2. Hector Amaya, "The Deterritorialized Political Economy of Narcocorridos in the United States," in *The Routledge Companion to Latina/o Media*, ed. María Elena Cepeda and Dolore Inés Casillas (New York: Taylor and Francis, 2016), 274–86.

3. Robert R. Alvarez Jr., "The Mexican-US Border: The Making of an Anthropology of Borderlands," *Annual Review of Anthropology* 24 (1995): 448.

4. See Josiah Heyman, "Contributions of U.S.-Mexico Border Studies to Social Science Theory," in *The U.S.-Mexico Transborder Region: Cultural Dynamics and Historical Interactions*, ed. Carlos Vélez-Ibáñez and Josiah Heyman (Tucson: University of Arizona Press, 2017), 44–64.

5. Alvarez, "Mexican-US Border," 462.

6. Héctor Gabriel Zazueta Beltrán, César Omar Sepúlveda Moreno, and Nora Teresa Millán López, "Influencia de narco-series y narco-corridos en las aspiraciones educativas de estudiantes de Sinaloa, México," in *Reconfigurando territorios a partir de la cultura, el empoderamiento de las mujeres y nuevos turismos*, ed. Mora Cantellano, Ma. del Pilar Alejandra, Serrano Oswald, Serena Eréndira y Mota Flores, and V. Enrique (Mexico City: UNAM-AMECIDER, 2022), 169–70.

7. A great deal of scholarship by Mexican social scientists exists in reference to narcoculture and youth. A full bibliography is available from the author upon request. See J. L. Cisneros, "Niños y jóvenes sicarios: Una batalla cruzada por la pobreza," *El cotidiano* 186 (2014): 7–18; Anajilda Mondaca, Gloria M. Cuamea, and Rocío del Carmen Payares, "Mujer, cuerpo y consumo en microproduccionesde narcocorridos," *Revista ComHumanitas* 6, no. 1 (2015): 170–88; Sayak Valencia Triana, "Capitalismo gore y necropolítica en México contemporáneo," *Relaciones internacionales* 19 (2012): 83–102; José Manuel Valenzuela, *Trazos de sangre y fuego: Bio-Necropolítica y juvenicidio en América Latina* (Mexico City: Transcript Verlag, 2019).

8. See Edmundo Pérez, *Que me entierren con narcocorrido las historias de los gruperos asesinadoss* (Mexico City: Grijalbo, 2012).

9. Miguel A. Cabañas, "El narcocorrido global y las identidades transnacionales," *Revista de Estudios Hispanos* 42, no. 3 (October 2008): 519–42.

10. See Frances Sola-Santiago, "Remembering Petra Herrera, the Unsung, Cross-Dressing Heroine of the Mexican Revolution," *Remezcla*, September 14, 2018, https://remezcla.com/features/culture/petra-herrera-mexican-revolution-heroine/.

11. See Carlos G. Vélez-Ibáñez et al., "Interrogating Early New Mexican Folklore y Lo Mexicano: The Literate Works of José Agapito Olivas," *Aztlán: A Journal of Chicano Studies* 44, no. 2 (Fall 2019): 85–112.

12. Juan Carlos Ramírez-Pimienta, "'El Pablote': Una nueva mirada al primer corrido dedicado a un traficante de drogas," *Mitologías Hoy* 14 (December 2016): 41–56. While Elijah Wald had earlier pinpointed the first thematic narcotic corrido to San Antonio, Texas, in 1934, the earlier date seems not debatable according to Ramírez-Pimienta's evidence. See Elijah Wald, *Narcocorrido: A Journey into the Music of Drugs, Guns and Guerrillas* (New York: HarperCollins, 2001), 13.

13. Ramírez-Pimienta, "'El Pablote,'" 42.

14. Ramírez-Pimienta, "'El Pablote,'" 44.

15. Ramírez-Pimienta, "'El Pablote,'" 52.

16. Omar Shamout, "Narcocorridos: The Drug War in Song," *Intersections, South LA*, January 16, 2012, https://intersectionssouthla.org/story/narcocorridos_the_drug_war_in_song/.

17. See "Prajin Music Group festeja 50 años de presencia internacional," *La Gorda Magazine*, February 2022, 67, https://www.yumpu.com/es/document/read/66314002/la-gorda-magazine-ano-8-edicion-numero-85-febrero-2022-portada-ana-barbara.

18. Juan Carlos Ramírez-Pimienta, "Narcocultura a ritmo norteño: El narcocorrido ante el nuevo milenio," *Latin American Research Review* 42, no. 2 (June 2007): 261.

19. Emiliano Villarreal, "Narcocultura as Cultural Capital for Latinx Youth Identity Work: An Online Ethnography" (PhD diss., University of Texas at El Paso, 2019), 10.

20. Oliva Solís, "Masculinidad y música latinoamericana," Entre Hombres México, accessed October 4, 2023, https://www.entrehombres.net/319-masculinidad-y-musica-latinoamericana-movimiento-alterado-dra-oliva-solis/.

21. Emilio (pseudonym), author's field notes, February and May 2023. All places and names have been changed for the sake of anonymity. Emilio knows the hierarchy, nomenclature, and operational details. He is an "informed informant" par excellence. All his bioethnography must be kept confidential, anonymous, and masked, given the rather risky data provided.

22. Emilio (pseudonym), author's field notes, February and May 2023. Emilio described this differentiation as well as their subtleties too complex to render here.

23. Olivia Adams, "Understanding the Dynamics of Femicide in Mexico," Vision of Humanity, accessed October 4, 2023, https://www.visionofhumanity.org/understanding-the-dynamics-of-femicide-of-mexico/.

24. Mark C. Edberg, "Narcocorridos: Narratives of a Cultural Persona and Power on the Border," in *Transnational Encounters: Music and Performance at the U.S.-Mexico Border*, ed. Alejandro L. Madrid (Oxford: Oxford University Press, 2011), 81.

25. Wald, *Narcocorrido*, 133.

NOTES TO PAGES 205–208

26. Amaya, "Deterritorialized Political Economy," 275. See also Mohamad Moslimani, Luis Noe-Bustamante, and Sono Shah, "Facts on Hispanics of Mexican Origin in the United States, 2021," Pew Research Center, August 16, 2023, https://www.pewresearch.org/race-and-ethnicity/fact-sheet/us-hispanics-facts-on-mexican-origin-latinos/.

27. This is probably created for the purpose of posting on social media—for on the website, there are other examples of user-created "quotes" (no source given for any of them) superimposed over graphics. Yet it is an example of a created image of wishful thinking giving equal power to women's roles when in actuality the drug enterprise is mostly in the hands of men, and few women except by inheritance succeed in gaining the notoriety and power that this male-dominated enterprise purports and supports. See Mayra Washington, "Puros Corridos Alterados Pariente!," Quotes-Gram, accessed October 4, 2023, https://quotesgram.com/img/puros-corridos-con-banda-quotes/11757446/.

28. Helena Simonett, "Subcultura musical: El narcocorrido comercial y el narcocorrido por encargo," *Caravelle*, no. 82 (June 2004): 188–90.

29. This is quite different in intention from "Trap Corridos," which focus on Chicano lives of working-class Mexican-origin youths and reject the capo-infused cartel type. Yet their accompanying YouTube videos still feature objectified young women, low-rider cars, alcohol consumption, and the artists provocatively displaying their anatomical features. See Gloria Malone, "Mexican Corrido for the New Era: The Evolution of a Genre," BElatina, November 6, 2019, https://belatina.com/mexican-corrido-evolution.

30. See Betto Arcos, "Drug Lords Pay This Mexican-American Singer to Write Their Ballads," *World*, December 11, 2013, https://theworld.org/stories/2013-12-11/drug-lords-pay-mexican-american-singer-write-their-ballads. Norteño music known as "trapteño" combines trap music and northern Sinaloan corridos. Leopoldo Medina explains that trapteño originates in Culiacán and describes the music created by Emmanuel Massu, alias "El Infermo." El Infermo's compositions focus on his neighborhood and his friends who had to move north seeking a better life, and who on their return found things to be different and gangs common. Leopoldo Medina, "A ritmo de Trapteño, Emmanuel Massú, 'El Enfermo,' comparte las historias de su barrio," *Noroeste*, July 19, 2023.

31. Victor Horacio Esparza Bernal, "Aproximación psicosocial a las juventudes y el narcotráfico en Sinaloa: Ingreso, prácticas, riesgos y (no) futuro" (PhD diss., Universidad Autónoma de Sinaloa, 2020), https://www.academia.edu/97706132/Aproximaci%C3%B3n_Psicosocial_a_las_Juventudes_y_el_Narcotr%C3%A1fico_en_Sinaloa_Ingreso_pr%C3%A1cticas_riesgos_y_no_Futuro.

32. Lilian Paola Ovalle, "Entre la indiferencia y la satanización: Representaciones sociales del narcotráfico desde la perspectiva de los universitarios de Tijuana," *Culturales* 1, no. 2 (2005): 63–89.

33. Ovalle, "Entre la indiferencia," 76–86.

34. David Moreno Candil, César Burgos Dávila, and Jairo Valdez Batiz, "Daño social y cultura del narcotráfico en México: Estudio de representaciones sociales en Sinaloa y Michoacán," *Mitologías Hoy* 14 (December 2016): 249–69.

35. Esparza Bernal, "Aproximación psicosocial a las juventudes," 38.

36. Esparza Bernal, "Aproximación psicosocial a las juventudes," 165–72.

37. David Moreno Candil and Fátima Flores Palacios, "Aceptación y rechazo al narcotráfico: Un studio intergeneracional sobre distancia social y nivel de contacto," *Alternativas en Psicología* 18, no. 32 (2015): 160–76.

38. Moreno Candil and Flores Palacios, "Aceptación y rechazo al narcotráfico."

39. It was also the site previously mentioned in chapter 3 where more than thirty marines were detained for human rights abuses.

40. Ariagor Manuel Almanza Avendaño et al., "Representaciones sociales acerca del narcotráfico en adolescentes de Tamaulipas," *Región y sociedad* 30, no. 72 (2018): 3–4.

41. Almanza Avendaño et al., "Representaciones sociales acerca del narcotráfico," 10–13.

42. Anel Hortensia Gómez San Luis and Ariagor Manuel Almanza Avendaño, "Impacto del narcotráfico en jóvenes de Tamaulipas, México: Drogas e inseguridad," *Revista de Psicología (PUCP)* 34, no. 2 (2016): 445–72.

43. Almanza Avendaño et al., "Representaciones sociales acerca del narcotráfico," 10–13.

44. Zazueta Beltrán, Sepúlveda Moreno, and Millán López, "Influencia de narco-series y narco-corridos."

45. Diego Vigil, "Community Dynamics and the Rise of Street Gangs," in *Latinos! Remaking America*, ed. Marcelo M. Suárez-Orozco and Mariela M. Páez (Berkeley: University of California Press with the David Rockefeller Center for Latin American Studies, Harvard University, 2002), 97–109.

46. One important medium not discussed here is drug culture's film and television representations, which César Albarrán-Torres has so ably examined in *Global Trafficking Networks on Film and Television: Hollywood's Cartel Wars* (New York: Routledge, 2021).

47. Zazueta Beltrán, Sepúlveda Moreno, and Millán López, "Influencia de narco-series y narco-corridos."

48. Zazueta Beltrán, Sepúlveda Moreno, and Millán López, "Influencia de narco-series y narco-corridos," 172.

49. Héctor Gabriel Zazueta Beltrán and José Carlos Pardini Moss, "Values and Educative Aspirations," *Chinese Business Review* 10, no. 3 (March 2011): 226–32.

50. Zazueta Beltrán, Sepúlveda Moreno, and Millán López, "Influencia de narco-series y narco-corridos," 172–73.

51. Zazueta Beltrán, Sepúlveda Moreno, and Millán López, "Influencia de narco-series y narco-corridos," 174.

52. Zazueta Beltrán, Sepúlveda Moreno, and Millán López, "Influencia de narco-series y narco-corridos," 184.

53. Zazueta Beltrán, Sepúlveda Moreno, and Millán López, "Influencia de narco-series y narco-corridos," 185.

54. Discussed in chapter 5; see also Chomczyński and Clark, "Crime and the Life Course."

55. For a bibliography of the literature, please contact the author. See Craig A. Anderson and Brad J. Bushman, "Media Violence and the General Aggression Model," *Journal of Social Issues* 74, no. 2 (2018): 386–413; Kim Dankoor, Dionne Stephens, and Tom Ter Bogt, "Drip Too Hard? Commercial Rap Music and Perceived Masculinity Ideals and Actual Self-Evaluations Among Black U.S. and Dutch Adolescent Men," *Sexuality & Culture* 27 (2023): 57–77; Peter Fischer and Tobias Greitemeyer, "Music and Aggression: The Impact of Sexual-Aggressive Song Lyrics on Aggression-Related Thoughts, Emotions, and Behavior Toward the Same and the Opposite Sex," *Personality and Social Psychology Bulletin* 32, no. 9 (2006): 1165–76; James D. Johnson et al., "Differential Gender Effects of Exposure to Rap Music on African American Adolescents' Acceptance of Teen Dating Violence," *Sex Roles: A Journal of Research* 33, no. 7–8 (1995): 597–605; Timothy Lauger and James A. Densley, "Broadcasting Badness: Violence, Identity, and Performance in the Online Gang Rap Scene," *Justice Quarterly* 35, no. 5 (2017): 816–41.

56. Pilar Fernandez Salgado, "Historical Controversy: Gangster Rap and its Relation to Aggression from a Psychological Perspective" (undergraduate thesis, National College of Ireland, 2023).

57. Vigil, "Community Dynamics"; James Diego Vigil and S. C. Yun, "A Cross-Cultural Framework for Understanding Gangs: Multiple Marginality and Los Angeles," in *Gangs in America*, 3rd ed., ed. C. Ronald Huff (Thousand Oaks, Calif.: Sage, 2002), 161–74.

58. Erik H. Erikson, *Identity, Youth and Crisis* (New York: W. W. Norton, 1968), 189.

59. Vigil, "Community Dynamics," 181.

60. Cati V. de los Rios, "'Los Músicos': Mexican Corridos, the Aural Border, and the Evocative Musical Renderings of Transnational Youth," *Harvard Educational Review* 89, no. 2 (Summer 2019): 177–201.

## Commentary and Conclusions

1. Glick-Schiller, "Explanatory Frameworks in Transnational Migration Studies," 2276.

2. Wolf, *Europe and the People Without History*, xxii–xxiii.

3. Bethany Blankley, "Border Agents Seize Enough Lethal Drugs This Fiscal Year to Kill More Than 6 Billion People," Center Square, April 14, 2023, https://www.the centersquare.com/national/article_590adb20-3aa3-11ee-aa43-3f89933ea37a.html.

4. On October 2, 2023, banners appeared in the northern state of Sinaloa announcing the banning of the manufacturing of fentanyl. Months previously, producers had received warnings not to continue production. Soon afterward, bodies were found covered with fentanyl pills, evidently to send a message. "El Chapo's Sons Bar Fentanyl Production in Sinaloa, According to Banners," Reuters, October 3, 2023, https://www.reuters.com/world/americas/el-chapos-sons-ban-fentanyl-production -sinaloa-according-banners-2023-10-03/.

5. Christina Baker, "Staging Narcocorridos: Las Reinas Chulas' Dissident Audio-Visual Performance," *Latin American Theater* 48, no. 1 (Fall 2014): 93–113.

# BIBLIOGRAPHY

Abbott, Bill. "Names on the Wall: A Closer Look at Those Who Died in Vietnam." History Net, June 12, 2006. https://www.historynet.com/names-on-the-wall-a-closer-look-at-those-who-died-in-vietnam/.

Abi-Habib, Maria. "In Mexico, One Cartel Is Cleared, but Others Storm." *New York Times*, May 4, 2022.

ACLU. "Supreme Court Keeps Title 42 Policy in Place for Now." December 27, 2022. https://www.aclu.org/press-releases/supreme-court-keeps-title-42-policy-place-now.

Albarrán-Torres, César. *Global Trafficking Networks on Film and Television: Hollywood's Cartel Wars*. New York: Routledge, 2021.

Adams, Olivia. "Understanding the Dynamics of Femicide in Mexico." Vision of Humanity. Accessed October 4, 2023. https://www.visionofhumanity.org/understanding-the-dynamics-of-femicide-of-mexico/.

Aldaz, Joe V., Jr. "Latino Veterans Fight for Victory." D'Aniello Institute for Veterans and Military Families, Syracuse University, September 14, 2020. https://ivmf.syracuse.edu/2020/09/14/latino-veterans-fight-for-victory.

Aldecoa, Janneth. "Declaraciones del alcalde son serias: CEDH." *Noroeste*, December 24, 2011.

Alexandrov, Nick. "Prevention Through Deterrence: The Strategy Shared by the El Paso Shooter and the U.S. Border Patrol." *Counter Punch*, August 16, 2019. https://www.counterpunch.org/2019/08/16/prevention-through-deterrence-the-strategy-shared-by-the-el-paso-shooter-and-the-u-s-border-patrol/.

Almanza Avedaño, Ariagor Manuel, Anel Hortensia Gómez San Luis, Diego Nahúm Guzmán González, and José Alfonso Cruz Montes. "Representaciones sociales acerca del narcotráfico en adolescentes de Tamaulipas." *Región y sociedad* 30, no. 72 (2018): 1–25.

Alvarez, Robert R., Jr. "The Mexican-US Border: The Making of an Anthropology of Borderlands." *Annual Review of Anthropology* 24 (1995): 447–70.

Amaya, Hector. "The Deterritorialized Political Economy of Narcocorridos in the United States." In *The Routledge Companion to Latina/o Media*, edited by María Elena Cepeda and Dolore Inés Casillas, 274–86. New York: Taylor and Francis, 2016.

American Battle Monuments Commission. "Jose C. Salazar." World War I Honor Roll. Accessed March 1, 2023. https://www.abmc.gov/decedent-search/salazar%3Djose-0.

Anderson, Craig A., and Brad J. Bushman. "Media Violence and the General Aggression Model." *Journal of Social Issues* 74, no. 2 (2018): 386–413.

Andreas, Peter. *Border Games: The Politics of Policing the U.S.–Mexico Divide.* Ithaca, N.Y.: Cornell University Press, 1998.

Aponte, David. *Los infiltrados: El narco dentro de los gobiernos.* Mexico City: Grijalbo, 2011.

Arce, Javier, and Joanna Jacobo Rivera. "Journalists Flee Violence in Mexico." *Arizona Republic*, August 8, 2022, 1–16A.

Arcos, Betto. "Drug Lords Pay This Mexican-American Singer to Write Their Ballads." *World*, December 11, 2013. https://theworld.org/stories/2013-12-11/drug-lords-pay-mexican-american-singer-write-their-ballads.

Ashby, Paul. "How Canada and Mexico Have Become Part of the U.S. Policing Regime." NACLA, December 12, 2014. https://nacla.org/blog/2014/12/01/how-canada-and-mexico-have-become-part-us-policing-regime.

Associated Press. "Arizona City Officials Want Troop-Installed Razor Wire Removed from Border Wall." *Military Times*, February 6, 2019. https://www.militarytimes.com/news/your-army/2019/02/07/arizona-city-officials-want-troop-installed-razor-wire-removed-from-border-wall.

Astorga, Luis. *Drogas sin fronteras.* Mexico City: Grijalbo Mondadori, S.A.-Junior, 2003.

Avalos, Héctor Silva. "States of Exception: The New Security Model in Central America." Washington Office on Latin America (WOLA), February 23, 2023. https://www.wola.org/analysis/states-of-exception-new-security-model-central-america.

Azaola, Elena. *Diagnóstico de las y los adolescentes que cometen delitos graves en México.* Mexico City: UNICEF, 2015.

Bailey, John, and Roy Godson, eds. *Organized Crime and Democratic Governability.* Pittsburgh: University of Pittsburgh Press, 2000.

Baker, Christina. "Staging Narcocorridos: Las Reinas Chulas' Dissident Audio-Visual Performance." *Latin American Theater* 48, no. 1 (Fall 2014): 93–113.

Bank of Mexico. "Income from Remittances, Distribution by Municipality." Economic Information System. Accessed July 20, 2023. https://www.banxico.org.mx/.

Beal, Tom. "12 Local Marines: From Barrio to Korea to Graves." *Arizona Daily Star*, May 27, 2002.

Beckett, Katherine, and Marco Brydolf-Horwitz. "A Kinder, Gentler Drug War? Race, Drugs, and Punishment in 21st Century America." *Punishment & Society* 22, no. 4 (May 2020): 509–33.

Beltrán, A. *Cosalá in the Context of Regional History*. Mexico City: Instituto Sinaloense de Cultura, Government of the State of Sinaloa, 2010.

Berlant, Lauren. 1997. *The Queen of America Goes to Washington City: Essays on Sex and Citizenship*. Durham, N.C.: Duke University Press.

Binford, Leigh, and Nancy Churchhill. "Lynching and States of Fear in Urban Mexico." *Anthropologica* 51, no. 2 (2009): 301–12.

Blatchford, Chris. *The Black Hand: The Story of Rene "Boxer" Enriquez and His Life in the Mexican Mafia*. New York: William Morrow, 2009.

Blankley, Bethany. "Border Agents Seize Enough Lethal Drugs This Fiscal Year to Kill More Than 6 Billion People." Center Square, April 14, 2023. https://www.thecenter square.com/national/article_590adb20-3aa3-11ee-aa43-3f89933ea37a.html.

Blust, Kendal. "Five Years Later, Still No Peace for Family of Slain Teen." *Nogales International*, October 12, 2017. https://www.nogalesinternational.com/news/five -years-later-still-no-peace-for-family-of-slain-teen/article_3fbbe8ae-af89-11e7 -b509-db4a32183492.html.

Boardman, Mark. "The Assassination of Charles Bent." *True West*, January 30, 2020. https://truewestmagazine.com/article/the-assassination-of-charles-bent/.

Brandt, William. "Tepito: Mexico City's Fierce Neighborhood." *Lensculture*, 2023. https://www.lensculture.com/articles/adriana-zehbrauskas-tepito-mexico-city-s -fierce-neighborhood.

Brewer, Stephanie. "Militarized Mexico: A Lost War That Has Not Brought Peace." Washington Office on Latin America, May 12, 2021. https://www.wola.org/analysis /militarized-mexico-a-lost-war/.

Burgueño, Nayeli. *Retorno a la comunidad: Migración y los fondos de identidad trasnacional*. Culiacán: Universidad Autónoma de Sinaloa, 2023.

Bush, George W. "Satellite Remarks to the League of United Latin American Citizens Convention." July 8, 2004. In *Public Papers of the Presidents of the United States: George W. Bush, 2004*, book 2, *July 1–September 30, 2004*. Washington, D.C.: US Government Printing Office, 2007.

Bustamante, Manuela. "Tiene Sinaloa registro de más de 3 mil personas desplazadas por la violencia." *El Sol de Sinaloa*, June 14, 2023. https://www.elsoldesinaloa.com .mx/local/tiene-sinaloa-registro-de-mas-de-3-mil-personas-desplazadas-por-la -violencia-10219281.html.

Cabañas, Miguel A. "El narcocorrido global y las identidades transnacionales." *Revista de Estudios Hispanos* 42, no. 3 (October 2008): 519–42.

Camhaji, Elías. "The Letter from 'El Mayo' Zambada That Widens the Scandal in Mexico: A Murder, a Capture and a Secret Meeting." *El Pais*, August 13, 2024. https://english.elpais.com/international/2024-08-13/the-letter-from-el-mayo -zambada-that-widens-the-scandal-in-mexico-a-murder-a-capture-and-a-secret -meeting.html.

Campbell, Howard. *Downtown Juarez: Underworlds of Violence and Abuse*. Austin: University of Texas Press, 2021.

Campbell, Howard, and Josiah Heyman. "Slantwise: Beyond Domination and Resistance on the Border." *Journal of Contemporary Ethnography* 36, no. 1 (February 2007): 3–30.

Caporal, José Antonio. *El cártel de Neza*. Mexico City: Debolsillo, 2012.

Castañeda Perez, José Ignacio. "Families in Sasabe Seek Refuge from Gangs." *Arizona Republic*, November 26, 2023, 1B.

Castellanos, Guillermo Valdés. "El nacimiento de un ejército criminal." *Nexos*, September 1, 2013. https://www.nexos.com.mx/?p=15460.

Castillo, Juan Camilo, Daniel Mejía, and Pascual Restrepo. *Scarcity Without Leviathan: The Violent Effects of Cocaine Supply Shortages in the Mexican Drug War*. Working Paper No. 356. Washington, D.C.: Center for Global Development, 2014. https://www.cgdev.org/publication/scarcity-without-leviathan-violent-effects-cocaine-supply-shortages-mexican-drug-war.

Cavallaro, Jim. "Transnational Litigation and Corporate Accountability: Mexico's Case Against Arms Traffickers, Keynote Speech." University of Arizona, May 24, 2023. Video, 4:15:50. https://www.youtube.com/watch?v=qga_ext341w.

Chavez, Leo R. *Anchor Babies and the Challenge of Birthright Citizenship*. Stanford: Stanford University Press, 2017.

Chavez, Leo R. *Covering Immigration: Popular Images and the Politics of the Nation*. Berkeley: University of California Press, 2001.

Chavez, Leo R. *The Latino Threat: Constructing Immigrants, Citizens, and the Nation*. Stanford: Stanford University Press, 2008.

Chomczyński, Piotr A., and Timothy W. Clark. "Crime and the Life Course in Another America: Collective Trajectory in Mexican Drug Cartel Dominated Communities." *Justice Quarterly* 40, no. 2 (2023): 291–314.

Chomczyński, Piotr, and Roger Guy. "'Our Biographies Are the Same': Juvenile Work in Mexican Drug Trafficking Organizations from the Perspective of a Collective Trajectory." *British Journal of Criminology* 61, no. 4 (July 2021): 946–64.

Cisneros, J. L. "Niños y jóvenes sicarios: Una batalla cruzada por la pobreza." *El cotidiano* 186 (2014): 7–18.

CONEVAL. *Poverty Indicators by Municipality*. Mexico City: Consejo Nacional de Evaluación de la Política de Desarrollo Social, 2022.

Congressional Medal of Honor Society. "David B. Barclay." Stories of Sacrifice. Accessed March 1, 2023. https://www.cmohs.org/recipients/david-b-barkeley.

Congressional Research Service. *Mexico: Organized Crime and Drug Trafficking Organizations*. Washington, D.C.: Congressional Research Service (CRS), 2020. https://crsreports.congress.gov.

Córdova Solís, Nery. "La narcocultura: Poder, realidad, iconografía y 'mito.'" *Cultura y representaciones sociales* 6, no. 12 (March 2012): 209–37.

Cruz-Torres, Maria L. *Pink Gold: Women, Shrimp, and Work in Mexico*. Austin: University of Texas Press, 2023.

Cuamea, Francisco. "Amenazan mi integridad: Arturo Santamaría." *Reporteros*, December 21, 2011. http://reporteroscom.blogspot.com/2011/12/amenazan-mi-integridad-arturo.html.

Curbelo, Silvia Álvarez. "The Color of War: Puerto Rican Soldiers and Discrimination During World War II." In *Beyond the Latino World War II Hero*, edited by Maggie Rivas-Rodriguez and Emilio Zamora, 110–24. Austin: University of Texas Press, 2009.

Dankoor, Kim, Dionne Stephens, and Tom Ter Bogt. "Drip Too Hard? Commercial Rap Music and Perceived Masculinity Ideals and Actual Self-Evaluations Among Black U.S. and Dutch Adolescent Men." *Sexuality & Culture* 27 (2023): 57–77.

D'Aubeterre, María Eugenia, and María Leticia Rivermar. "Migración de retorno en la sierra norte de Puebla a raíz de la crisis económica estadounidense." In *Nuevas experiencias de la migración de retorno*, edited by Elaine Levine, Silvia Nuñez García, and Mónica Verea, 159–80. Mexico City: Universidad Nacional Autónoma de México, Instituto Matías Romero, 2016.

Davidson, John Daniel. "A Drug Cartel Just Defeated the Mexican Military in Battle." *The Federalist*, October 21, 2019, https://thefederalist.com/2019/10/21/a-drug-cartel-just-defeated-the-mexican-military-in-battle/.

Deare, Craig A. *Militarization "a la AMLO": How Bad Can It Get?* Washington, D.C.: Wilson Center, Mexico Institute, 2021. https://www.wilsoncenter.org/sites/default/files/media/uploads/documents/Militarization_a_la_AMLO_Deare%20.pdf.

del Castillo, Griswold. *The Treaty of Guadalupe Hidalgo*. Norman: University of Oklahoma Press, 1990.

de los Rios, Cati V. "'Los Músicos': Mexican Corridos, the Aural Border, and the Evocative Musical Renderings of Transnational Youth." *Harvard Educational Review* 89, no. 2 (Summer 2019): 177–201.

del Valle, Pedro A. *Semper Fidelis: An Autobiography*. Hawthorne: Christian Book Club of America, 1976.

de Marcos Collado, Noelia. "Asesinada Gisela Mota Ocampo horas después de asumir su cargo." *Periodismo Internacional*, January 4, 2016. https://periodismo internacional.org/asesinada-gisela-mota-ocampo-horas-despues-de-asumir-su-cargo/.

Department of Homeland Security. "Department of Homeland Security (DHS): Strategic Outlook for 2021–2022." GovWin, Washington, D.C., 2021. https://info.deltek.com/DHS-Strategic-Outlook-2021-2022-GovWin-Deltek.

Díaz-Barriga, Miguel, and Margaret E. Dorsey. *Fencing in Democracy: Border Walls, Necrocitizenship, and the Security State*. Durham, N.C.: Duke University Press, 2020.

Dickerson, Caitlin. "A Rare Look Inside Trump's Immigration Crackdown Draws Legal Threats." *New York Times*, July 23, 2020.

Dimas, Peter, dir. *Los Veteranos of World War II*. Phoenix: Braun-Sacred Heart Center, 2007.

Duffin, Erin. "Enacted Border Patrol Program Budget in the United States from 1990–2020." Statista. Accessed January 4, 2023. https://www.statista.com/statistics/455587/enacted-border-patrol-program-budget-in-the-us/#statisticContainer.

Dunn, Timothy J. *The Militarization of the U.S.-Mexico Border, 1998–1972: Low-Intensity Conflict Doctrine Comes Home*. Austin: CMAS Books, 1996.

Durin, Séverine. *¡Salvese quien pueda! Violencia generalizada y desplazamiento forzado en el noreste de México*. Mexico City: CIESAS, 2019.

DW Documentary. "Uncovering Crime and Corruption—Anabel Hernández Takes on Mexico's Drug Cartels." May 3, 2022. Video, 51:54. https://www.youtube.com/watch?v=HYm7aJqXK8A&ab.

Edberg, Mark C. "Narcocorridos: Narratives of a Cultural Persona and Power on the Border." In *Transnational Encounters: Music and Performance at the U.S.-Mexico Border*, edited by Alejandro L. Madrid, 67–82. Oxford: Oxford University Press, 2011.

Egeland, Elizabeth. "Marine Survived War by 'Grace of God.'" *Narratives: Stories of U.S. Latinos and Latinas in World War II* 4, no. 1 (Spring 2003): 23.

Elder, G. H. "Perspectives on the Life Course." In *Life Course Dynamics*, edited by G. H. Elder, 23–49. Ithaca, N.Y.: Cornell University Press, 1985.

Enciso Higuera, Froylán. *Nuestra historia narcótica: Pasajes para (re) legalizar las drogas en México*. Mexico City: Debate, 2017.

Erikson, Erik H. *Identity, Youth and Crisis*. New York: W. W. Norton, 1968.

Ernst, Falko. "The Life and Death of a Mexican Hitman." InSight Crime, February 18, 2019. https://www.insightcrime.org/news/analysis/the-life-and-death-of-a-mexican-hitman/.

Esberg, Jane. "More Than Cartels: Counting Mexico's Crime Rings." International Crisis Group, May 8, 2020. https://www.crisisgroup.org/latin-america-caribbean/mexico/more-cartels-counting-mexicos-crime-rings.

Esparza Bernal, Victor Horacio. "Aproximación psicosocial a las juventudes y el narcotráfico en Sinaloa: Ingreso, prácticas, riesgos y (no) futuro." PhD diss., Universidad Autónoma de Sinaloa, 2020. https://www.academia.edu/97706132/Aproximaci%C3B3n_Psicosocial_a_las_Juventudes_y_el_Narcotr%C3%A1fico_en_Sinaloa_Ingreso_pr%C3%A1cticas_riesgos_y_no_Futuro.

Ewing, Walter A. "'Enemy Territory': Immigration Enforcement in the US-Mexico Borderlands." *Journal on Migration and Human Security* 2, no. 3 (2014): 198–222.

Fernandez Salgado, Pilar. "Historical Controversy: Gangster Rap and Its Relation to Aggression from a Psychological Perspective." Undergraduate thesis, National College of Ireland, 2023. https://norma.ncirl.ie/6700/.

Fernández-Velázquez, Juan Antonio. "La operación Cóndor en los Altos de Sinaloa: La labora del estado durante los primeros años de la Campaña antidroga." *Ra Ximhai* 14, no. 1 (2018): 63–84.

Fernández-Velázquez, Juan Antonio, and Félix Brito Rodríguez. "Pistolerismo y narcotráfico: Escenarios de la violencia cotidiana en Sinaloa, 1940–1980." *Escripta* 2, no. 4 (July–December 2020): 125–58.

Fischer, Peter, and Tobias Greitemeyer. "Music and Aggression: The Impact of Sexual-Aggressive Song Lyrics on Aggression-Related Thoughts, Emotions, and Behavior Toward the Same and the Opposite Sex." *Personality and Social Psychology Bulletin* 32, no. 9 (2006): 1165–76.

Garay y Salamanca, Luis Jorge, and Eduardo Salcedo-Albarán, eds. *Narcotráfico, corrupción y estados.* Mexico City: Penguin Random House Grupo Editorial México, 2012.

Garcia, Angela. *The Pastoral Clinic: Addiction and Dispossession Along the Rio Grande.* Berkeley: University of California Press, 2010.

Garcia, Guillermo X. "War Gave Soldier Confidence to Strive for More." *Narratives: Stories of U.S. Latinos and Latinas in World War II* 3, no. 1 (Fall 2001): 15.

García, Mario T. *The Latino Generation: Voices of the New America.* Chapel Hill: University of North Carolina Press, 2018.

Garrison, Jessica, Wendy Fry, and Alexandra Mendoza. "Baja California Tries to Return to Normal After a Weekend of Cartel Violence." *Los Angeles Times,* August 14, 2022.

Gentry, Blake, Geoffrey Alan Boyce, Jose M. Garcia, and Samuel N. Chambers. "Indigenous Survival and Settler Colonial Dispossession on the Mexican Frontier? The Case of Cedagï Whaia and Wo'oson O'oDham Indigenous Communities." *Journal of Latin American Geography* 18, no. 1 (2019): 65–93.

Glass, Andrew. "U.S. Enacts First Immigration Law, March 26, 1790." Politico, March 26, 2012. https://www.politico.com/story/2012/03/the-united-states-enacts -first-immigration-law-074438.

Glick-Schiller, Nina. "Explanatory Frameworks in Transnational Migration Studies: The Missing Multi-scalar Global Perspective." *Ethnic and Racial Studies* 38, no. 13 (2015): 2275–82.

Gómez San Luis, Anel Hortensia, and Ariagor Manuel Almanza Avendaño. "Impacto del narcotráfico en jóvenes de Tamaulipas, México: Drogas e inseguridad." *Revista de Psicología (PUCP)* 34, no. 2 (2016): 445–72.

Gonzales-Barrera, Ana. "More Mexicans Leaving Than Coming to the U.S." Pew Research Center, November 19, 2015. https://www.pewresearch.org/hispanic/2015 /11/19/more-mexicans-leaving-than-coming-to-the-u-s/.

González Torres, Josue Ángel. "Mexico y el mercado mundial de drogas en 2022." *Diario Contra Replica,* June 29, 2022. https://www.contrareplica.mx/nota-Mexico-y -el-mercado-mundial-de-drogas-en-2022-20222864.

González-Valdes, Ronaldo. *Sinaloa, una sociedad demediada.* Culiacán: H. Ayuntamiento de Culiacán, Dirección de Cultura, 2007.

Goodman-Meza, David, Maria Elena Medina-Mora, Carlos Magis-Rodríguez, Raphael J. Landovitz, Steve Shoptaw, and Dan Werb. "Where Is the Opioid Use Epidemic in Mexico? A Cautionary Tale for Policymakers South of the US–Mexico Border." *American Journal of Public Health* 109, no. 1 (January 1, 2019): 73–82.

Gottesdiener, Laura. "Mexican Navy Offers Rare Apology over Missing People in Border Town." Reuters, July 13, 2021. https://www.reuters.com/world/americas/mexican -navy-offers-rare-apology-over-missing-people-border-town-2021-07-13/.

Grant, Ulysses S. *The Personal Memoirs of Ulysses S. Grant*. Old Saybrook: Konecky & Konecky Press, 1992.

Grillo, Loan. "Opinion: How Mexico's Drug Cartels Are Profiting from the Pandemic." *New York Times*, July 7, 2020.

Guerra, Tere. "Palabra de lector: Crítica desde la crítica." *Noroeste*, December 10, 2011.

Hass, Antonio. "Comentario." *Revista Siempre*, March 23, 1988.

Heyman, Josiah. "Constructing a Perfect Wall: Race, Class, and Citizenship in US-Mexico Border Policing." In *Migration in the Twenty-First Century*, edited by Pauline Gardiner Barber and Winnie Lem, 153–74. New York: Routledge, 2012.

Heyman, Josiah. "Contributions of U.S.-Mexico Border Studies to Social Science Theory." In *The U.S.-Mexico Transborder Region: Cultural Dynamics and Historical Interactions*, edited by Carlos G. Vélez-Ibáñez and Josiah Heyman, 44–64. Tucson: University of Arizona Press, 2017.

Heyman, Josiah. "Who Is Watched? Racialization of Surveillance Technologies and Practices in the US-Mexico Borderlands." *Information & Culture* 57, no. 2 (May 2022): 123–49.

Howell, Rachel. "High Grades Landed Nurse a Job Working in Operating Room." *Narratives: Stories of U.S. Latinos and Latinas in World War II* 4, no. 1 (Spring 2003): 35.

Hu-DeHart, Evelyn. "Immigrants to a Developing Society: The Chinese in Northern Mexico, 1875–1932." *Journal of Arizona History* 21 (Autumn 1980): 49–86.

Ibarra, Guillermo Eduardo. *Ensayos sobre el desarrollo económico regional de Sinaloa, México*. Culiacán: Universidad Autónoma de Sinaloa, Instituto Sinaloense de Cultura, 2009.

Illades, Carlos, and Teresa Santiago. *Estado de guerra: De la guerra sucia a la narcoguerra*. Mexico City: Ediciones Era, 2014.

*Informe de la Presidencia de la Comision para la Verdad y Acceso a la Justicia del Caso*. Mexico City: Gobierno de México, Ayotzinapa, 2022. https://comisionayotzinapa.segob.gob.mx/es/Comision_para_la_Verdad/Segundo_Informe.

Institute for Economics and Peace. *Mexico Peace Index 2022: Identifying and Measuring the Factors That Drive Peace*. Sydney: Institute for Economics and Peace, 2022.

Institute for Women in Migration / Instituto para las Mujeres en la Migración (IMUMI). *Now Where To? The Challenges Facing Transnational Migrant Families Between the United States and Mexico*. Mexico City: IMUMI, 2013.

Instituto Nacional de Estadística, Geografía e Informática (INEGI). *Encuesta Nacional de Victimización y Percepción sobre Seguridad Pública 2022*. Mexico City: INEGI, Government of Mexico, 2022.

Instituto Nacional de Estadística, Geografía e Informática (INEGI). *Population and Housing Census 2020*. Mexico City: INEGI, Government of Mexico, 2020.

Jensen, Bryant, Rebeca Mejía Arauz, and Rodrigo Aguilar Zepeda. "La enseñanza equitativa para los niños retornados a México." *Sinéctica*, no. 48 (2017). https://www.redalyc.org/journal/998/99856084005/html/.

Johnson, James D., Mike S. Adams, Leslie Ashburn, and William Reed. "Differential Gender Effects of Exposure to Rap Music on African American Adolescents' Acceptance of Teen Dating Violence." *Sex Roles: A Journal of Research* 33, no. 7–8 (1995): 597–605.

Jones, Reece. *Nobody Is Protected: How the Border Patrol Became the Most Dangerous Police Force in the United States*. Berkeley: Counterpoint, 2022.

Jusionyte, Ieva. *Threshold: Emergency Responders on the U.S.-Mexico Border*. Berkeley: University of California Press, 2018.

Kearney, Michael. "Borders and Boundaries of State and Self at the End of Empire." *Journal of Historical Sociology* 4, no. 1 (March 1991): 52–74.

Kerr, Audrey Elisa. *The Paper Bag Principle: Class, Complexion, and Community in Black Washington, D.C.* Knoxville: University of Tennessee Press, 2006.

Kline, Victoria. "And Now Where Do We Go? The Challenges Faced by Transnational Migrant Families Between the United States and Mexico." In *Nuevas experiencias de la migración de retorno*, edited by Elaine Levine, Silvia Núñez, and Mónica Verea, 45–58. Mexico City: UNAM, Instituto Matías Romero, 2016.

Kulka, Richard A., William E. Schlenger, John A. Fairbank, Richard L. Hough, B. Kathleen Jordan, Charles R. Marmar, and Daniel S. Weiss. *Contractual Report of Findings from the National Vietnam Veterans Readjustment Study*. Volume 1, *Executive Summary, Description of Findings, and Technical Appendices*. Research Triangle Park: Research Triangle Institute, 1988.

Kulka, Richard A., William E. Schlenger, John A. Fairbank, Richard L. Hough, B. Kathleen Jordan, Charles R. Marmar, and Daniel S. Weiss. *Trauma and the Vietnam War Generation: Report of Findings from the National Vietnam Veteran's Readjustment Study*. New York: Brunner Mazel, 1990.

Lara, Alfonso. "The Other Soldiers." *Narratives: Stories of U.S. Latinos and Latinas in World War II* 3, no. 2 (Spring 2002): 32–33.

Lardieri, Alexa. "Arizona City Officials Demand Government Remove Razor Wire from Border Wall." *U.S. News*, February 7, 2019. https://www.usnews.com/news /politics/articles/2019-02-07/arizona-city-officials-demand-government-remove -razor-wire-from-border-wall.

Lauger, Timothy, and James A. Densley. "Broadcasting Badness: Violence, Identity, and Performance in the Online Gang Rap Scene." *Justice Quarterly* 35, no. 5 (2017): 816–41.

Laurell, Asa Cristina. "Three Decades of Neoliberalism in Mexico: The Destruction of Society." *International Journal of Health Services* 45, no. 2 (2015): 246–64.

Lazcano y Ochoa, Manuel, and Nery Córdova. *Una vida en la vida sinaloense*. Sinaloa: Universidad de Occidente, 1992.

Lecke, Robert. *The March to Glory*. New York: Bantam Books, 1990.

Lee, Allison Elizabeth. "US-Mexico Border Militarization and Violence: Dispossession of Undocumented Laboring Classes from Puebla, Mexico." *Migraciones Internacionales* 9, no. 4 (July–September 2018): 212–38.

Lettieri, Michael. "U.S. Military Training of Mexican Armed Forces and Law Enforcement." Mexico Violence Resource Project, 2022. https://www.mexicoviolence.org /military-training.

Levario, Miguel Antonio. *Militarizing the Border: When Mexicans Became the Enemy.* College Station: Texas A&M University Press, 2012.

Lim, Julian. *Porous Borders: Multiracial Migrations and the Law.* Chapel Hill: University of North Carolina Press, 2017.

Lim, Yvonne. "Boyhood Dream Led to Career as Fighter Ace." *Narratives: Stories of U.S. Latinos and Latinas in World War II* 4, no. 1 (Spring 2003): 72.

Lizárraga-Hernández, Arturo. *Nos llevó la ventolera: El proceso de la emigración rural al extranjero en Sinaloa.* Culiacán: Universidad Autónoma de Sinaloa, 2004.

Lizárraga-Hernández, Arturo, ed. *Procesos y efectos de la emigración sinaloense al extranjero.* Mexico City: Universidad Autónoma de Sinaloa, 2010.

Lizárraga-Hernández, Arturo, Ernestine Lizárraga, and Jorge Abel Guerrero Velasco. "Sinaloa: Migración, pobreza, narcotráfico y crisis económica." In *De aquí, de allá: Migración y desarrollo local,* edited by Eduardo Meza Ramos and Lourdes Pacheco Ladrón de Guevara, 59–80. Mexico City: Unidad Académica de Economía, Universidad Autónoma de Nayarit, 2010.

Los Angeles Almanac. "Gang-Related Crime Los Angeles County." Crime and Justice. Accessed July 7, 2023. https://www.laalmanac.com/crime/cr03x.php#homicides.

Mack, Karin A., Christopher M. Jones, and Michael F. Ballesteros. "Illicit Drug Use, Illicit Drug Use Disorders, and Drug Overdose Deaths in Metropolitan and Non-metropolitan Areas—United States." *Morbidity and Mortality Weekly Report* 66, no. 19 (October 2017): 1–12.

Malone, Gloria. "Mexican Corrido for the New Era: The Evolution of a Genre." BElatina, November 6, 2019. https://belatina.com/mexican-corrido-evolution.

Marchbanks, Rachael. "The Borderline: Indigenous Communities on the International Frontier." *Journal of American Indian Tribal Education* 26, no. 3 (February 2015). https://tribalcollegejournal.org/borderline-indigenous-communities-inter national-frontier/.

Mares, Teresa. *Life on the Other Border: Farmworkers and Food Justice in Vermont.* Berkeley: University of California Press, 2020.

Marizco, Michael. "Was Sonora Shootout a First Act?" *Nogales International,* July 8, 2010. https://www.nogalesinternational.com/news/was-sonora-shootout-a-first -act/article_eeae9ae1-6132-557a-92fa-9a75e4b6802d.html.

Masferrer, Claudia, Erin R. Hamilton, and Nicole Denier. "Half a Million American Minors Now Live in Mexico." The Conversation, July 1, 2019. https://theconver sation.com/half-a-million-american-minors-now-live-in-mexico-119057.

Massey, Douglas, Jorge Durand, and Karen A. Pren. "Border Enforcement and Return Migration by Documented and Undocumented Mexicans." *Journal of Ethnic and Migration Studies* 41, no. 7 (2015): 1015–40.

Matloff, Judith. "The Tale of New York and Neza York." *Al Jazeera*, January 18, 2014. http://america.aljazeera.com/features/2014/1/the-tale-of-new-yorkandnezayork .html.

Mattson, Christine L., Lauren J. Tanz, Kelly Quinn, Mbabazi Kariisa, Priyam Patel, and Nicole L. Davis. "Trends and Geographic Patterns in Drug and Synthetic Opioid Overdose Deaths—United States, 2013–2019." *Morbidity and Mortality Weekly Report* 70, no. 6 (February 2021): 202–7.

Mbembe, Achille. *Necropolitics*. Translated by Steve Corcoran. Durham, N.C.: Duke University Press, 2019.

McCarty, Dawn. "The Impact of the North American Free Trade Agreement (NAFTA) on Rural Children and Families in Mexico: Transnational Policy and Practice Implications." *Journal of Public Child Welfare* 1, no. 4 (2007): 105–23.

McDonald, James H. "The Cultural Effects of the Narcoeconomy in Rural Mexico." *Journal of International and Global Studies* 1, no. 1 (2009): 1–23.

McDonald, James H. "The Narcoeconomy and Small-Town, Rural Mexico." *Human Organization* 64, no. 2 (Summer 2005): 115–24.

McDonald, James H. "Reconfiguring the Countryside: Power, Control, and the (Re) organization of Farmers in West Mexico." *Human Organization* 60, no. 3 (2001): 247–58.

Medina, Leopoldo. "A ritmo de Trapteño, Emmanuel Massú, 'El Enfermo,' comparte las historias de su barrio." *Noroeste*, July 19, 2023.

Menchaca, Martha. *The Mexican American Experience in Texas*. Austin: University of Texas Press, 2022.

Menchaca, Martha. *Recovering History, Constructing Race: The Indian, Black, and White Roots of Mexican Americans*. Austin: University of Texas Press, 2001.

Midgette, Gregory, Steven Davenport, Jonathan P. Caulkins, and Beau Kilmer. *What America's Users Spend on Illegal Drugs, 2006–2016*. Santa Monica: RAND Corporation, 2019.

Miranda, Gabriela. "US Suspends Avocado Imports from Mexico After Inspector Receives Threats." *USA Today*, February 16, 2022.

Miroff, Nick, Scott Higham, Steven Rich, Salwan Georges, and Erin Patrick O'Connor. "Cause of Death: Washington Faltered as Fentanyl Gripped America." *Washington Post*, December 12, 2022.

Molina y Vedia, Silvia, and Rubén Hernández Duarte. "Aportaciones de la transmigración: Mexicanos en Estados Unidos, mexicanos en tránsito y en sus comunidades de origen." In *Migración, organizaciones civiles y transmigración: Redes e interdependencia*, edited by Alejandro Méndez Rodríguez, Jeanette de Rosas Quintero, Miguel Ángel Márquez Zárate, Silvia Molina y Vedia, and V. Castillo, 143–80. Mexico City: UNAM, 2014.

Molnar, Petra. "Robo Dogs and Refugees: The Future of the Global Border Industrial Complex." *Border Chronicle*, February 17, 2022. https://www.theborderchronicle .com/p/robo-dogs-and-refugees-the-future.

Mondaca, Anajilda, Gloria M. Cuamea, and Rocío del Carmen Payares. "Mujer, cuerpo y consumo en microproduccionesde narcocorridos." *Revista ComHumanitas* 6, no. 1 (2015): 170–88.

Montejano, David. *Anglos and Mexicans in the Making of Texas, 1836–1986*. Austin: University of Texas Press, 1987.

Montes, Juan, and David Luhnow. "Mexico's Leader Has Answer for All His Needs: The Army." *Washington Post*, May 28, 2020.

Montoya, Erika, and Arturo Santamaría. "De ida y de regreso: Migración Sinaloa-Arizona en medio de las políticas antimigrantes, violencia y desempleo." In *Visiones de aquí y de allá: Implicaciones de la apolítica antiinmigrante en las comunidades de origen mexicano en Estados Unidos y México*, edited by Carlos G. Vélez-Ibáñez, Roberto Sánchez Benítez, and M. Maríangela Rodríguez, 247–78. Mexico City: Universidad Nacional Autónoma de México, Tempe: Arizona State University; Ciudad Juárez: Universidad Autónoma de Ciudad Juárez, 2015.

Moreno Candil, David, César Burgos Dávila, and Jairo Valdez Batiz. "Daño social y cultura del narcotráfico en México: Estudio de representaciones sociales en Sinaloa y Michoacán." *Mitologías Hoy* 14 (December 2016): 249–69.

Moreno Candil, David, and Fátima Flores Palacios. "Aceptación y rechazo al narcotráfico: Un studio intergeneracional sobre distancia social y nivel de contacto." *Alternativas en Psicología* 18, no. 32 (2015): 160–76.

Murdza, Katy. "New Border Surveillance Technology Raises Privacy Concerns and Could Increase Deaths." Immigration Impact, March 4, 2022. https://immigration impact.com/2022/03/04/border-surveillance-technology-privacy-deaths/.

Murillo, Eduardo. "Asegura SEDENA 6 laboratorios clandestinos del Cártel de Sinaloa." *La Jornada*, July 6, 2022. https://www.jornada.com.mx/notas/2022/06/07/politica /asegura-sedena-seis-laboratorios-clandestinos-del-cartel-de-sinaloa/.

Moslimani, Mohamad, Luis Noe-Bustamante, and Sono Shah. "Facts on Hispanics of Mexican Origin in the United States, 2021." Pew Research Center, August 16, 2023. https://www.pewresearch.org/race-and-ethnicity/fact-sheet/us-hispanics -facts-on-mexican-origin-latinos/.

Nelsen, Aaron. "Former UT President to Teach Course on the Border." *San Antonio Express-News*, December 23, 2017.

Neves, Yuri. "What's Behind the Killings of Mexico's Mayors?" InSight Crime, May 28, 2019. https://www.insightcrime.org/news/analysis/killings-of-mexico-mayors/.

Nuño, Analy. "Mexico's Citizens Caught in Crossfire as Cartels Launch Attacks Across the Country." *The Guardian*, August 18, 2022.

O'Connor, Mike. "Gunmen Rule Neza and the Press on Outskirts of Mexico City." Committee to Protect Journalists, February 2014. https://cpj.org/2014/02/attacks -on-the-press-mexico-analysis.

O'Donnell-Rosales, John. *Hispanic Confederates from the Gulf Coast States*. Baltimore: Clearfield, 2009.

Office of Border Patrol. "Message from the Commissioner." In *National Border Patrol Strategy*, n.p. Washington, D.C.: U.S. Customs and Border Protection, 2004.

Office of Deputy Assistant Secretary of Defense for Equal Opportunity and Safety Policy. *Hispanics in America's Defense*. Washington, D.C.: Department of Defense, 1980.

Olea, Héctor R. *Badiraguato: Visión Panorámica de su historia*. Mexico City: DIFOCUR-Ayuntamiento de Badiraguato, 1988.

Onaran, Özlem. *Wage Share, Globalization, and Crisis: The Case of the Manufacturing Industry in Korea, Mexico, and Turkey*. Working Paper 132. Political Economy Research Institute, University of Massachusetts, Amherst, March 2007.

O'Neill, Kevin Lewis. "Moral Failure: A Jeremiad of the War on Drugs in Guatemala." *Journal of the Royal Anthropological Institute* 28 (2021): 52–70.

Ovalle, Lilian Paola. "Entre la indiferencia y la satanización: Representaciones sociales del narcotráfico desde la perspectiva de los universitarios de Tijuana." *Culturales* 1, no. 2 (2005): 63–89.

Pansters, Wil G., ed. *Violence, Coercion, and State-Making in Twentieth-Century Mexico*. Stanford: Stanford University Press, 2012.

Park, Joseph E. "The History of Mexican Labor in Arizona During the Territorial Period." Master's thesis, University of Arizona, 1961.

Parker, William D. *U. S. Marine Corps Civil Affairs in I Corps: Republic of South Vietnam, April 1966–April 1967*. Washington, D.C.: Historical Division Headquarters, U.S. Marine Corps, 1970.

Passel, Jeffrey S., and Paul Taylor. "Unauthorized Immigrants and Their U.S.-Born Children." Pew Research Center, August 11, 2010. https://www.pewresearch.org/hispanic/2010/08/11/unauthorized-immigrants-and-their-us-born-children/.

Pérez, Edmundo. *Que me entierren con narcocorrido las historias de los gruperos asesinadoss*. Mexico City: Grijalbo, 2012.

Pillai, Drishti, and Samantha Artiga. "Title 42 and Its Impact on Migrant Families." KFF, May 26, 2022. https://www.kff.org/racial-equity-and-health-policy/issue-brief/title-42-and-its-impact-on-migrant-families/.

Pintor-Sandoval, Renato. "The Habitus and Transnational Fields in the Process of Migrant Transnationalism." *International Migrations* 6, no. 2 (2011): 159–92.

Plascencia, Luis F. B. "Where Is 'the Border'? The Fourth Amendment, Boundary Enforcement and the Making of an Inherently Suspect Class." In *The U.S.-Mexico Transborder Region: Cultural Dynamics and Historical Interactions*, edited by Carlos G. Vélez-Ibáñez and Josiah Heyman, 244–80. Tucson: University of Arizona Press, 2017.

Plascencia, Luis F. B., and Gloria Cuadras. *Mexican Workers and the Making of Arizona*. Tucson: University of Arizona Press, 2018.

Pratt, Mary Louise. *Imperial Eyes: Travel Writing and Transculturation*. New York: Routledge, 1992.

Ramírez-Pimienta, Juan Carlos. "'El Pablote': Una nueva mirada al primer corrido dedicado a un traficante de drogas." *Mitologías Hoy* 14 (December 2016): 41–56.

Ramírez-Pimienta, Juan Carlos. "Narcocultura a ritmo norteño: El narcocorrido ante el nuevo milenio." *Latin American Research Review* 42, no. 2 (June 2007): 253–61.

Ramírez-Sánchez, Rubén Darío. "Del edén al infierno: Inseguridad y construcción estatal en Tabasco." *LiminaR: Estudios Sociales y Humanísticos* 17, no. 2 (July–December 2019): 196–216.

Ramos, Henry A. J. *The American G.I. Forum: In Pursuit of the Dream, 1948–1983.* Houston: Arte Público Press, 1998.

Ravelo, Ricardo. *Herencia Maldita: El reto de Calderón y el nuevo mapa del narcotráfio.* Mexico City: Grijalbo, 2007.

Rivera-Sánchez, L. "Sujetos móviles y pertenencías urbanas: Notas en torno a una investigación sobre prácticas y experiencias de reinserción social de migrantes retornados a espacios urbanos." *Estudios sociológicos* 33, no. 97 (2015): 169–96.

Rocha Moya, Rubén. "UAS: De la libertad a la censura." *El Debate*, January 10, 2012.

Rocha Moya, Rubén, Andomar Ahumada Quintero, Jorge Medina Viedas, and David Moreno Lizárraga. "Nuestra solidaridad con el Doctor Arturo Santamaría Gómez." *Noroeste*, December 29, 2011.

Rodríguez, Agustín. "Ejército asegura a 6 laboratorios clandestinos de droga en Sinaloa." TV Azteca, June 7, 2022. https://www.tvazteca.com/aztecanoticias/ejercito-laboratorios-sinaloa-jvgl.

Rodríguez Nicholls, Mariángela. *Esclavitud posmoderna: Flexibilización, migración y cambio cultural.* Mexico City: CIESAS, 2010.

Román, Iván. "When a Fallen Mexican American War Hero Was Denied a Wake, a Civil Rights Push Began." History, October 9, 2020. https://www.history.com/news/mexican-american-rights-longoria-lyndon-johnson-hector-garcia.

Roosevelt, Theodore. "Appendix A. Muster-Out Roll." In *The Rough Riders*, 233–81. New York: P. F. Collier & Son, 1899.

Saenz, J. Luz. *Los mexico-americanos en la Gran Guerra: Y su contingente en pro de la democracia, la humanidad y la justicia.* San Antonio: Artes Gráficas, 1933.

Sánchez, George I. *Forgotten People: A Study of New Mexicans.* Albuquerque: University of New Mexico Press, 1967.

Sánchez-Talanquer, Mariano, and Kenneth F. Greene. "Is Mexico Falling into the Authoritarian Trap?" *Journal of Democracy* 32, no. 4 (2021): 56–71.

Santa Ana, Otto. *Brown Tide Rising: Metaphors of Latinos in Contemporary American Public Discourse.* Austin: University of Texas Press. 2000.

Santamaría Gómez, Arturo. *Las jefas del narco: El ascenso de las mujeres en el crimen organizado.* Mexico City: Random House Mondradon, 2012.

Santamaría Gómez, Arturo. *De carnaval, reinas y narco: El terrible poder de la belleza.* Mexico City: Grijalbo, 2014.

Santamaría Gómez, Arturo. "¿Si México es un narco estado, desde cuándo?" *Noroeste*, February 18, 2023.

Santamaría Gómez, Arturo, Pedro Brito Osuna, and Luis Antonio Martínez Peña. *Morir en Sinaloa: Violencia, narco y cultura.* Culiacán: Universidad de Sinaloa, 2009.

Santiago, Tony. "Major Oscar Francis Perdomo." *Aviation Online Magazine.* Accessed March 5, 2023. http://www.avstop.com/history/hispanic_aviators/major_oscar_francis_perdomo.htm.

Scheiner, Patricia Campos. "Californio Resistance to the U.S. Invasion of 1846." Master's thesis, California State University, East Bay, 2009.

Secretaría de Gobernación. "Índices de intensidad migratoria México-Estados Unidos." Consejo Nacional de Población, Gobierno de México, 2010. https://www.gob.mx/conapo/documentos/indices-de-intensidad-migratoria-mexico-estados-unidos-2010.

Servín, Manuel P. "The Legal Basis for the Establishment of Spanish Colonial Sovereignty: The Act of Possession." *New Mexico Historical Review* 53, no. 4 (1978): 295–303.

Shamout, Omar. "Narcocorridos: The Drug War in Song." *Intersections, South LA*, January 16, 2012. https://intersectionssouthla.org/story/narcocorridos_the_drug_war_in_song/.

Sheridan, Thomas E. *Arizona: A History*. Tucson: University of Arizona Press, 2013.

Sheridan, Thomas E., and Randal H. McGuire. "Introduction: The Border and Its Bodies: The Embodiment of Risk Along the U.S.-Mexico Line." In *The Border and Its Bodies: The Embodiment of Risk Along the U.S.-Mexico Line*, edited by Thomas E. Sheridan and Randal H. McGuire, 3–40. Tucson: University of Arizona Press, 2019.

Shoichet, Catherine E. "Robot Dogs Could Patrol the U.S.-Mexico Border." CNN, February 9, 2020. https://www.cnn.com/2022/02/19/us/robot-dogs-us-mexico-border-patrol-cec/index.html.

Simonett, Helena. "Subcultura musical: El narcocorrido comercial y el narcocorrido por encargo." *Caravelle*, no. 82 (June 2004): 179–93.

Slack, Jeremy, and Daniel E. Martínez. "Postremoval Geographies: Immigration Enforcement and Organized Crime on the U.S.-Mexico Border." *Annals of the American Association of Geographers* 111, no. 4 (2020): 1062–78.

Smith, Benjamin T. *The Dope: The Real History of the Mexican Drug Trade*. New York: W. W. Norton, 2021.

Sola-Santiago, Frances. "Remembering Petra Herrera, the Unsung, Cross-Dressing Heroine of the Mexican Revolution." Remezcla, September 14, 2018. https://remezcla.com/features/culture/petra-herrera-mexican-revolution-heroine/.

Solis, Gustavo, and Matthew Bowler. "Officials Doing Little as More Migrants Drown in Imperial County Canal." KPBS, February 8, 2022. https://www.kpbs.org/news/local/2022/02/08/officials-doing-little-as-more-migrants-drown-in-imperial-county-canal.

Solís, Oliva. "Masculinidad y música latinoamericana." Entre Hombres México. Accessed October 4, 2023. https://www.entrehombres.net/319-masculinidad-y-musica-latinoamericana-movimiento-alterado-dra-oliva-solis/.

Stanford, Kristin. "Sixth Brother in Uniform." *Narratives: Stories of U.S. Latinos and Latinas in World War II* 3, no. 2 (Spring 2002): 10.

Stanley, F. *The Civil War in New Mexico*. Santa Fe: Sunstone, 2011.

State Public Security Council. *Diagnóstico Febrero 2021*. Culiacán: Coordinación General del Consejo Estatal de Seguridad Pública del Estado de Sinaloa, 2021.

Sullivan, John P. "Maras Morphing: Revisiting Third Generation Gangs." *Global Crime* 7, no. 3–4 (August–November 2006): 487–504.

Sullivan, John P. "Transnational Gangs: The Impact of Third Generation Gangs in Central America." *Air and Space Power Journal*, July 2008.

Sundberg, Juanita. "The State of Exception and the Imperial Way of Life in the United States–Mexico Borderlands." *Environment and Planning D: Society and Space* 33, no. 2 (2015): 209–28.

Swanson, Doug J. *Cult of Glory: The Bold and Brutal History of the Texas Rangers.* New York: Viking, 2020.

Timmons, Patrick. "Trump's Wall at Nixon's Border: How Richard Nixon's Operation Intercept Laid the Foundation for Decades of U.S.-Mexico Border Policy, Including Trump's Wall." *NACLA Report on the Americas* 49, no. 1 (2017): 15–24.

Traphagan, Amanda. "Young Woman Found Freedom as Navy Nurse." *Narratives: Stories of U.S. Latinos and Latinas in World War II* 4, no. 1 (Spring 2003): 34.

Trejo, Guillermo, and Sandra Ley. *Votes, Drugs, and Violence: The Political Logic of Criminal Wars in Mexico.* Cambridge: Cambridge University Press, 2020.

Trickey, Erick. "The Little-Remembered Ally Who Helped America Win the Revolution." *Smithsonian Magazine*, January 13, 2017. https://www.smithsonianmag .com/history/little-remembered-ally-who-helped-america-win-revolution-1809 61782/.

Turner, D. L. "Arizona's Twenty-Four Hour War: The Arizona Rangers and the Cananea Copper Strike of 1906." *Journal of Arizona History* 48, no. 3 (Autumn 2007): 257–88.

Turner, Victor W. *Dramas, Fields, and Metaphors: Symbolic Action in Human Society.* Ithaca, N.Y.: Cornell University Press, 1974.

Unidad de Política Migratoria, Registros e Identidad de Personas. *Diagnóstico de la movilidad humana en Sinaloa.* Mexico City: Secretaría de Gobernación, 2020.

United Nations Office on Drugs and Crime (UNODC). "¿Qué dice el Informe mundial sobre las drogas 2022 de las tendencias de América Latina y el Caribe?" Centro de Excelencia UNODC-INEGI, July 8, 2022. https://www.cdeunodc.inegi.org.mx /index.php/2022/07/08/dice-informe-mundial-las-drogas-2022-las-tendencias -america-latina-caribe.

U.S. Department of Labor. "Earnings Disparities by Race and Ethnicity." Office of Federal Contract Compliance Programs. Accessed July 4, 2023. https://www.dol .gov/agencies/ofccp/about/data/earnings/race-and-ethnicity.

U.S. General Accountability Office. *Border Patrol: Available Data on Interior Checkpoints Suggest Differences in Sector Performance.* Report to Congressional Requesters. Washington, D.C.: Government Printing Office, 2005.

U.S. General Accountability Office. "Firearms Trafficking: U.S. Efforts to Disrupt Gun Smuggling into Mexico: Would Benefit from Additional Data and Analysis," *GAO 100 Highlights*, February 2021. https://www.gao.gov/assets/d21322high.pdf.

U.S. General Accountability Office. *Illegal Immigration: Southwest Border Strategy Results Inconclusive; More Evaluation Needed.* Report to the Committee on the Judiciary, US Senate and the Committee on the Judiciary, House of Representatives. Washington, D.C.: Government Printing Office, 1997.

U.S. Immigration and Customs Enforcement, Department of Homeland Security. "Arrestos migratorios de ERO ICE aumentan casi un 40 por ciento en comparación con el año pasado." Comunicados de Prensa, May 17, 2017. https://www.ice .gov/es/news/releases/arrestos-migratorios-de-ero-ice-aumentan-casi-un-40 -por-ciento-en-comparacion-con-el.

Valdez, Al. "The Origins of Southern California Latino Gangs." In *Maras: Gang Violence and Security in Central America*, edited by Thomas Bruneau, Lucía Dammert, and Elizabeth Skinner, 23–42. Austin: University of Texas Press, 2011.

Valencia Triana, Sayak. "Capitalismo gore y necropolítica en México contemporáneo." *Relaciones internacionales* 19 (2012): 83–102.

Valenzuela, José Manuel. *Trazos de sangre y fuego: Bio-Necropolítica y juvenicidio en América Latina.* Mexico City: Transcript Verlag, 2019.

van Gennep, Arnold. *The Rites of Passage.* Translated by M. B. Vizedom and G. L. Caffee. Chicago: University of Chicago Press, 1960.

Van Herk, Glen. "Organized Crime Controls 35% of Mexico." *Yucatan Times*, March 23, 2021. https://www.theyucatantimes.com/2021/03/organized-crime-controls-35-of -mexico/.

Vega, Miguel Ángel. "Cuando Jesus Maria se convertido en zona de guerras." *Río Doce*, January 15, 2023. https://riodoce.mx/2023/01/17/cuando-jesus-maria-se -convirtio-en-zona-de-guerra/.

Veiras, Pardo, and José Luis y Íñigo Arredondo. "Opinión: Una guerra inventada y 350,000 muertos en México." *Washington Post*, June 14, 2021.

Velázquez, Carlos. "Asesinan a Héctor Melesio Cuén, diputado electo del PAN-PRI-PRD, en Sinaloa." *El Financiero*, July 26, 2024. https://www.elfinanciero.com.mx /estados/2024/07/26/asesinan-a-hector-melesio-cuen-diputado-electo-del-pan -pri-prd-en-sinaloa/.

Velazquez, Loreta Janeta. *The Woman in Battle: A Narrative of the Exploits, Adventures, and Travels of Madame Loreta Janeta Velazquez, Otherwise Known as Lieutenant Harry T. Buford, Confederate States Army.* Richmond, Va.: Dustin, Gilman & Co., 1876.

Vélez-Ibáñez, Carlos G. *Border Visions: Mexican Cultures of the Southwest United States.* Tucson: University of Arizona Press, 1996.

Vélez-Ibáñez, Carlos G. "Continuity and Contiguity of the Southwest North American Region: The Dynamics of a Common Political Ecology." In *The U.S. Mexico Transborder Region*, edited by Carlos G. Vélez-Ibáñez and Josiah Heyman, 11–43. Tucson: University of Arizona Press, 2017.

Vélez-Ibáñez, Carlos G. *Hegemonies of Language and Their Discontents: The Southwest North American Region Since 1540.* Tucson: University of Arizona Press, 2017.

Vélez-Ibáñez, Carlos. G. *An Impossible Living in a Transborder World: Culture, Confianza, and Economy of Mexican-Origin Populations.* Tucson: University of Arizona Press, 2017.

Vélez-Ibáñez, Carlos G. *Rituals of Marginality: Politics, Process, and Cultural Change in Urban Mexico, 1969–1974.* Berkeley: University of California Press, 1983.

Vélez-Ibáñez, Carlos G., Phillip Gonzales, Luis Plascencia, and Jesús Rosales. "Interrogating Early New Mexican Folklore y Lo Mexicano: The Literary Works of José Agapito Olivas." *Aztlán: A Journal of Chicano Studies* 44, no. 2 (Fall 2019): 85–112.

Vélez-Ibáñez, Carlos G., and James B. Greenberg. "Formation and Transformation of Funds of Knowledge Among US-Mexican Households." *Anthropology and Education Quarterly* 23, no. 4 (December 1992): 313–35.

Verini, James. "Death in the Desert: How U.S. Policy Turned the Sonoran Desert into a Graveyard for Migrants." *New York Times Magazine*, August 18, 2020.

Vigil, Diego. "Community Dynamics and the Rise of Street Gangs." In *Latinos! Remaking America*, edited by Marcelo M. Suárez-Orozco and Mariela M. Páez, 97–109. Berkeley: University of California Press with the David Rockefeller Center for Latin American Studies, Harvard University, 2002.

Vigil, James Diego. *Chicano High Schoolers in a Changing Los Angeles.* Columbus, Ohio: Biblio, 2020.

Vigil, James Diego. *Gang Redux: A Balanced Anti-gang Strategy.* Long Grove: Waveland, 2010.

Vigil, James Diego, and Steve C. Yun. "A Cross-Cultural Framework for Understanding Gangs: Multiple Marginality and Los Angeles." In *Gangs in America*, edited by C. Ronald Huff, 161–74. 3rd ed. Thousand Oaks, Calif.: Sage, 2002.

Villahermosa, Gilberto. "America's Hispanics in America's Wars." *Army Magazine*, September 2002. https://www.valerosos.com/HispanicsMilitary.html.

Villarreal, Emiliano. "Narcocultura as Cultural Capital for Latinx Youth Identity Work: An Online Ethnography." PhD diss., University of Texas at El Paso, 2019.

Vivanco, Roxana. "El texto pone a Santamaría de cuerpo entero: Cuén." *Noroeste*, December 23, 2011.

Vivanco, Roxana. "'Sin precedente en la UAS agresión contra Santamaría.'" *Noroeste*, November 9, 2015.

Waghelstein, John D. "Low-Intensity Conflict in the Post-Vietnam Period." Transcript of presentation at American Enterprise Institute, Washington, D.C., January 17, 1985.

Wald, Elijah. *Narcocorrido: A Journey into the Music of Drugs, Guns and Guerrillas.* New York: HarperCollins, 2001.

Washington, Mayra. "Puros Corridos Alterados Pariente!" QuotesGram. Accessed October 4, 2023. https://quotesgram.com/img/puros-corridos-con-banda-quotes /11757446/.

Wessler, Seth Freed. "Thousands of Kids Lost from Parents in U.S. Deportation System." Colorlines, November 2, 2011. https://colorlines.com/article/thousands -kids-lost-parents-us-deportation-system/.

West, Brooke. "Despite Anti-Hispanic Bias Staff Sergeant Led a Dozen Men." *Narratives: Stories of U.S. Latinos and Latinas in World War II* 4, no. 1 (Spring 2003): 31.

Wolf, Eric R. *Europe and the People Without History*. Berkeley: University of California Press, 1997.

Woody, Christopher. "Mexicans in the World's Most Violent City Are Taking Barbed Wire Right Off the Border Wall to Protect Their Own Homes." Business Insider, March 20, 2019. https://www.businessinsider.com/tijuana-residents-stealing -concertina-barbed-wire-on-border-for-homes-2019-3.

World Population Review. "New Mexico Poverty by Race." New Mexico Population 2023. Accessed July 4, 2023. https://worldpopulationreview.com/states/new -mexico-population.

Zazueta Beltrán, Héctor Gabriel, and José Carlos Pardini Moss. "Values and Educative Aspirations." *Chinese Business Review* 10, no. 3 (March 2011): 226–32.

Zazueta Beltrán, Héctor Gabriel, César Omar Sepúlveda Moreno, and Nora Teresa Millán López. "Influencia de narco-series y narco-corridos en las aspiraciones educativas de estudiantes de Sinaloa, México." In *Reconfigurando territorios a partir de la cultura, el empoderamiento de las mujeres y nuevos turismos*, edited by Mora Cantellano, Ma. del Pilar Alejandra, Serrano Oswald, Serena Eréndira y Mota Flores, and V. Enrique, 169–86. Mexico City: UNAM-AMECIDER, 2022.

# INDEX

All-American Canal: completion, 31; earlier material form of prevention through deterrence, 34–35; and migrant death, 31

Alvarez Jr., Robert R.: contradictions between state regulatory actions and human actions, 200; on migration states and migrants as labor, 200

Amaya, Hector: on the "deterritorialization" of commodities (narcocorridos), 199; narcocorridos link Mexican origin persons to Mexico, 205

AMLO. *See* López Obrador, Andrés Manuel (president)

Asbhy, Paul, 223n3; Canada and Mexico as part of U.S. policing regime, 6; link between policing and NAFTA, 6; and "NAFTA-land Security," 6

American Intervention (U.S.-Mexico War, 1846–1848), 64, 135, 232–33n9; relevance for necrocitizenship, 64; represented in YouTube, 206; set the stage for the Civil War, 64; U.S. invasion of Mexico, 21; various labels for, 233n14

American Mexican Triangle, 204, 205; absence of research on Chicano/Mexican American youth, 212, 215; altered corridos as, 205; described, 16, 215, 221; emergence of, 201; and impact of narco novelas and narcocorridos on adolescents, 210; importance of structural inequality in, 213–14; limitations of research, 212; link to Twiins Culiacán production company (Los Angeles), 204; materialistic culture and youth, 211; and narcocorridos, 16, 200, 203, 212–13; other research, 209, 210; portrayed on YouTube, 206; and the production of a dominant subculture, 211; relevance of "multiple marginality" in examining, 137, 213; research in Tamaulipas, 209–10; research on *alterados* and youth, 211; research on youth in Sinaloa and Michoacán, 200, 208–9; research on youth in Tijuana, 208; structural context for, 213; and values, 204

Biden, Joseph R., Jr. (president): continued use of Title 42, 31, 63; part of Obama administration's deportations, 52; on Trump asylum policies, 51–52

Border Patrol: enactment of low-intensity warfare, 26; Mexican-origin officers, 23; violence by, 31, 228n14

*Border Security Wall Construction* (videogame), 31–32, *33*

Burgueño A., Nayeli, 224n18; agricultural and livestock work, 119; change in Mexico's federal law regarding admission to public schools, 122; conjunction of necro-narco citizenship, 127, 128; creation of transnational community, 117; crisis returnees, 111; decision to return, 118; and difficulties faced by U.S.-born returnees, 112–13, 121–23, 125; displacement of rural communities due to violence, 127; exclusion of returnee children from health-care system, 122; and extreme violence in Cosalá, 113, 124; families send their U.S.-born children back to the U.S., 124, 125, 126, 220–21; federal law on revalidation of schooling in the U.S., 122; five phases of migration, 115; forced returnees, 111; and the fracturing of families, 126, 220; high proportion of families with U.S.-born children, 120; high rates of homicides, 119; history of mining, 113–14; illegal status of returnee children, 122, 123; and the importance of extended family, 119; incorporation of youth into drug-trafficking organizations, 125; increased vulnerability of returned migrants, 112, 120, 125; increase in forced return of migrants, 111, 118; layered identities of youth, 124; link between drug production and violence, 119–20; Mexican state ignoring returned migrant families, 123; migration as a major avenue to escape economic conditions, 114; migration corridor, 115; most returned to Mexico are family units, 111, 121; "new migration phase,"

111; normalization of violence, 124, 128; and poverty in Cosalá, 114; precarious wages and medical care, 119; re-emergence of mining by Americas Gold and Silver Corporation (Canadian), 114; and remittances, 117; return of mixed-status families, 112; schools do not recognize English knowledge of children, 121–22; tri-directional changes in transnational families, 126–27; value of kinship relations, 120; youth plan to return to the U.S., 125, 126

Cabañas, Miguel A.: and deterritorialization of origins, 201; on narcocorridos as transnational phenomena linked to transnational migration, 201

cartels, Mexican: and Pedro Avilés, 161; Battle of Culiacán, 91; business model of, 91–92; capture and release of Ovidio Guzmán López, 44, 91; Cártel de Sinaloa, 172; collusion between government officials and, 89; commodities promoting popular acceptance of, 51; and control agricultural and trade goods, 219; and control of cities, 44; corporate-oriented organization of, 152; depend on U.S. drug demand, 43; dominate civil, educational, political institutions, and capitalist enterprises, 89, 219; as drug-trafficking organizations, 125; expansion into legitimate businesses, 89; extensive geographic reach in Mexico, 100; and Miguel Ángel Félix Gallardo, 161; formation of standard cartel units and militarized cartel units, 46; and former Mexican and Guatemalan tactical operations soldiers, 46, 90; gained control of entire parts of cities, 220; and Genaro García Luna, 44; in government, 172–73; growth of,

91, 161; impact on the Indigenous O'odham community (Arizona), 98; income from *huachicoleo* (illicit sale of fuel), 89; incorporation of tactical soldiers trained by the U.S., 90; killing as rational approach, 104; killing of elected officials, 44–45; known, 91; La Familia's impact in Michoacán, 94–95; later emergence of the Sinaloa, 161; leaders distinguish women as *catedrales* and *capillas*, 204; legitimate businesses as foundation of cultural complex, 89–90; and Los Zetas, 90–91; maturational seepage in local control by La Familia, 95; militarization and cultural architecture in, 9, 90; murder as a control mechanism, 97–98; nonreporting by journalist of activity of, 103–4; penetrated local, municipal, and state elections, 219; place limits on academic freedom and journalism, 172; power and control over much of Sinaloa, 170, 172; preference for assault rifles, 45–46; sale of "protection" and extraction of "social rent" by Los Zetas, 91–92; seepage into civil and military structures, 90; siphoning of state-transported gasoline, 219; *situado* (situated) as link to a cartel, 49; splintering and regrouping dynamics, 43; use of government to weaken rival cartels, 174; "vertical integration" encompassing local gangs, military, police, and politicians, 89, 219, 220; warnings to residents about planned "*limpiados*" (cleaning out) of opponents, 150. *See also* Mexican journalists killed or disappeared; Mexico; narcocitizenship; Santamaría Gómez, Arturo; United States

Chavez, Leo R., 224n15, 226n14; the deployment of criminal trope, 22, 25; on infectious "Others," 25

Cienfuegos, Salvador (general): arrest and conviction, 46; release, 46; secretary of defense, 46

Civil War (U.S.), 60; and Mexican-origin soldiers, 64

colonial hegemony: as imperial and settler, 20; Mexican Republican rationalization as, 20; Spanish colonialism as, 20; U.S. manifest destiny as, 20

*confianza* (mutual trust), 224n16; as a central core value, 6; and security of private schools attended by children of cartel members, 150; violence and destruction of ties based on, 93

Constitution-Free Zone, 52, 230n39, 231n58

Cuén Ojeda, Héctor Melesio: on absurdity of article supporting, 167; assassinated in Sinaloa, 174, 198, 249–50n17; and Cuenta Conmigo political organization, 164, 186; directors and professors at UAS publish document supporting, 166–67; as *dirigente corte caciquil y autoritario*, 182; and emergence of individuals seeking to empower themselves and use the university as a political institution, 160–61; emulated his grandfather's caciquism, 169, 192; family's extensive ownership of properties and businesses, 163, 185–86; as "fascist" and "cacique," 165–66; and implicit death threat against Arturo Santamaría Gómez, 166, 188–89; Mayor of Culiacán, 165; in operation of Universidad Autónoma de Sinaloa (UAS) as Mayor of Culiacán, 164, 168–69; patrimonial enrichment of, 162–63; politician of the University Party/Sinaloa Party (PAS), 160, 182; politicized and destabilized UAS, 162; as representing "illiterate despotism," 169, 192; Rubén Rocha Moya critical of, 168; Santamaría Gómez's filed com-

Cuén Ojeda, Héctor Melesio (*continued*) plaint against, 169. Tere Guerra and campaign of inquisition by, 168, 191. *See also* Santamaría Gómez, Arturo cycles of attraction and expulsion of Mexicans, 8

death funnels, 24, 34; as part of low-intensity warfare, 24

Díaz-Barriga, Miguel: conjunto festival in honor of Eligio Escobar, 81; contrast between "patriotic citizenship" and "necrocitizenship," 57; El Veterano Conjunto Festival, 81–82; inclusion of an Iwo Jima survivor, 83; linking of Day of the Dead and national patriotism, 82; necrocitizenship's emotional and ritual dynamic, 81; normalization of militarism among Mexican Americans, 57; symbols of sacrifice and citizenship-worthiness, 82. *See also* necrocitizenship

Dorsey, Margaret: conjunto festival in honor of Eligio Escobar, 81; contrast between "patriotic citizenship" and "necrocitizenship," 57; El Veterano Conjunto Festival, 81–82; inclusion of an Iwo Jima survivor, 83; linking of Day of the Dead and national patriotism, 82; necrocitizenship's emotional and ritual dynamic, 81; normalization of militarism among Mexican Americans, 57; symbols of sacrifice and citizenship-worthiness, 82. *See also* necrocitizenship

drug supplying sectors: Asia, 19; Mexico, 19; South America, 19

fear of obedience, 128; emigration driven by, 126; and impact on U.S.-born returnees, 221; involves cartel control of physical, emotional, and social space, 103; link to narcocitizenship,

103; killing of innocent civilians as a strategy to induce obedience, 132; and loss of cultural contexts of security and predictability in the everyday, 103; university politics and imprinting of, 152–53

Glick-Schiller, Nina: and accumulation and concentration of wealth and power, 18; "global historical conjunctures," 12, 17, 18, 218; 224n17, 224n1

global capitalism: centrality of neoliberal economic policies in, 6; and development of the necro/narco transtate network, 12, 127; and erasure of allegiance to place, territory, or persons, 199; hidden dimensions of, 217; link to U.S. empire, 199; long history in the political relationship of the U.S. with Mexico, 12, 17–18; and narcocorridos, 213; and systems of extraction, 6; quotidian dimensions of, 217

Heyman, Josiah: on neoliberalization and capitalist wealth accumulation, 9; policing regimes as political theater, 19–20; surveillance technologies, 227n16; U.S. military power and framing as foreign policy and diplomacy, 19–20

Hu-DeHart, Evelyn: and Chinese and other foreign migrants in northern Mexico, 229–30n31

Illegal Immigration Reform and Immigrant Responsibility Act (IIRIRA, 1996), 118

Jones, Reece: on the Border Patrol as the most dangerous police force, 228n14

Kearney, Michael, 223n4; "decline of the unitedstatesian empire," 7, 199; separation of production and reproduction, 7

INDEX

late-stage capitalism: and American Mexican Triangle, 215; described, 6–7; link to narcocorridos, 203, 206, 213; as motherless, 199; produces casualties, 6–7. *See also* American Mexican Triangle; global capitalism

Levario, Miguel Antonio: and construction of Mexicans as an "enemy other," 62; on development and deployment of "low-intensity warfare" on the Mexico-U.S. boundary area, 62

living at a slant, 224n16; defined, 11; as a survival strategy in a context of low-intensity warfare, 53

López Obrador, Andrés Manuel (president): advocated military role in construction of public works, 47, 221–22; agreements with the Sinaloa Cartel, 173, 196; arrested Ovidio Guzmán López, 44; corruption of individuals in the presidency of, 89; created the National Guard (2019), 48, 88; failed to defeat drug trafficking, 172; failure of "hugs, not bullets" campaign against criminal networks, 109; governmental Cuarta Transformación (Fourth Transformation), 172, 195; mandated release of Salvador Cienfuegos, 46; militarization of Mexico's southern border, 51–52, 88; and narcostate, 174, 197; ordered release of Guzmán López, Ovidio, 44, 109; Sinaloa Cartel is protected by, 173, 197

Marine Corps League. *See* Mexican and Latina/o/x populations and militarization

Mbembe, Achille, necropower, 26

Mexican and Latina/o/x populations and militarization: controversy and casualties in the Vietnam War, 72; diagnosis of post-traumatic stress disorder among, 73; enlistment of

Latinas, 69; and formation of the GI Forum, 68–69; Felix Longoria burial controversy, 232n3; and GI Bill, 71–72; legitimacy through the military, 73–74; Los Chavalones of E Company, 74–81; and E Company of Marine Corps League, 11, 74–78; men in the 65th Regiment exonerated, 71; Mexican noncitizens participation in U.S. wars, 73; Mexicans as the enemy of the state after U.S. conquest, 61–62; Mexicans killed in action in WWII, 70; Mexican support for U.S. wars, 63; military work and furthering of civil rights, 64, 66; mixed view of Korean War, 70; participation in anti–Vietnam War movement, 72; participation in the Gulf War (1990–1991), 73; presence in U.S. wars, 60, 62, 63, 64–72, 74, 84; Puerto Rican accommodation and resistance to U.S. militarization, 63–64; U.S. public view of Mexicans as "cheap labor," 63; World War II as a watershed for Latinas, 69

Mexican journalists killed or disappeared, 44; Jorge Armenta, 103–4; Miroslava Breach, 103–4; Jorge Camero Zazueta, 107–8; María de Jesús Peters, 104–5; estimated number of, 105; José Luis Gamboa Arenas, 107; Juan de Dios García Davish, 104–5; Marco Ernesto Islas Flores, 107; Armando Linares López, 108; Heber López Vásquez, 104, 105–6; Lourdes Maldonado López, 104, 106–7; Margarito Martínez Esquivel, 104, 106; Juan Carlos Muñiz, 108; Roberto Toledo, 106; Javier Valdez, 104, 171–72

Mexican labor: elaborately rationalized by state regulations, 199; elastic supply of, 21–22, 226n12; overproduced and underproduced, 199; recruitment and expulsion of, 199; use and misuse of, 54

Mexico: Army and Marines involved in extrajudicial killings in, 47; collusion of the state and organized crime, 89; corrupt purchase of a French railroad engine and cars, 152; corrupt sale and purchase of oil pipes, 152; corruption and expansion of the narcostate, 89; direct challenge to civil authorities by cartels, 109; disintegration of the efficacy of Tabasco, 102–3; and drug money as foreign exchange, 51; as emerging site for the consumption of illicit drugs, 132, 219; enactment of neoliberalism, 8–9; impact of drug-associated deported cholos on rural areas, 93–97, impact of narco transstate networks in, 39, 43; incessant corruption of all sectors in, 110; as living next to the worlds' largest drug consumer market and arms seller, 50–51; loss of Texas territory, 21; major crimes facilitated by the military, police, civil authorities, and governmental offices, 104; massacre at Ayotzinapa as a "state crime," 109; Mérida Initiative/Plan Mexico, 19; and mestizo hegemony, 20; military expenditures (2012–2020), 48; military role in construction of public works, 47, 221–22; and narco/military development, 53; as a narcostate, 110, 172; narcostate dependence on the U.S. drug consumption economy, 88–89; Navy special operation units pulled from active drug enforcement operations, 47; phases of colonial hegemony, 20; ports of entry and airports placed under military control, 47; presence of *ley fuga* in rural communities, 92–93; remittances supersede oil revenues, 51; and state-ignored returned migrant families, 123; U.S.-born children residing in, 121

migration: conflation of authorized and unauthorized, 22; and deportation, 22; displacement induced, 50, 219; fostered by late capitalism, 18–19; fostered by War of Commission, 43; Guatemalan and Mexican unauthorized workers in Vermont, 52; induced by local violence and insecurity, 95, 98; military operations in Sinaloa induce U.S.-bound, 116–17; originating in Guerrero, Michoacán, and Sinaloa, 219; reemigration due to violence in communities of origin, 126; to the U.S., 9; U.S.-born children as culturally "illegal," 221; use of Title 42 to prohibit, 24; within Mexico, 9

militarization, 8, 22, 54; Border Patrol agents, 23; consequences of, 8; of Canada-Mexico-U.S. territory, 6; Department of Homeland Security and military communications network, 24; emergence of a militarized transnational superstate-like network, 7, 54; Mexican-origin Border Patrol agents, 23; Mexico's expansion of tactical training for low intensity warfare, 47; as product of late-stage postindustrial global capitalism, 55; robotic surveillance dogs, 23; salient role in production of violence as the norm, 24; of the Southwest North American Region (SWNAR), 20; use of Ghost Robotics robo-dogs, 22. *See* Southwest North American Region (SWNAR)

narcocitizenship: avoidance of discussion of, 50; cholos provided ritual space in the celebration of the Virgen de Guadalupe in Acachuén (Puebla), 96–97; counterpart to necrocitizenship, 85; cultural complex, 89–90; described, 13, 85; driven by high demand for illicit drugs in the U.S. and Europe, 85, 88; elements associated with, 85–86; elusive military operations against drug cartels, 87; experience of Clarissa Gómez, 98–100; experience of Manuel (Maya ancestry), 100–102; and Felipe Calderón and a War on Drugs on behalf of the U.S., 87; incipient, 94; includes Mexican Special Forces members trained by the U.S. and Israel, 219; involves trusting no one and remaining private, 101; in Mexico, 17; militarization of the Mexican armed forces by the U.S., 87; as normative civic status, 220; as an outcome of Wars of Commission and Wars of Omission, 110; parallel enactment of low-intensity warfare by cartels, 219; political pact with the PRI, 86–87; powerless objectification of circumstance in communities controlled by cartels, 95; public works military complex, 87–88; reliance on a low-intensity warfare strategy, 86; seeking avoidance of violence, 98; views of those affected by, 85. *See also* cartels, Mexican; Mexico

narcocorrido, 16–17; "American," 203; American Mexican, 204; as anthems of narcoculture and necro/narco citizenship, 16, 200, 221; as anthems to the Wars of Commission and Wars of Omission, 16; and devaluing those who are poor, 211; earlier versions condemned narcotrafficking, 203; "El Pablote" as an early precursor, 202–3; as fantasy for wealth, status, and power, 206; on impact on youth, 208–10; links to traditional corridos, 201–2; as model for poor Mexican youth becoming more than just an "other," 206; as *movimientos alterados*, 204, 210; as opiate of poor youth, 215;

parallel to gangsta rap and hip-hop, 204, 205; production, 200, 203, 204; Reinas Chulas critique of, 221; two dimensions in the creation of, 207; violence, objectification of women, and accumulation of money in, 204, 205–6, 211, 215. *See also* American Mexican Triangle

narcoculture, 15; as cultural hegemony, 211; description of, 206–7; emergence of narcotours, 100; narcocultural complex, 95, 101, 102; and television narcodramas, 51

narco/necro state structures: cartel control of Mexico, 43; cartel power over political authority, 39–40; characterized by flexibility, inequality, and asymmetry, 54; contradictions between U.S. necrostate apparatus and Mexican narcostate, 40; double victimization, 41; and emergence of drug cartels, 37; and emergence of narcostate network, 48; estimate of Mexicans disappeared, 43; impact of militarization, 39; link between the twin-state structures, 10; link to criminal connections, 49; and manifestations of narcocitizenship, 39; in Mexico, 10; massacre of Ayotzinapa students, 39; Mexico resembling a narcostate, 39; Mexican state governors involvement with cartels, 49; Mexican states most impacted by, 39, 43; middle-class exodus to U.S. border cities, 39; narcostate fostering cultural dislocations, 97; network defined, 17; ongoing presence of violence or its possibility, 89; persons killed or murdered under, 43, 44; and policing policies, 19; as transstate network, 13; in the U.S., 10. *See also* narcocitizenship; Operation Intercept; Operation Condor necrocitizenship: and adherence to ideologies of sacrifice and death, 59, 64, 218; contrast with civilly associated citizenship, 57–58; and death as the raison d'être for living, 221; deployment of terror by migration officials to suppress negative reports, 29–30; described, 13, 25, 31, 57; double-faced and hydra-headed, 25–26; dying to belong, 218; importance of American-Mexican War to, 64; institutions shaping, 58–59; Pledge of Allegiance as initial site of, 25–26; premises and rituals of, 58; ritualization of, 59–60; and rituals of marginality, 83–84; role of U.S. Customs and Border Protection, 26–27; state sovereignty and, 26; and structures of legitimacy, 58; and syncretism of necroartifacts, 83; tactics within one-hundred-mile border zone and at international airports, 27–28; tools of militarization (1978–1992), 28–29; in the U.S., 17; violence in building the border wall, 32, 34; War of Commission and, 31, 57, 60; and weaponization of the political ecology, 34; as a weaponized expression of "patriotism," 57; youth and the formation of "necrocitizens," 58

North American Free Trade Agreement (NAFTA): date of implementation, 9, 18; and evolution of neoliberal policy, 9; and foreign direct investment (FDI), 18; instituted by Carlos Salinas de Gortari, 9; and militarization, 6; as a U.S. policing regime, 6. *See also* Ashby, Paul; United States-Mexico-Canada Agreement (USMCA)

Onaran, Özlem: negative effect of foreign direct investments (FDIs), 18
Operation Condor (Operación Condor, 1970s), 42, 115, 159, 172, 180–81, 183, 195, 242nn18–20; estimated deaths under, 116; impact of, 42, 116, 161; objective and actions under, 116; rape and torture by Mexican soldiers, 116
Operation Intercept (1969), 42, 230n39
opium: early links between U.S. Mafia and Mexican facilitators, 41; early tensions between political protection and law enforcement, 41; introduction in Mexico by Chinese migrants, 40; Spanish introduction of ornamental opium plants, 40; transition from a cottage industry to larger enterprises, 41; violence induced emigration, 41

PRD (Partido de la Revolución Democrática): moderate left-party created in 1989, 160, 182
prevention through deterrence, 34; death of Primero Luis, Roberto, 36; estimate of deaths based on recovered bodies, 35; migration enforcement more complex than, 53; number of deaths between 1998 and 2017, 35; policy drafted by Sandia National Laboratories (1993), 35; use of All-American Canal and weaponizing of political ecology as, 34–35
PRI (Partido Institucional Revolucionario), 152; alliance with Cuenta Conmigo in Sinaloa, 164, 167, 187, 190; arrangement between military and, 86; drop in corruption transparency under Enrique Peña Nieto, 49; and expansion of drug trafficking organizations, 9; governors in jail or under investigation, 49

rotating savings and credit associations (*tandas*), 6, 224n16; in Ciudad Nezahualcóyotl (Mexico), 141

Santamaría Gómez, Arturo: abandoned party militancy, 154, 175; awards, 155, 176–77; collaborated with Juan Gómez-Quiñonez, 155, 177; considerado "un sicario de la pluma," 188–89; early activism, 153–54, 156, 174–75; education, 154, 155, 156, 176, 178; efforts to discredit, 170; el caciquismo en la UAS, 185; emergence of right-wing university party, 160; escenario de alta violencia criminal y miedo social, 183; faculty and student links to drug trafficking, 159; faculty participation in leadership of criminal groups, 159; and Héctor Melesio Cuén Ojeda, 162, 185; journalism, 157, 176, 179; la Universidad Autónoma de Sinaloa como un instrumento patrimonialista y politico, 183; Los Enfermos, 180; los universitarios pasaron de ser radicalmente críticos a ser extremadamente pasivos, 184; message from Sinaloa cartel to, 170; and Miguel Ángel Félix Gallardo and UAS Culiacán Central Library, 159, 181; partidos politicos y sus amoríos con el crimen, 197–98; political and administrative dynamics at the UAS, 156, 158–59; politics of obtaining fulltime professorship and researcher status, 156–57, 177; professor at the UAS, 153–55, 175–76, 180; publications, 156–57, 171, 178–79, 194–95; research carried out by, 155–57, 176–78; scholar and journalist, 151; shift of UAS students from radically critical to extremely passive, 161; university transformed into a political instrument under Héctor Melesio Cuén Ojeda, 162. *See also* cartels, Mexican; Cuén Ojeda, Héctor Melesio

SB 1070 (Arizona law), 22, 112, 226n13

Southwest North American Region (SWNAR), 3, 223n2; definition of, 4; global capitalism within the, 12, 17–18; historical presence of corridos within the, 202; impact of low-intensity military warfare on residents in the, 7–8, 219; imperial and colonial hegemonies as context of current militarization in the, 20, 61; importance of Mexican cohort identities within the, 146; importance of understanding the complex economic, political and social practices in the, 16; long history of complex methods of survival in the, 4; map of, 5; and necrocitizenship, 26; necro/narco structure in the, 10; normative presence of illicit drugs in the, 129, 200; part of a War of Omission, 17; perceptions of Mexicans as foreigners in the, 60; Wars of Commission and Omission in the, 15

Spanish empire, 20; encomienda, 225–6n7; established notions of "whiteness" and "pure blood" through the caste system, 61; hegemony, 4, 20, 226n9; imposed colonialism, 20, 135; imposition of Catholicism, 20; incessant discontent against hegemony of, 226n9; introduced an ornamental opium plant, 40; oppressive hegemony of, 20; rationalization for mercantile and imperial hegemony, 20; repartimiento, 225–26n7; requerimiento, 225–26n7

superstate militarized network, 7; cartel duplication of U.S. and Mexican low-intensity warfare, 48; importance of the U.S. illicit drug market, 7; and low-intensity military doctrine, 7; as mechanism of control, surveillance, suppression, exploitation, and violence, 7; Mexico's parallel low-intensity warfare, 48; and "total war at the grassroots level, 7; U.S. integration of regional low-intensity warfare, 48; and "warrior" cultural formations, 7

Treaty of Guadalupe Hidalgo (1848), 21, 233n14; granted a form of whiteness to Mexicans living in acquired territory, 61

Trump, Donald J. (president): activated special teams against protesters, 29; application of Title 42 to prevent entry of migrants, 63; daily migrant apprehensions, 118; de facto relocation of U.S. boundary line to southern Mexico, 51; deployment of authoritarian narrative, 221; labeling of all Mexican migrants as "illegals," 22; and the United States-Mexico-Canada Agreement (USMCA, 2020), 224–25n2; used defense funds in building of a border wall, 52; and Wars of Commission, 31–34, 48

United States: application of the hegemonic state apparatus to achieve border control, 200; budget of the Department of Homeland Security (DHS), 23; Colombian Plan, 19; conquest and occupation in hegemony over Mexico, 61; as dominant hegemony over Mexico, 54; drug seeking sector in, 19, 43; economic dependence on Mexican labor, 18; estimate of consumers' expenditures on illicit drugs (2016), 43; expansion of militarization and 9/11 attacks, 10; filibuster expeditions in Mexican territory, 62; invasion of Mexico, 21; large transfer of funds to Mexican military and public works, 10; Mérida Initiative/Plan Mexico, 19; Mexican labor elasticity, 21–22; Mexicans as foreigners in annexed territory, 21; personnel at DHS, 23; primary source of weapons obtained by cartels, 45; principal U.S. states supplying weapons obtained by cartels, 46; recruitment and banishment of Mexican persons, 21–22; role in formation of Wars of Omission, 17; states, whole or in part, annexed from Mexico, 21, 61; unabated demand for illicit drugs and continuing poverty in Mexico, 217; War on Drugs, 10, 19

United States Customs and Border Protection (CBP): activities carried out by, 27–28; core elements of, 26–27; officer force level, 27–28

United States-Mexico-Canada Agreement (USMCA), 224–25n2

Universidad Autónoma de Sinaloa (UAS). *See* Cuén Ojeda, Héctor Melesio; Santamaría Gómez, Arturo

Velásquez, Loreta Janeta ("Buford, Harry"), 65

Wars of Commission: actions by the necrostate, 34; articulation with Wars of Omission, 13, 51; cartels able to shut down regions and impose curfews, 130; cartel takeover of highway toll booths, 131; casualty toll in Culiacán, 132; described, 12, 218; desolate Mexican border towns as "dead zones," 130; enactment of checkpoints, *34*, 34–35; homicide rate, 130; men killed in Tubutama (Sonora), 130; murder to induce obedience and silence, 132; narcocitizenship among members of cartels, 131; and resultant low-intensity warring capacities, 219; second shut down of Culiacán, 131; severe trauma among Mexican children, 132; and structures and policies encompassing interdiction strategies, 218

Wars of Omission, 14: articulation with Wars of Commission, 13, 51; cartel control of Netzahualcóyotl (near Mexico City), 141; cartel infiltration of all levels of Mexican society, 145; casualties of, 6–7; comparison of average weekly earnings by race/ethnicity, 135–36; consumption of methamphetamines in Mexico, 132; criminal gangs take-over of Tepito neighborhood (Mexico City), 139; defined, 12. 17; deportation and transnationalization of criminal activities, 137; emergence of globally oriented gangs, 137; emergence of vulnerable youth in Tepito, 139–40; fentanyl drug overdoses in California, 133; and foreign direct investments, 18; growth in the number of gangs in Los Angeles County, 138; high rate of drug overdose in New Mexico, 134; historical summary of gangs in Los Angeles, 136–37; link between anti-drug campaigns and non-white communities, 134; link to global capitalism and neoliberalism, 6; Mayor of Mexico City asserts that there are no cartels there, 143; Mexico as the primary nation in the manufacture and trafficking of methamphetamines, 133; options for residents in communities controlled by drug trafficking organizations, 140; overdose deaths as KIAs, 130, 132; silencing of journalist by the La Familia Michoacana cartel, 143; U.S. deaths due to drug overdoses, 133; violent confrontation in El Salvador, 138; and youth as primary casualties of, 129, 220;

Wolf, Eric R., 16, 218, 224n19

# ABOUT THE AUTHOR

**Carlos G. Vélez-Ibáñez** received a PhD in anthropology (USCD, 1975). His intellectual interests are broadly comparative and applied and his publications include twelve books in English and Spanish as well as many articles and chapters. Three of his English-language books have been translated into Spanish. He has held tenured professorships in anthropology at UCLA and the University of Arizona, where in 1982 he founded the Bureau of Applied Research in Anthropology. He is Regents' Professor in the School of Transborder Studies and the School of Human Evolution and Social Change at Arizona State University and Motorola Presidential Professor of Neighborhood Revitalization.